3 0116 01587022 1

Sherdog & Takeru Wajima

Story: Yuma Ando   Art: Yuki Sato

CHARACTERS

Takeru Wajima

A second-year at London Academy High School, he is an ordinary student who loves dogs. He is Sherdog's owner and the one person who can understand him. When Sherdog saw his name, he misread it as Watson, and appointed Takeru his assistant. Perhaps through some trick of fate, the two are mixed up in all kinds of difficult mysteries.

Sherdog
(Sherlock Holmes)

The mixed-breed puppy that Takeru adopted. His true identity is that of the world-famous detective, Sherlock Holmes. When he has the Wajima family's heirloom pipe in his mouth, he can speak to Takeru. He solves crimes with Takeru, learning about the modern world in the process.

Airin Wajima

Takeru's sister, an inspector in the Violent Crimes Division. She is quite an attractive woman. Sherdog calls her Irene.

Miki Arisaka

A second-year at London Academy High School. Takeru's friend since childhood, and member of the school newspaper staff. Takeru's crush.

THE STORY SO FAR

"Hello, my dear Watson."
The dog spoke! Takeru took a dog home from the pound, and he turned out to be Sherlock Holmes! But apparently Takeru is the only one who can understand him speak. Named for Sherlock Holmes, but with a canine spin, Sherdog and his master Takeru find themselves surrounded by mysterious crimes in modern-day Japan!!

STORY

Volume.2

CONTENTS

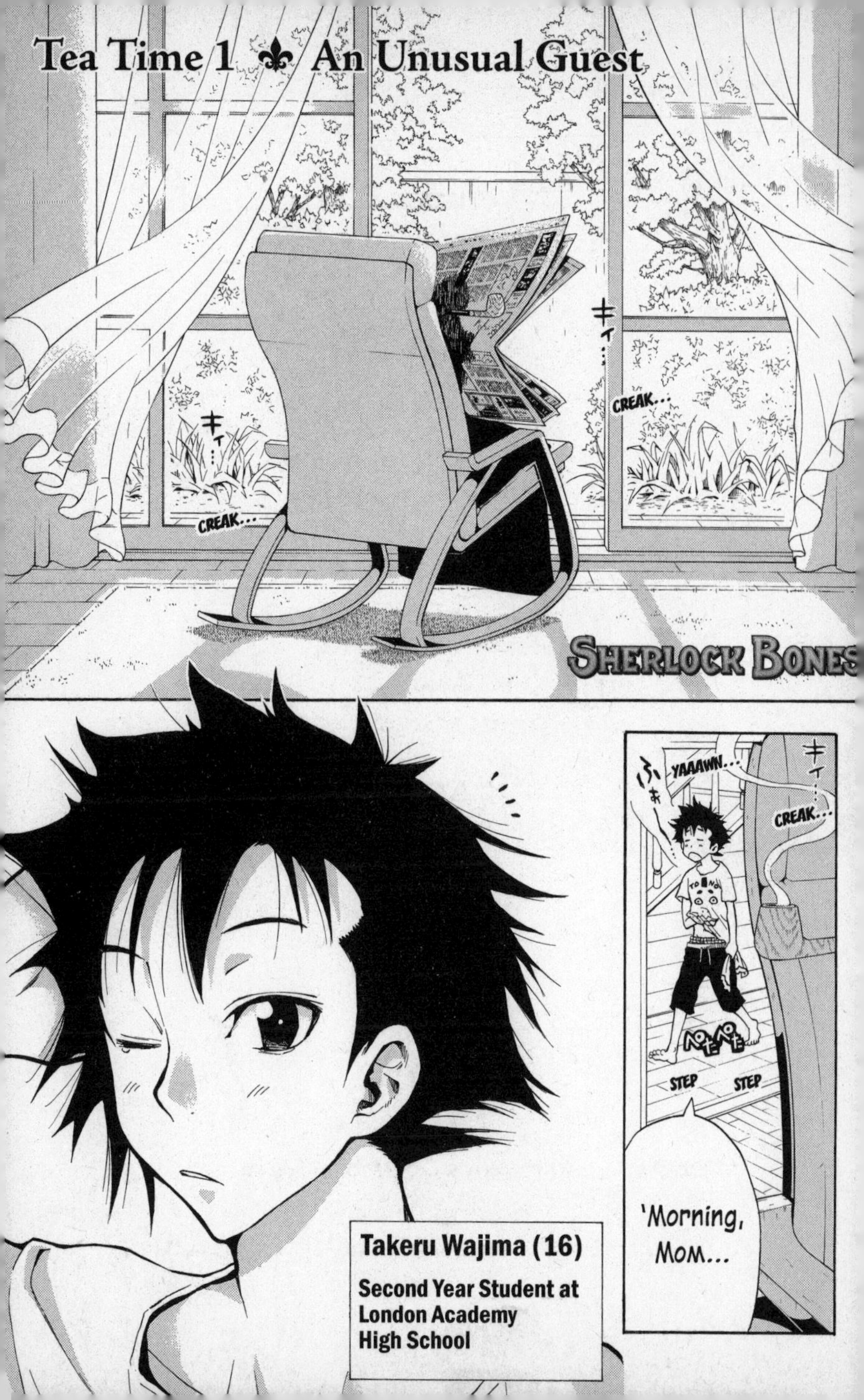
Tea Time 1 ⚜ An Unusual Guest
CREAK...
CREAK...
SHERLOCK BONES
YAAAWN...
CREAK...
STEP STEP
'Morning, Mom...
Takeru Wajima (16)
Second Year Student at London Academy High School

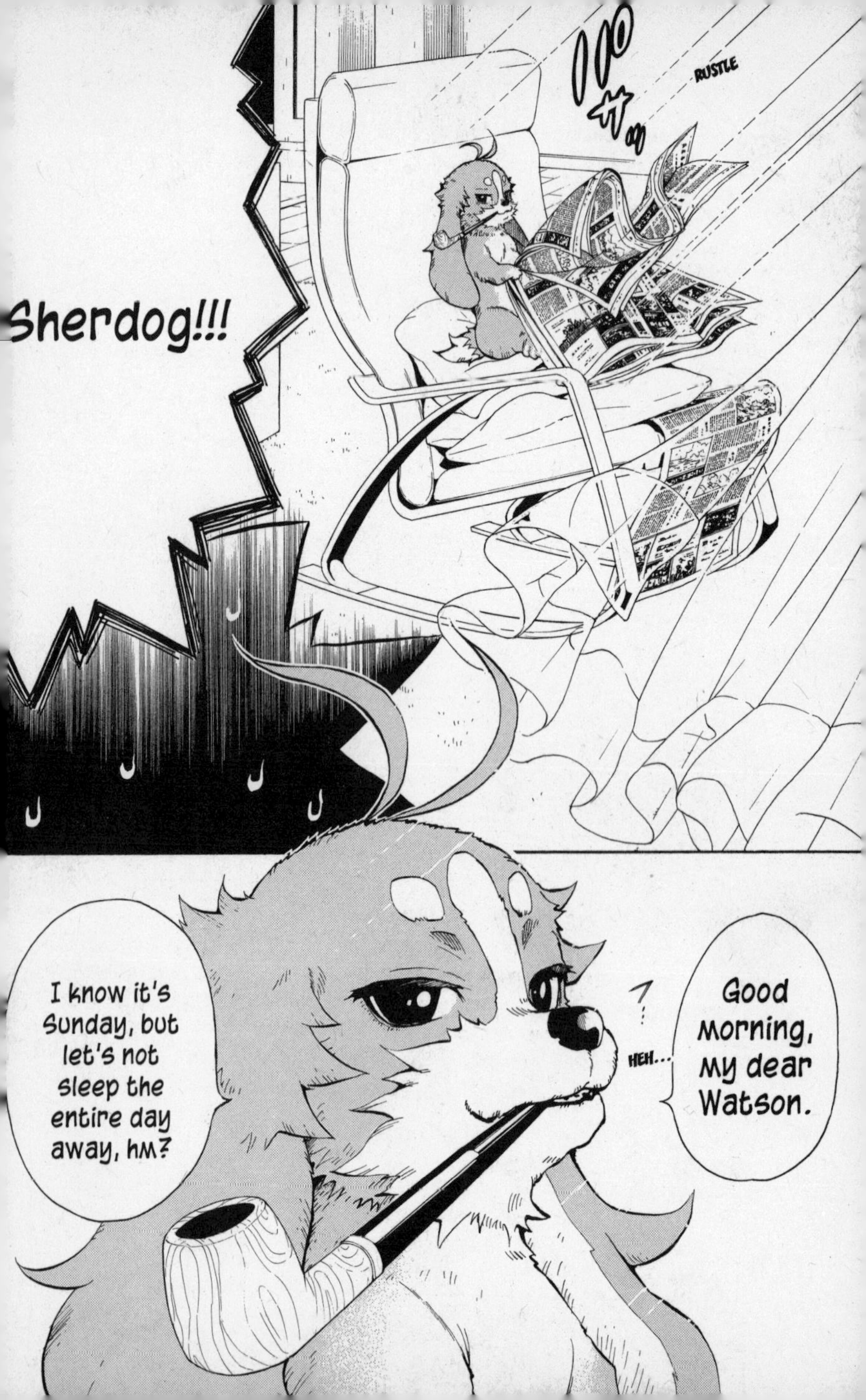
RUSTLE
Sherdog!!!
Good Morning, My dear Watson.
HEH...
I know it's Sunday, but let's not sleep the entire day away, hm?

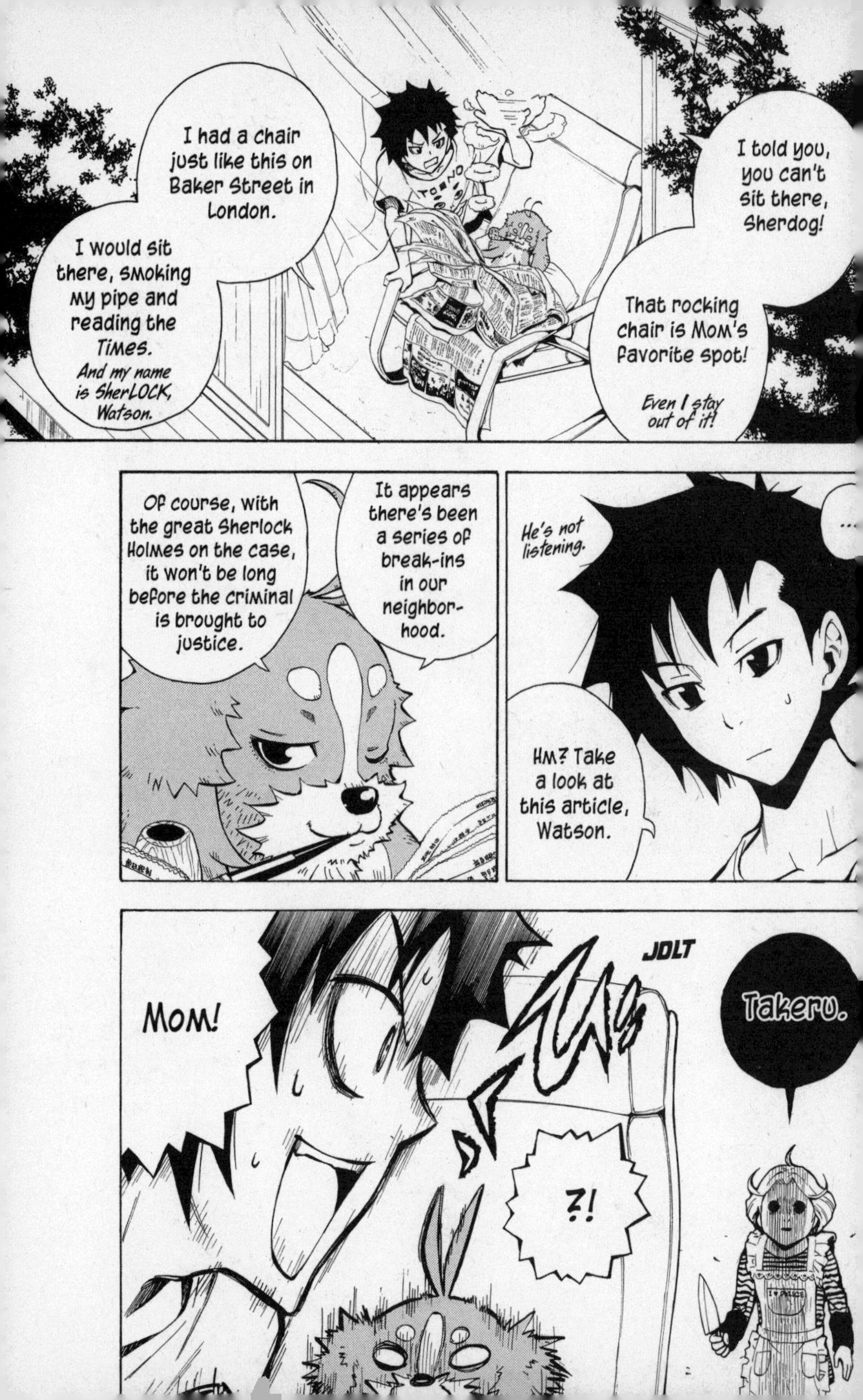
I told you, you can't sit there, Sherdog!
That rocking chair is Mom's favorite spot!
Even I stay out of it!
I had a chair just like this on Baker Street in London.
I would sit there, smoking my pipe and reading the Times.
And my name is SherLOCK, Watson.
...
He's not listening.
Hm? Take a look at this article, Watson.
It appears there's been a series of break-ins in our neighbor-hood.
Of course, with the great Sherlock Holmes on the case, it won't be long before the criminal is brought to justice.
Takeru.
JOLT
?!
Mom!

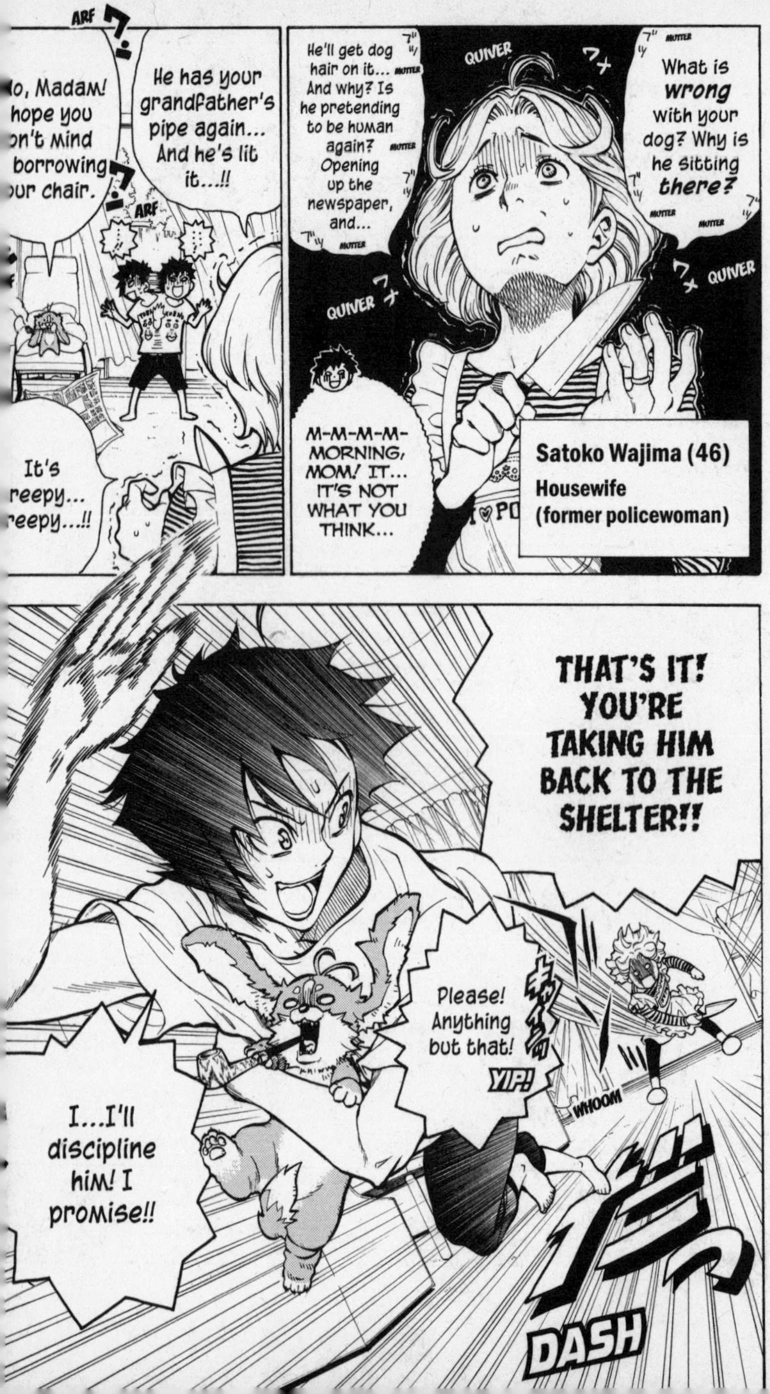

What is wrong with your dog? Why is he sitting there?
MUTTER
QUIVER
He'll get dog hair on it... MUTTER And why? Is he pretending to be human again? MUTTER Opening up the newspaper, and... MUTTER
QUIVER
Satoko Wajima (46)
Housewife (former policewoman)
M-M-M-M-MORNING, MOM! IT... IT'S NOT WHAT YOU THINK...
He has your grandfather's pipe again... And he's lit it...!!
ARF
lo, Madam! hope you on't mind borrowing our chair.
ARF
It's reepy... reepy...!!
THAT'S IT! YOU'RE TAKING HIM BACK TO THE SHELTER!!
WHOOM
Please! Anything but that!
YIP!
I...I'll discipline him! I promise!!
DASH

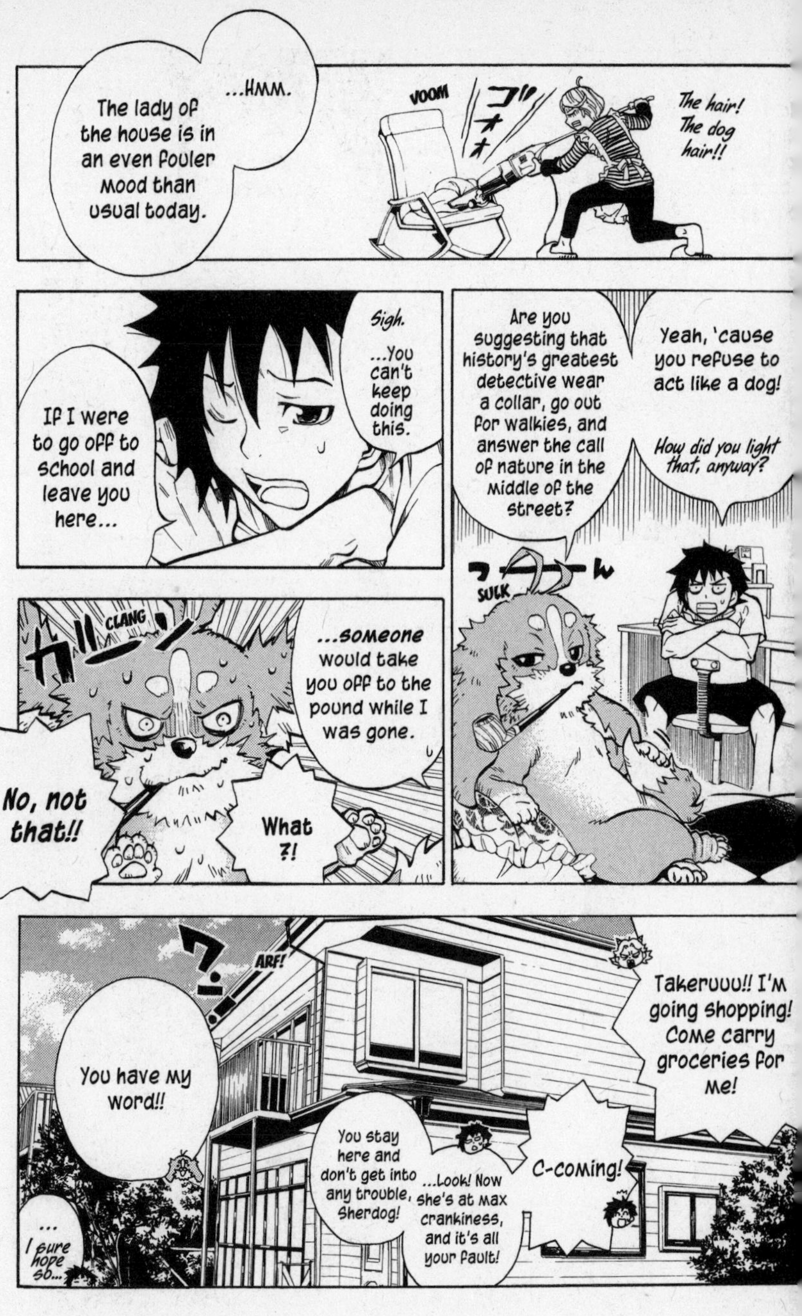
The hair! The dog hair!!
VOOM
...HMM.
The lady of the house is in an even fouler mood than usual today.
Are you suggesting that history's greatest detective wear a collar, go out for walkies, and answer the call of nature in the middle of the street?
Yeah, 'cause you refuse to act like a dog!
How did you light that, anyway?
SULK
Sigh.
...You can't keep doing this.
If I were to go off to school and leave you here...
...someone would take you off to the pound while I was gone.
What?!
CLANG
No, not that!!
Takeruuu!! I'm going shopping! Come carry groceries for me!
ARF!
You have my word!!
C-coming!
...Look! Now she's at max crankiness, and it's all your fault!
You stay here and don't get into any trouble, Sherdog!
... I sure hope so...

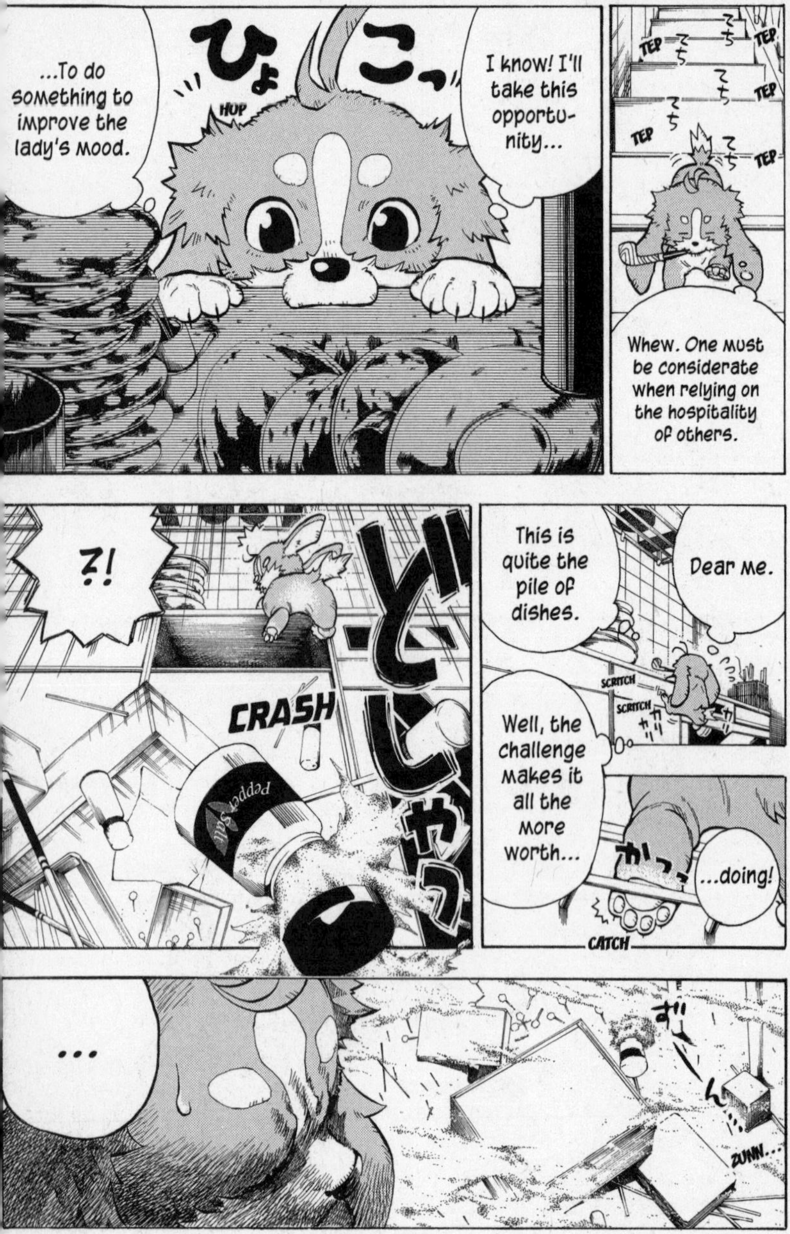
TEP
TEP
TEP
TEP
TEP
Whew. One must be considerate when relying on the hospitality of others.
I know! I'll take this opportu-nity...
HOP
...To do something to improve the lady's mood.
Dear me.
This is quite the pile of dishes.
SCRITCH
SCRITCH
Well, the challenge makes it all the more worth...
...doing!
CATCH
?!
CRASH
Pepper Salt
ZUNN...
...

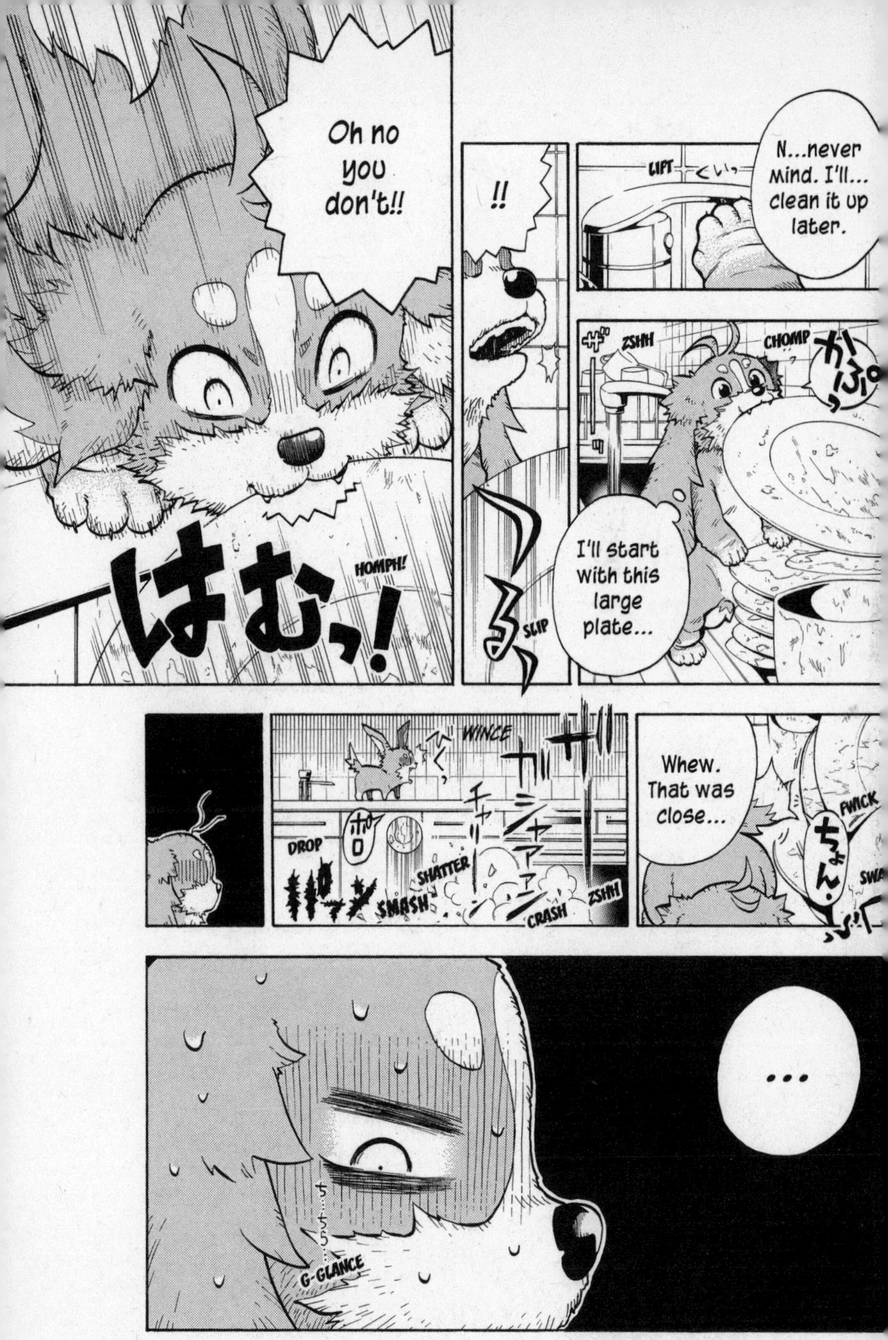
N...never mind. I'll... clean it up later.
LIFT
CHOMP
ZSHH
I'll start with this large plate...
!!
SLIP
Oh no you don't!!
HOMPH!
はむっ!
Whew. That was close...
FWICK
ちょん.
WINCE
DROP
SHATTER
SMASH
CRASH
ZSHH
...
G-GLANCE

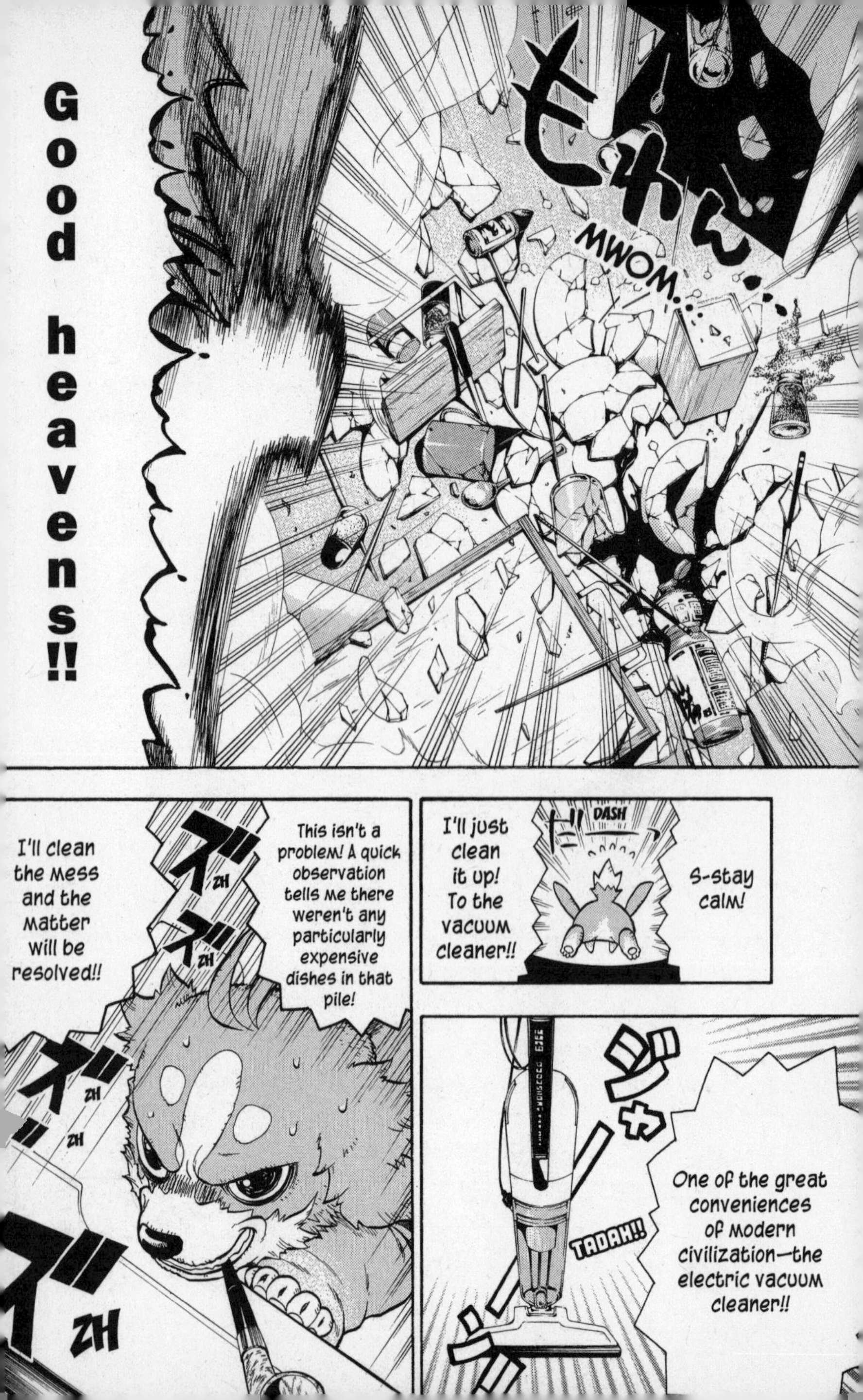

MWOM...
Good heavens!!
S-stay calm!
DASH
I'll just clean it up! To the vacuum cleaner!!
One of the great conveniences of modern civilization—the electric vacuum cleaner!!
TADAH!!
This isn't a problem! A quick observation tells me there weren't any particularly expensive dishes in that pile!
ZH
ZH
I'll clean the mess and the matter will be resolved!!
ZH
ZH
ZH

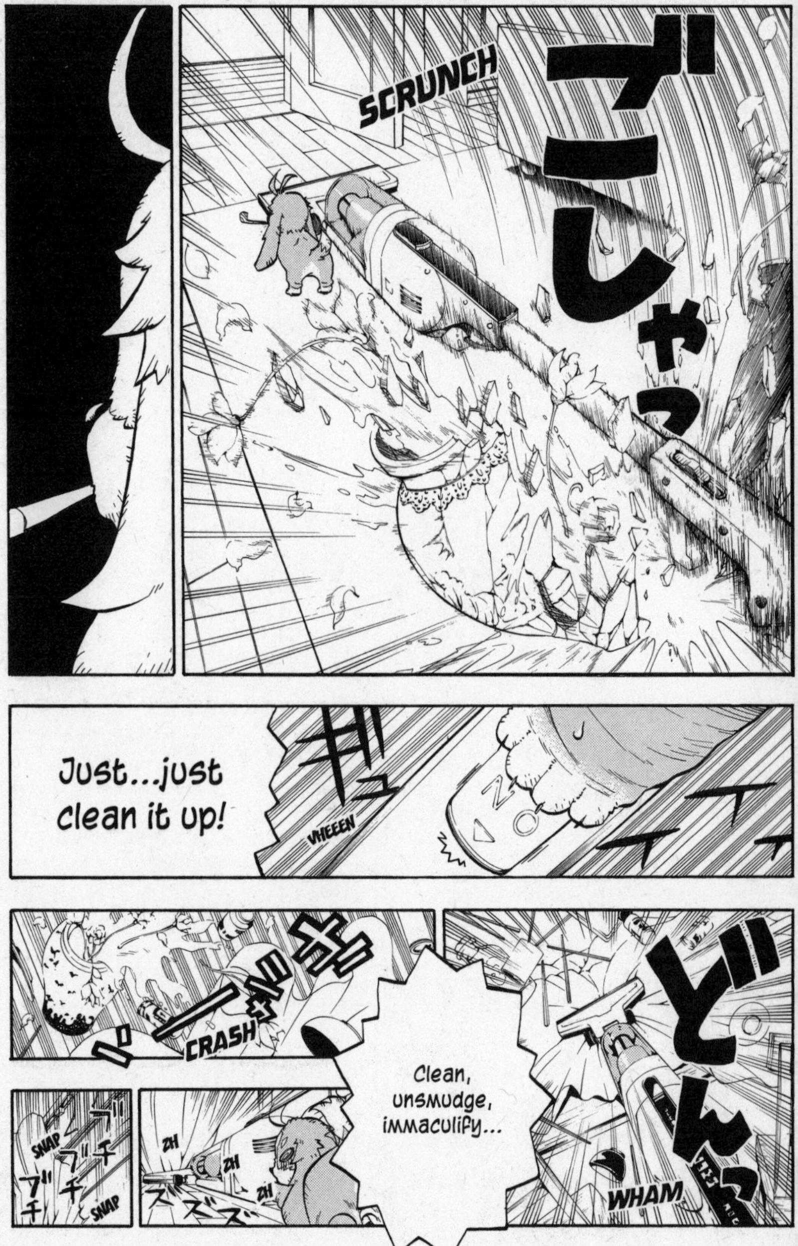
SCRUNCH
ごしゃっ
Just...just clean it up!
ギュ
VHEEEN
WHAM
どんっ
Clean, unsmudge, immaculify...
CRASH
ZH
ZH
ZH
SNAP
SNAP

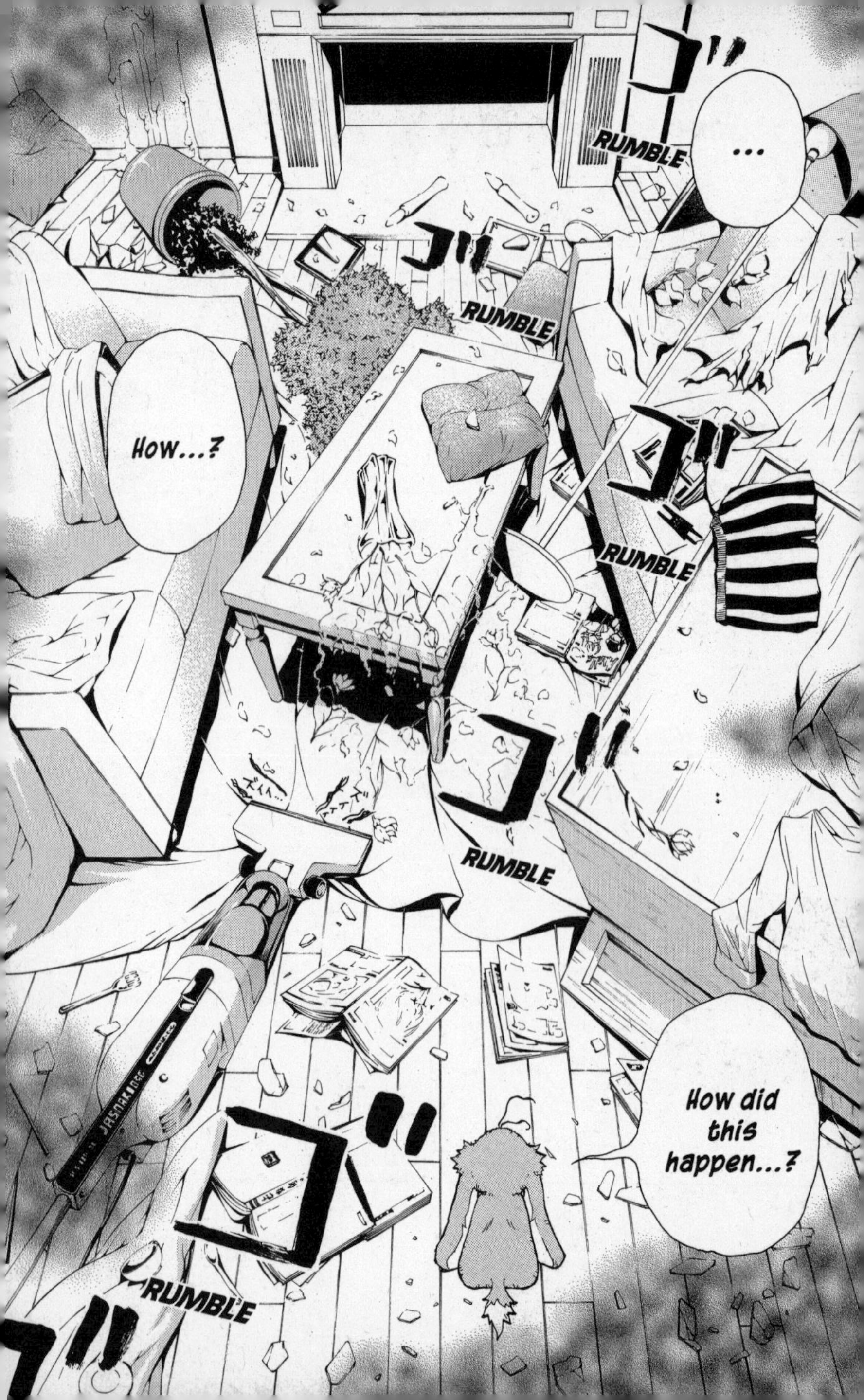
...
RUMBLE
RUMBLE
How...?
RUMBLE
How did this happen...?
RUMBLE
RUMBLE

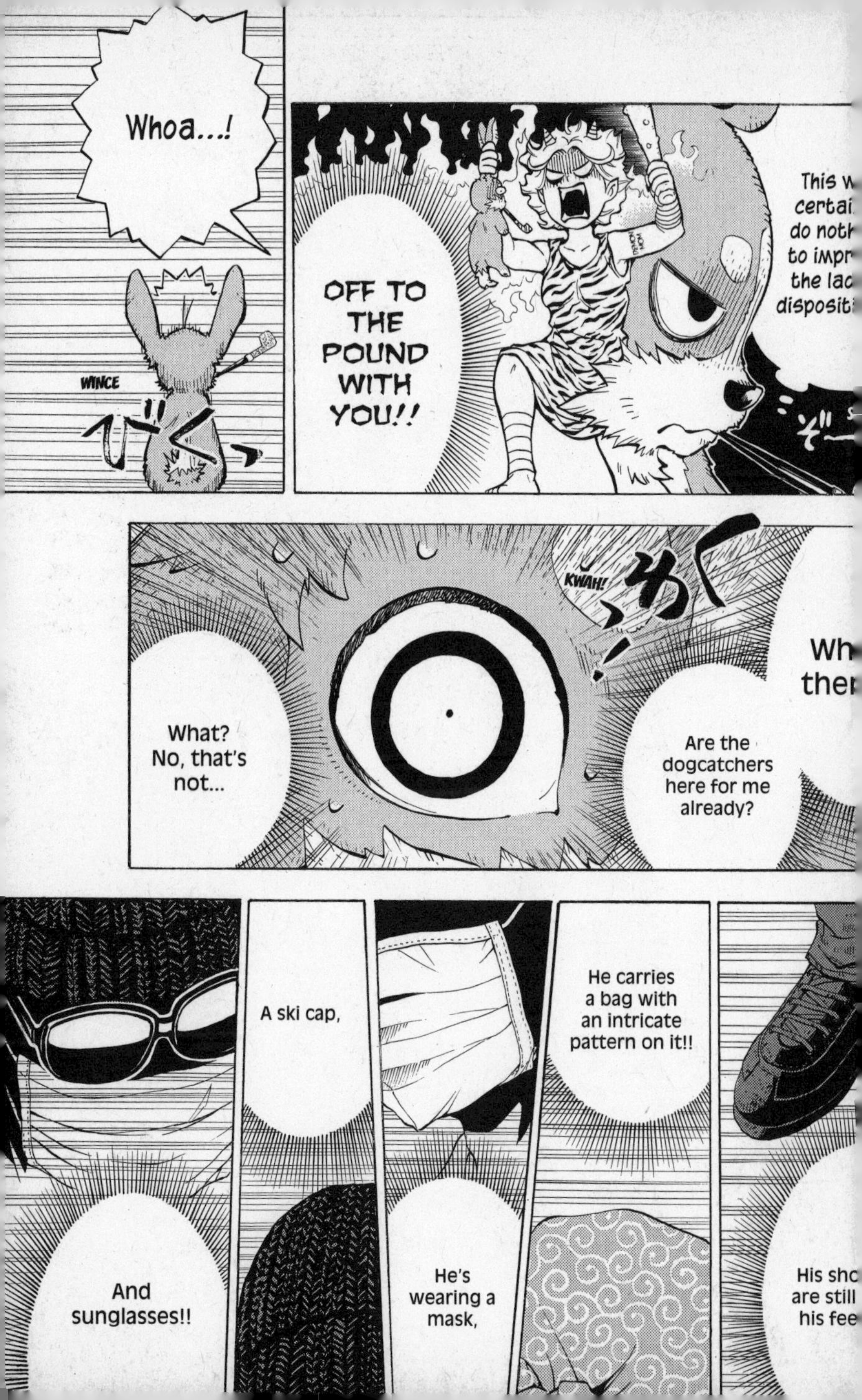
This w
certai
do noth
to impr
the lac
disposit
OFF TO THE POUND WITH YOU!!
Whoa...!
WINCE
Wh
ther
Are the dogcatchers here for me already?
KWAH!
What? No, that's not...
His sho
are still
his fee
He carries a bag with an intricate pattern on it!!
He's wearing a mask,
A ski cap,
And sunglasses!!

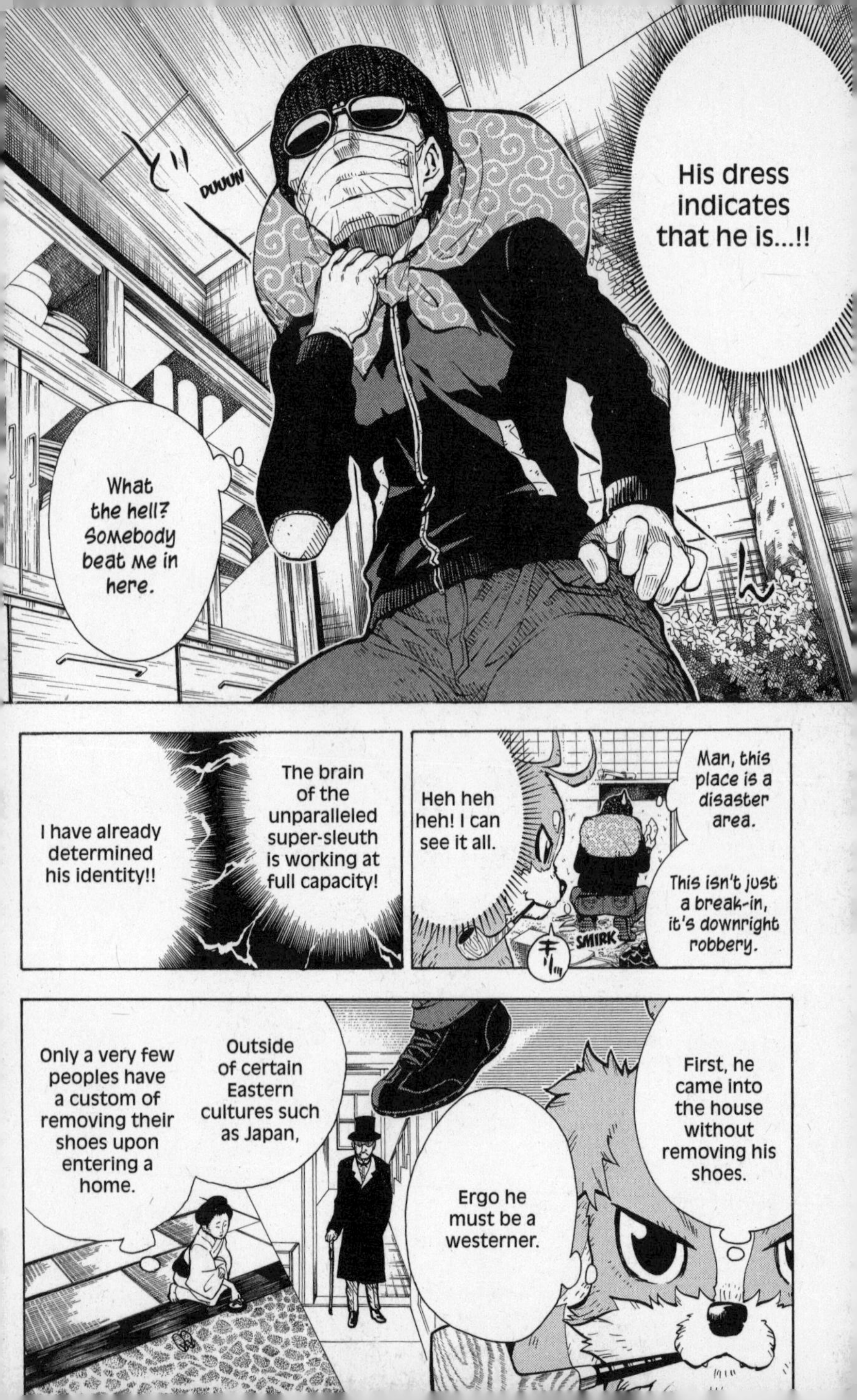
His dress indicates that he is...!!
DUUUN
What the hell? Somebody beat me in here.
Man, this place is a disaster area.
Heh heh heh! I can see it all.
This isn't just a break-in, it's downright robbery.
SMIRK
The brain of the unparalleled super-sleuth is working at full capacity!
I have already determined his identity!!
First, he came into the house without removing his shoes.
Ergo he must be a westerner.
Outside of certain Eastern cultures such as Japan,
Only a very few peoples have a custom of removing their shoes upon entering a home.

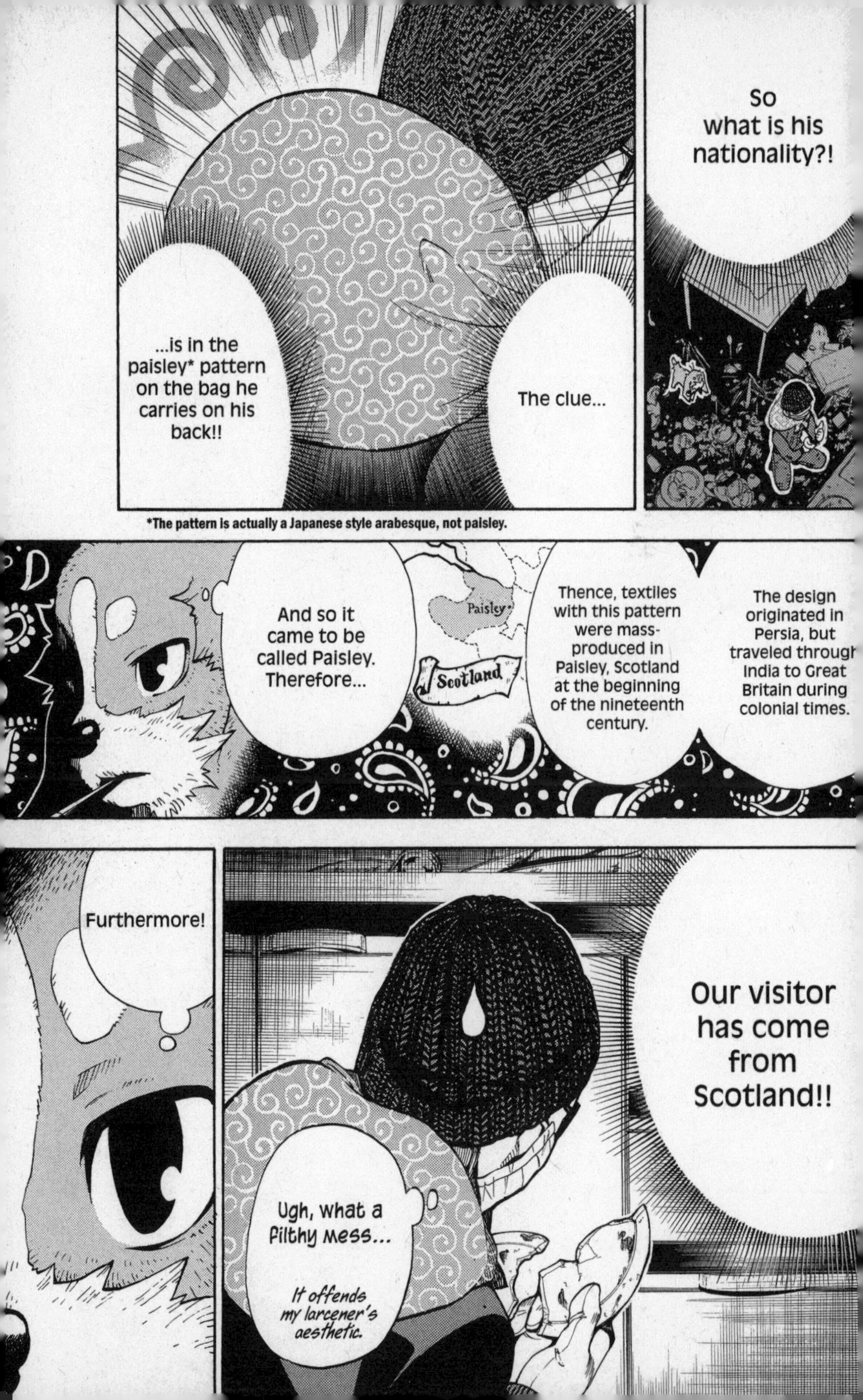
So what is his nationality?!
The clue...
...is in the paisley* pattern on the bag he carries on his back!!
*The pattern is actually a Japanese style arabesque, not paisley.
The design originated in Persia, but traveled through India to Great Britain during colonial times.
Thence, textiles with this pattern were mass-produced in Paisley, Scotland at the beginning of the nineteenth century.
Paisley
Scotland
And so it came to be called Paisley. Therefore...
Our visitor has come from Scotland!!
Ugh, what a filthy mess...
It offends my larcener's aesthetic.
Furthermore!

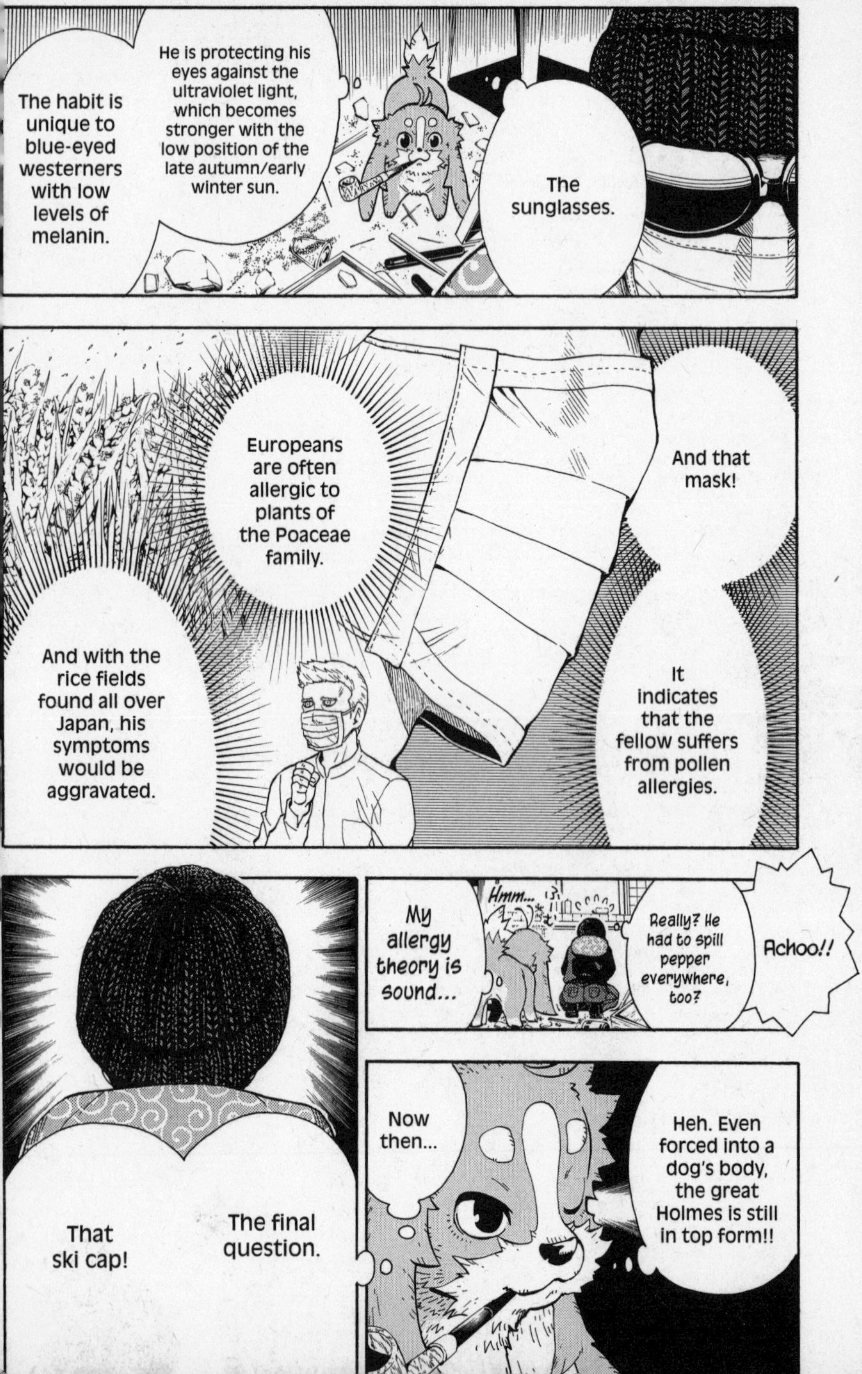
The sunglasses.
He is protecting his eyes against the ultraviolet light, which becomes stronger with the low position of the late autumn/early winter sun.
The habit is unique to blue-eyed westerners with low levels of melanin.
And that mask!
Europeans are often allergic to plants of the Poaceae family.
It indicates that the fellow suffers from pollen allergies.
And with the rice fields found all over Japan, his symptoms would be aggravated.
Achoo!!
Really? He had to spill pepper everywhere, too?
Hmm...
My allergy theory is sound...
Heh. Even forced into a dog's body, the great Holmes is still in top form!!
Now then...
The final question.
That ski cap!

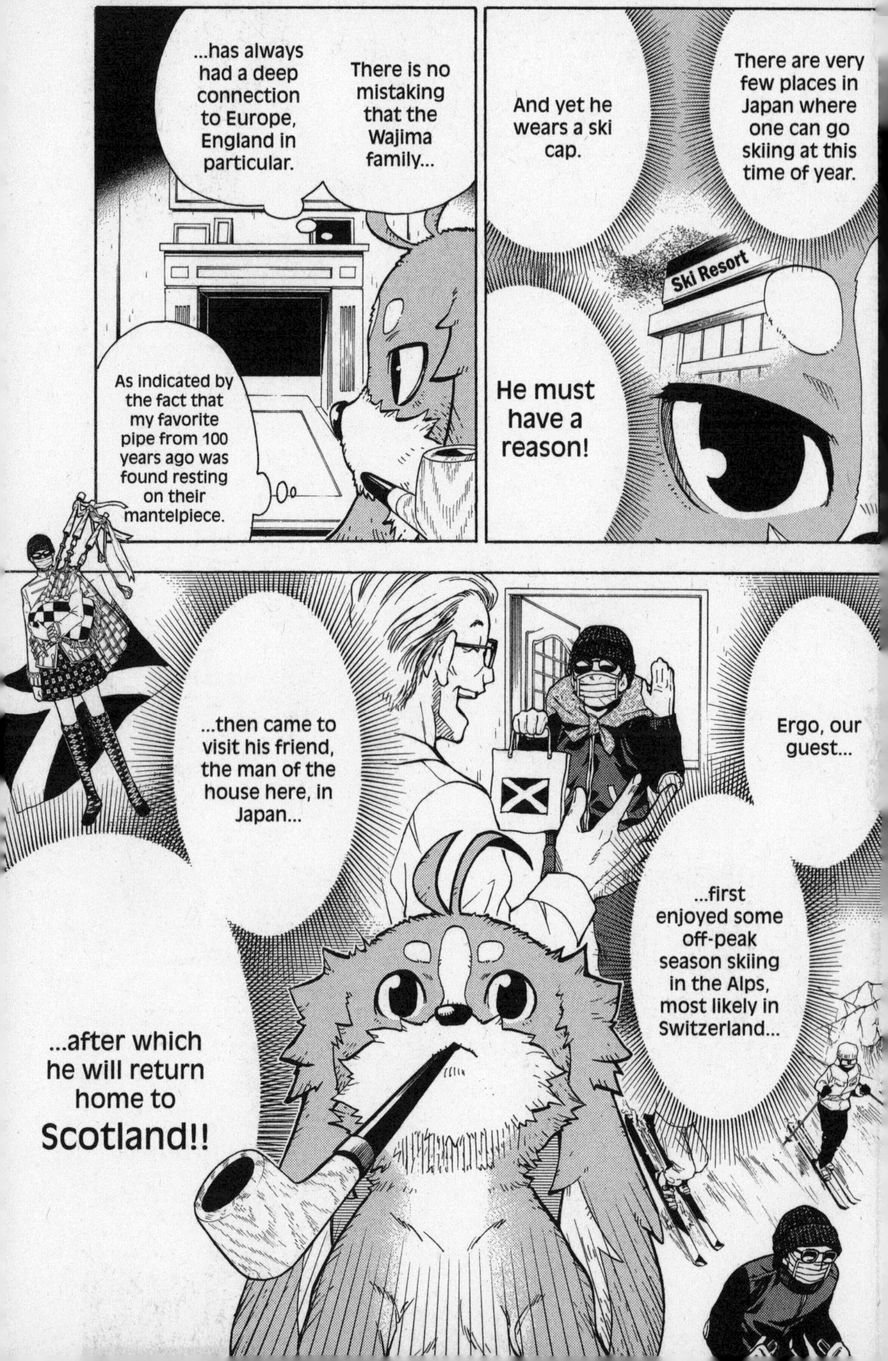
There are very few places in Japan where one can go skiing at this time of year.
And yet he wears a ski cap.
Ski Resort
He must have a reason!
There is no mistaking that the Wajima family...
...has always had a deep connection to Europe, England in particular.
As indicated by the fact that my favorite pipe from 100 years ago was found resting on their mantelpiece.
Ergo, our guest...
...first enjoyed some off-peak season skiing in the Alps, most likely in Switzerland...
...then came to visit his friend, the man of the house here, in Japan...
...after which he will return home to Scotland!!

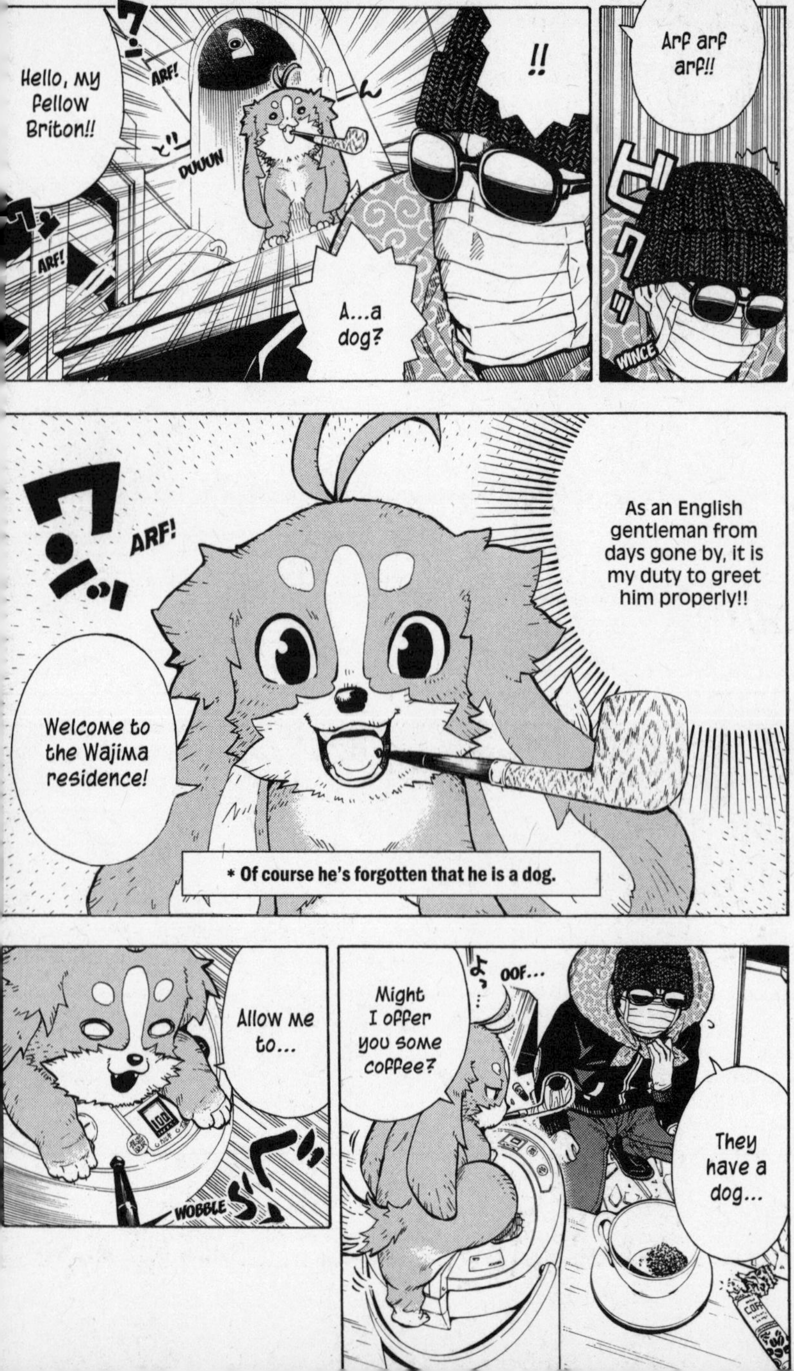
Arf arf arf!!
WINCE
!!
A...a dog?
ARF!
Hello, my fellow Briton!!
DUUUN
ARF!
As an English gentleman from days gone by, it is my duty to greet him properly!!
ARF!
Welcome to the Wajima residence!
* Of course he's forgotten that he is a dog.
They have a dog...
OOF...
Might I offer you some coffee?
Allow me to...
WOBBLE

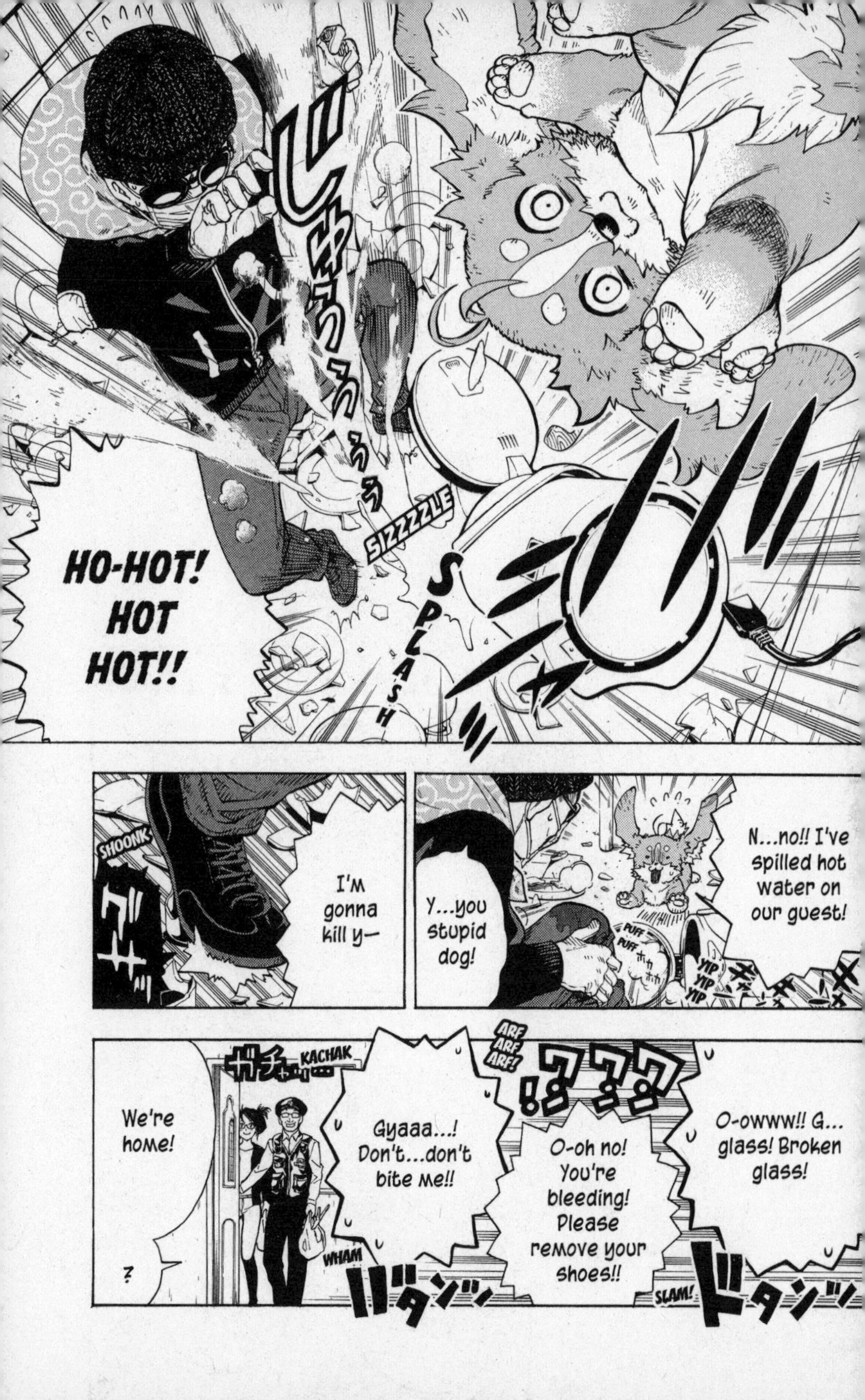
HO-HOT! HOT HOT!!
SIZZZZLE
SPLASH
N...no!! I've spilled hot water on our guest!
YIP YIP YIP
PUFF PUFF
Y...you stupid dog!
I'm gonna kill y—
SHOONK
O-owww!! G... glass! Broken glass!
SLAM!
O-oh no! You're bleeding! Please remove your shoes!!
ARF ARF ARF!
Gyaaa...! Don't...don't bite me!!
WHAM
KACHAK
We're home!
?

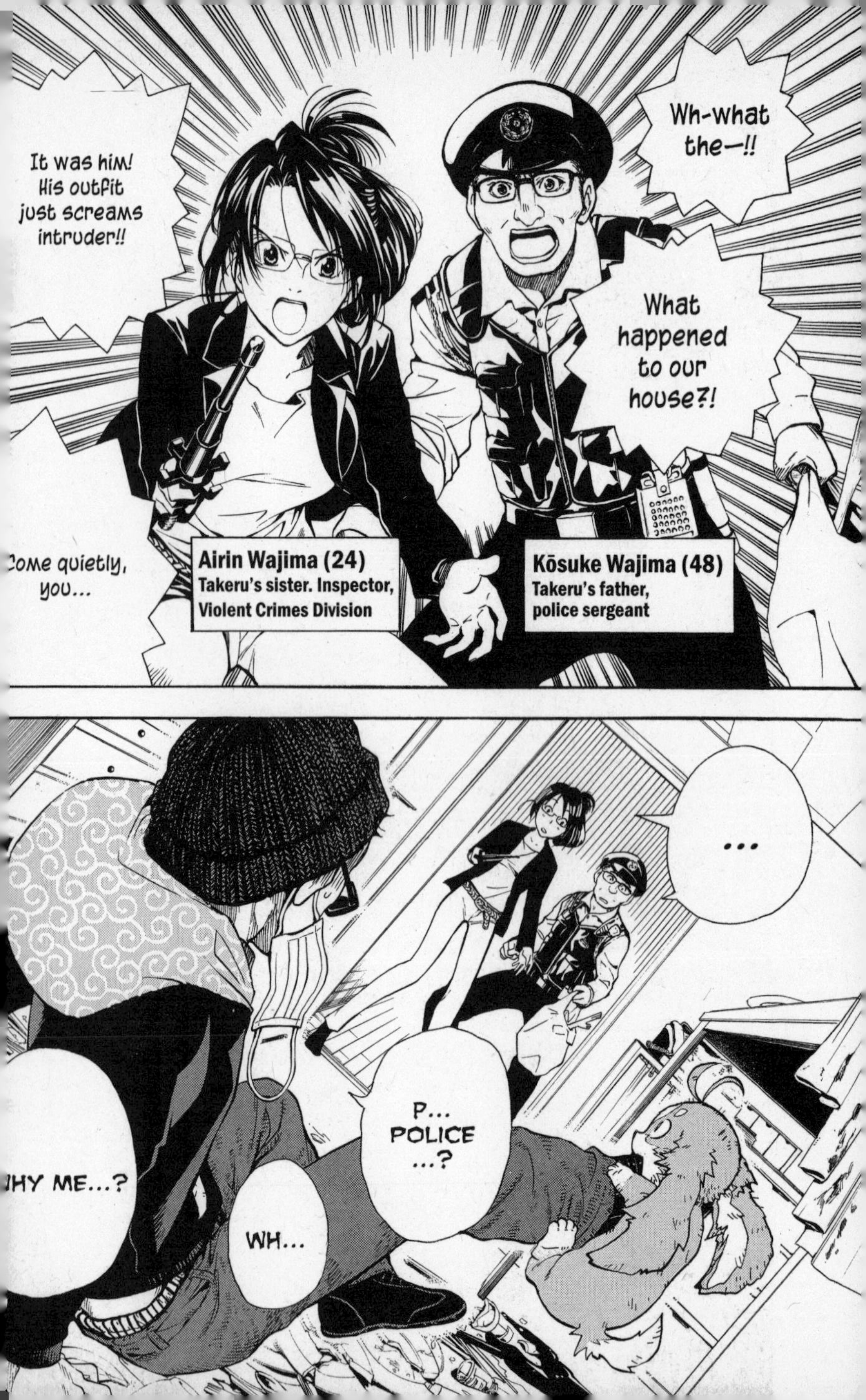
Wh-what the—!!
What happened to our house?!
Kōsuke Wajima (48) Takeru's father, police sergeant
It was him! His outfit just screams intruder!!
Airin Wajima (24) Takeru's sister. Inspector, Violent Crimes Division
Come quietly, you...
...
P... POLICE ...?
WH...
HY ME...?

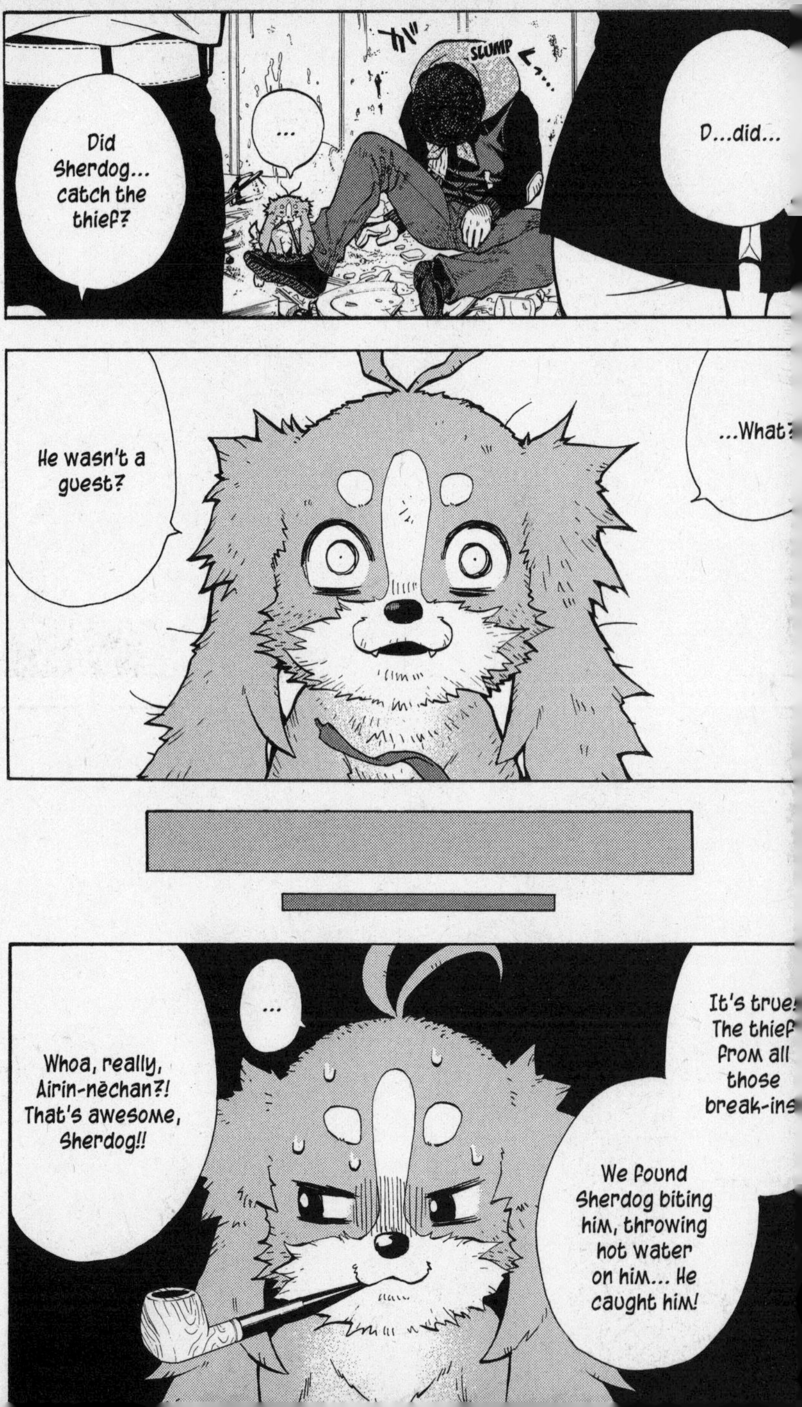
D...did...
SLUMP
...
Did Sherdog... catch the thief?
...What?
He wasn't a guest?
It's true! The thief from all those break-ins
We found Sherdog biting him, throwing hot water on him... He caught him!
...
Whoa, really, Airin-nēchan?! That's awesome, Sherdog!!

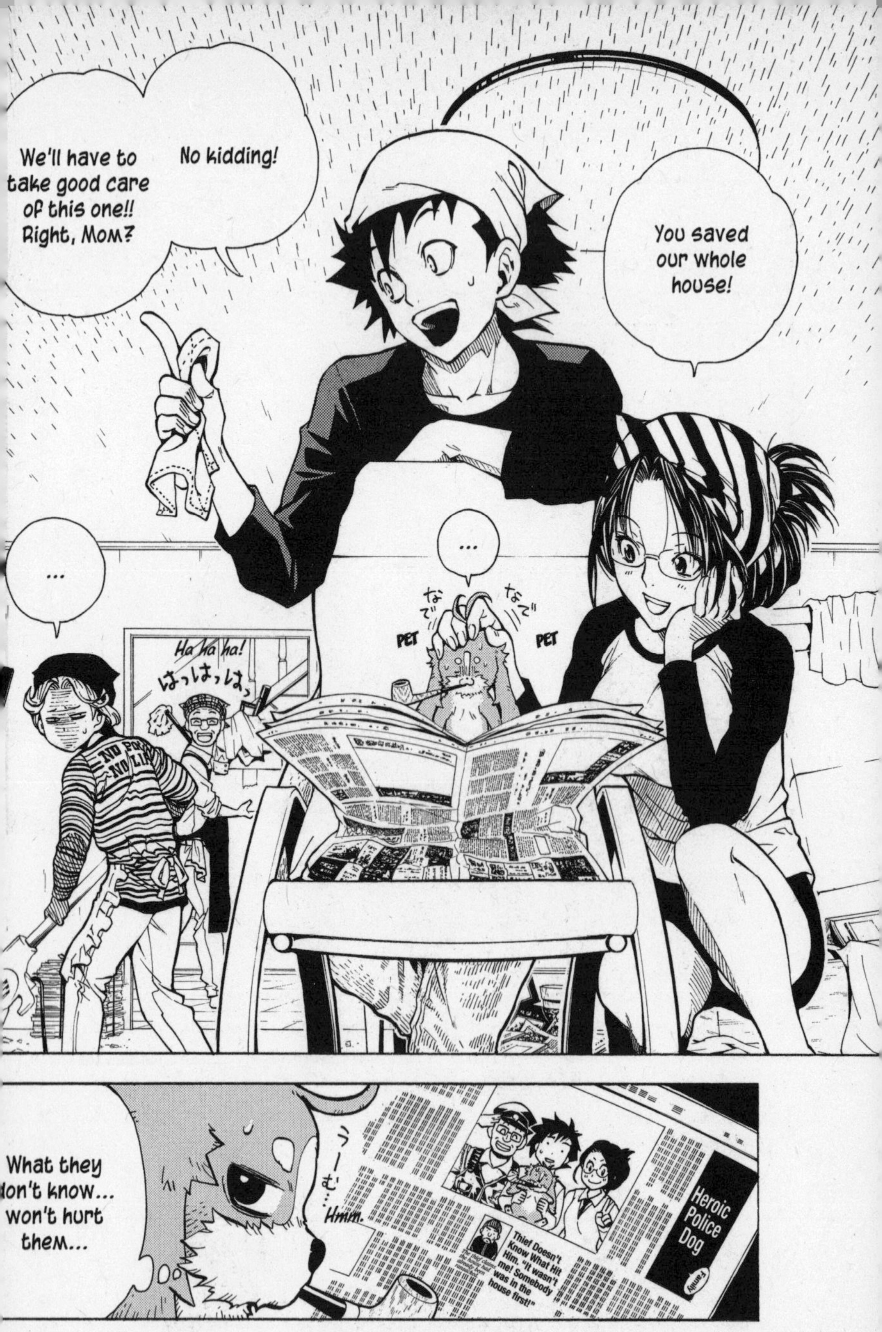

You saved our whole house!
No kidding!
We'll have to take good care of this one!! Right, Mom?
...
なでなで
PET
なでなで
PET
...
Ha ha ha!
はっはっは
うーむ…
Hmm.
Heroic Police Dog
Family
Thief Doesn't Know What Hit Him. "It wasn't me! Somebody was in the house first!"
What they don't know... won't hurt them...

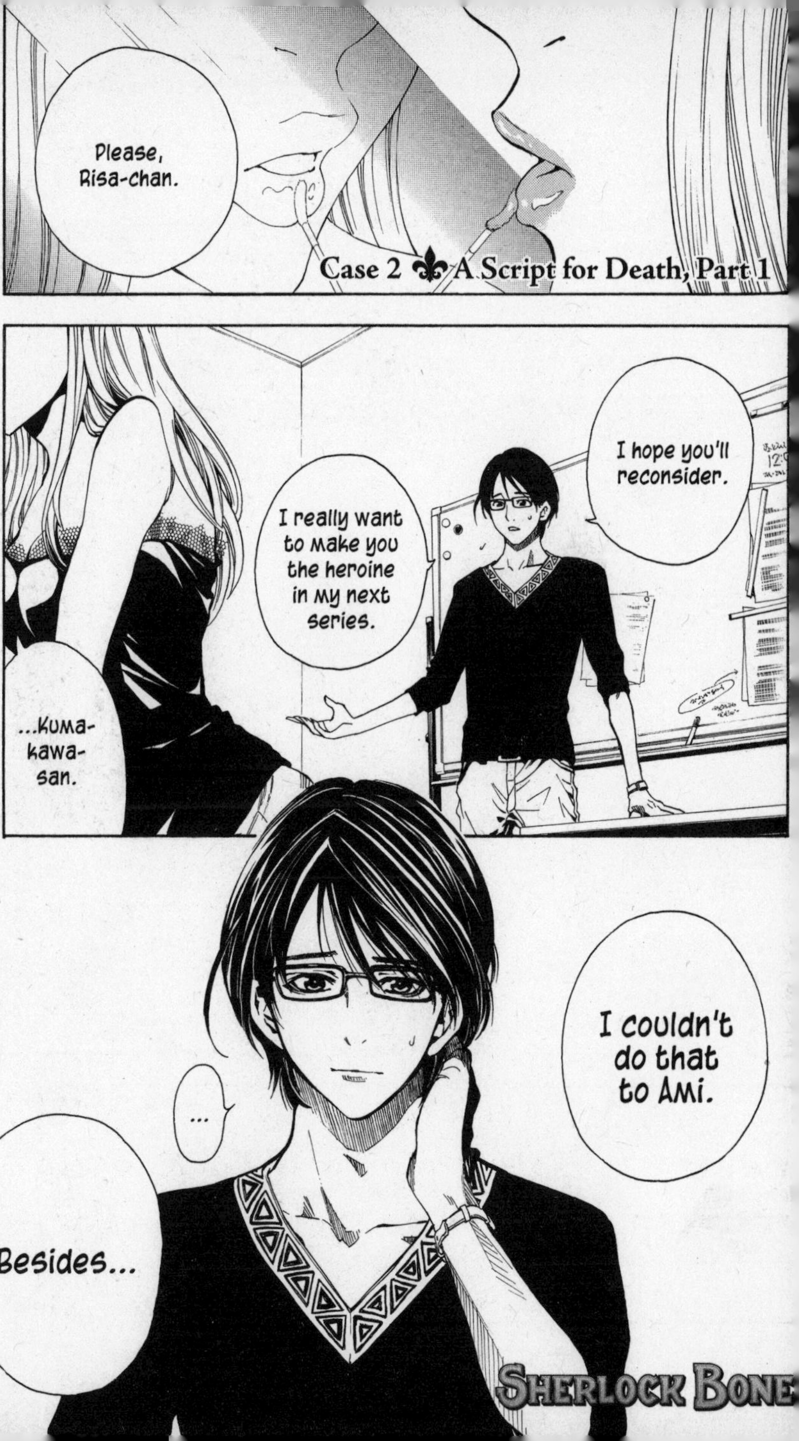
Please, Risa-chan.
Case 2 ⚜ A Script for Death, Part 1
I hope you'll reconsider.
I really want to make you the heroine in my next series.
...Kuma-kawa-san.
I couldn't do that to Ami.
...
Besides...
SHERLOCK BONE

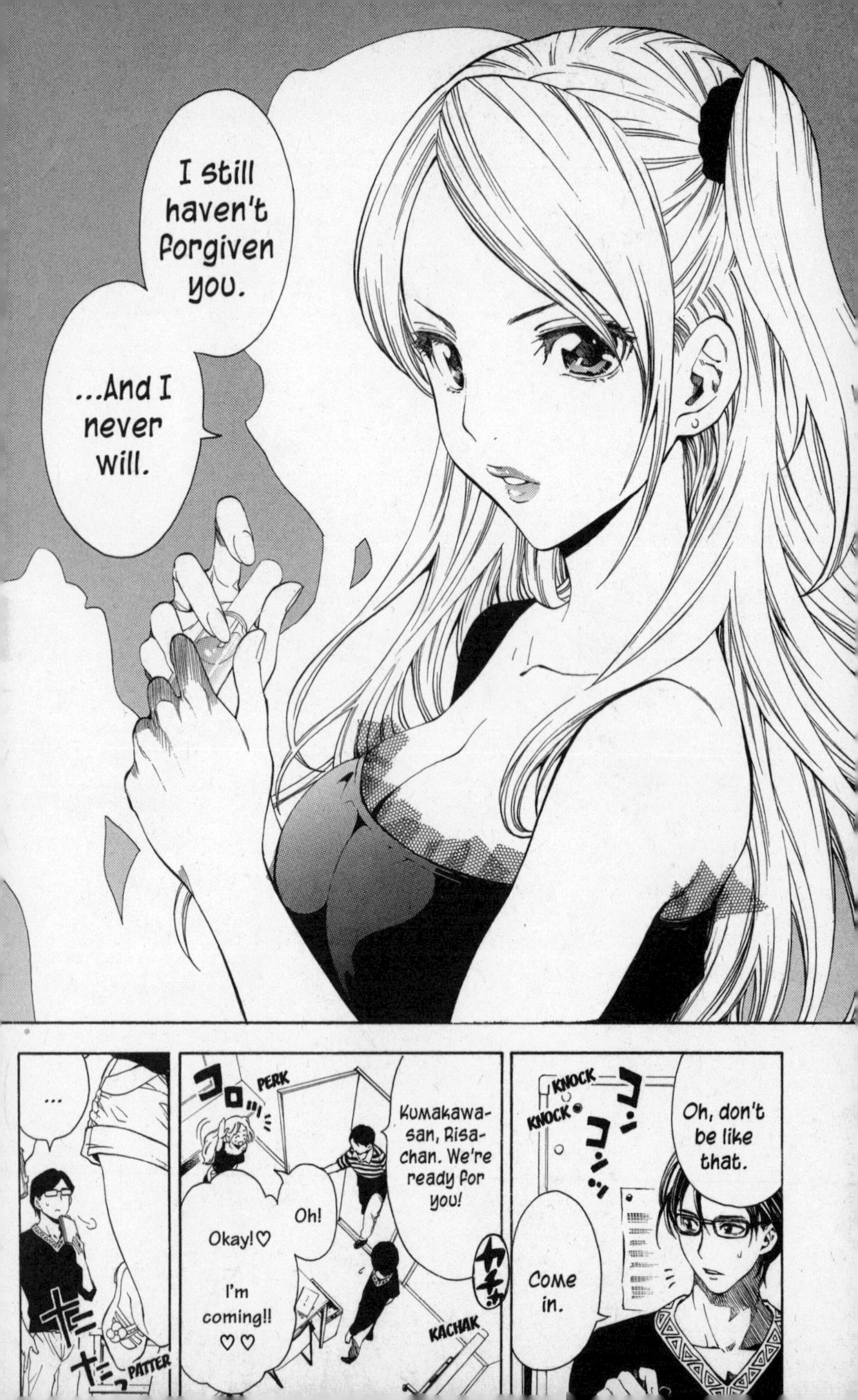
I still haven't forgiven you.
...And I never will.
Oh, don't be like that.
KNOCK
KNOCK
Come in.
Kumakawa-san, Risa-chan. We're ready for you!
KACHAK
PERK
Oh!
Okay!♡ I'm coming!! ♡♡
...
PATTER

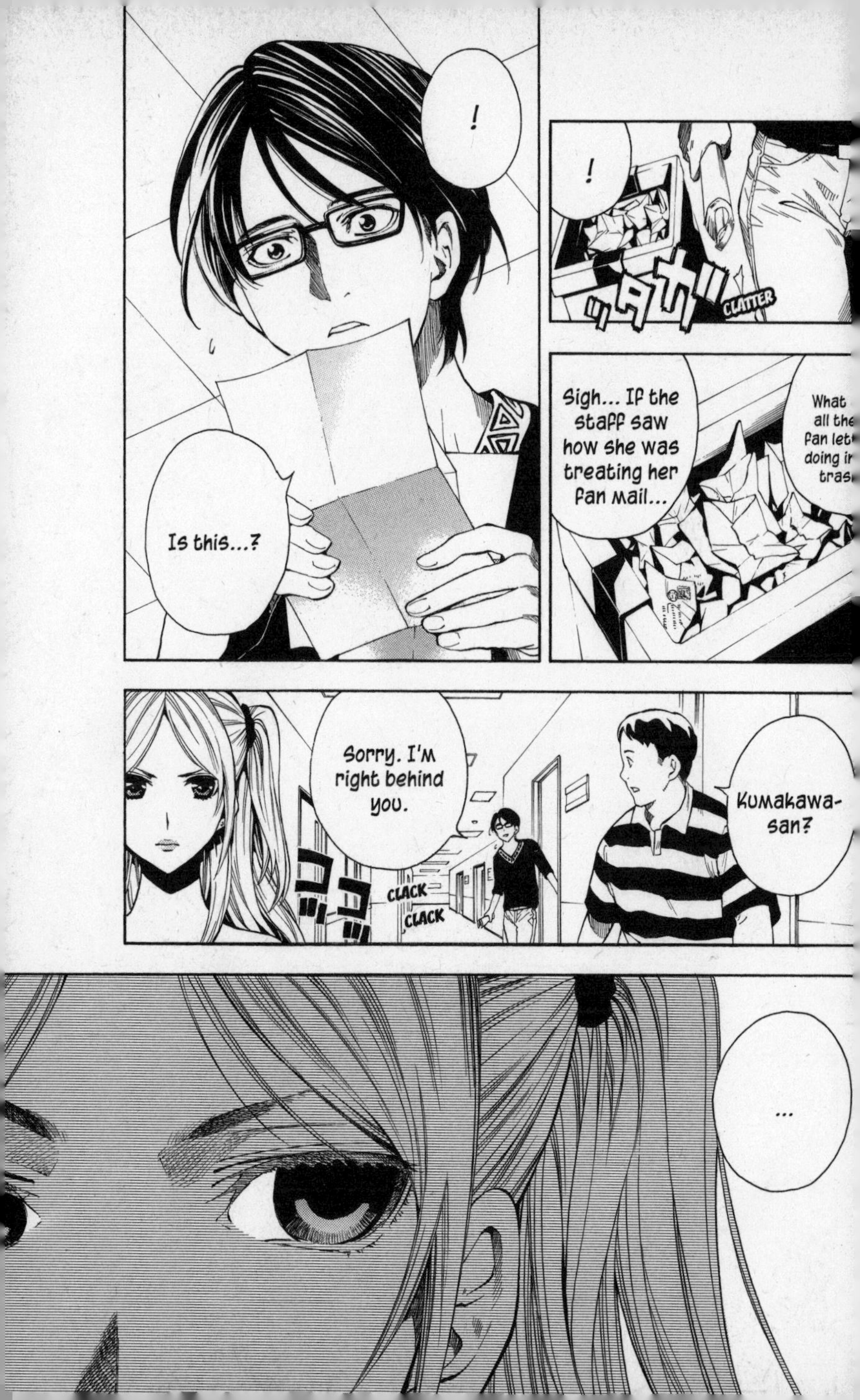
!
CLATTER
What all the fan let doing ir tras
Sigh... If the staff saw how she was treating her fan mail...
!
Is this...?
Kumakawa-san?
Sorry. I'm right behind you.
CLACK
CLACK
...

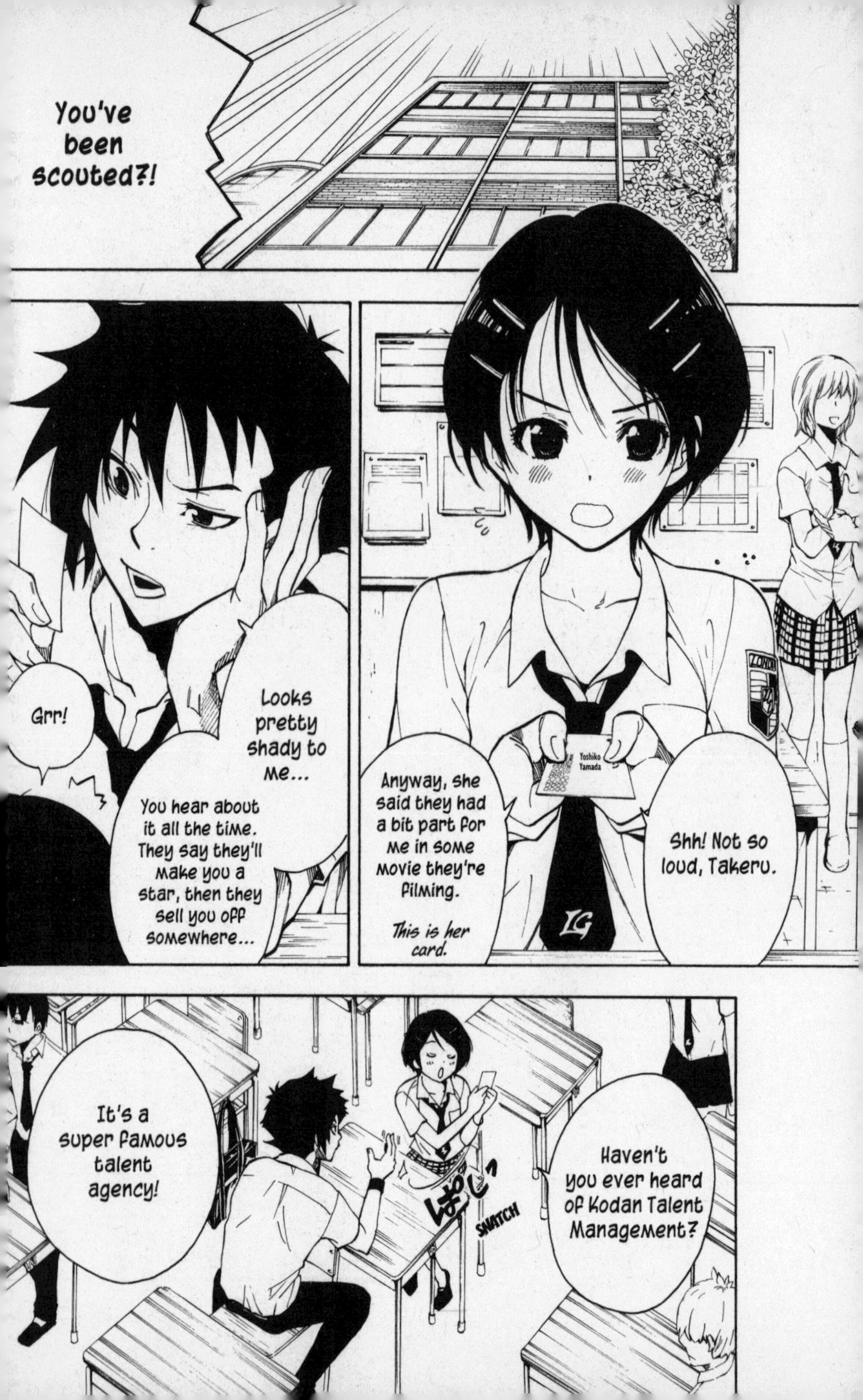
You've been scouted?!
Shh! Not so loud, Takeru.
Anyway, she said they had a bit part for me in some movie they're filming.
This is her card.
Yoshiko Yamada
Looks pretty shady to me...
You hear about it all the time. They say they'll make you a star, then they sell you off somewhere...
Grr!
Haven't you ever heard of Kodan Talent Management?
SNATCH
It's a super famous talent agency!

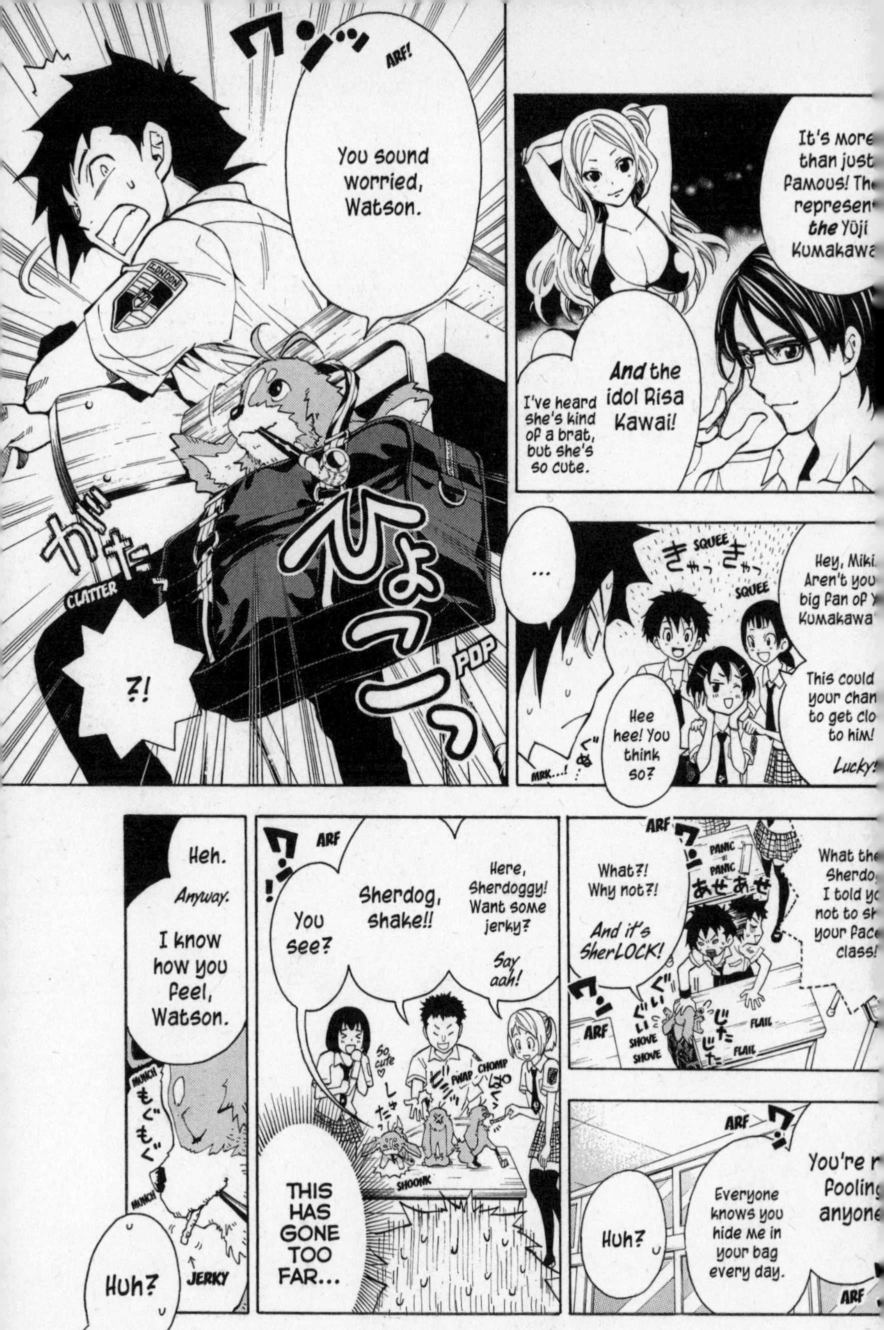
It's more than just famous! Th represen the Yūji Kumakawa
And the idol Risa Kawai!
I've heard she's kind of a brat, but she's so cute.
SQUEE きゃっ きゃっ SQUEE
Hey, Miki. Aren't you big fan of Y Kumakawa
This could your chan to get clo to him!
Lucky!
Hee hee! You think so?
...
ぐぬ MRK...!
ワンッ ARF!
You sound worried, Watson.
ひょこっ POP
がたっ CLATTER
?!
What the Sherdo I told yo not to sh your face class!
ワン ARF
PANIC PANIC あせあせ
What?! Why not?!
And it's SherLOCK!
ぐいぐい SHOVE SHOVE
じたじた FLAIL FLAIL
ワン ARF
You're fooling anyone
ARF ワ?
Everyone knows you hide me in your bag every day.
Huh?
ARF
Here, Sherdoggy! Want some jerky?
Say aah!
Sherdog, shake!!
ワン! ARF
You see?
So cute ♡
FWAP CHOMP
SHOONK
THIS HAS GONE TOO FAR...
Heh.
Anyway.
I know how you feel, Watson.
MUNCH もぐもぐ MUNCH
JERKY
Huh?

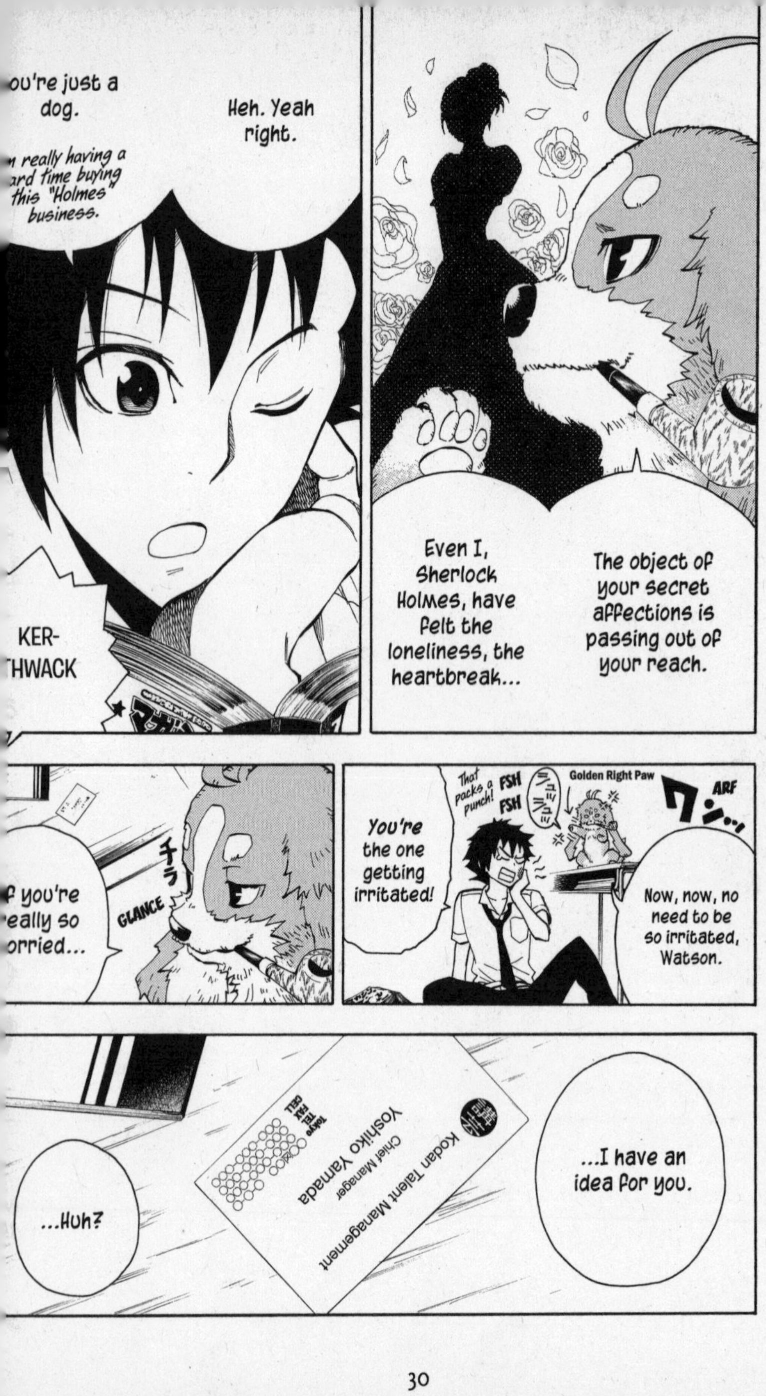
The object of your secret affections is passing out of your reach.
Even I, Sherlock Holmes, have felt the loneliness, the heartbreak...
Heh. Yeah right.
ou're just a dog.
n really having a ard time buying this "Holmes" business.
KER-THWACK
ARF
Golden Right Paw
Now, now, no need to be so irritated, Watson.
FSH FSH
That packs a punch!
You're the one getting irritated!
GLANCE
f you're eally so orried...
...I have an idea for you.
Kodan Talent Management
Chief Manager
Yoshiko Yamada
Tokyo
TEL
FAX
CELL
...Huh?

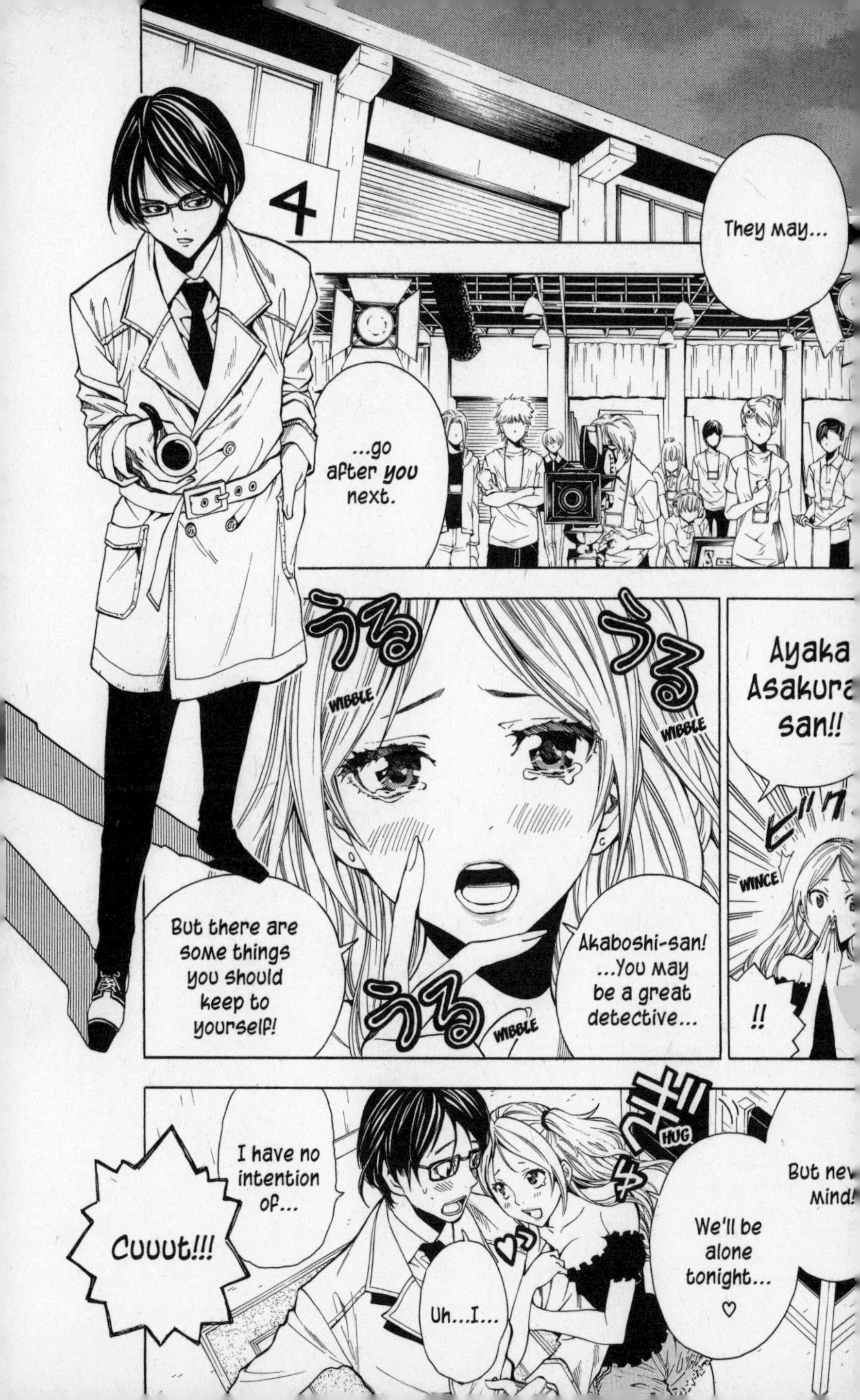

They may...
...go after you next.
Ayaka Asakura-san!!
WINCE
!!
うる
WIBBLE
うる
WIBBLE
Akaboshi-san! ...You may be a great detective...
うる
WIBBLE
But there are some things you should keep to yourself!
But nev Mind!
ぎゅ
HUG
We'll be alone tonight... ♡
Uh...I...
I have no intention of...
Cuuut!!!

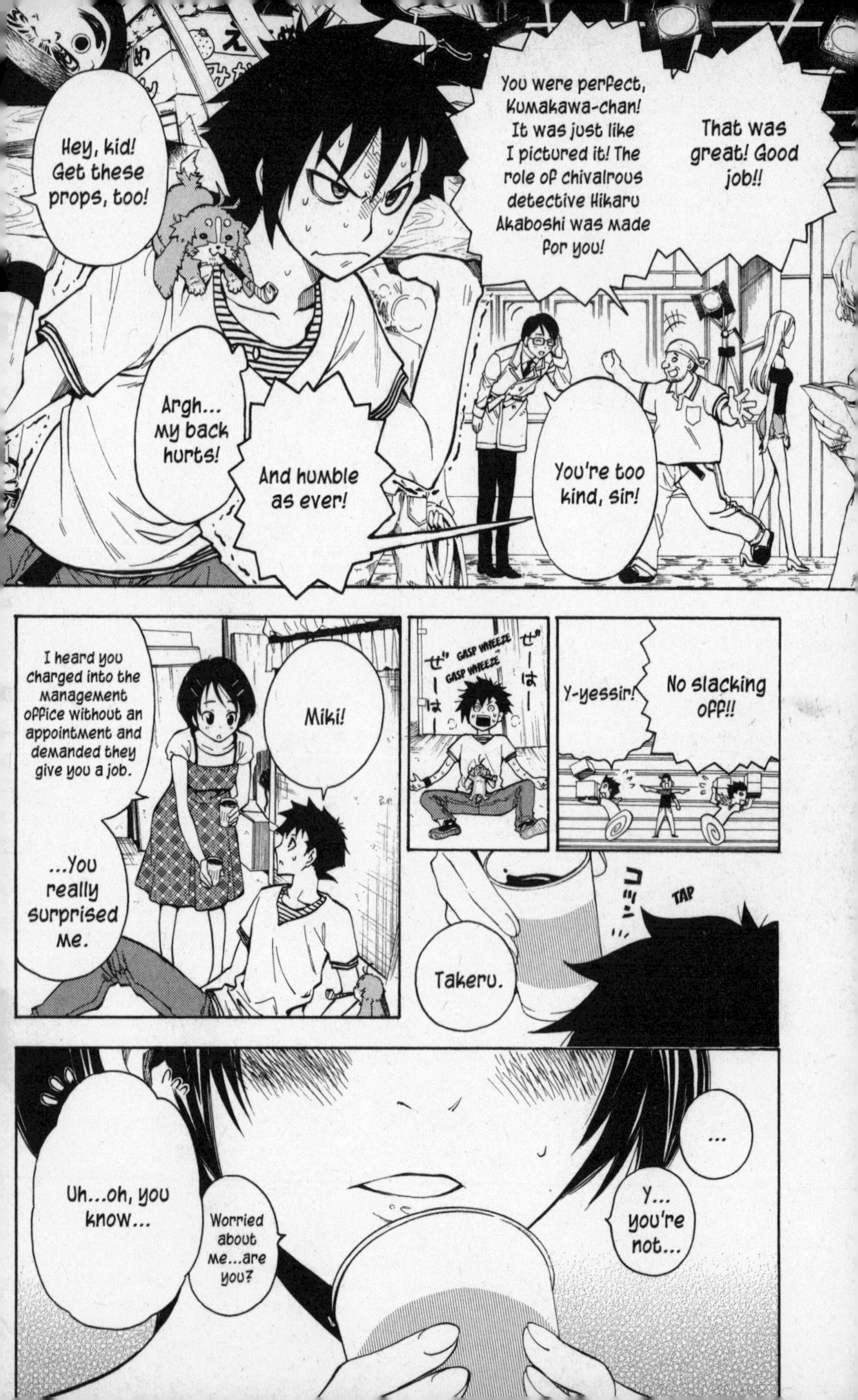
That was great! Good job!!
You were perfect, Kumakawa-chan! It was just like I pictured it! The role of chivalrous detective Hikaru Akaboshi was made for you!
You're too kind, sir!
And humble as ever!
Argh... my back hurts!
Hey, kid! Get these props, too!
No slacking off!!
Y-yessir!
ぜーはー
GASP WHEEZE
ぜーはー
GASP WHEEZE
コツ
TAP
Takeru.
Miki!
I heard you charged into the management office without an appointment and demanded they give you a job.
...You really surprised me.
...
Y... you're not...
Worried about me...are you?
Uh...oh, you know...

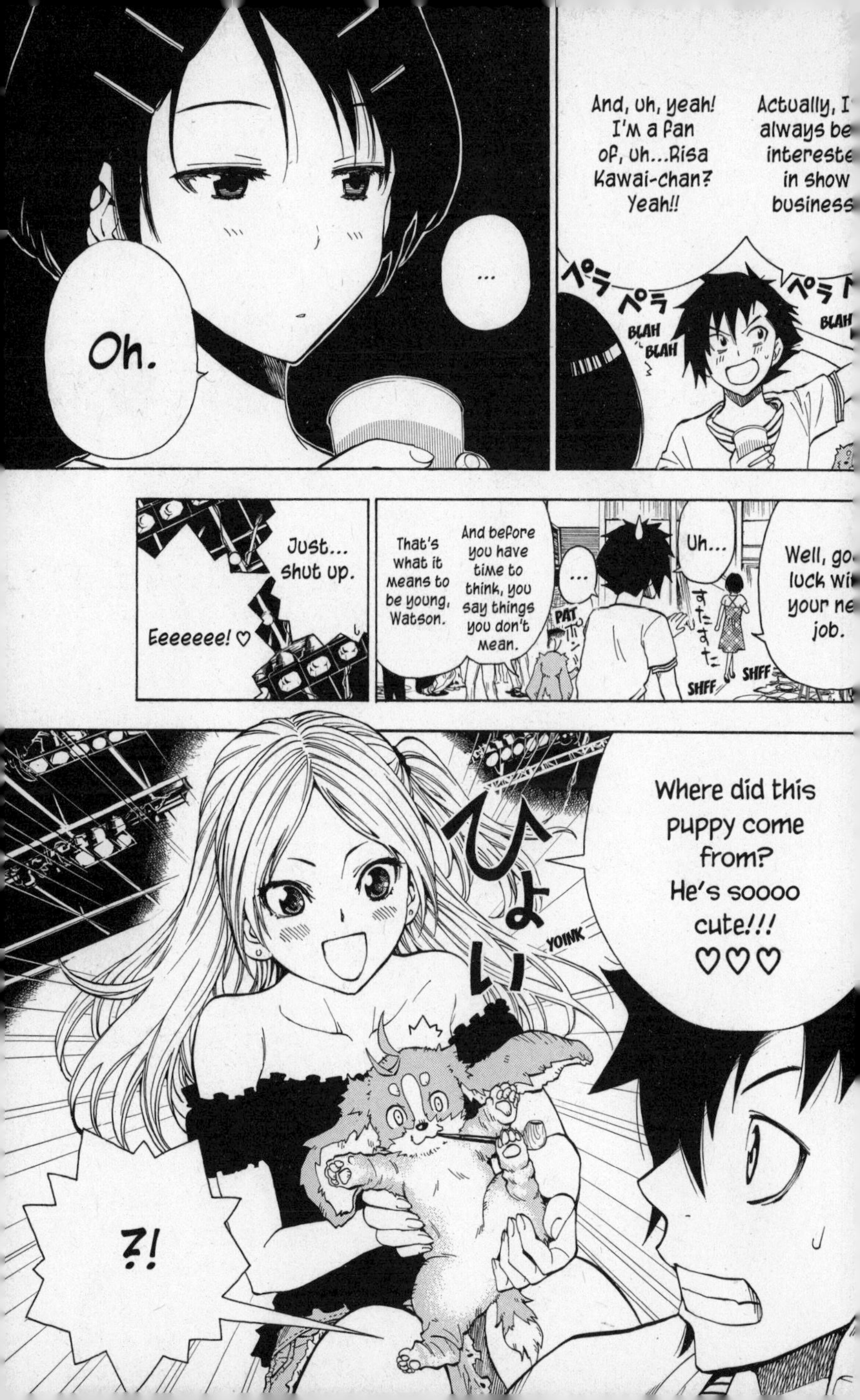

Actually, I always be intereste in show business
And, uh, yeah! I'm a fan of, uh...Risa Kawai-chan? Yeah!!
ペラ ペラ ペラ
BLAH BLAH BLAH
...
Oh.
Well, go luck wi your ne job.
Uh...
すたすた
SHFF SHFF
...
ポン
PAT
And before you have time to think, you say things you don't mean.
That's what it means to be young, Watson.
Just... shut up.
Eeeeeee! ♡
Where did this puppy come from? He's soooo cute!!! ♡♡♡
ひょい
YOINK
?!

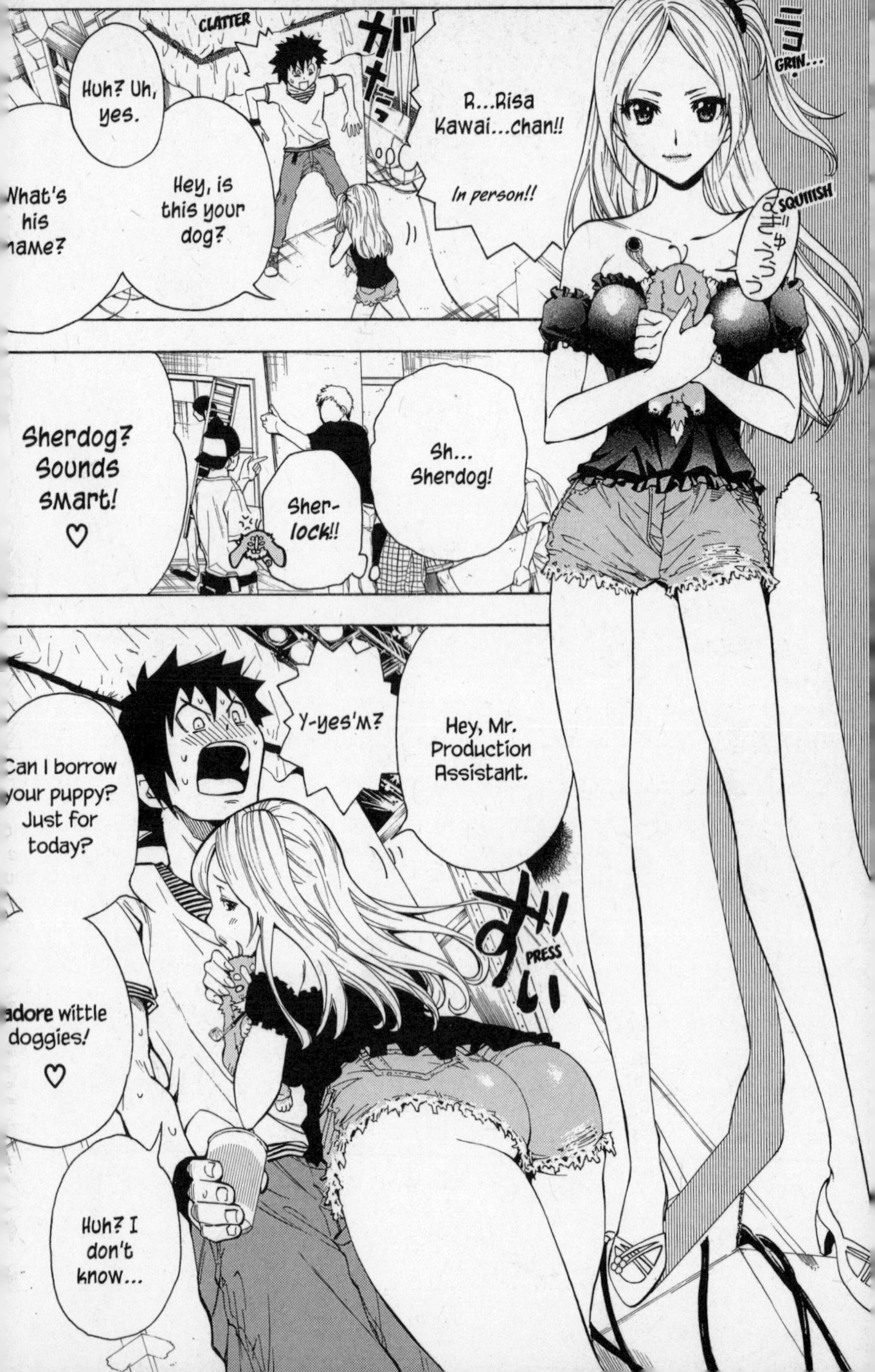
GRIN...
SQUIIISH
CLATTER
R...Risa Kawai...chan!!
In person!!
Hey, is this your dog?
Huh? Uh, yes.
What's his name?
Sh... Sherdog!
Sher-lock!!
Sherdog? Sounds smart! ♡
Hey, Mr. Production Assistant.
Y-yes'm?
PRESS
Can I borrow your puppy? Just for today?
adore wittle doggies! ♡
Huh? I don't know...

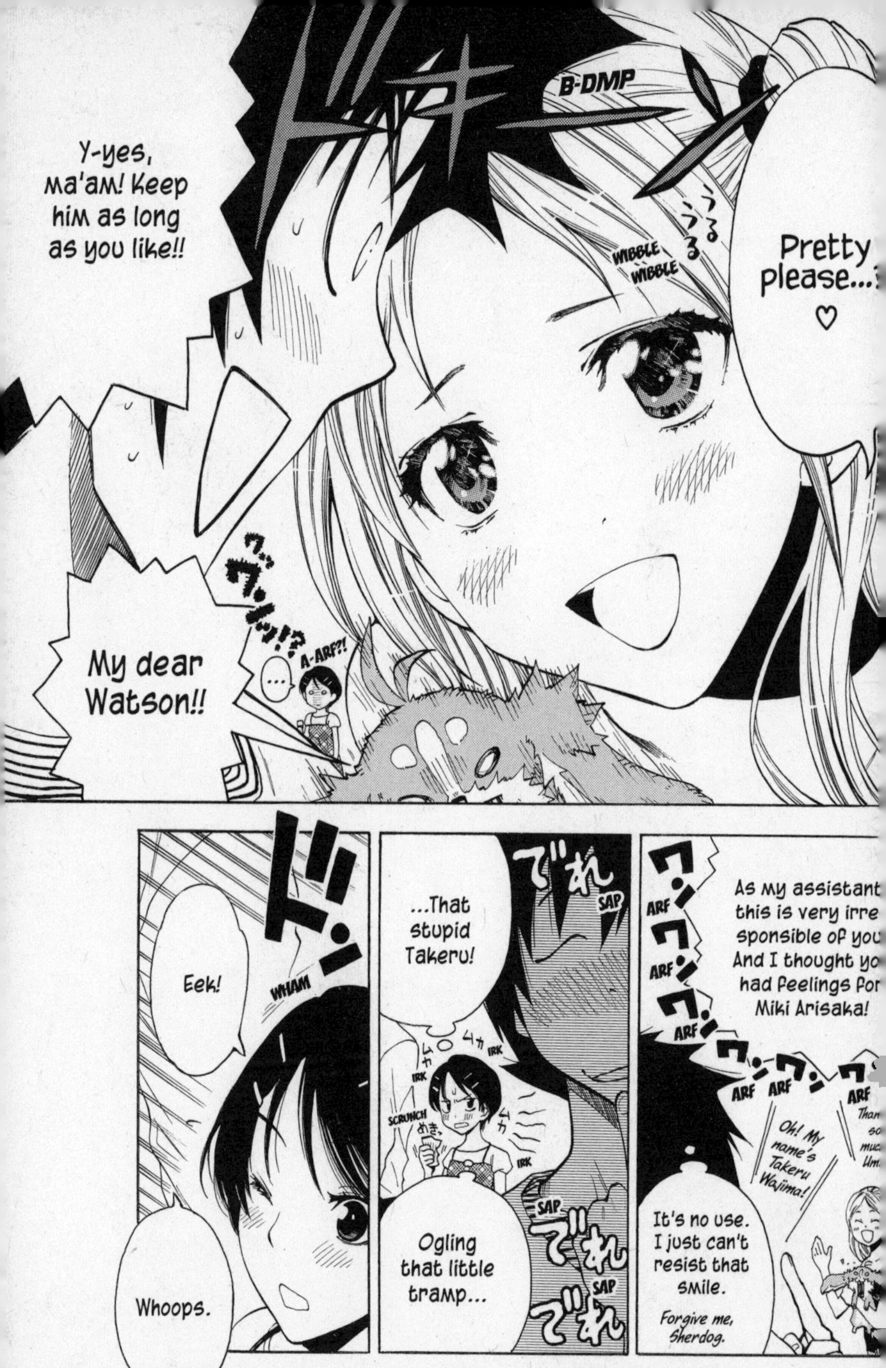
B-DMP
Pretty please...♡
WIBBLE WIBBLE
Y-yes, ma'am! Keep him as long as you like!!
A-ARF?!
...
My dear Watson!!
ARF ARF ARF ARF ARF ARF
As my assistant this is very irre sponsible of you And I thought yo had feelings for Miki Arisaka!
Oh! My name's Takeru Wajima!
It's no use. I just can't resist that smile.
Forgive me, Sherdog.
SAP
...That stupid Takeru!
IRK IRK IRK
SCRUNCH
SAP SAP
Ogling that little tramp...
WHAM
Eek!
Whoops.

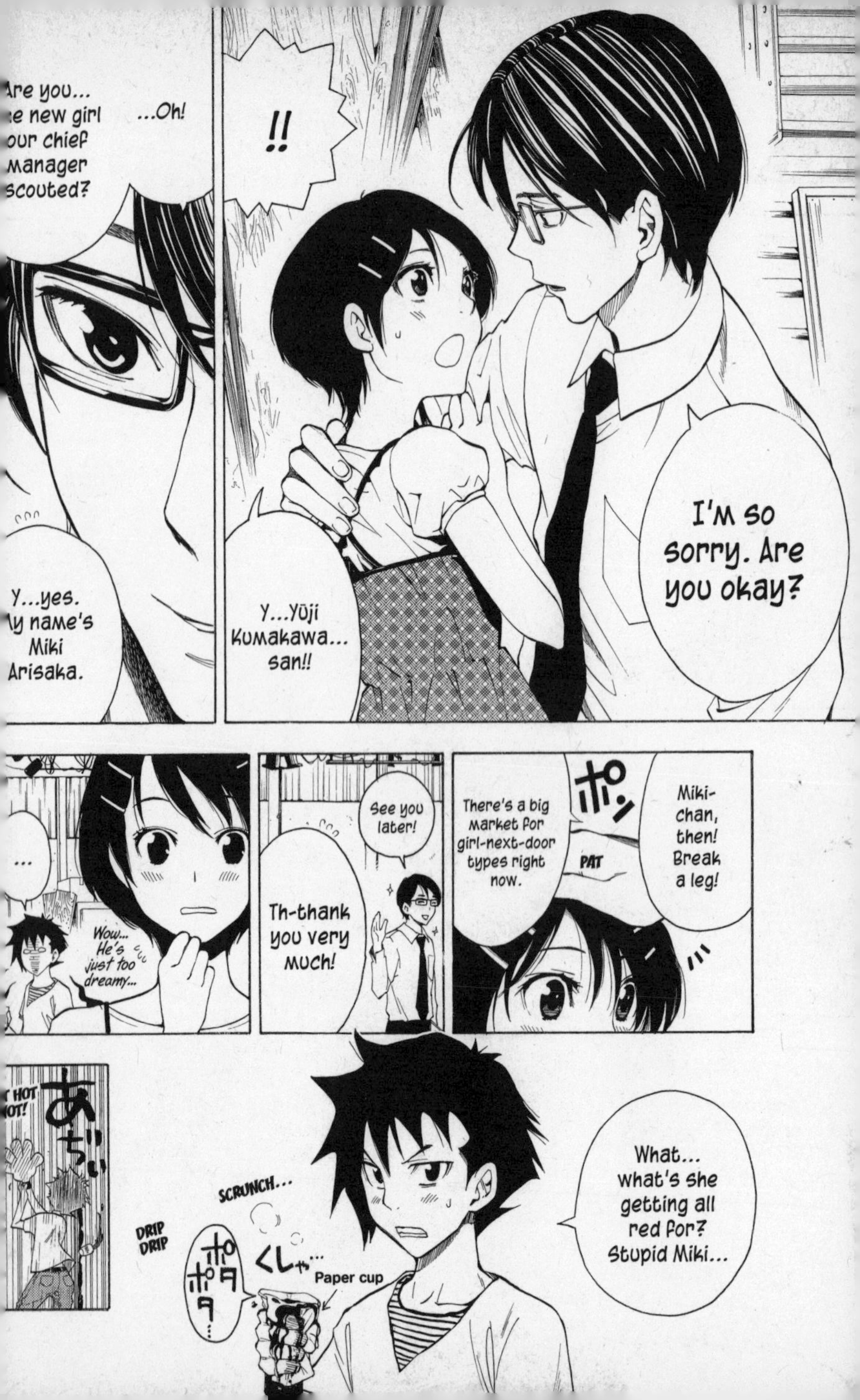
I'm so sorry. Are you okay?
!!
Y...Yūji Kumakawa... san!!
...Oh!
Are you... e new girl our chief manager scouted?
Y...yes. y name's Miki Arisaka.
Miki-chan, then! Break a leg!
ポン
PAT
There's a big market for girl-next-door types right now.
See you later!
Th-thank you very much!
...
Wow... He's just too dreamy...
What... what's she getting all red for? Stupid Miki...
SCRUNCH...
くしゃ...
Paper cup
ポタポタ...
DRIP DRIP
あちっ
T HOT OT!

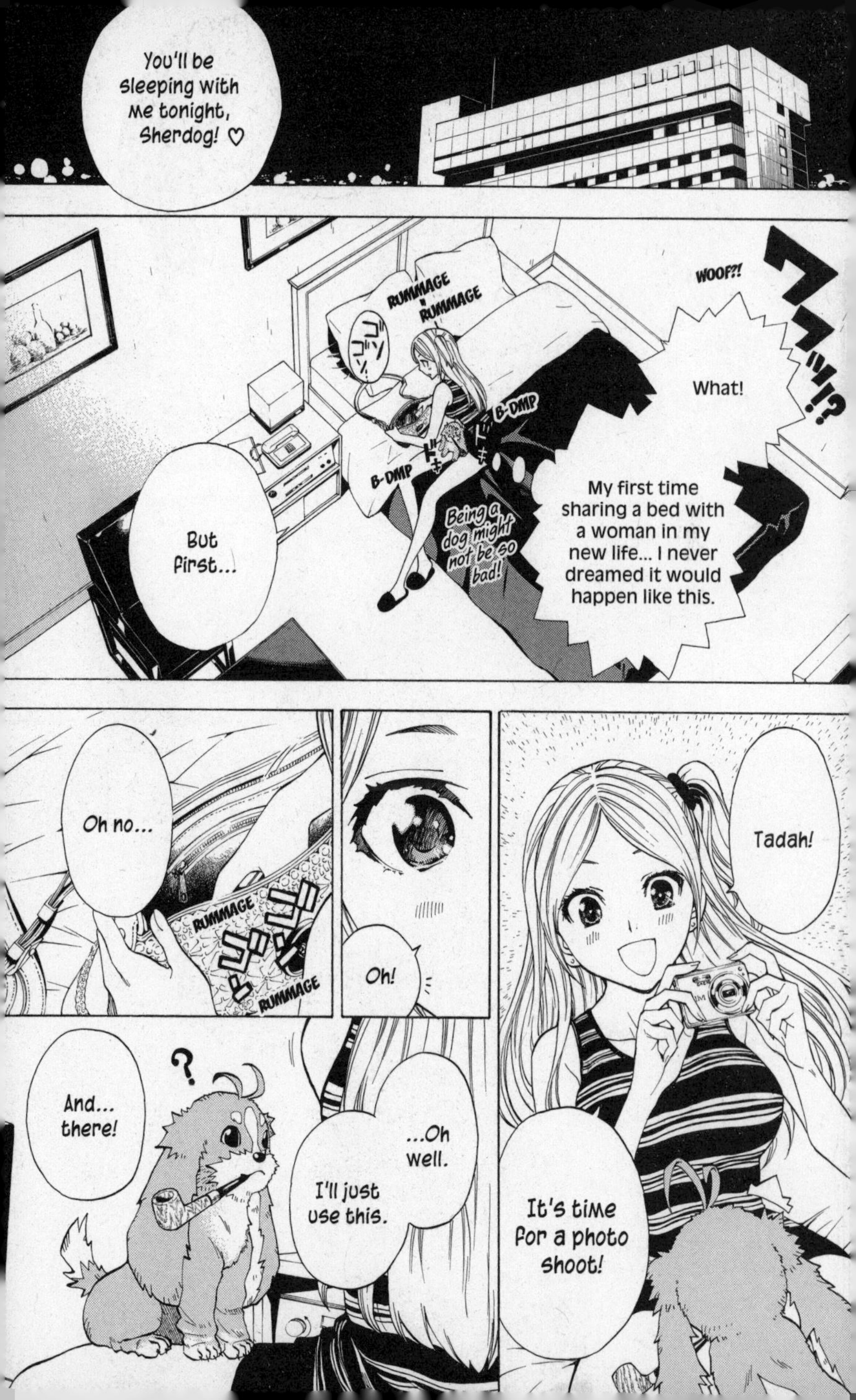
You'll be sleeping with me tonight, Sherdog! ♡
WOOF?!
What!
My first time sharing a bed with a woman in my new life... I never dreamed it would happen like this.
Being a dog might not be so bad!
RUMMAGE RUMMAGE
B-DMP
B-DMP
But first...
Tadah!
It's time for a photo shoot!
Oh!
Oh no...
RUMMAGE
RUMMAGE
...Oh well.
I'll just use this.
And... there!
?

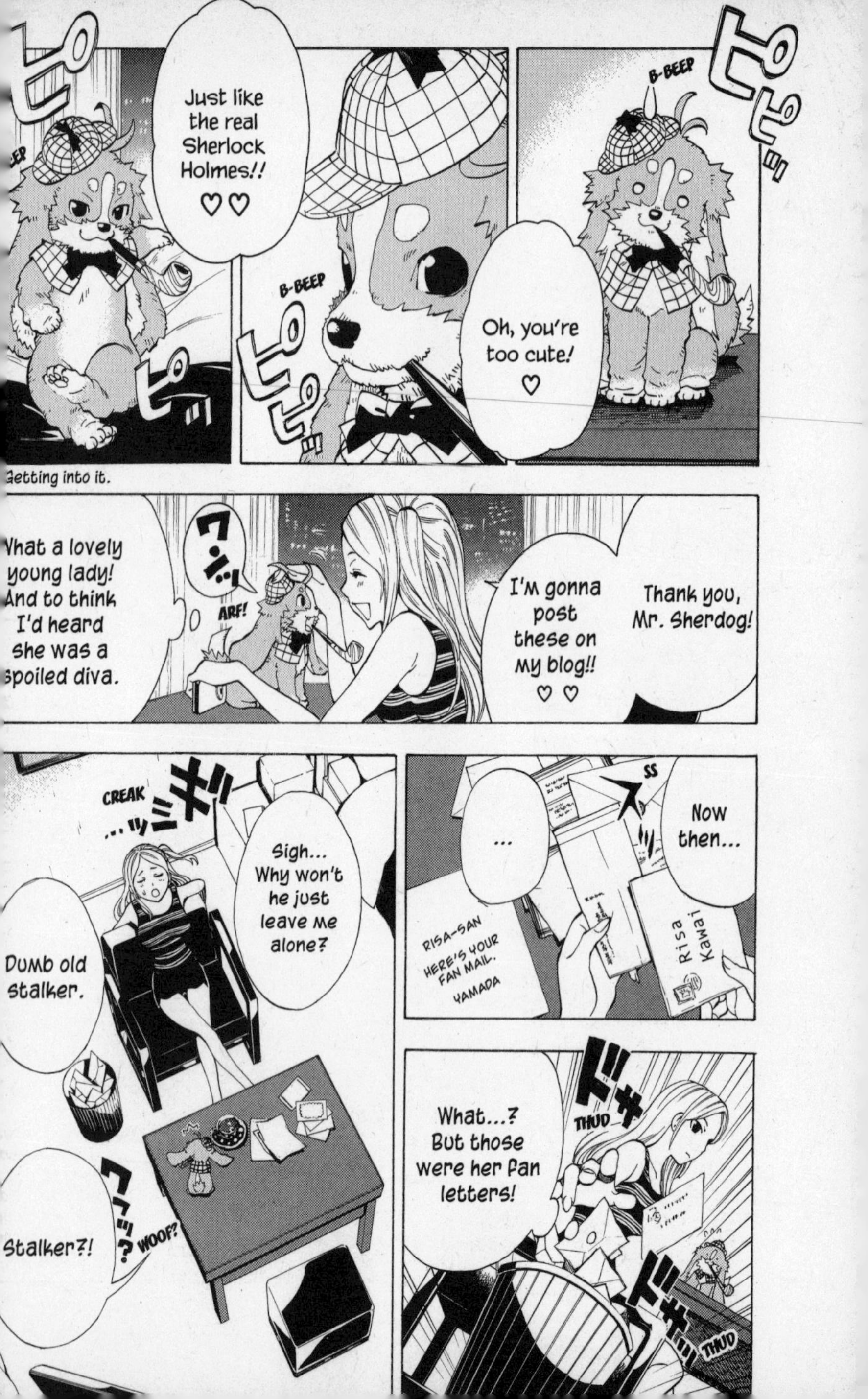
B-BEEP
ピピッ
Oh, you're too cute! ♡
B-BEEP
ピピッ
Just like the real Sherlock Holmes!! ♡ ♡
BEEP
ピッ
Getting into it.
Thank you, Mr. Sherdog!
I'm gonna post these on my blog!! ♡ ♡
ワン
ARF!
What a lovely young lady! And to think I'd heard she was a spoiled diva.
Now then...
SS
...
RISA-SAN
HERE'S YOUR FAN MAIL.
YAMADA
Risa Kawai
THUD
What...? But those were her fan letters!
THUD
CREAK
Sigh... Why won't he just leave me alone?
Dumb old stalker.
WOOF?
Stalker?!

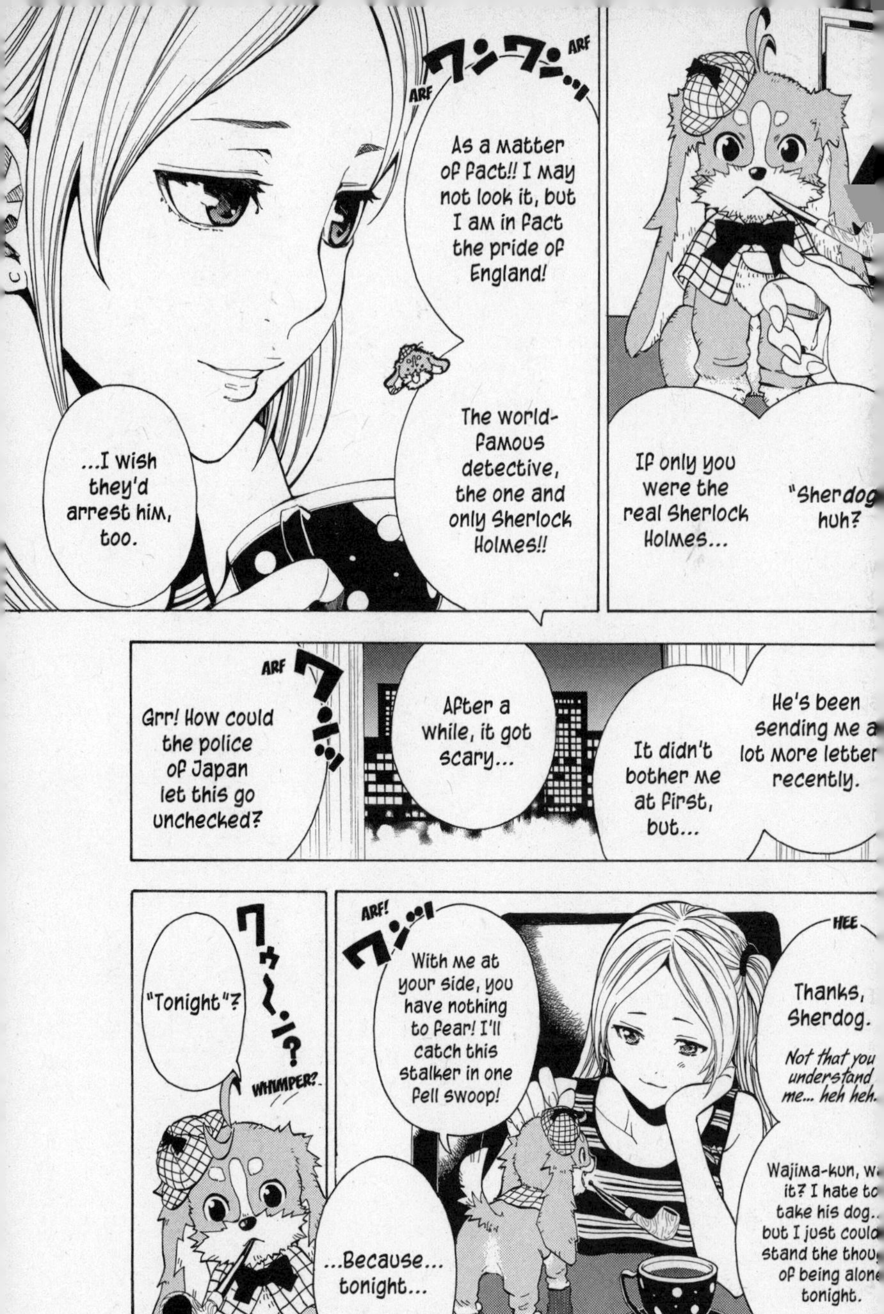
"Sherdog
huh?
If only you were the real Sherlock Holmes...
ARF
ARF
As a matter of fact!! I may not look it, but I am in fact the pride of England!
The world-famous detective, the one and only Sherlock Holmes!!
...I wish they'd arrest him, too.
He's been sending me a lot more letter recently.
It didn't bother me at first, but...
After a while, it got scary...
ARF
Grr! How could the police of Japan let this go unchecked?
HEE
Thanks, Sherdog.
Not that you understand me... heh heh.
Wajima-kun, w it? I hate to take his dog.. but I just could stand the thou of being alone tonight.
ARF!
With me at your side, you have nothing to fear! I'll catch this stalker in one fell swoop!
...Because... tonight...
WHIMPER?
"Tonight"?

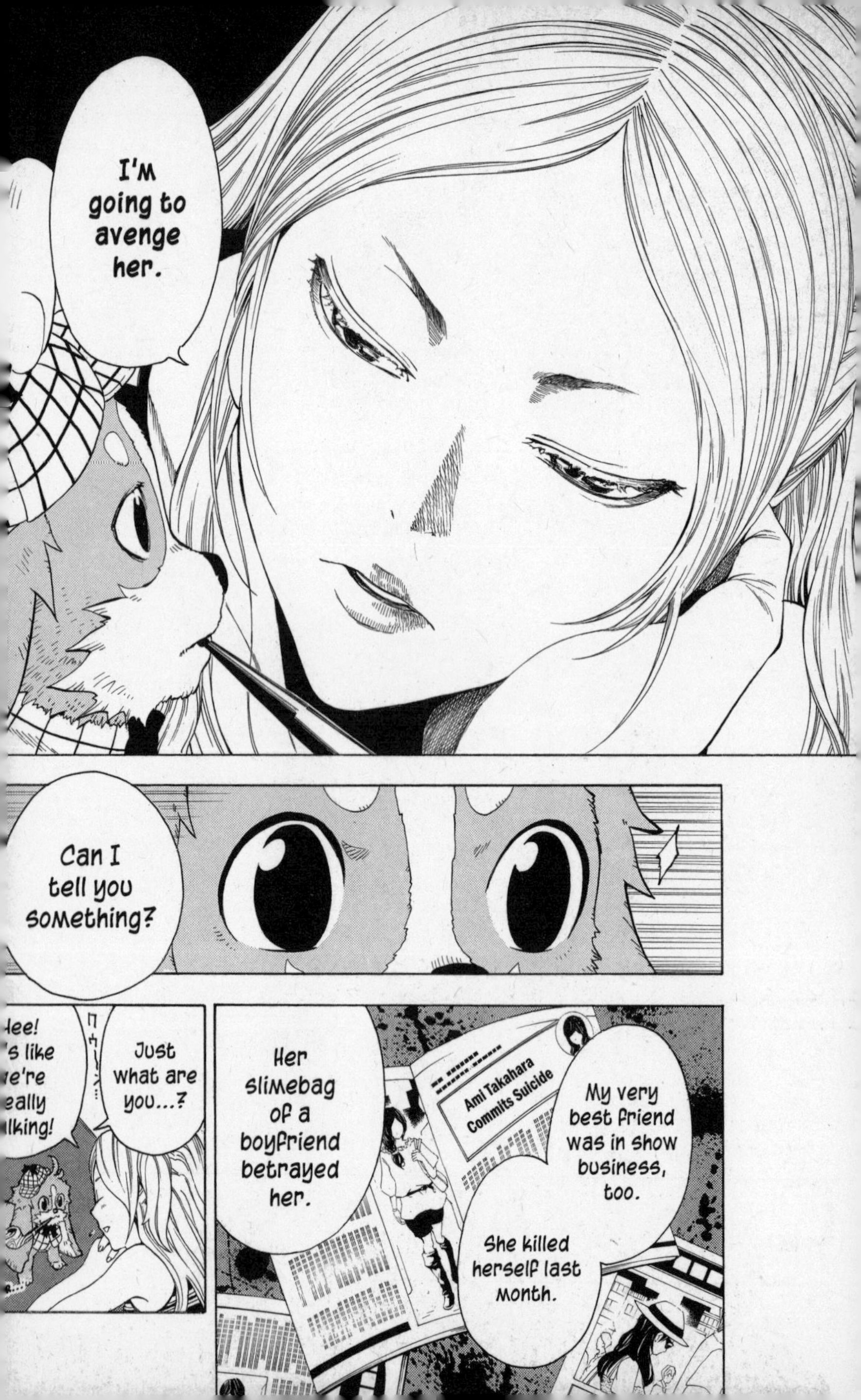
I'M going to avenge her.
Can I tell you something?
Ami Takahara Commits Suicide
My very best friend was in show business, too.
She killed herself last month.
Her slimebag of a boyfriend betrayed her.
Just what are you...?
Hee! 's like e're eally lking!

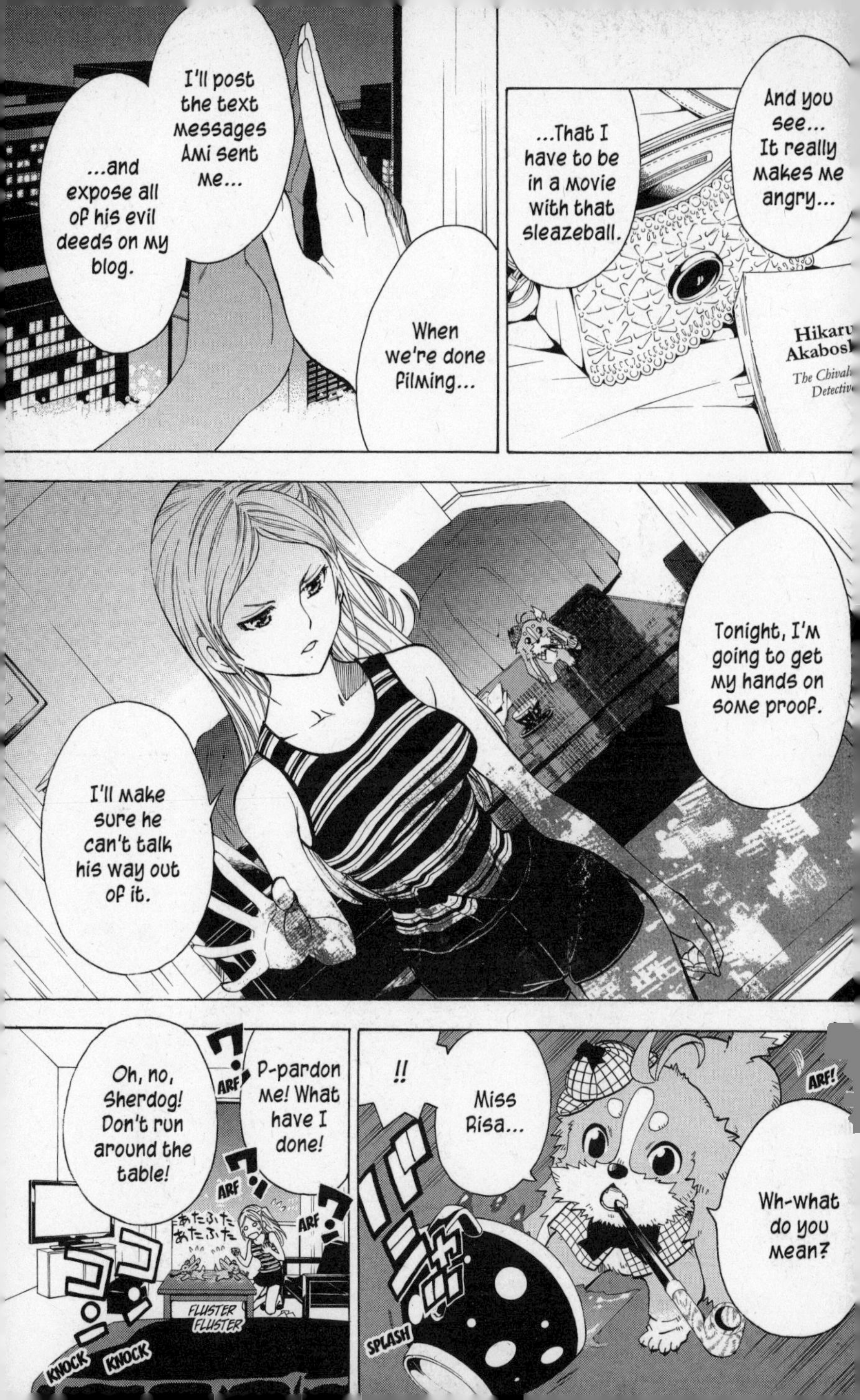
And you see... It really makes me angry...
...That I have to be in a movie with that sleazeball.
When we're done filming...
I'll post the text messages Ami sent me...
...and expose all of his evil deeds on my blog.
Tonight, I'm going to get my hands on some proof.
I'll make sure he can't talk his way out of it.
ARF!
Wh-what do you mean?
Miss Risa...
!!
SPLASH
ARF
P-pardon me! What have I done!
Oh, no, Sherdog! Don't run around the table!
ARF
ARF
あたふた
あたふた
FLUSTER
FLUSTER
KNOCK
KNOCK

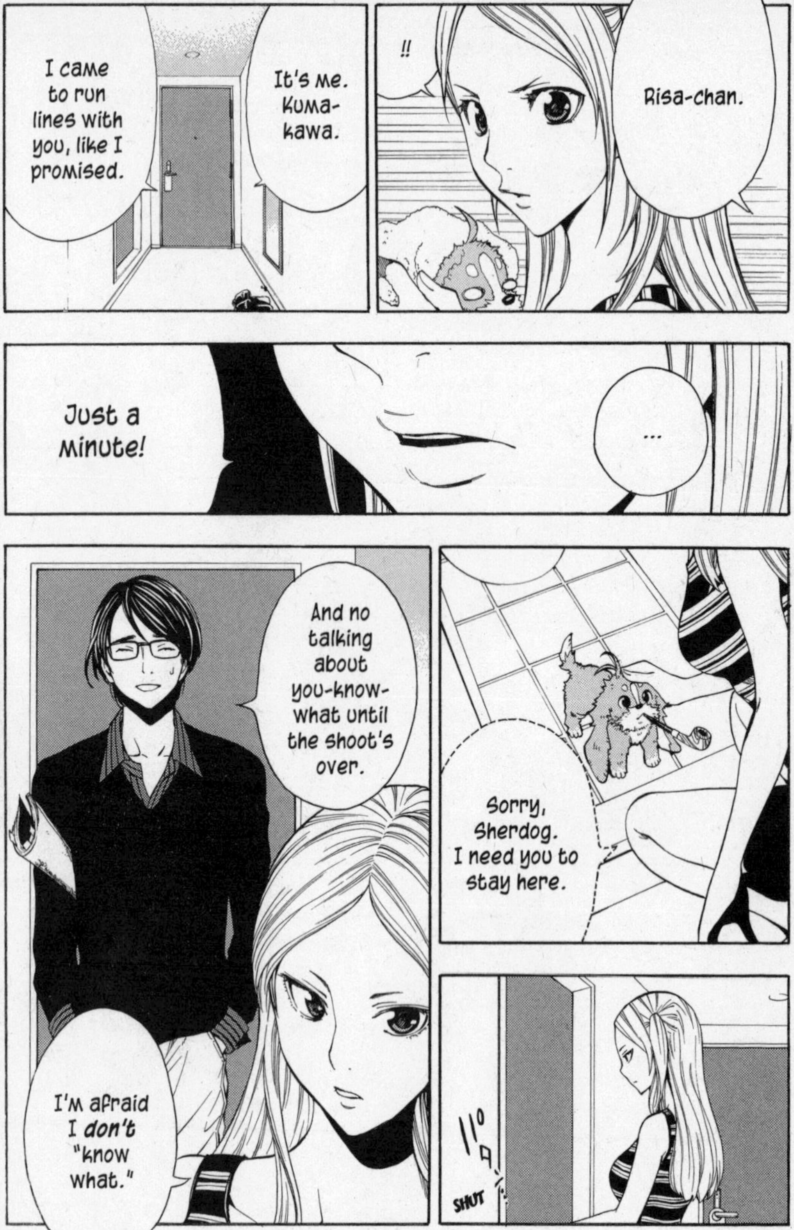
Risa-chan.
!!
It's me. Kuma-kawa.
I came to run lines with you, like I promised.
...
Just a minute!
Sorry, Sherdog. I need you to stay here.
SHUT
And no talking about you-know-what until the shoot's over.
I'm afraid I *don't* "know what."

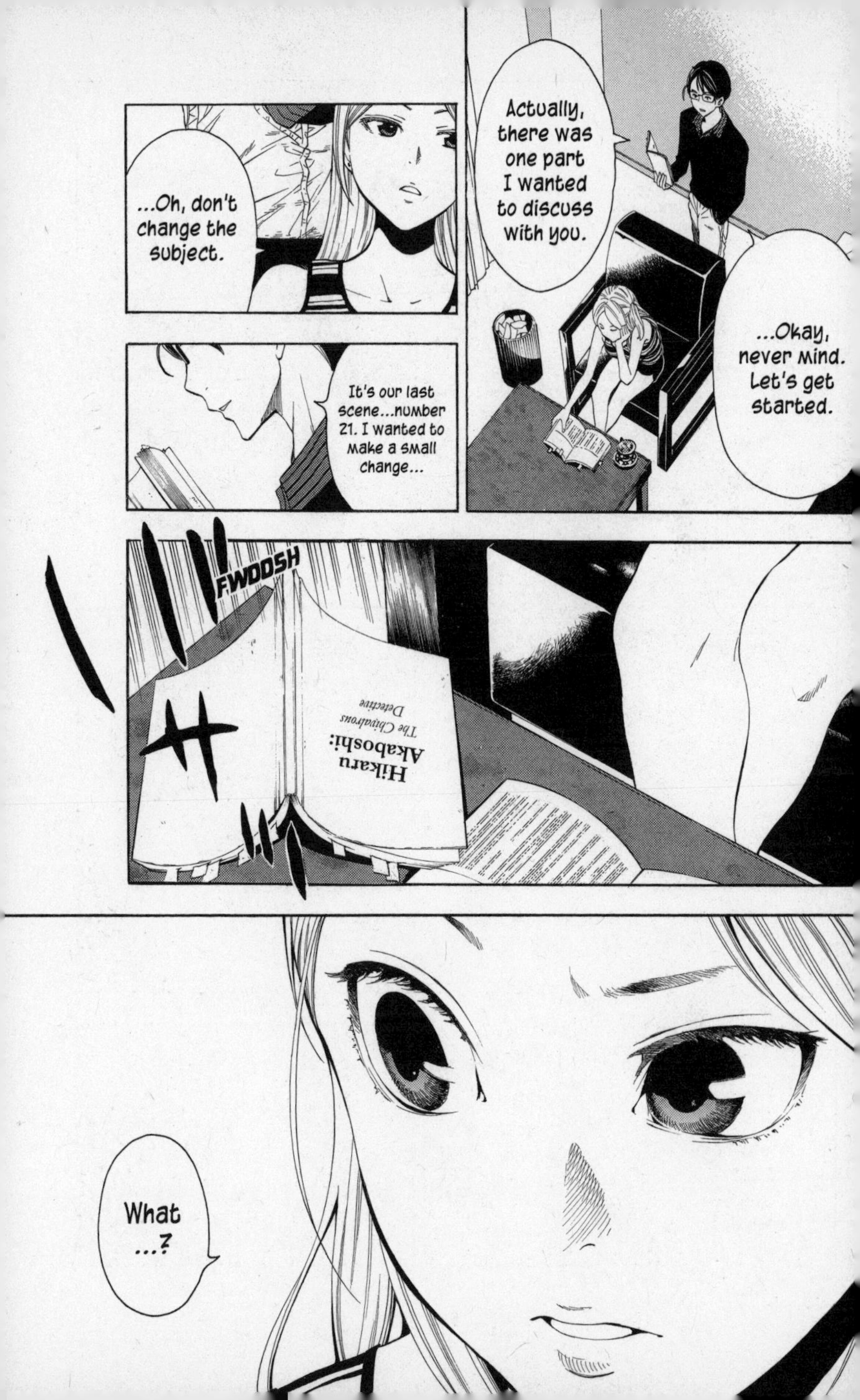
...Okay, never mind. Let's get started.
Actually, there was one part I wanted to discuss with you.
...Oh, don't change the subject.
It's our last scene...number 21. I wanted to make a small change...
FWOOSH
Hikaru Akaboshi: The Chivalrous Detective
What ...?

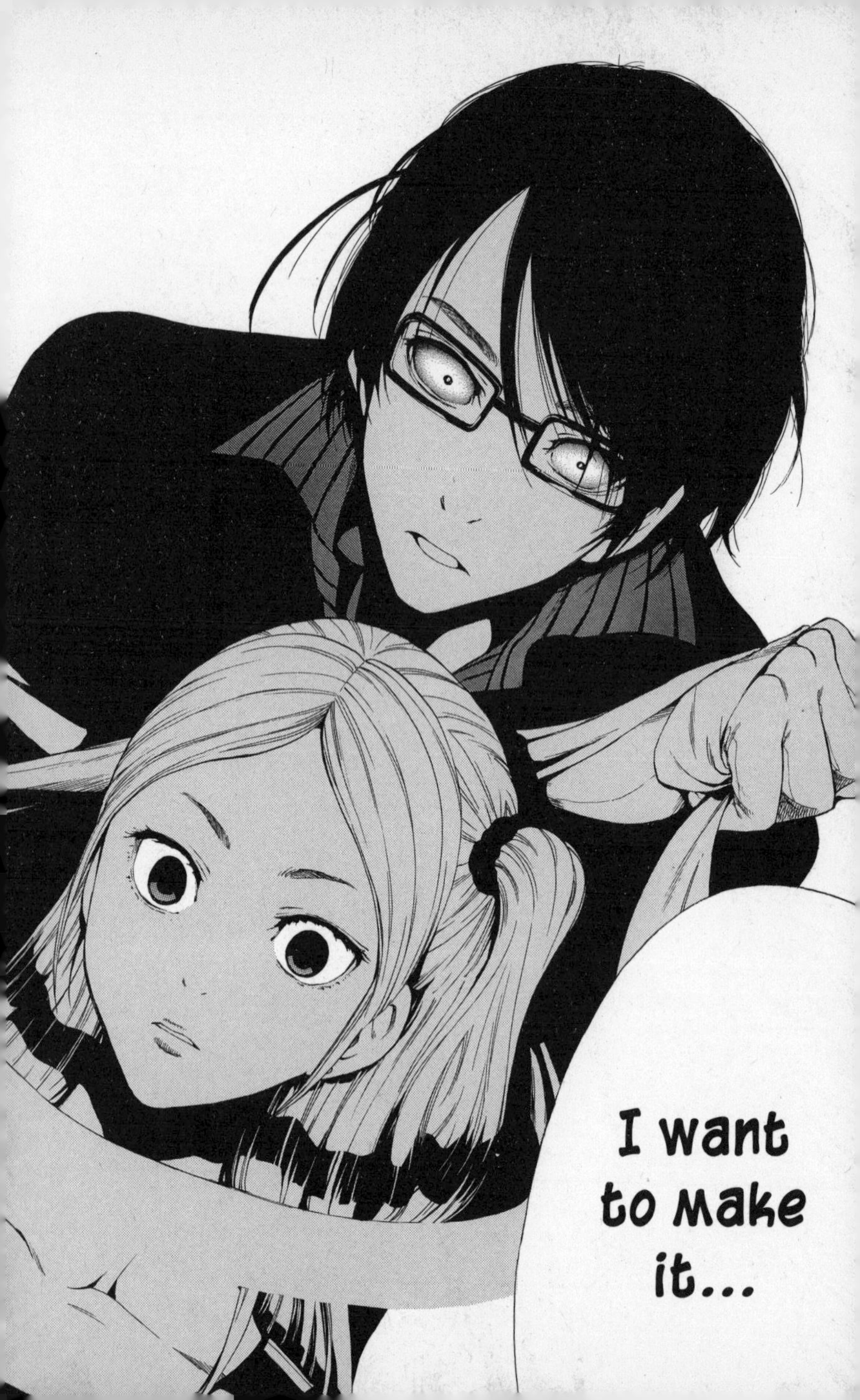
I want to make it...

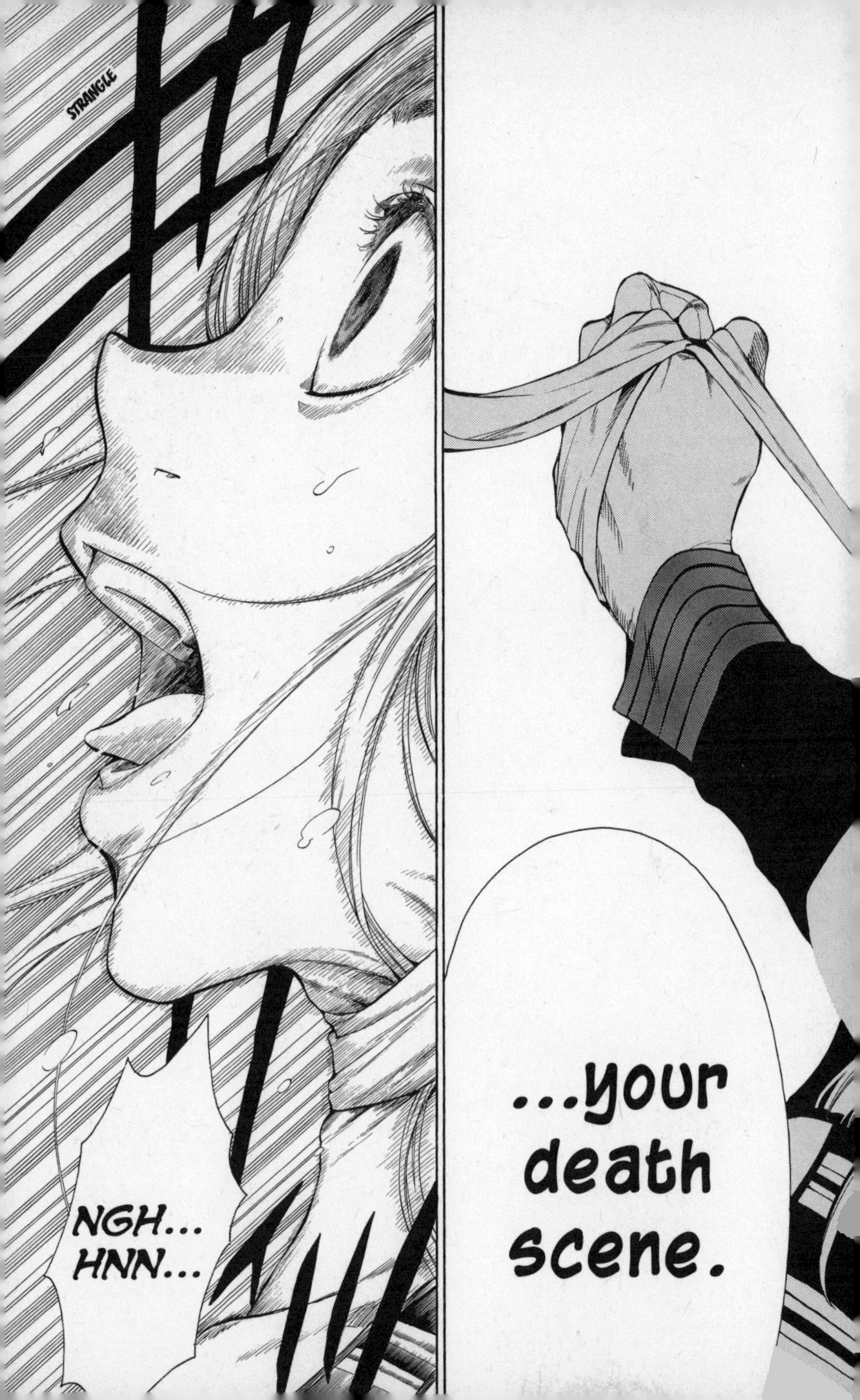
...your death scene.
STRANGLE
NGH... HNN...

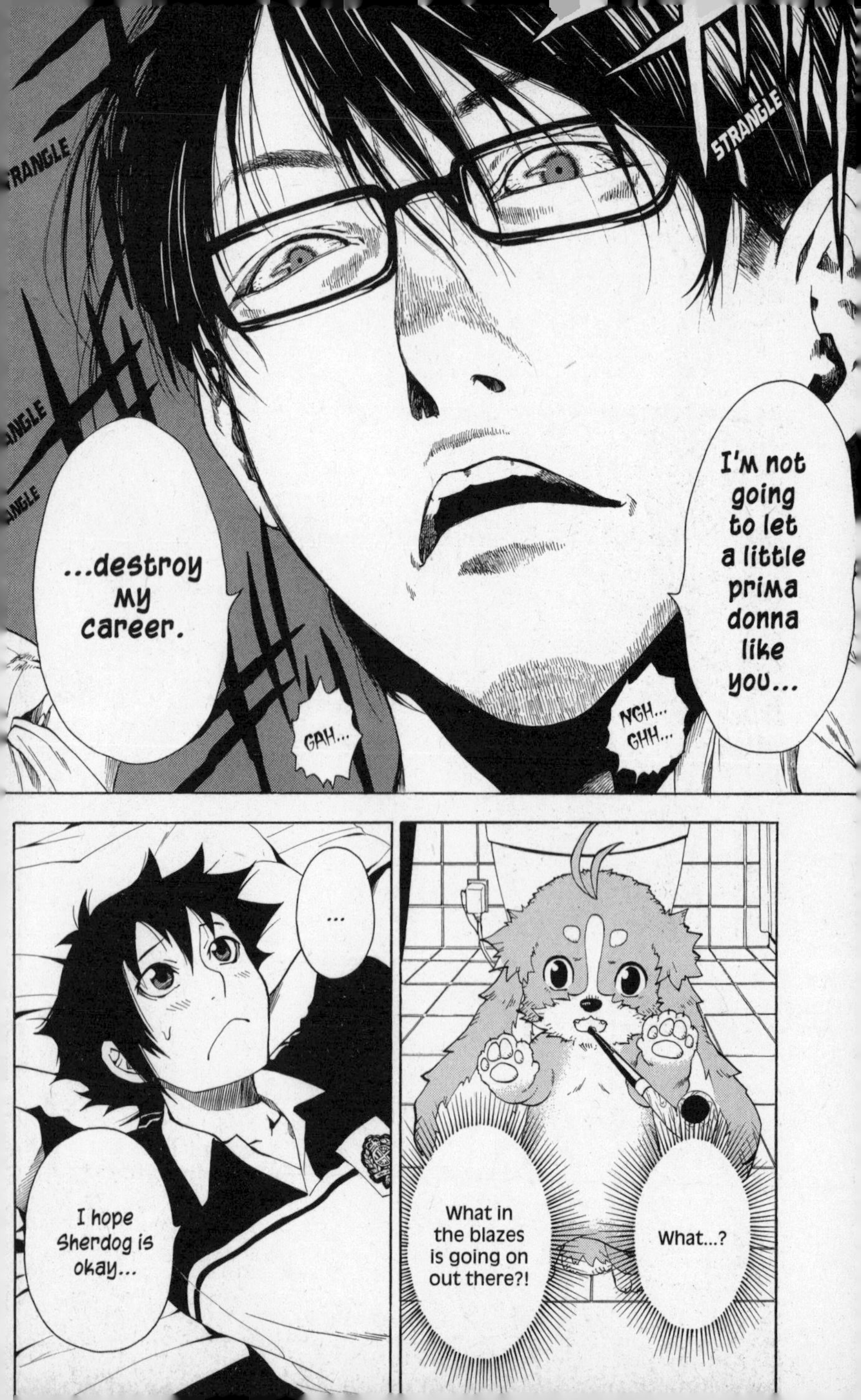
STRANGLE
I'm not going to let a little prima donna like you...
NGH... GHH...
GAH...
...destroy my career.
What...?
What in the blazes is going on out there?!
...
I hope Sherdog is okay...

Case 2 ⚜ A Script for Death, Part 2

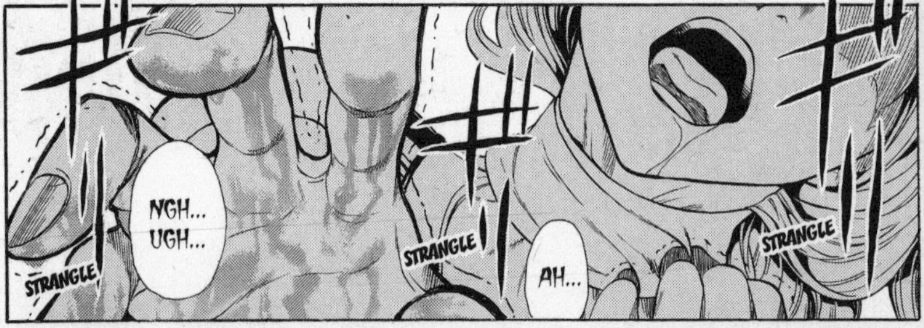
STRANGLE
AH...
STRANGLE
NGH... UGH...
STRANGLE

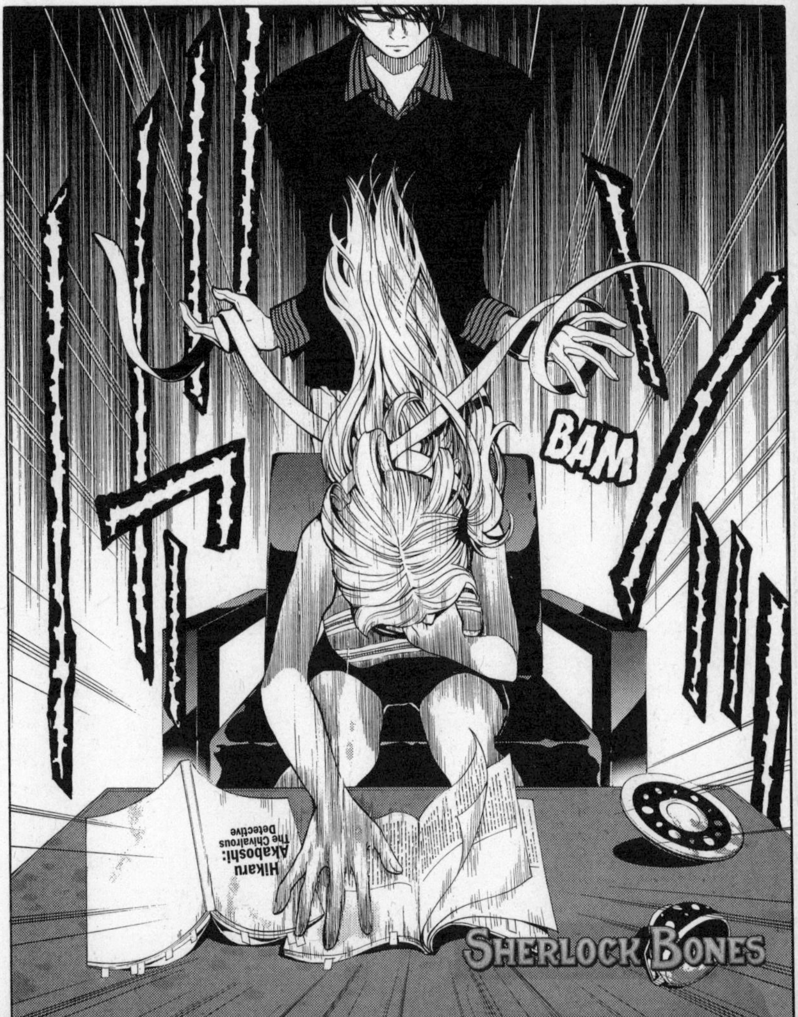
BAM
Hikaru Akaboshi: The Chivalrous Detective
SHERLOCK BONES

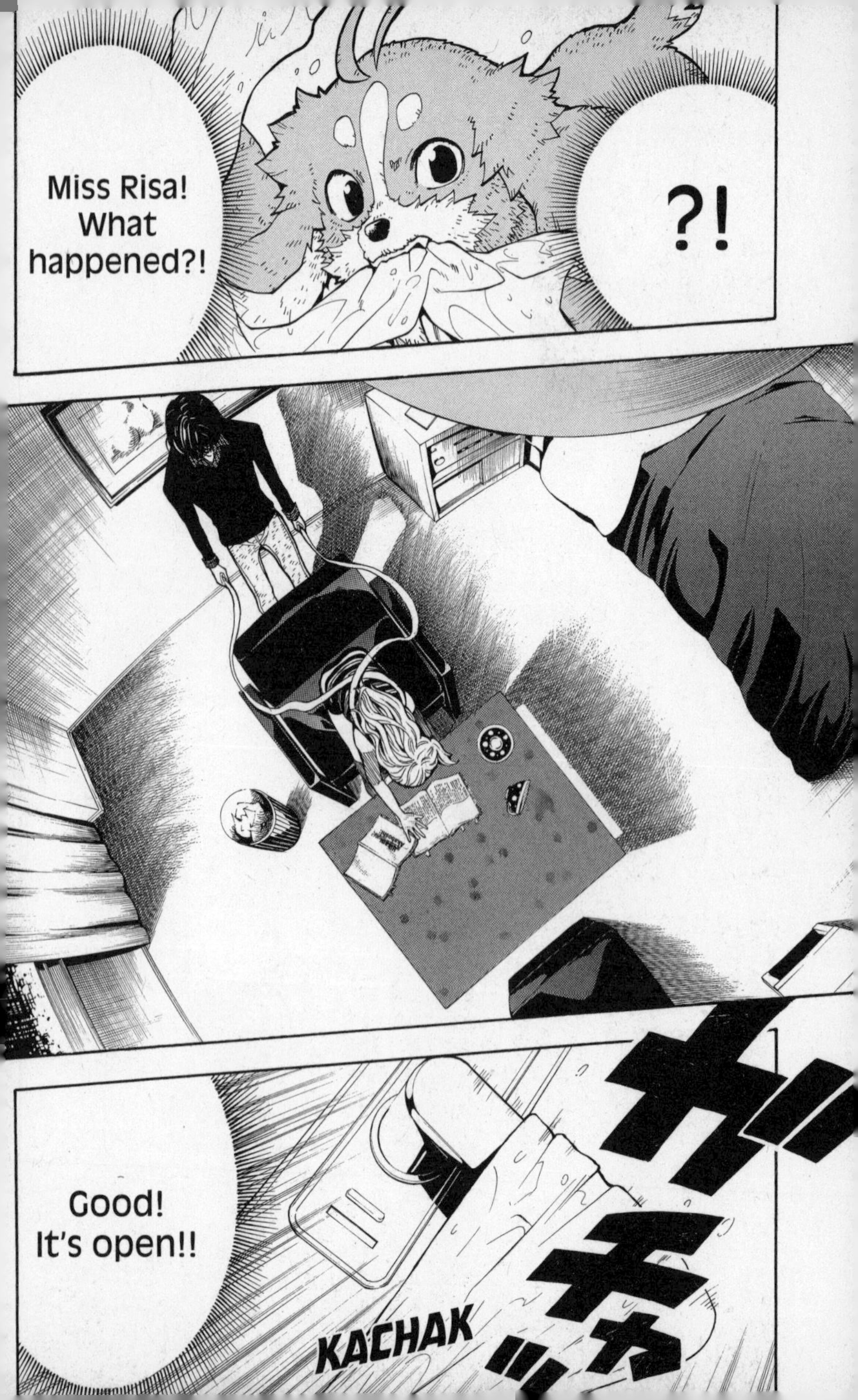
?!
Miss Risa! What happened?!
ガチャッ
KACHAK
Good! It's open!!

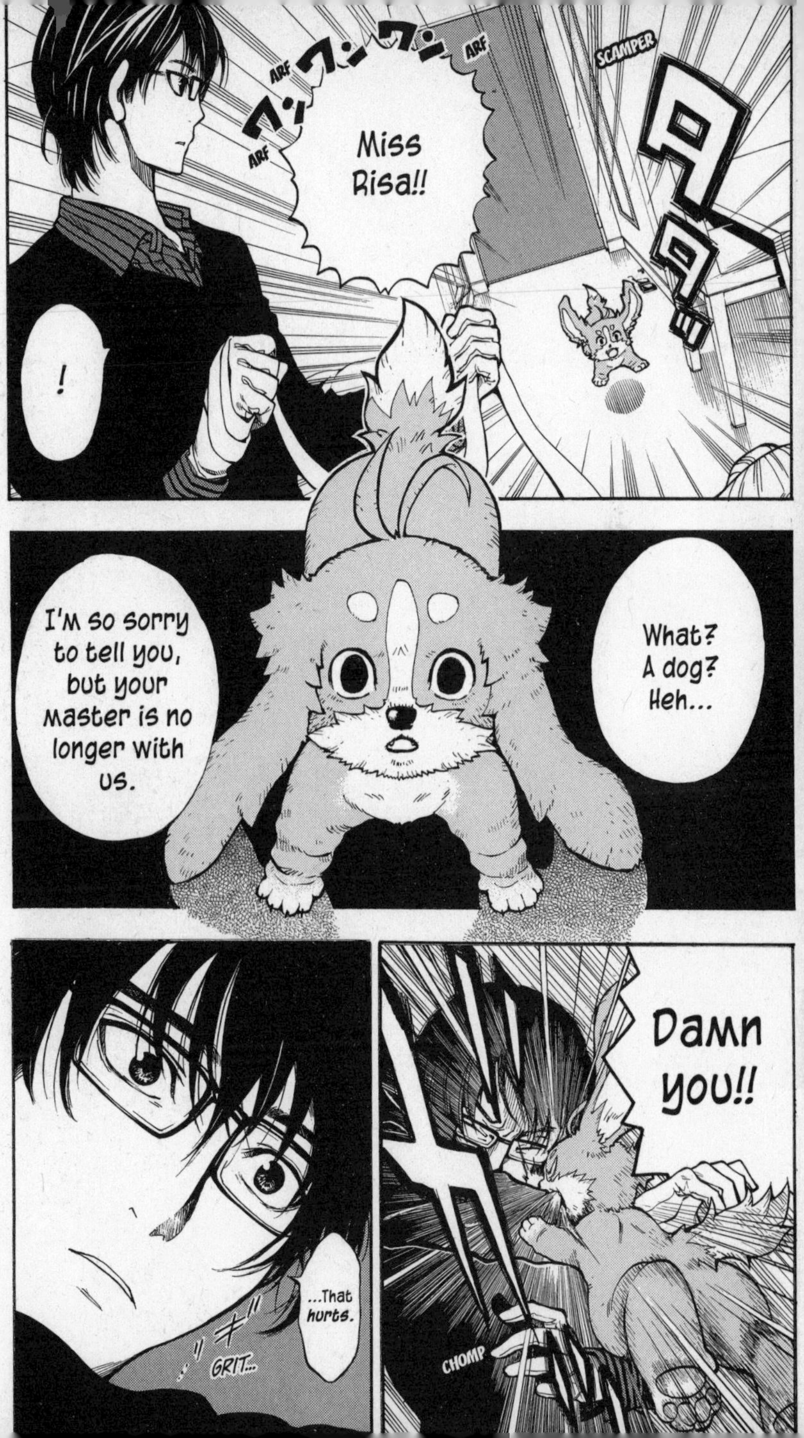
SCAMPER
ARF
ARF
ARF
ARF
Miss Risa!!
!
What? A dog? Heh...
I'm so sorry to tell you, but your master is no longer with us.
Damn you!!
CHOMP
...That hurts.
GRIT...

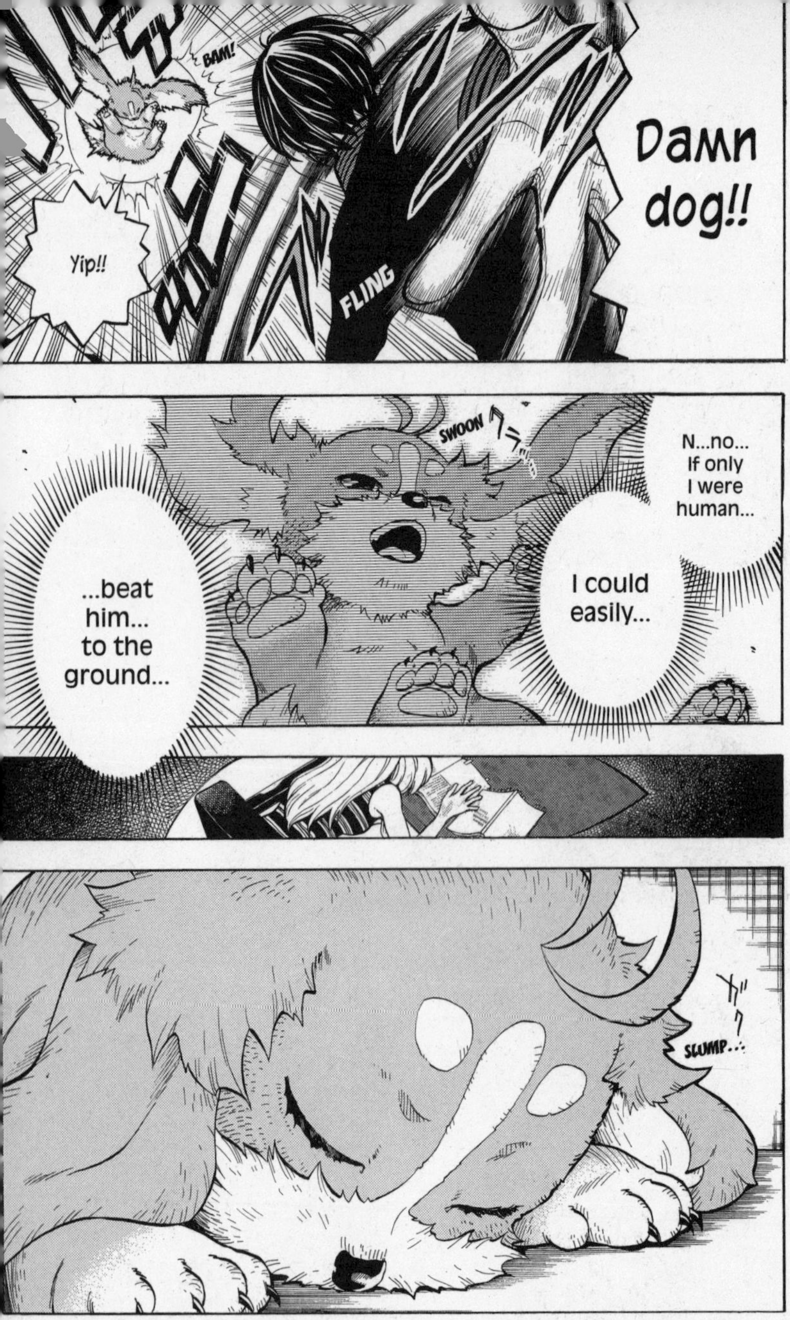
Damn dog!!
BAM!
FLING
Yip!!
N...no... If only I were human...
SWOON
I could easily...
...beat him... to the ground...
SLUMP...

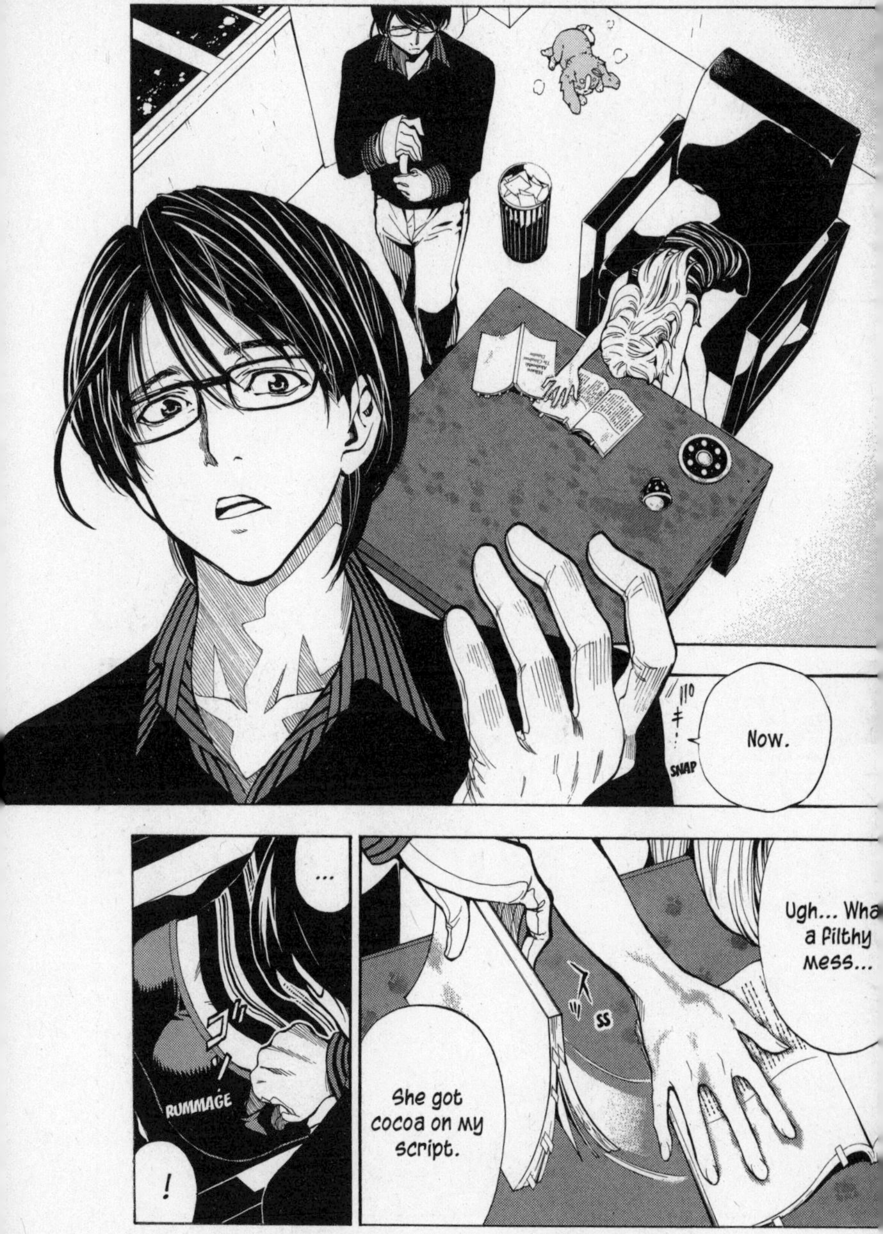
SNAP
Now.
Ugh... Wha
a filthy
mess...
SS
She got cocoa on my script.
...
RUMMAGE
!

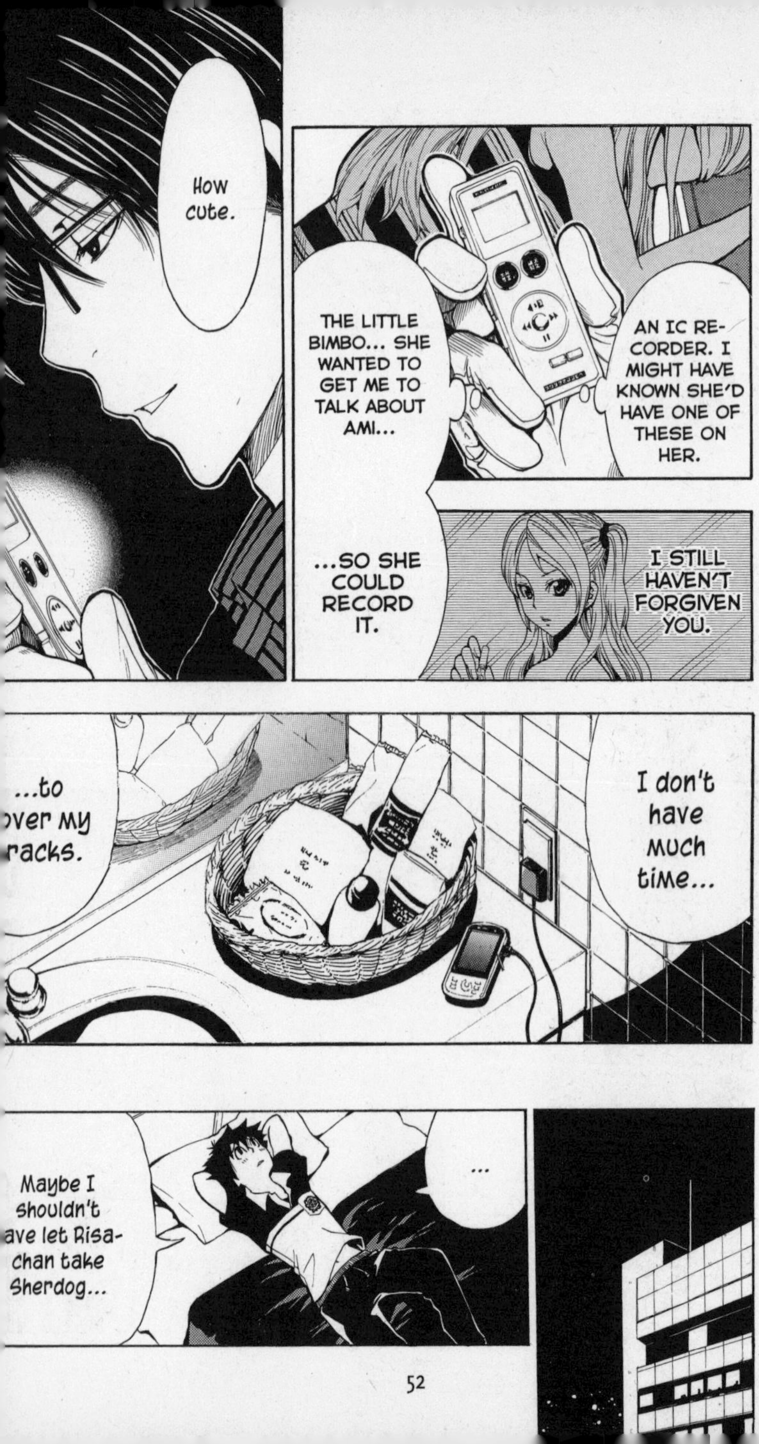
AN IC RE-CORDER. I MIGHT HAVE KNOWN SHE'D HAVE ONE OF THESE ON HER.
THE LITTLE BIMBO... SHE WANTED TO GET ME TO TALK ABOUT AMI...
I STILL HAVEN'T FORGIVEN YOU.
...SO SHE COULD RECORD IT.
How cute.
I don't have much time...
...to over my racks.
...
Maybe I shouldn't ave let Risa-chan take Sherdog...

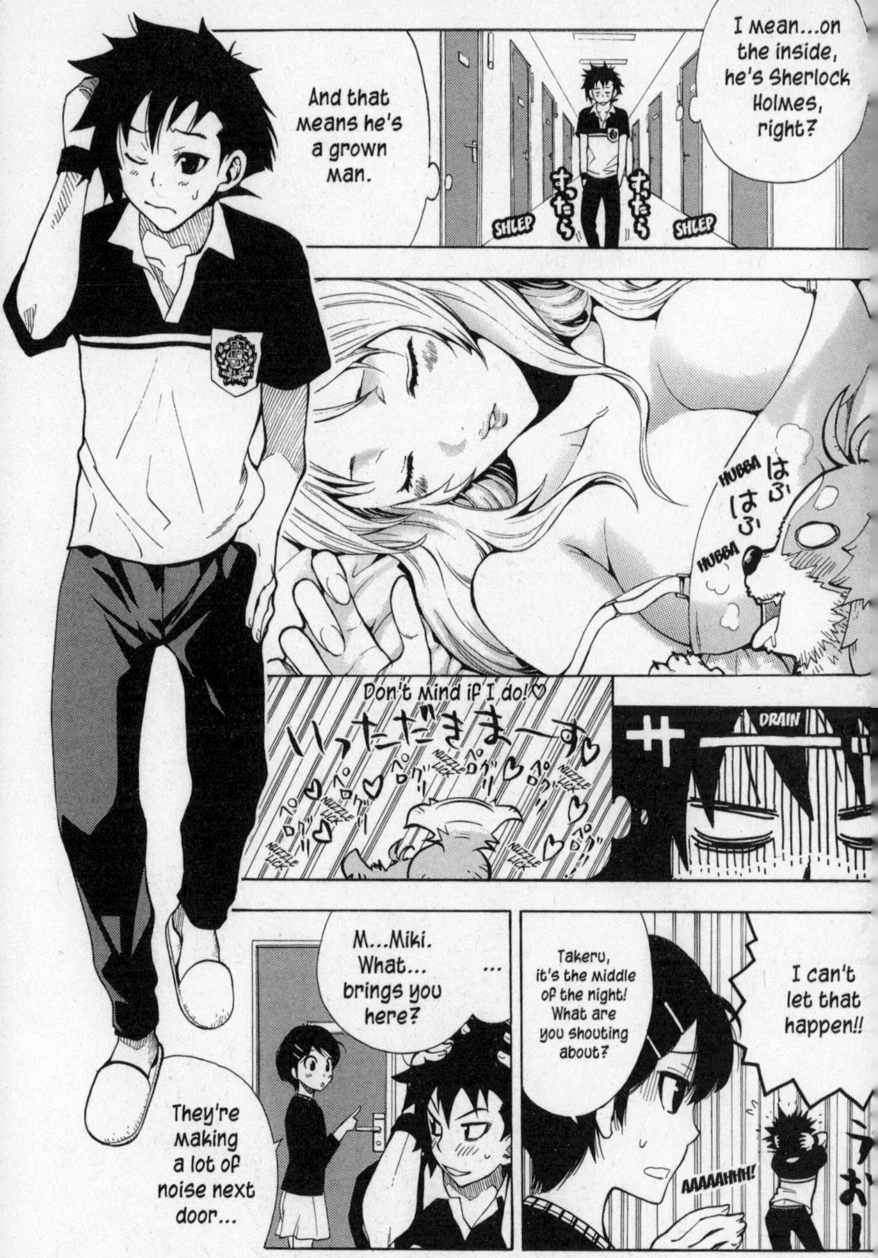
I mean...on the inside, he's Sherlock Holmes, right?
And that means he's a grown man.
SHLEP
SHLEP
HUBBA
HUBBA
はふ はふ
DRAIN
Don't mind if I do!♡
いっただきまーす♡
NUZZLE LICK
NUZZLE LICK
NUZZLE LICK
NUZZLE LICK
I can't let that happen!!
AAAAAHHH!
Takeru, it's the middle of the night! What are you shouting about?
M...Miki. What... brings you here?
...
They're making a lot of noise next door...

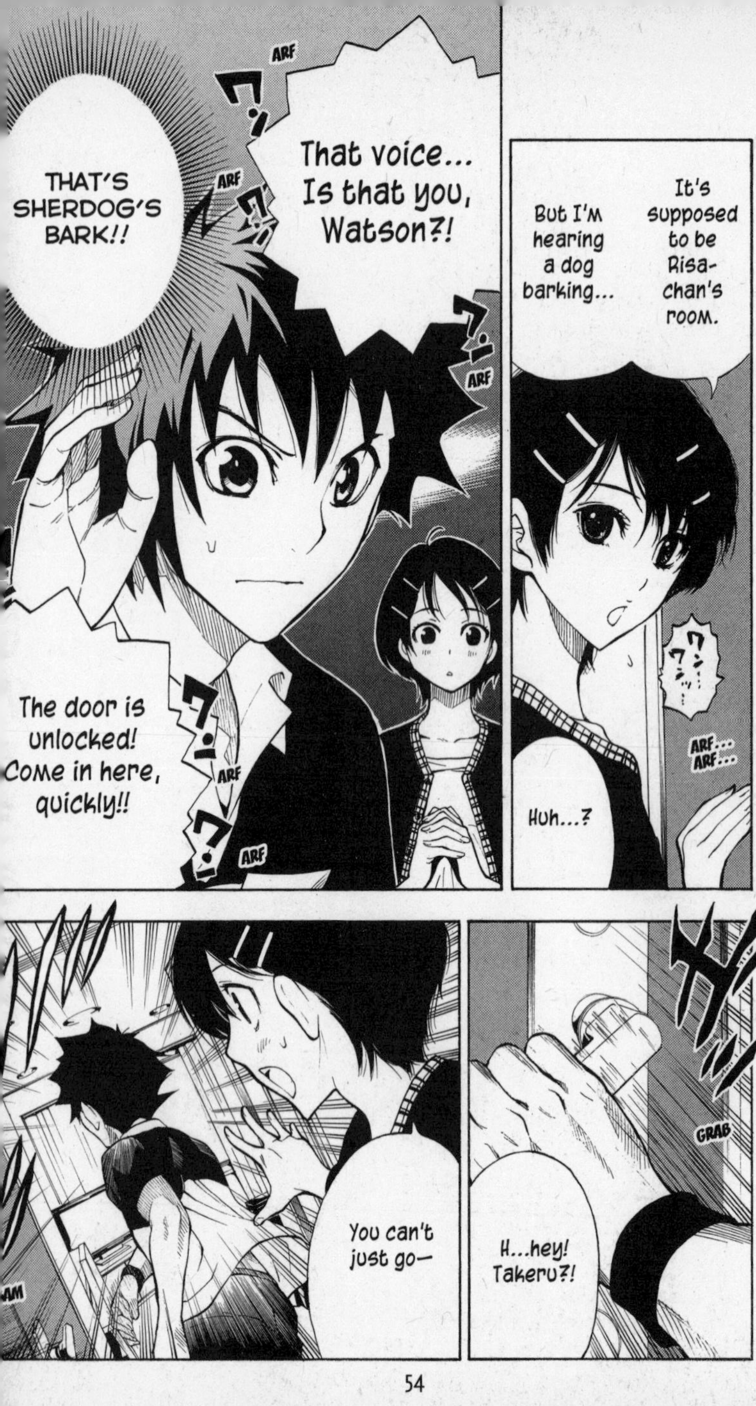
It's supposed to be Risa-chan's room.
But I'm hearing a dog barking...
ARF... ARF...
Huh...?
ARF
That voice... Is that you, Watson?!
THAT'S SHERDOG'S BARK!!
ARF
ARF
The door is unlocked! Come in here, quickly!!
ARF
ARF
GRAB
H...hey! Takeru?!
You can't just go—

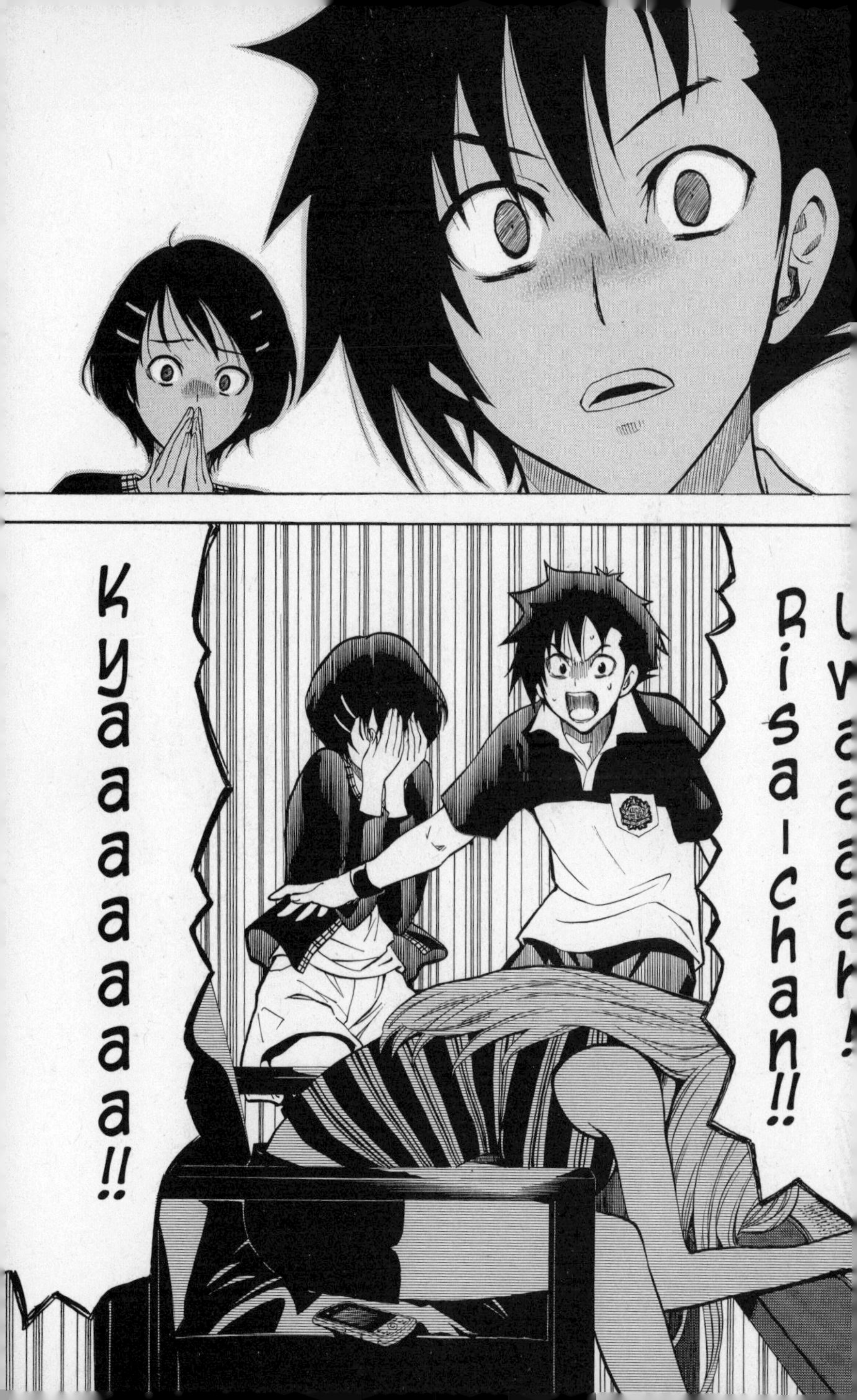
Uwaaaah!
Risa-chan!!
Kyaaaaaaa!!

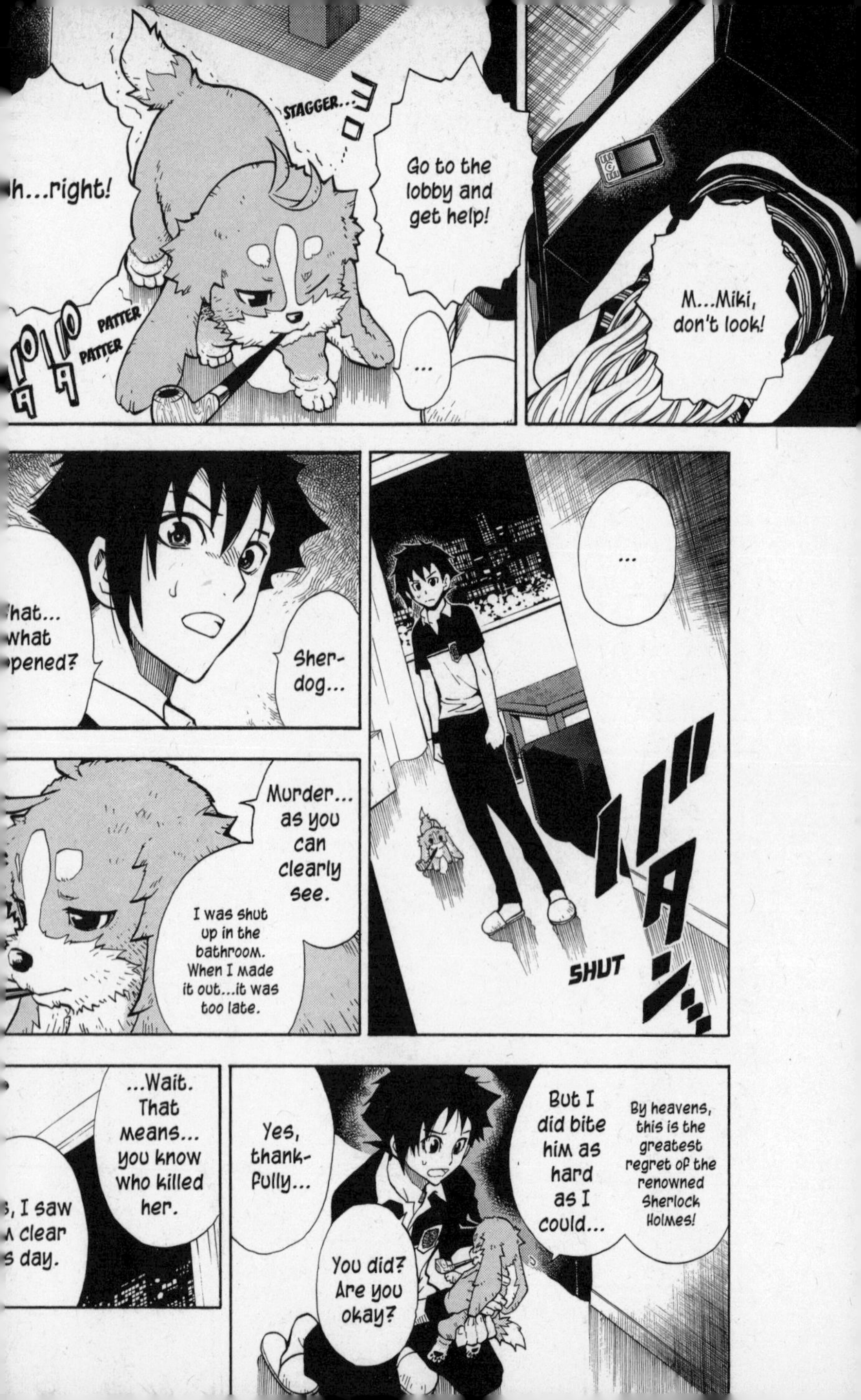
M...Miki, don't look!
Go to the lobby and get help!
STAGGER...
h...right!
...
PATTER PATTER
...
SHUT
Sher-dog...
hat... what pened?
Murder... as you can clearly see.
I was shut up in the bathroom. When I made it out...it was too late.
By heavens, this is the greatest regret of the renowned Sherlock Holmes!
But I did bite him as hard as I could...
Yes, thankfully...
You did? Are you okay?
...Wait. That means... you know who killed her.
s, I saw a clear s day.

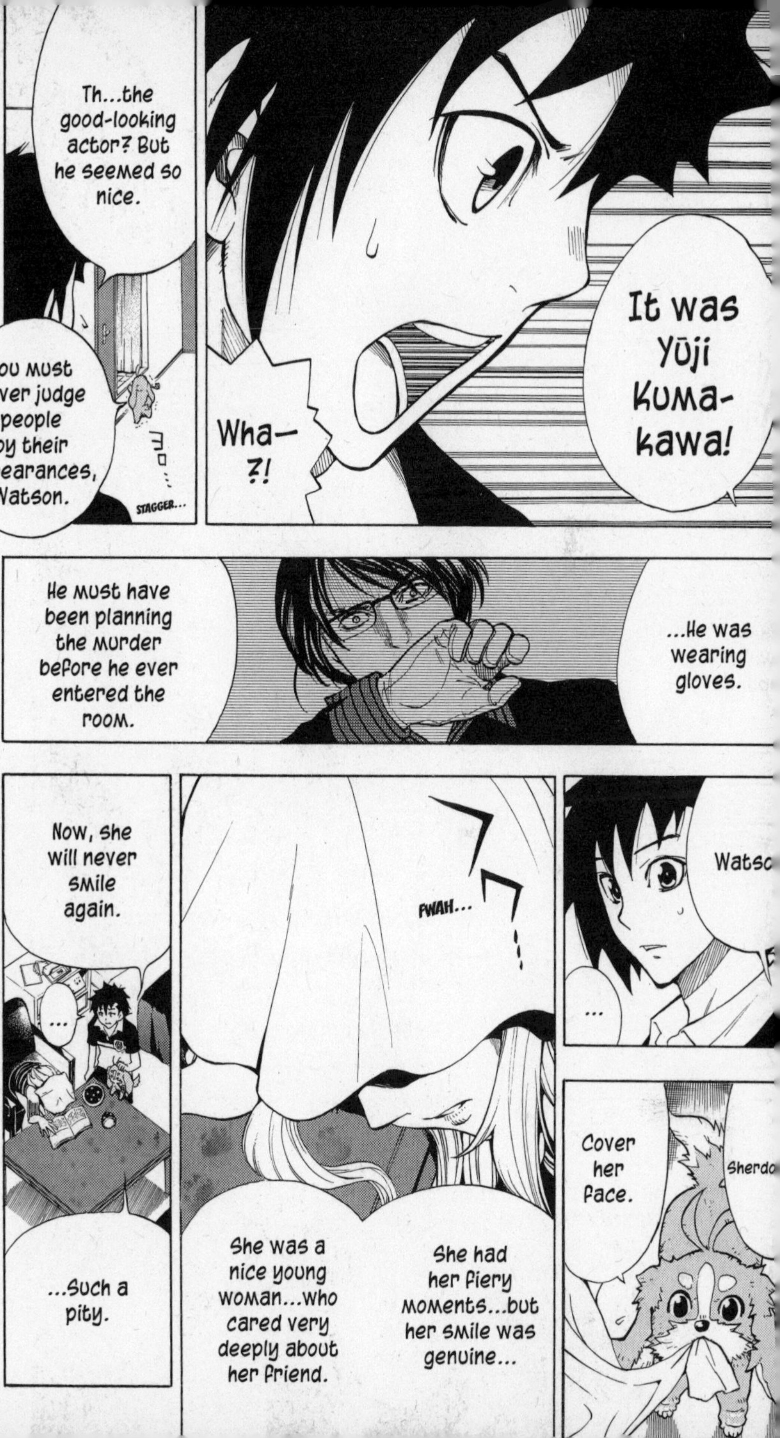
It was Yūji Kumakawa!
Wha—?!
Th...the good-looking actor? But he seemed so nice.
You must never judge people by their appearances, Watson.
STAGGER...
...He was wearing gloves.
He must have been planning the murder before he ever entered the room.
Watso
...
Sherdo
Cover her face.
FWAH...
She had her fiery moments...but her smile was genuine...
She was a nice young woman...who cared very deeply about her friend.
Now, she will never smile again.
...
...Such a pity.

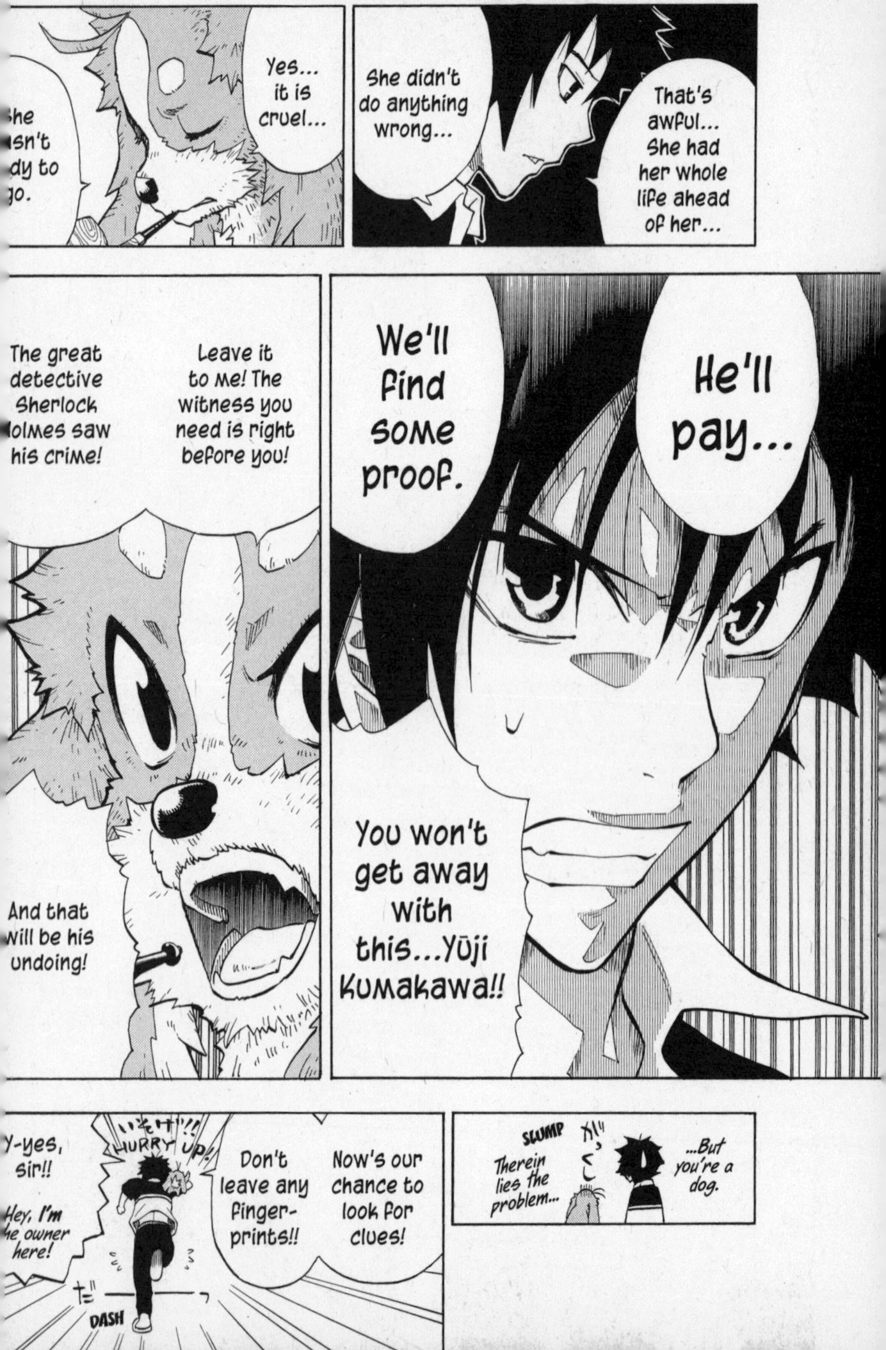
That's awful... She had her whole life ahead of her...
She didn't do anything wrong...
Yes... it is cruel...
he sn't dy to o.
He'll pay...
We'll find some proof.
You won't get away with this...Yūji Kumakawa!!
Leave it to me! The witness you need is right before you!
The great detective Sherlock olmes saw his crime!
And that ill be his undoing!
...But you're a dog.
SLUMP
Therein lies the problem...
Now's our chance to look for clues!
Don't leave any finger-prints!!
HURRY UP!
Y-yes, sir!!
Hey, I'm e owner here!
DASH

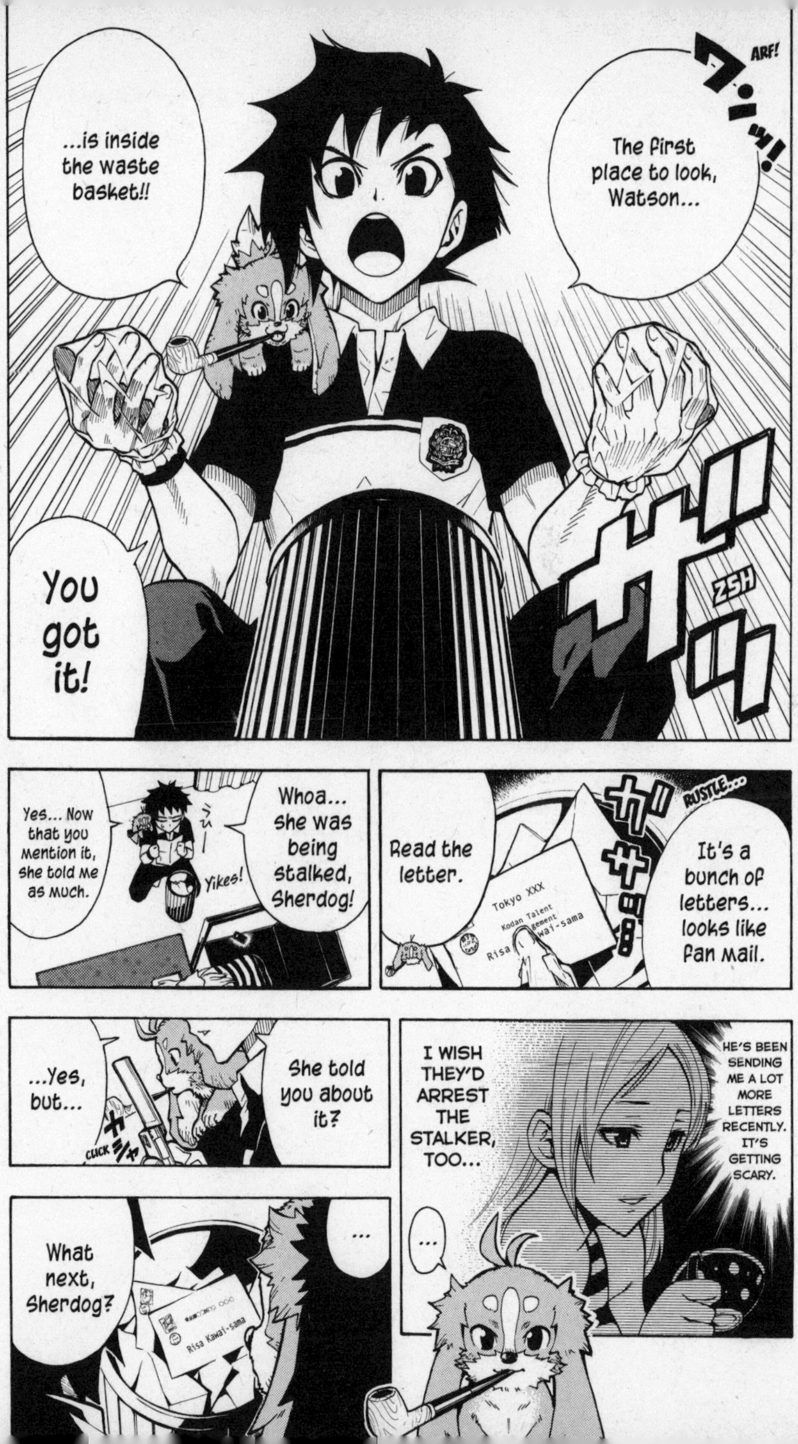
ARF!
The first place to look, Watson...
...is inside the waste basket!!
ZSH
You got it!
RUSTLE...
It's a bunch of letters... looks like fan mail.
Read the letter.
Whoa... she was being stalked, Sherdog!
Yikes!
Yes... Now that you mention it, she told me as much.
HE'S BEEN SENDING ME A LOT MORE LETTERS RECENTLY. IT'S GETTING SCARY.
I WISH THEY'D ARREST THE STALKER, TOO...
...
She told you about it?
...Yes, but...
CLICK
...
What next, Sherdog?
Risa Kawai-sama

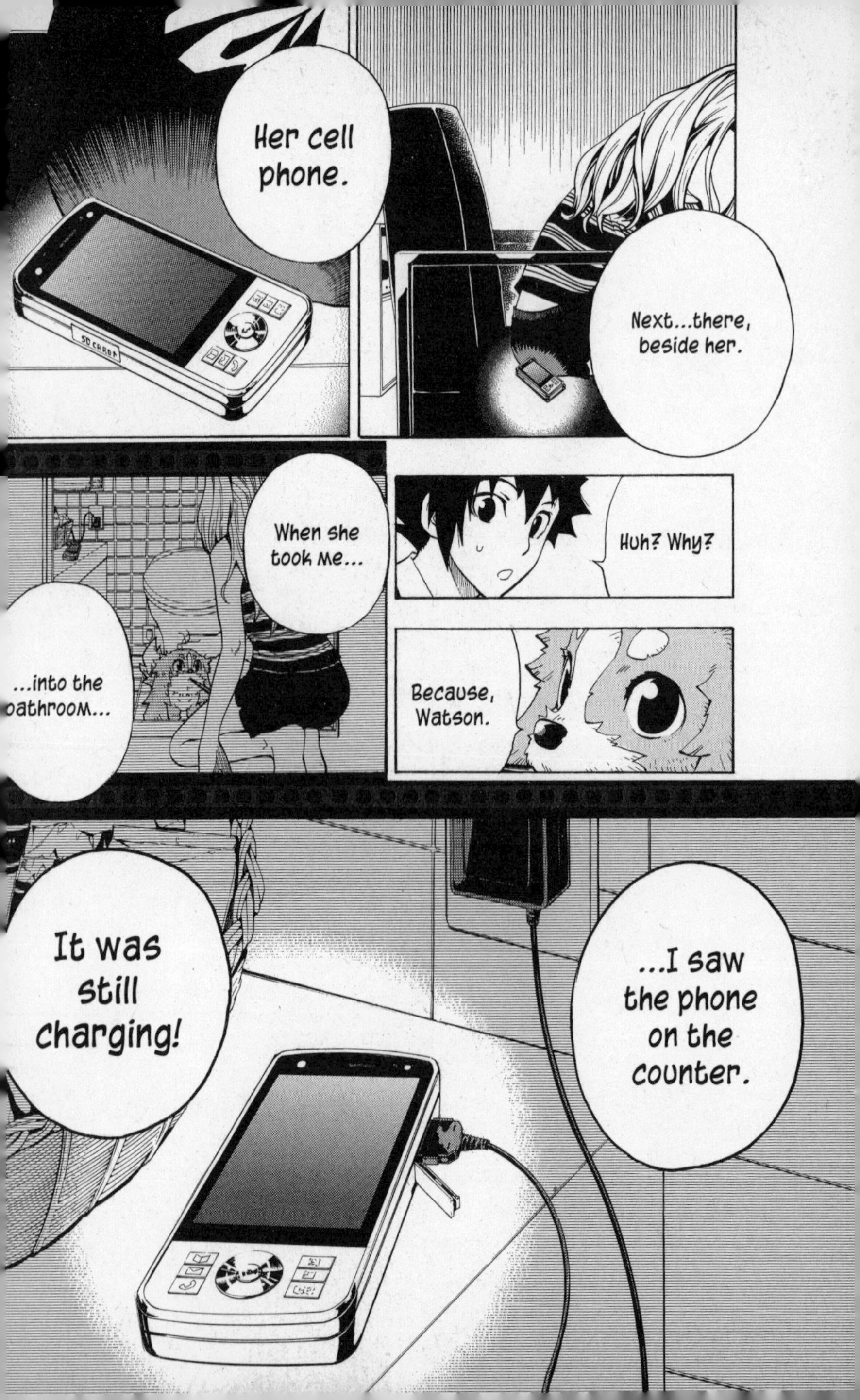
Next...there, beside her.
Her cell phone.
Huh? Why?
Because, Watson.
When she took me...
...into the bathroom...
...I saw the phone on the counter.
It was still charging!

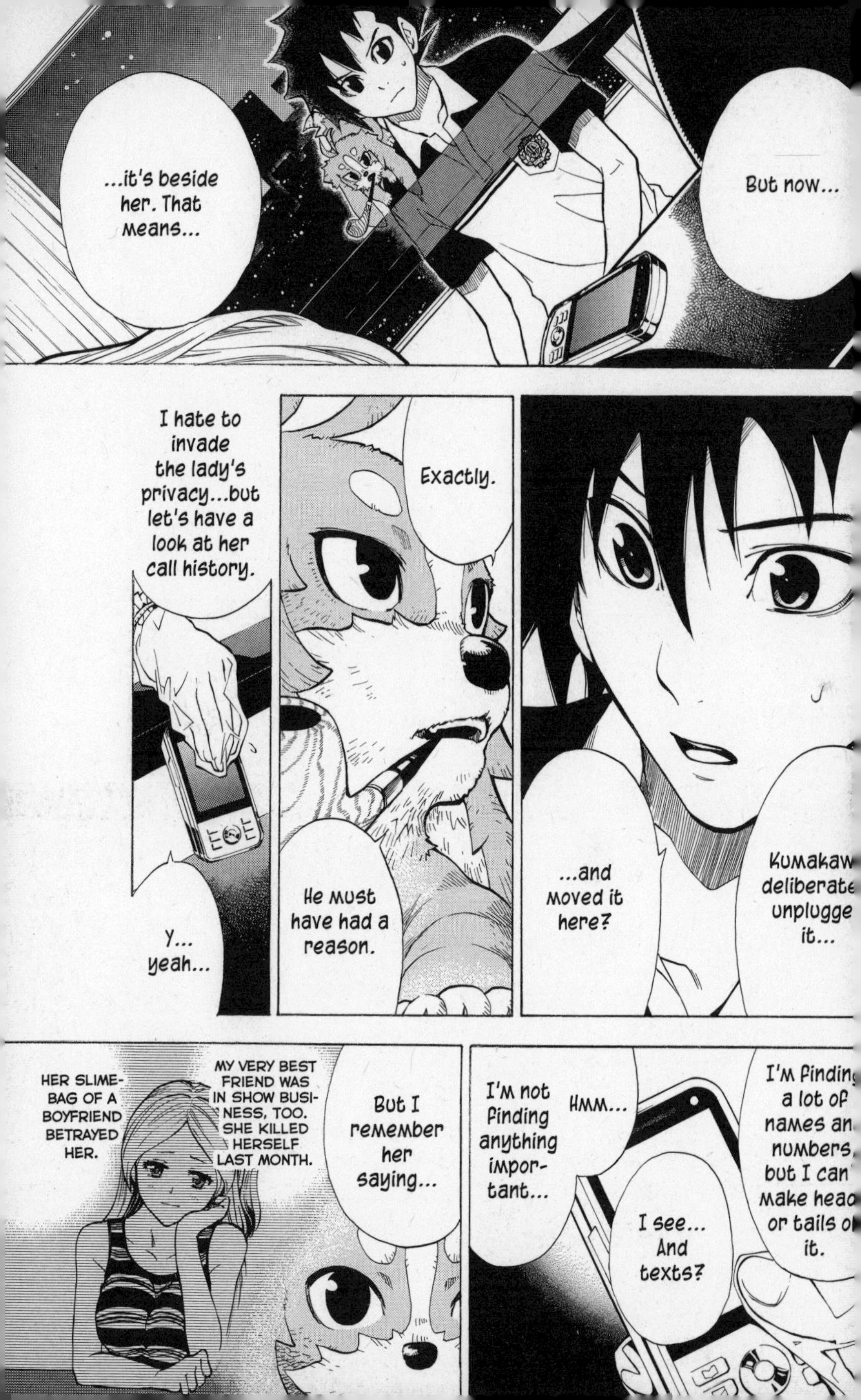
But now...
...it's beside her. That means...
Kumakaw deliberate unplugge it...
...and moved it here?
Exactly.
He must have had a reason.
I hate to invade the lady's privacy...but let's have a look at her call history.
Y... yeah...
I'm findin a lot of names an numbers, but I can make head or tails o it.
HMM...
I'm not finding anything impor-tant...
I see... And texts?
But I remember her saying...
MY VERY BEST FRIEND WAS IN SHOW BUSI-NESS, TOO. SHE KILLED HERSELF LAST MONTH.
HER SLIME-BAG OF A BOYFRIEND BETRAYED HER.

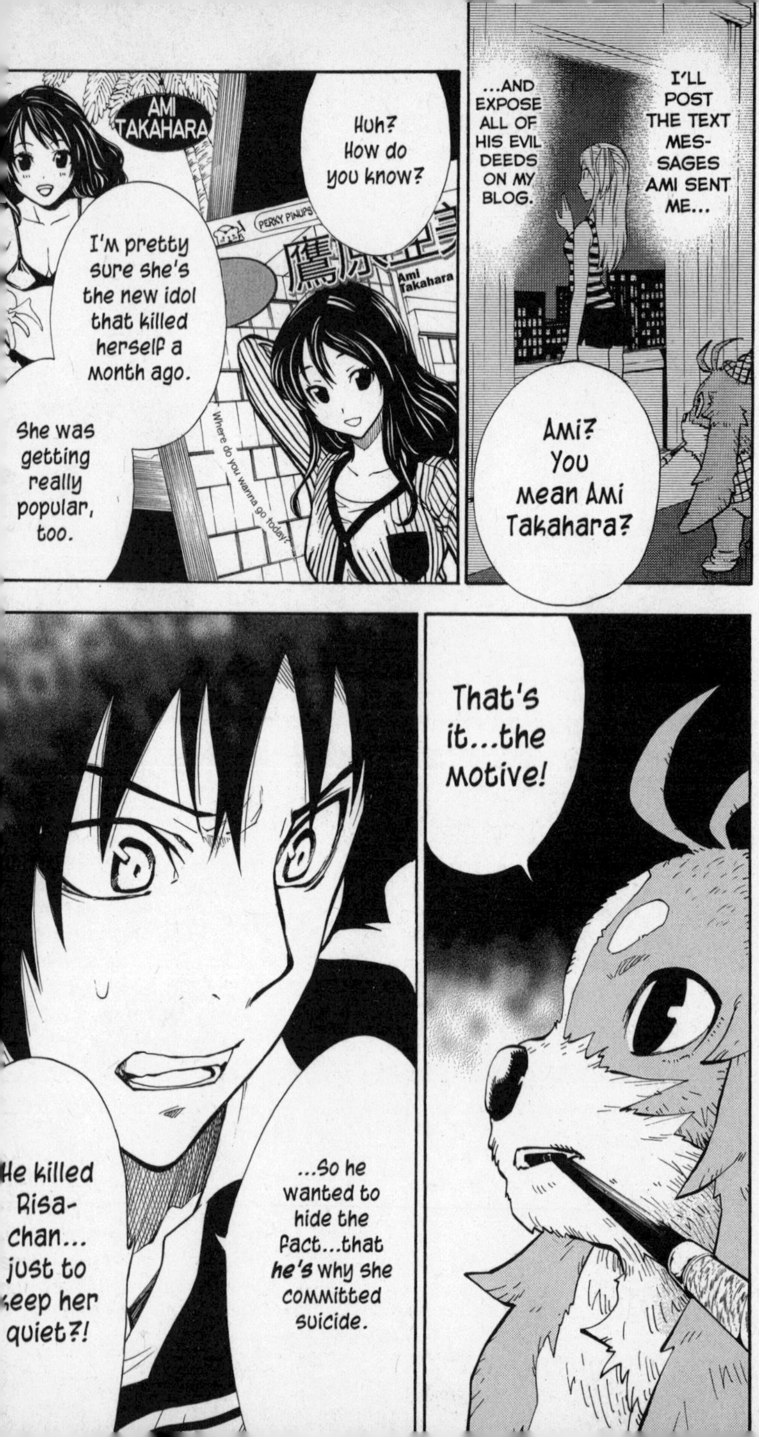
I'LL POST THE TEXT MES-SAGES AMI SENT ME...
...AND EXPOSE ALL OF HIS EVIL DEEDS ON MY BLOG.
Ami? You mean Ami Takahara?
Huh? How do you know?
AMI TAKAHARA
PERKY PINUPS
Ami Takahara
I'm pretty sure she's the new idol that killed herself a month ago.
Where do you wanna go today?
She was getting really popular, too.
That's it...the motive!
...So he wanted to hide the fact...that *he's* why she committed suicide.
He killed Risa-chan... just to keep her quiet?!

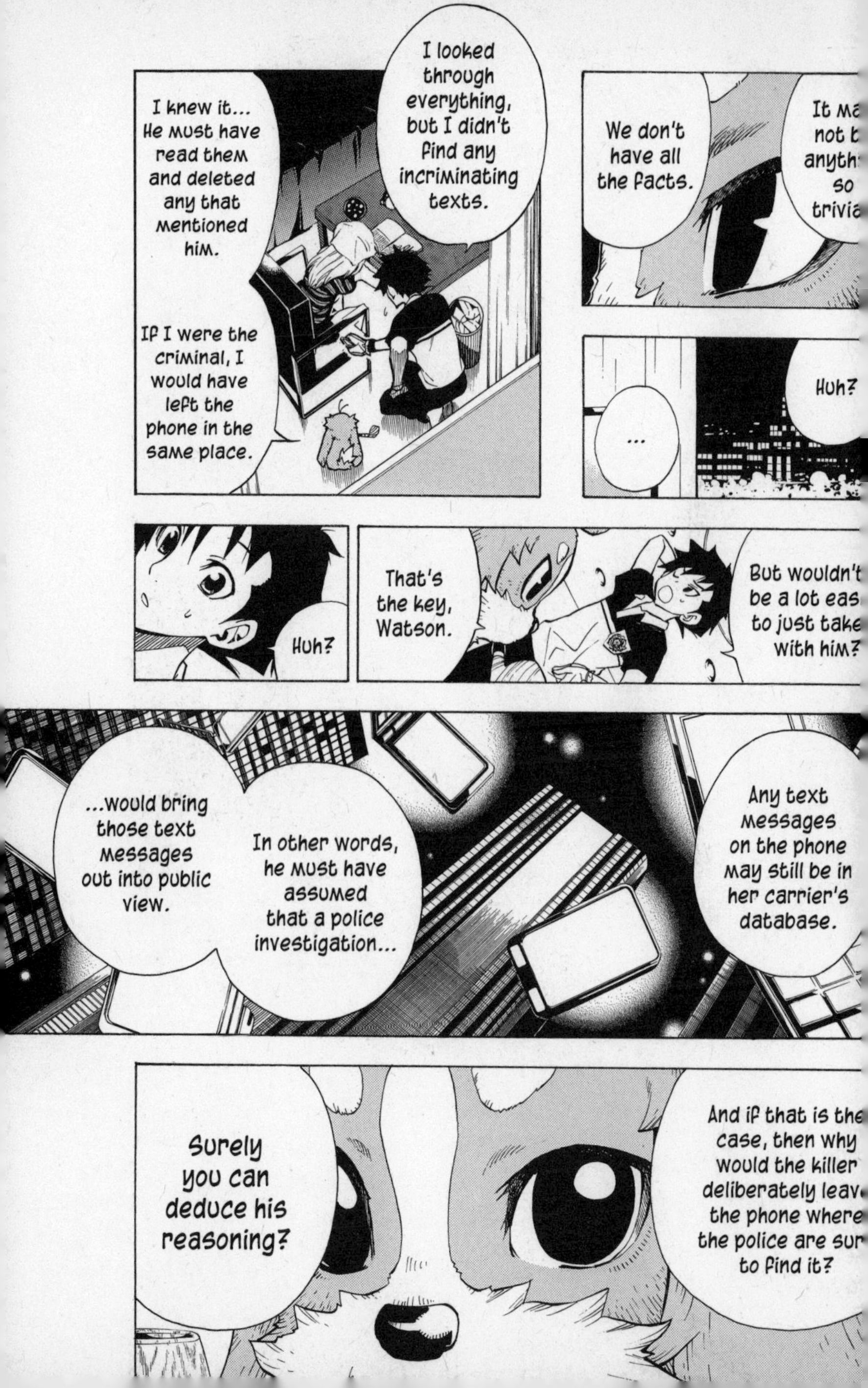

It ma not b anyth so trivia
We don't have all the facts.
Huh?
...
I looked through everything, but I didn't find any incriminating texts.
I knew it... He must have read them and deleted any that mentioned him.
If I were the criminal, I would have left the phone in the same place.
But wouldn't be a lot eas to just take with him?
That's the key, Watson.
Huh?
Any text messages on the phone may still be in her carrier's database.
In other words, he must have assumed that a police investigation...
...would bring those text messages out into public view.
And if that is the case, then why would the killer deliberately leav the phone where the police are sur to find it?
Surely you can deduce his reasoning?

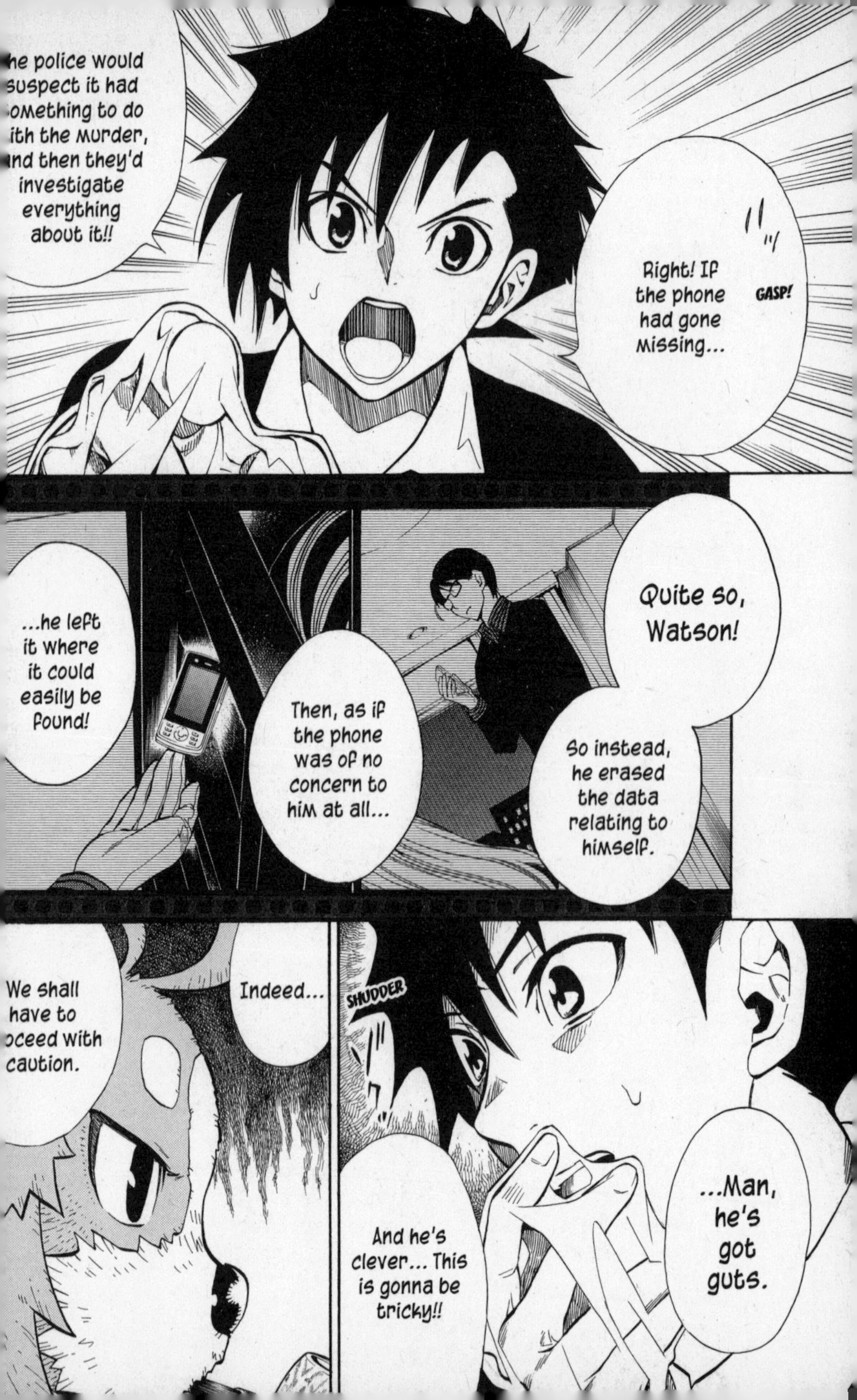
GASP!
Right! If the phone had gone missing...
he police would suspect it had omething to do ith the murder, nd then they'd investigate everything about it!!
Quite so, Watson!
So instead, he erased the data relating to himself.
Then, as if the phone was of no concern to him at all...
...he left it where it could easily be found!
...Man, he's got guts.
SHUDDER
And he's clever... This is gonna be tricky!!
Indeed...
We shall have to oceed with caution.

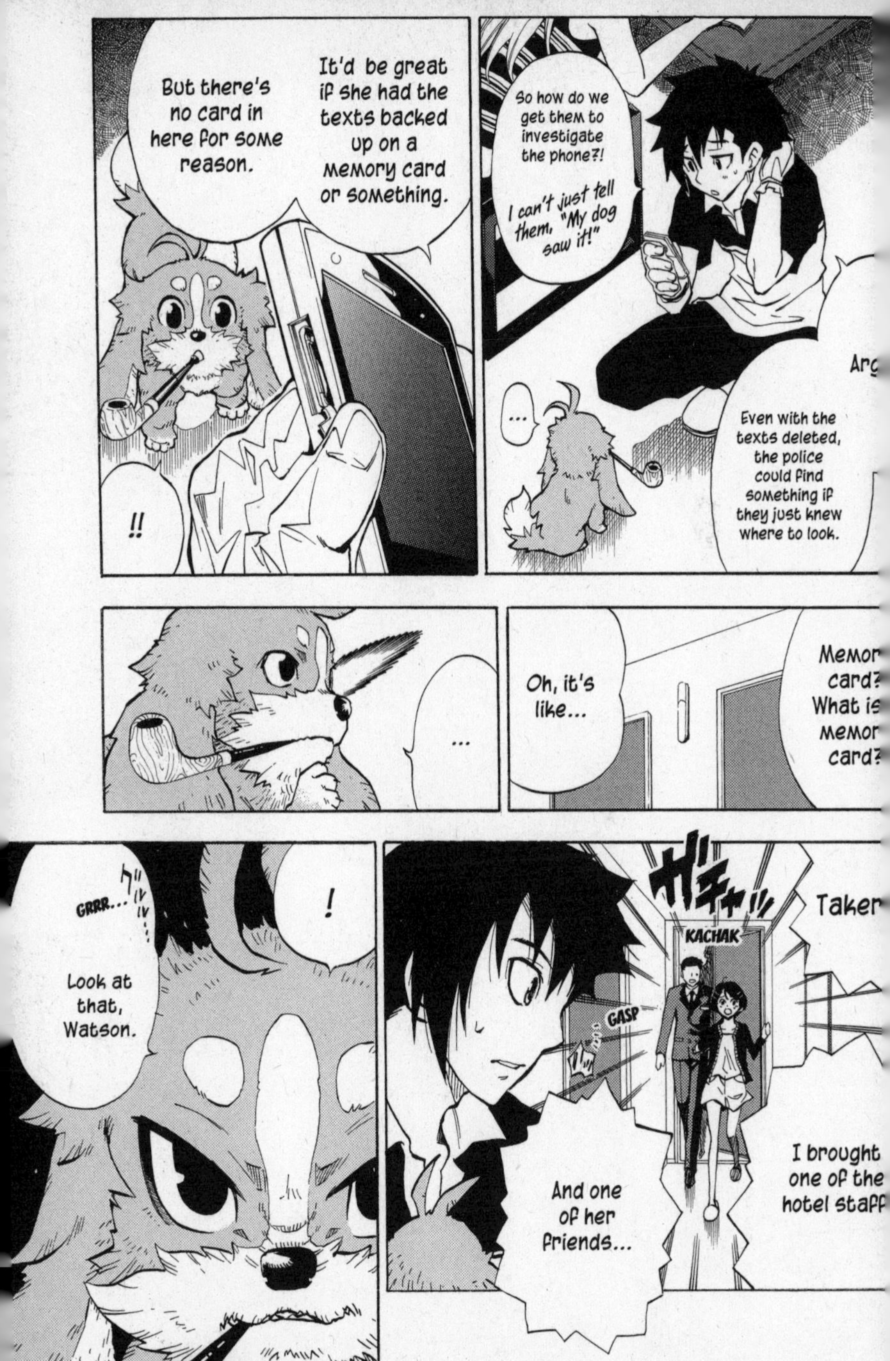
So how do we get them to investigate the phone?!
I can't just tell them, "My dog saw it!"
Arg
...
Even with the texts deleted, the police could find something if they just knew where to look.
It'd be great if she had the texts backed up on a memory card or something.
But there's no card in here for some reason.
!!
Memor card? What is memor card?
Oh, it's like...
...
Taker
KACHAK
GASP
I brought one of the hotel staff
And one of her friends...
!
GRRR...
Look at that, Watson.

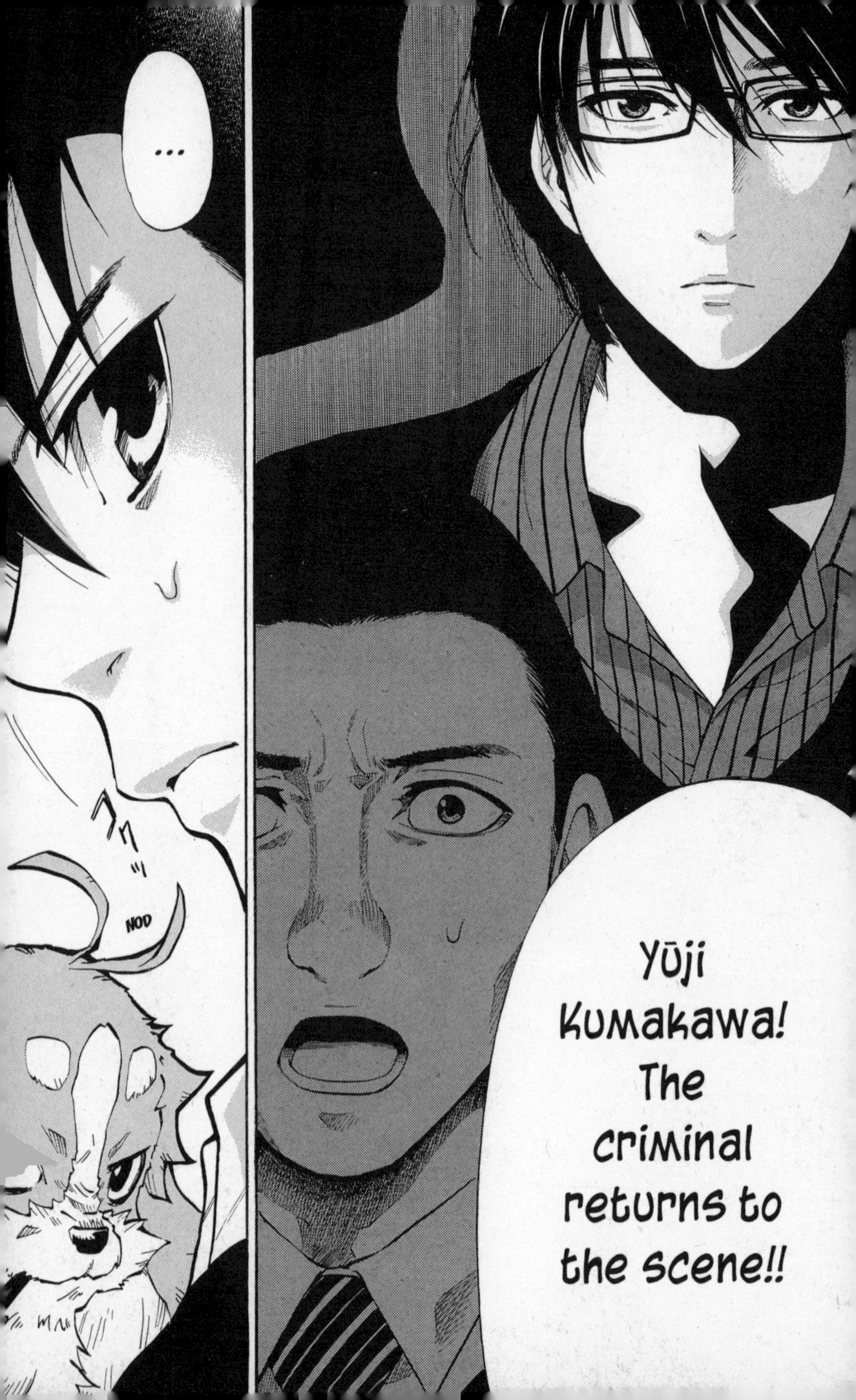
Yūji Kumakawa! The criminal returns to the scene!!
...
NOD

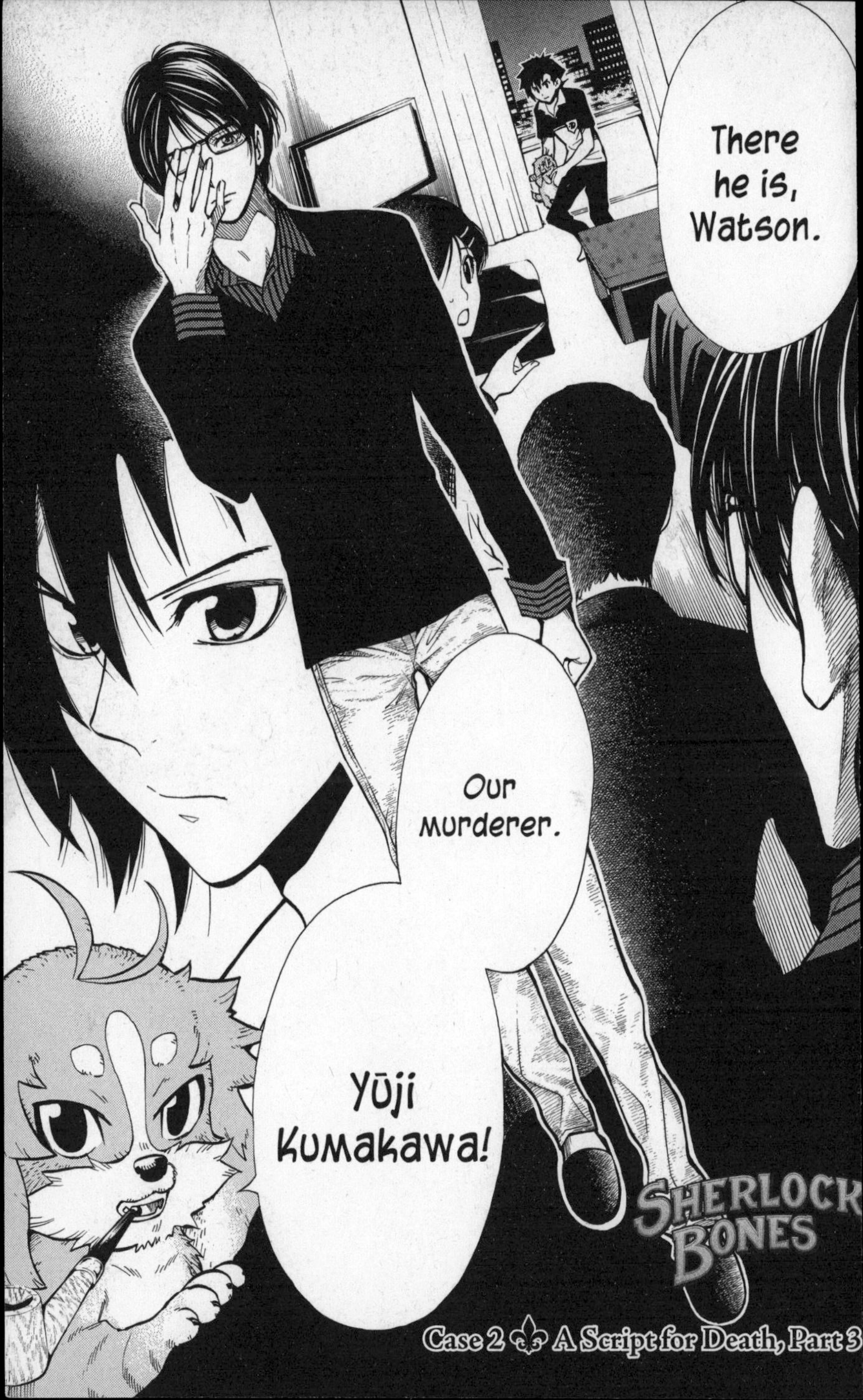
There he is, Watson.
Our murderer.
Yūji Kumakawa!
SHERLOCK BONES
Case 2 A Script for Death, Part 3

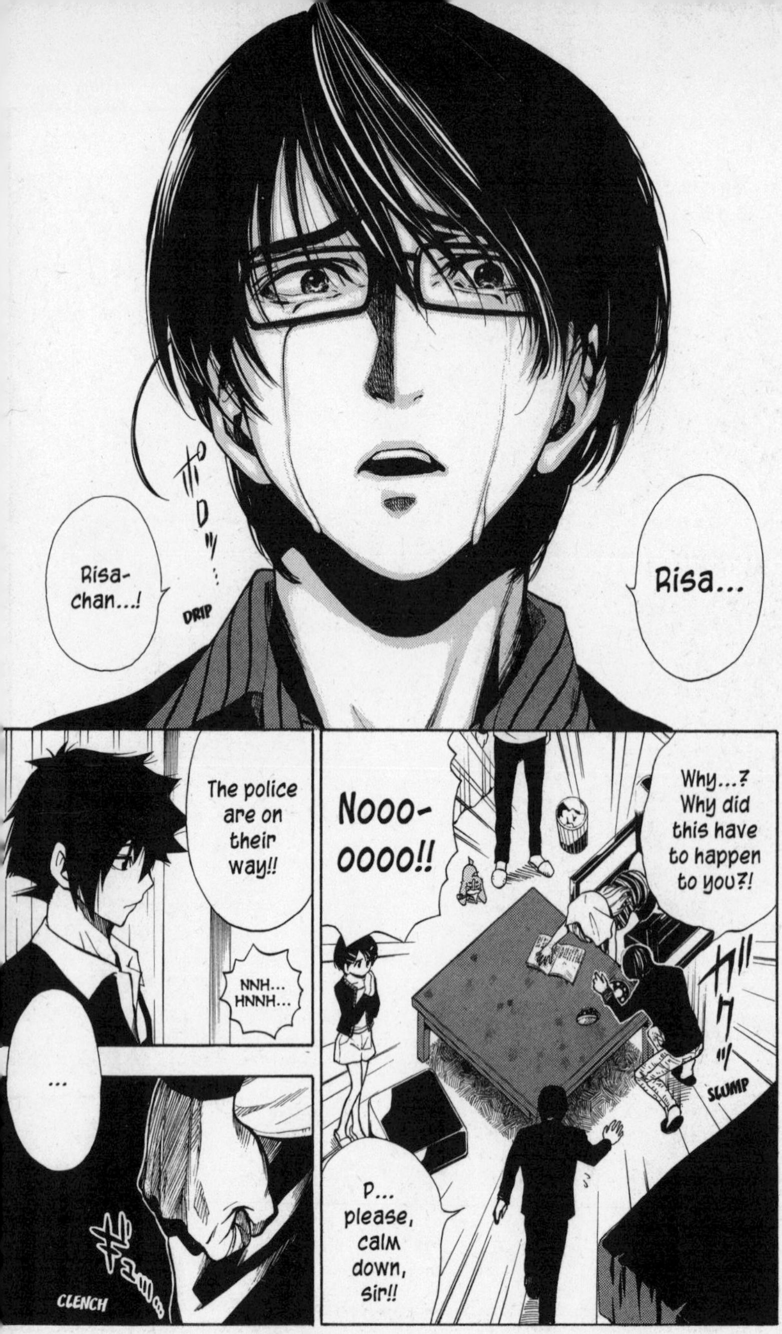
Risa...
Risa-chan...!
DRIP
Why...? Why did this have to happen to you?!
SLUMP
Nooo-oooo!!
P... please, calm down, sir!!
The police are on their way!!
NNH... HNNH...
...
CLENCH

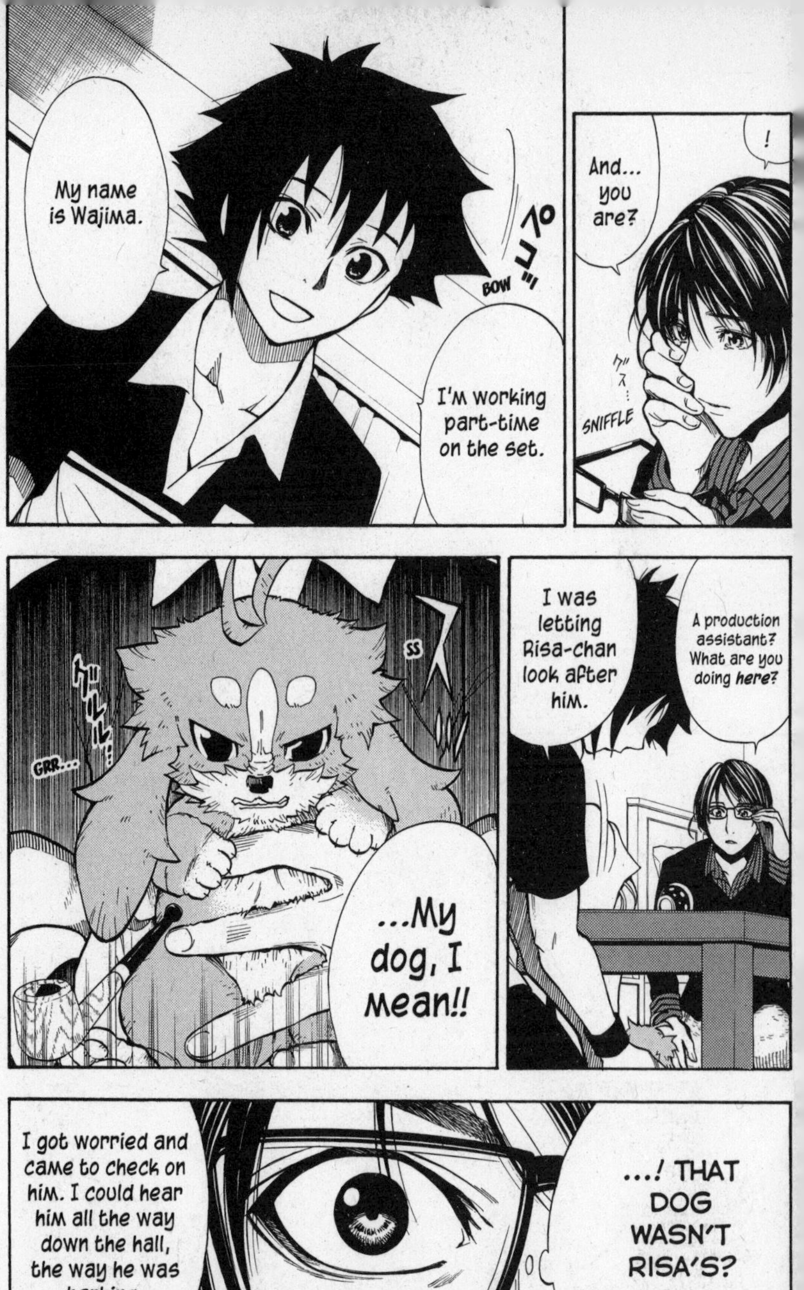
!
And... you are?
SNIFFLE
My name is Wajima.
BOW
I'm working part-time on the set.
A production assistant? What are you doing here?
I was letting Risa-chan look after him.
SS
GRR...
...My dog, I mean!!
...! THAT DOG WASN'T RISA'S?
I got worried and came to check on him. I could hear him all the way down the hall, the way he was barking.

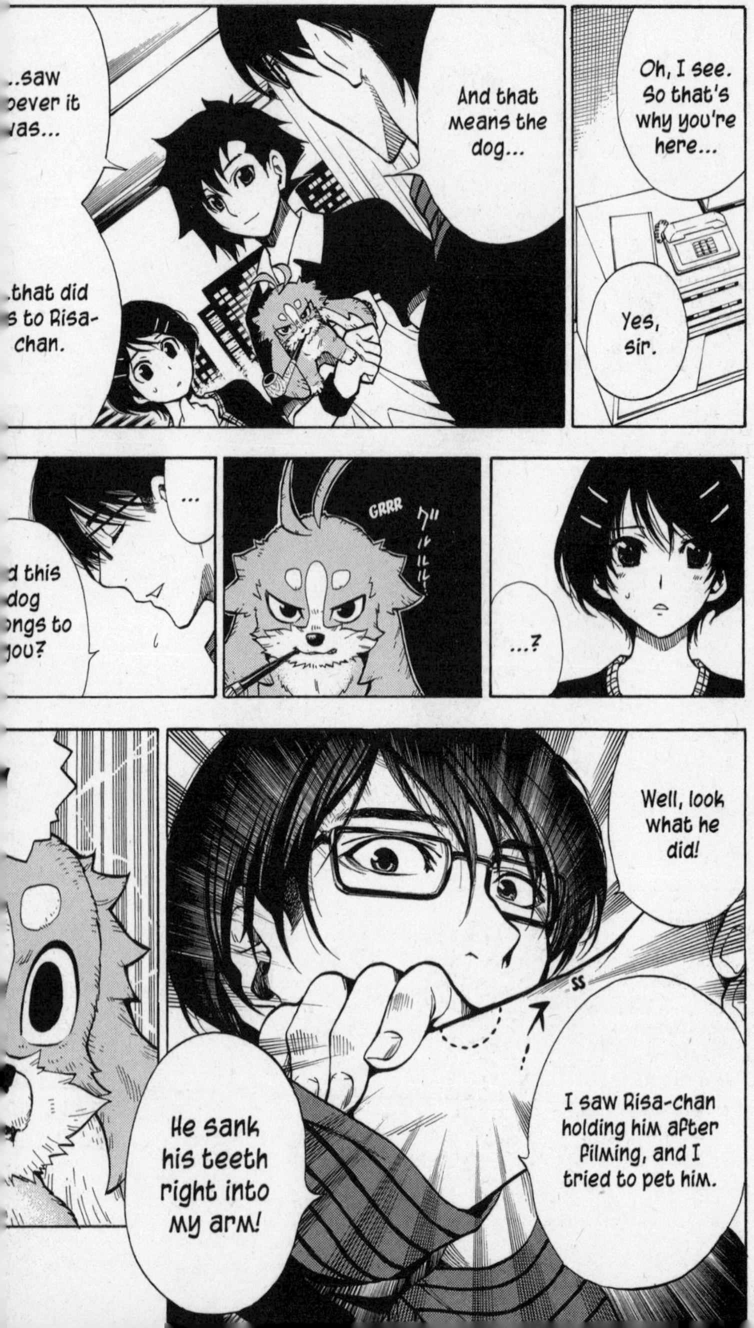

Oh, I see. So that's why you're here...
Yes, sir.
And that means the dog...
..saw
oever it
vas...
.that did
s to Risa-
chan.
...?
GRRR
グルルル
...
d this
dog
ongs to
you?
Well, look what he did!
I saw Risa-chan holding him after filming, and I tried to pet him.
SS
He sank his teeth right into my arm!

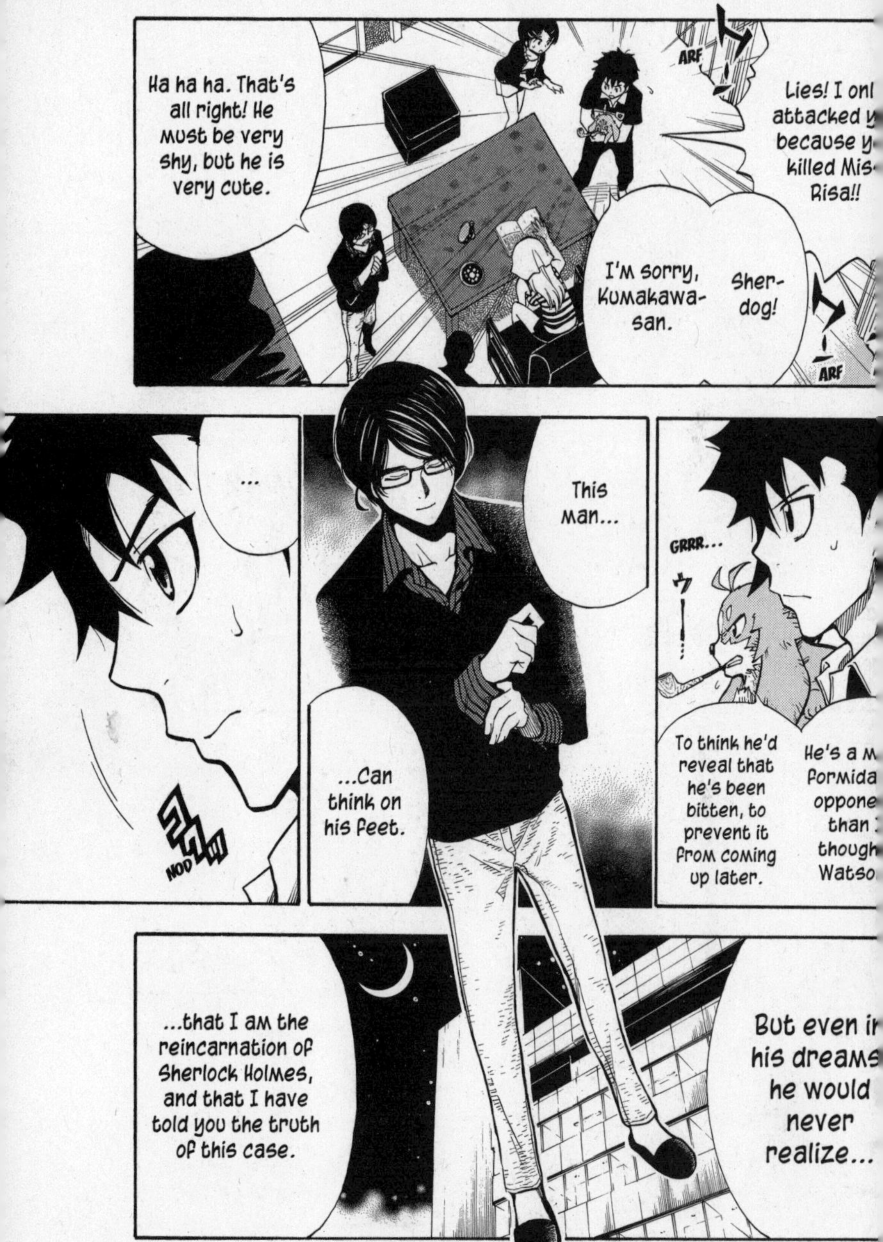
Lies! I onl attacked y because y killed Mis Risa!!
ARF
Sher-dog!
I'm sorry, Kumakawa-san.
ARF
Ha ha ha. That's all right! He must be very shy, but he is very cute.
He's a m formida oppone than I though Watso
To think he'd reveal that he's been bitten, to prevent it from coming up later.
GRRR...
ウー
This man...
...Can think on his feet.
...
NOD
But even i his dreams he would never realize...
...that I am the reincarnation of Sherlock Holmes, and that I have told you the truth of this case.

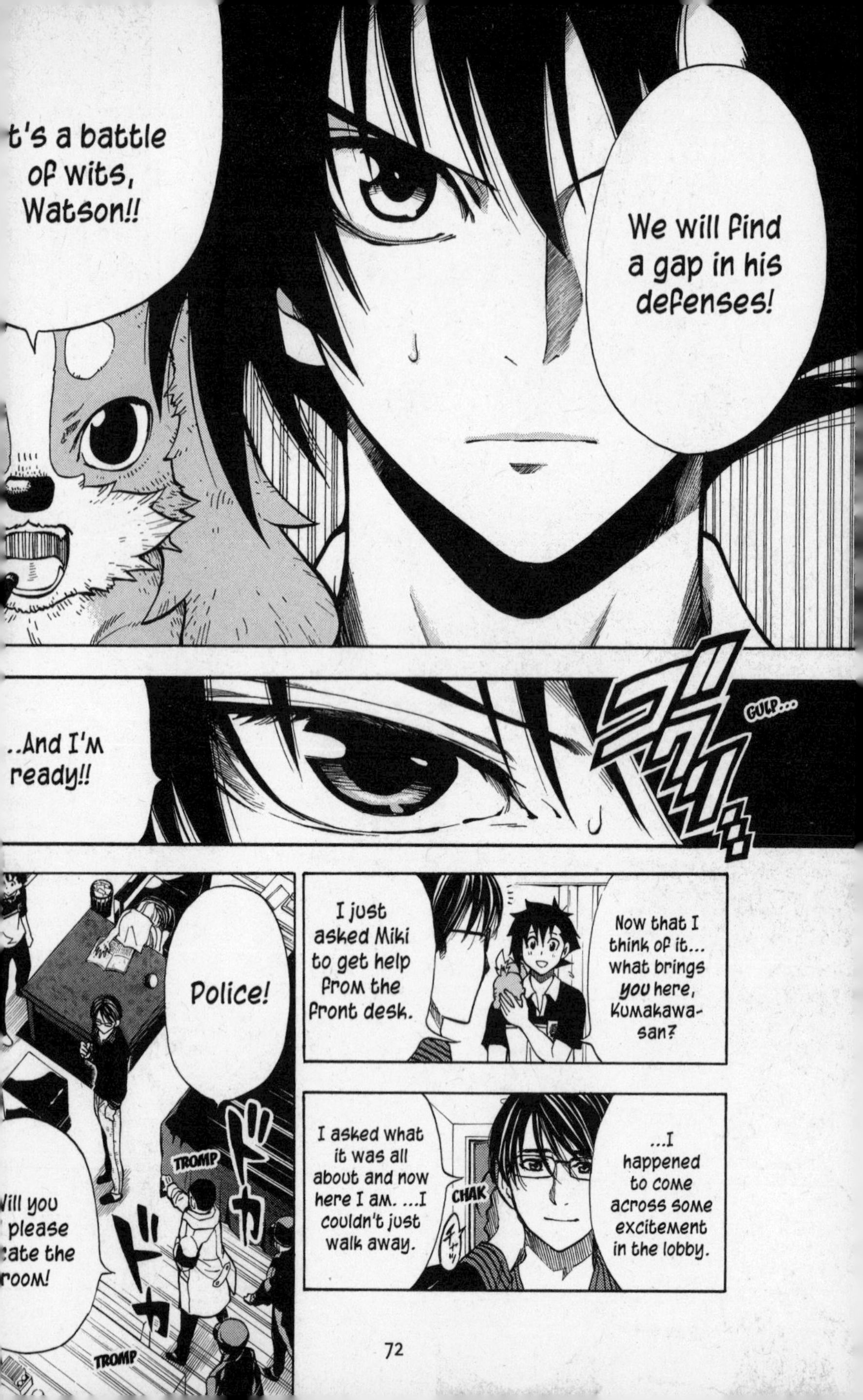
We will find a gap in his defenses!
t's a battle of wits, Watson!!
GULP...
..And I'm ready!!
Now that I think of it... what brings you here, Kumakawa-san?
I just asked Miki to get help from the front desk.
...I happened to come across some excitement in the lobby.
CHAK
I asked what it was all about and now here I am. ...I couldn't just walk away.
Police!
TROMP
ill you please cate the room!
TROMP

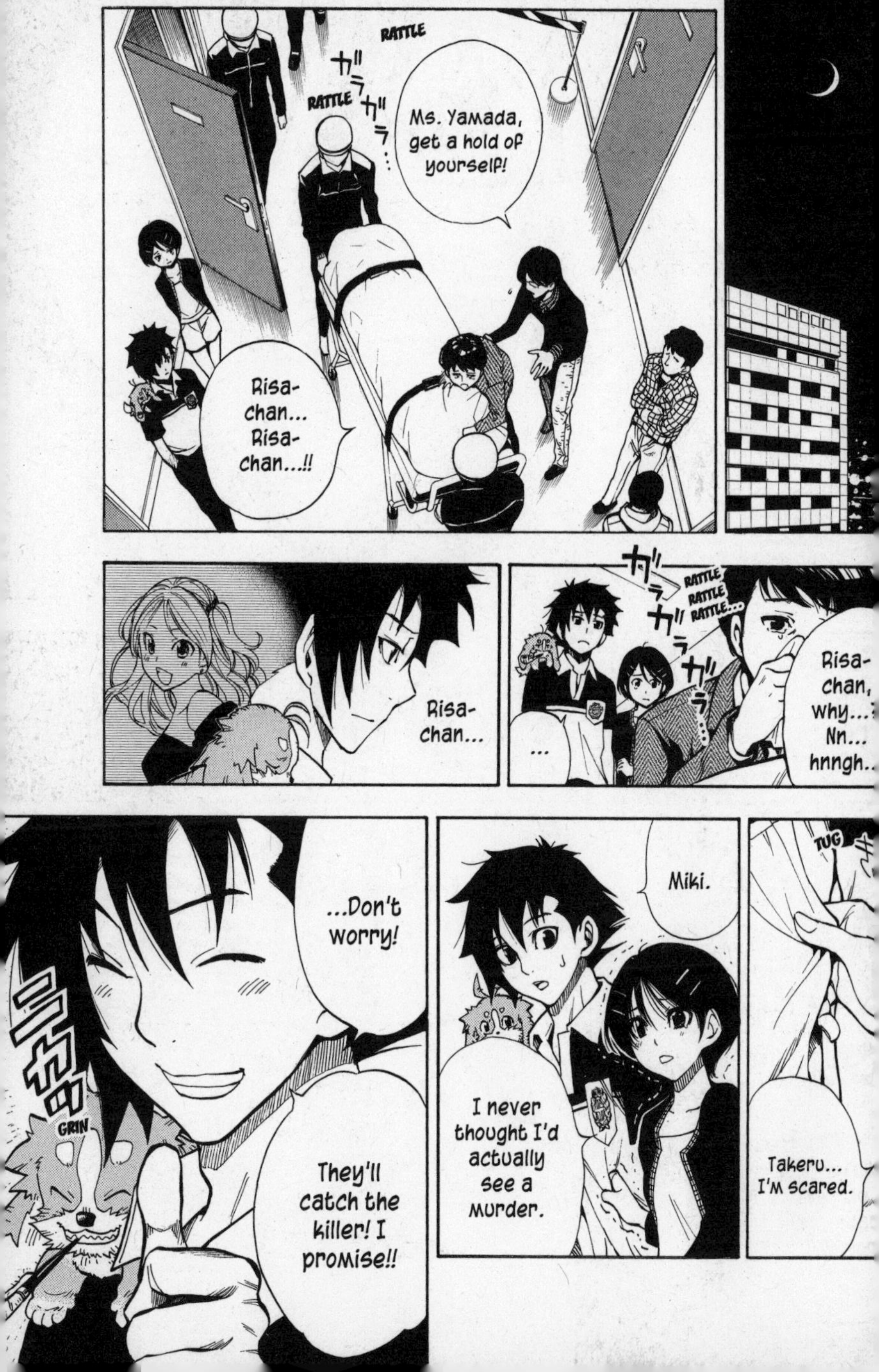

RATTLE
ガラガラ...
RATTLE
Ms. Yamada, get a hold of yourself!
Risa-chan... Risa-chan...!!
Risa-chan, why... Nn... hnngh...
RATTLE RATTLE RATTLE...
ガラガラガラ...
...
Risa-chan...
TUG
Takeru... I'm scared.
Miki.
I never thought I'd actually see a murder.
...Don't worry!
They'll catch the killer! I promise!!
GRIN

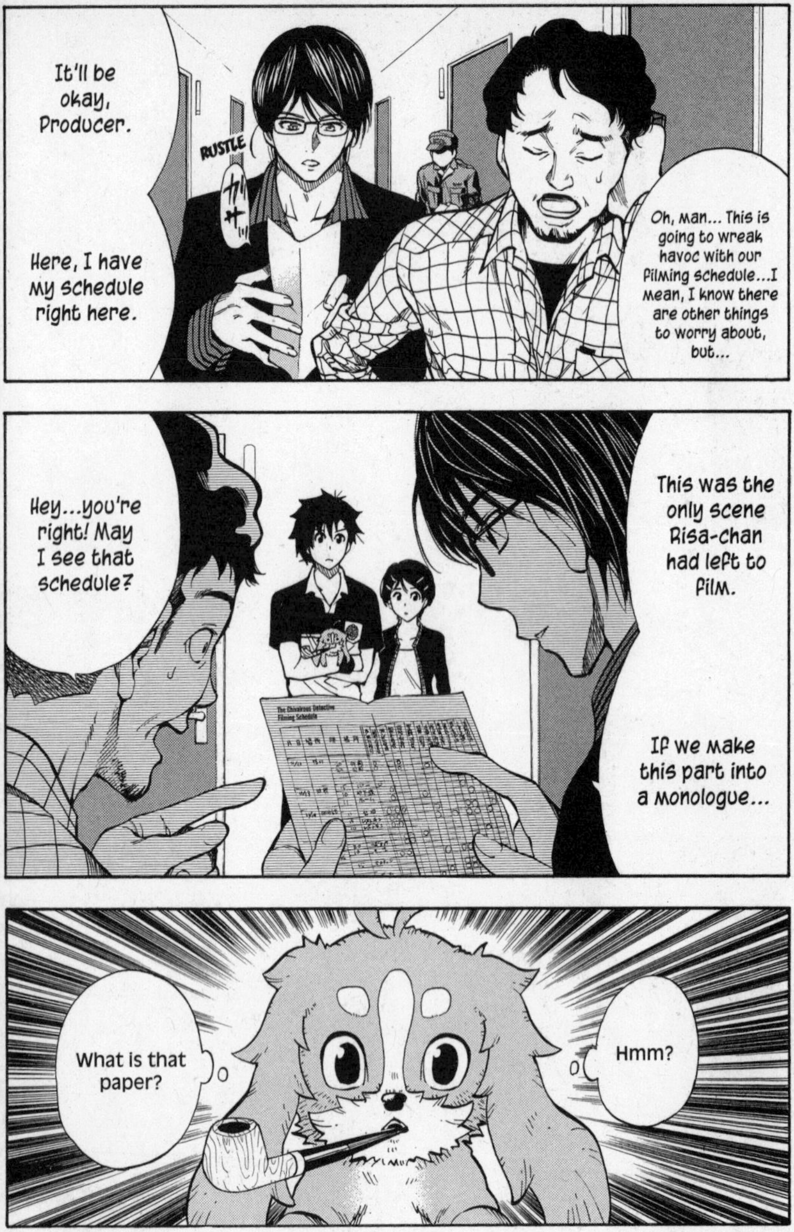
Oh, man... This is going to wreak havoc with our filming schedule...I mean, I know there are other things to worry about, but...
RUSTLE
It'll be okay, Producer.
Here, I have my schedule right here.
This was the only scene Risa-chan had left to film.
If we make this part into a monologue...
Hey...you're right! May I see that schedule?
Hmm?
What is that paper?

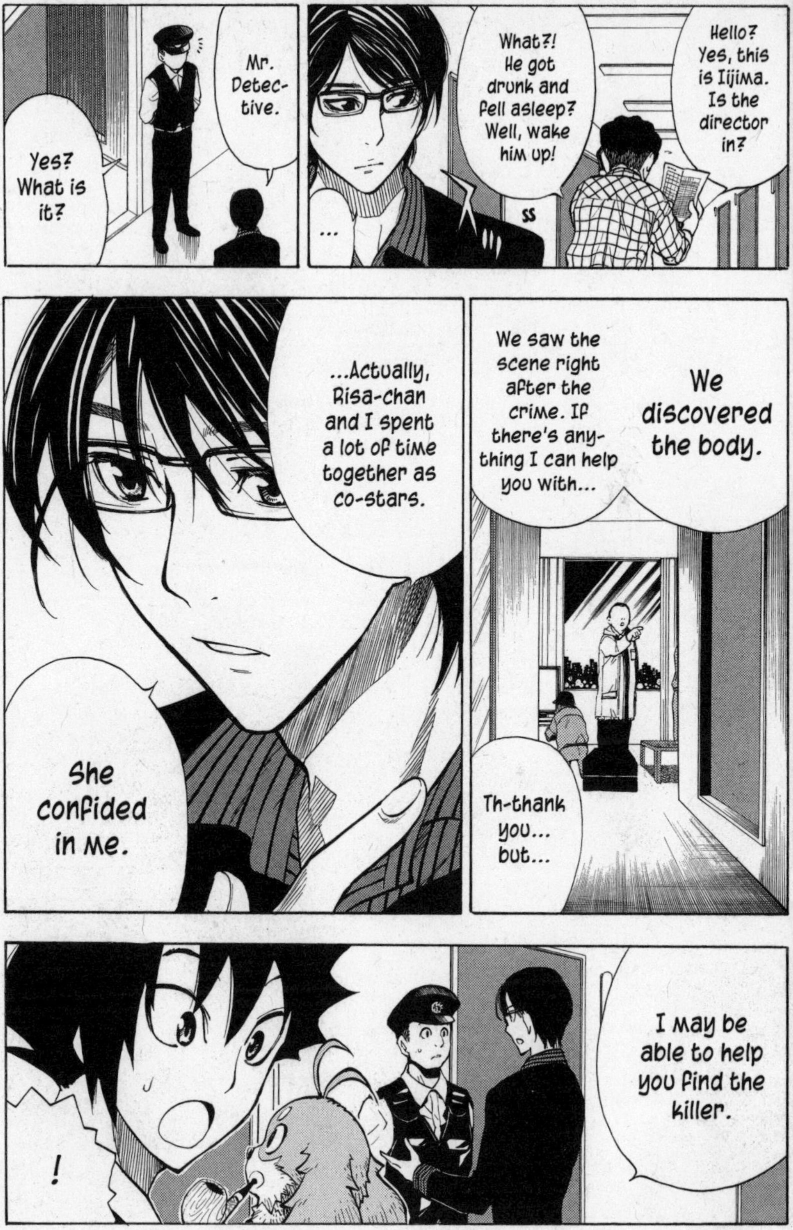
Hello? Yes, this is Iijima. Is the director in?
What?! He got drunk and fell asleep? Well, wake him up!
SS
...
Mr. Detective.
Yes? What is it?
We discovered the body.
We saw the scene right after the crime. If there's anything I can help you with...
Th-thank you... but...
...Actually, Risa-chan and I spent a lot of time together as co-stars.
She confided in me.
I may be able to help you find the killer.
!

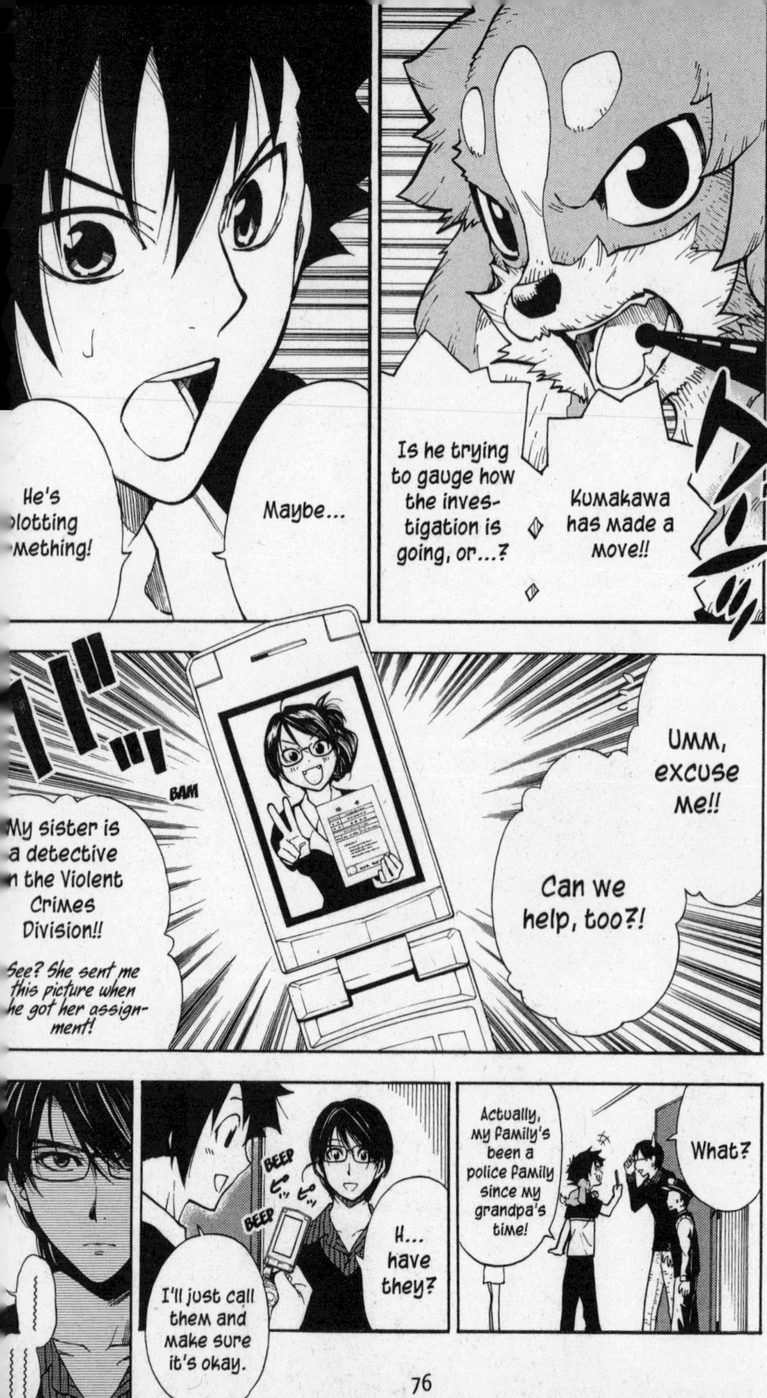
ARF!
Kumakawa has made a move!!
Is he trying to gauge how the inves-tigation is going, or...?
Maybe...
He's lotting mething!
Umm, excuse me!!
Can we help, too?!
BAM
My sister is a detective n the Violent Crimes Division!!
ee? She sent me this picture when he got her assign-ment!
What?
Actually, my family's been a police family since my grandpa's time!
H... have they?
BEEP
BEEP
I'll just call them and make sure it's okay.

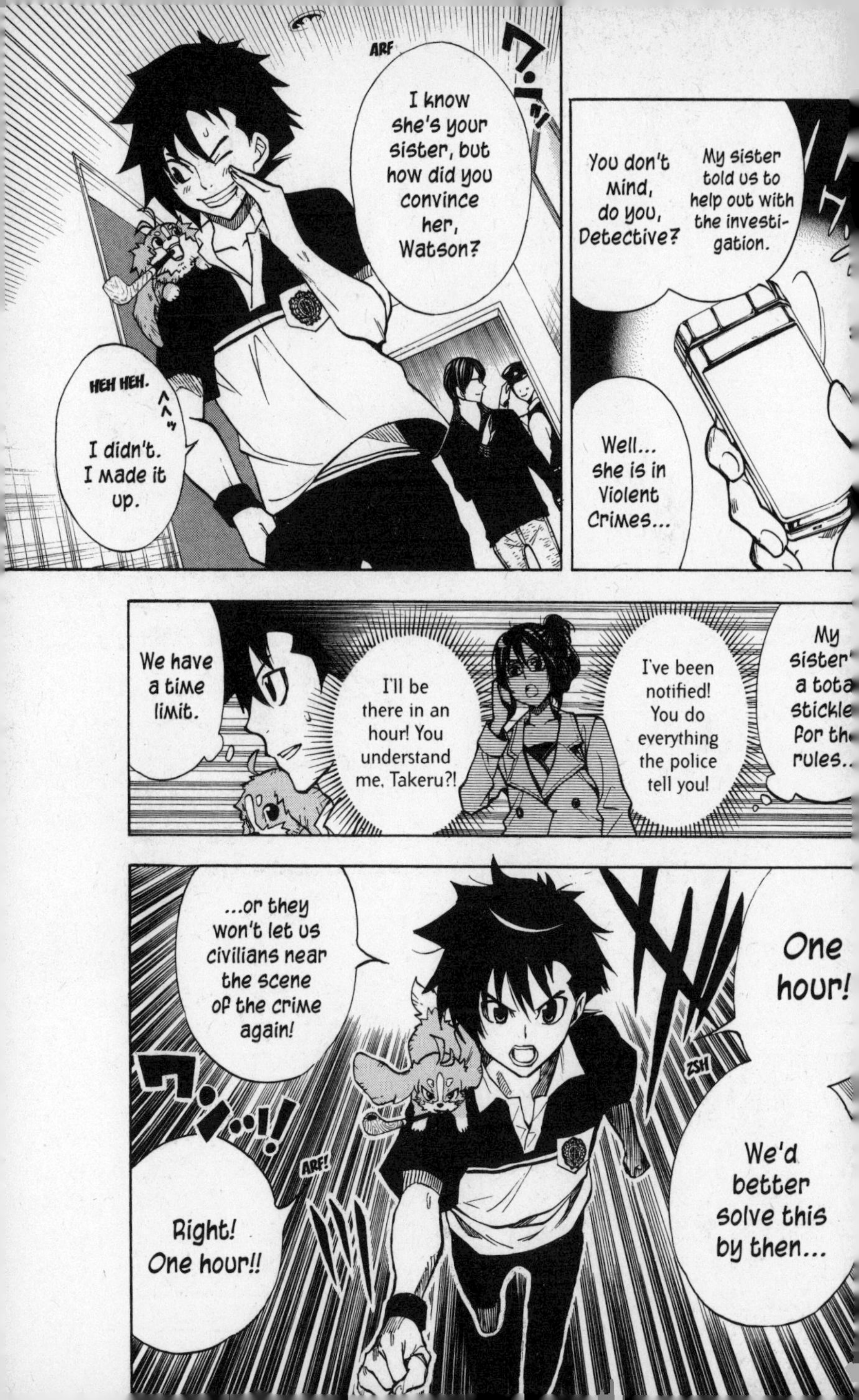
My sister told us to help out with the investigation.
You don't mind, do you, Detective?
Well... she is in Violent Crimes...
ARF
I know she's your sister, but how did you convince her, Watson?
HEH HEH.
I didn't. I made it up.
My sister' a tota stickle for th rules..
I've been notified! You do everything the police tell you!
I'll be there in an hour! You understand me, Takeru?!
We have a time limit.
One hour!
...or they won't let us civilians near the scene of the crime again!
ZSH
We'd better solve this by then...
ARF!
Right! One hour!!

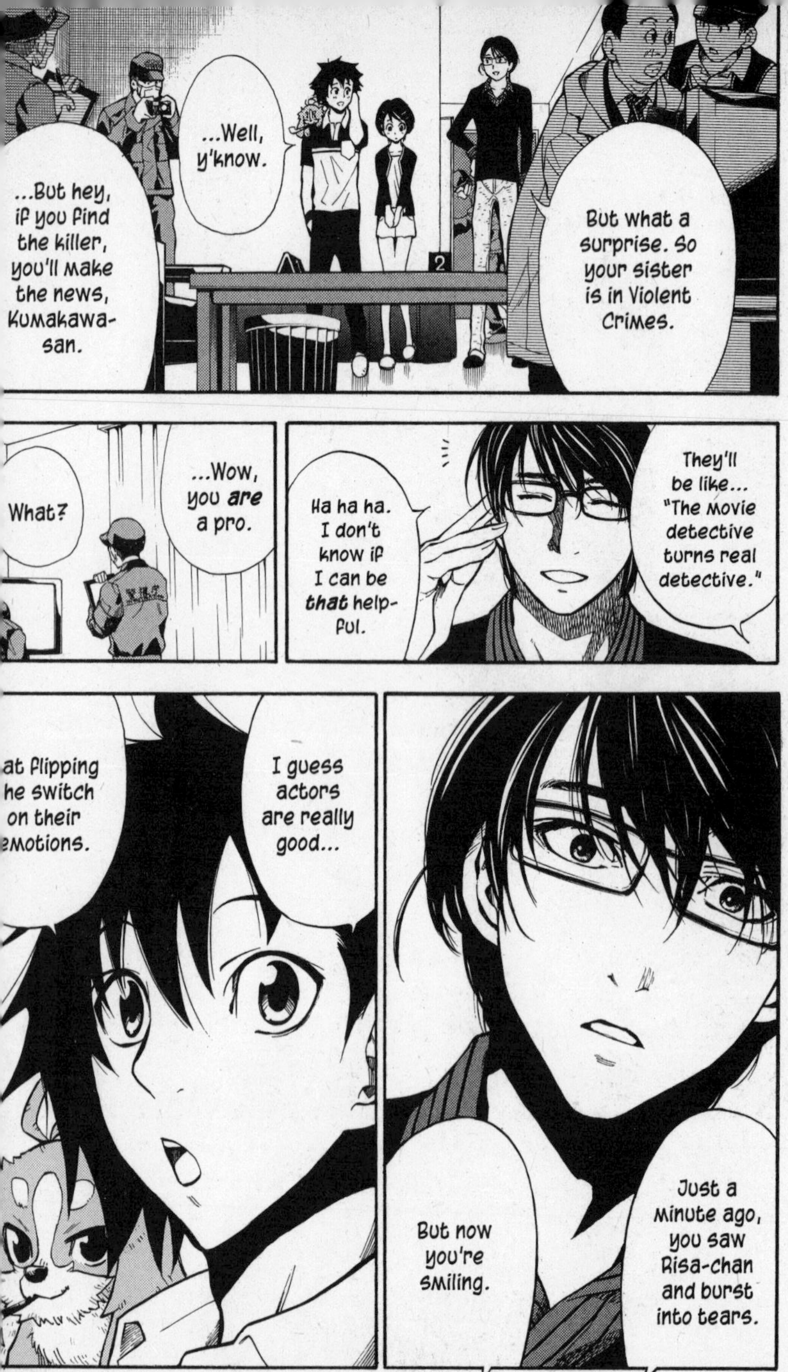
But what a surprise. So your sister is in Violent Crimes.
...Well, y'know.
...But hey, if you find the killer, you'll make the news, Kumakawa-san.
They'll be like... "The movie detective turns real detective."
Ha ha ha. I don't know if I can be *that* helpful.
...Wow, you *are* a pro.
What?
Just a minute ago, you saw Risa-chan and burst into tears.
But now you're smiling.
I guess actors are really good...
at flipping he switch on their emotions.

Oh...I'm sorry. You just made me think of Risa-chan sitting there, and...

...!

Ha ha... I'm hopeless. I thought...I could act cool about this...

Oh! Kumakawa-san...

Hey...stop it, Takeru! You're being rude.

DRIP

DRIP

DRIP

SERIOUSLY, LEAVE IT TO AN ACTOR...

W... WOW...

I'm sorry if...I made you feel uncomfortable, Wajima-kun.

I just...I want to catch the murderer so badly...

...

CREAK

We have to make this movie a success... for her.

I had one scene left with Risa-chan, but I think I can do it without her.

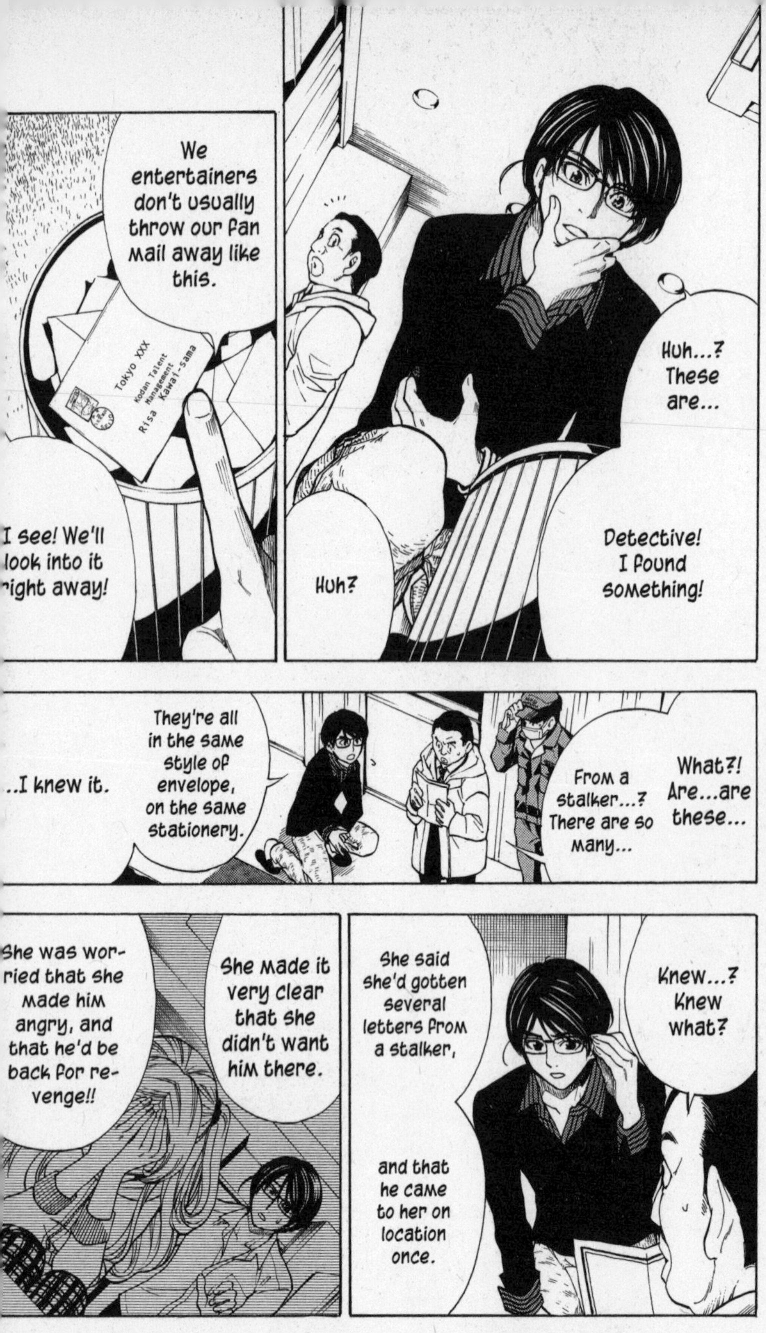
Huh...? These are...
Detective! I found something!
Huh?
We entertainers don't usually throw our fan mail away like this.
Tokyo XXX Kodan Talent Management Risa Kawai-sama
I see! We'll look into it right away!
What?! Are...are these...
From a stalker...? There are so many...
They're all in the same style of envelope, on the same stationery.
...I knew it.
Knew...? Knew what?
She said she'd gotten several letters from a stalker,
and that he came to her on location once.
She made it very clear that she didn't want him there.
She was worried that she made him angry, and that he'd be back for revenge!!

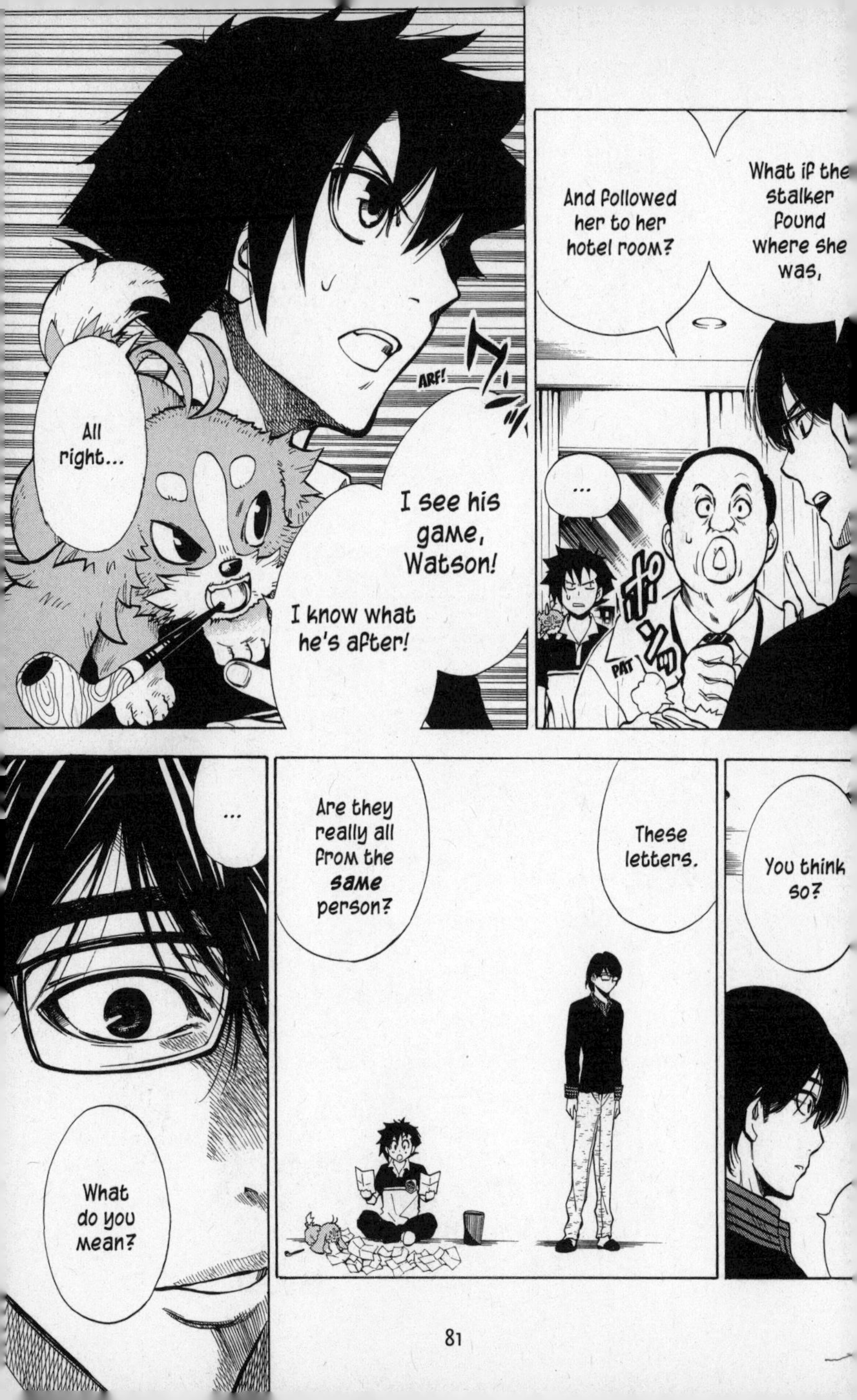
What if the stalker found where she was,
And followed her to her hotel room?
...
PAT
I see his game, Watson!
I know what he's after!
ARF!
All right...
You think so?
These letters.
Are they really all from the same person?
...
What do you mean?

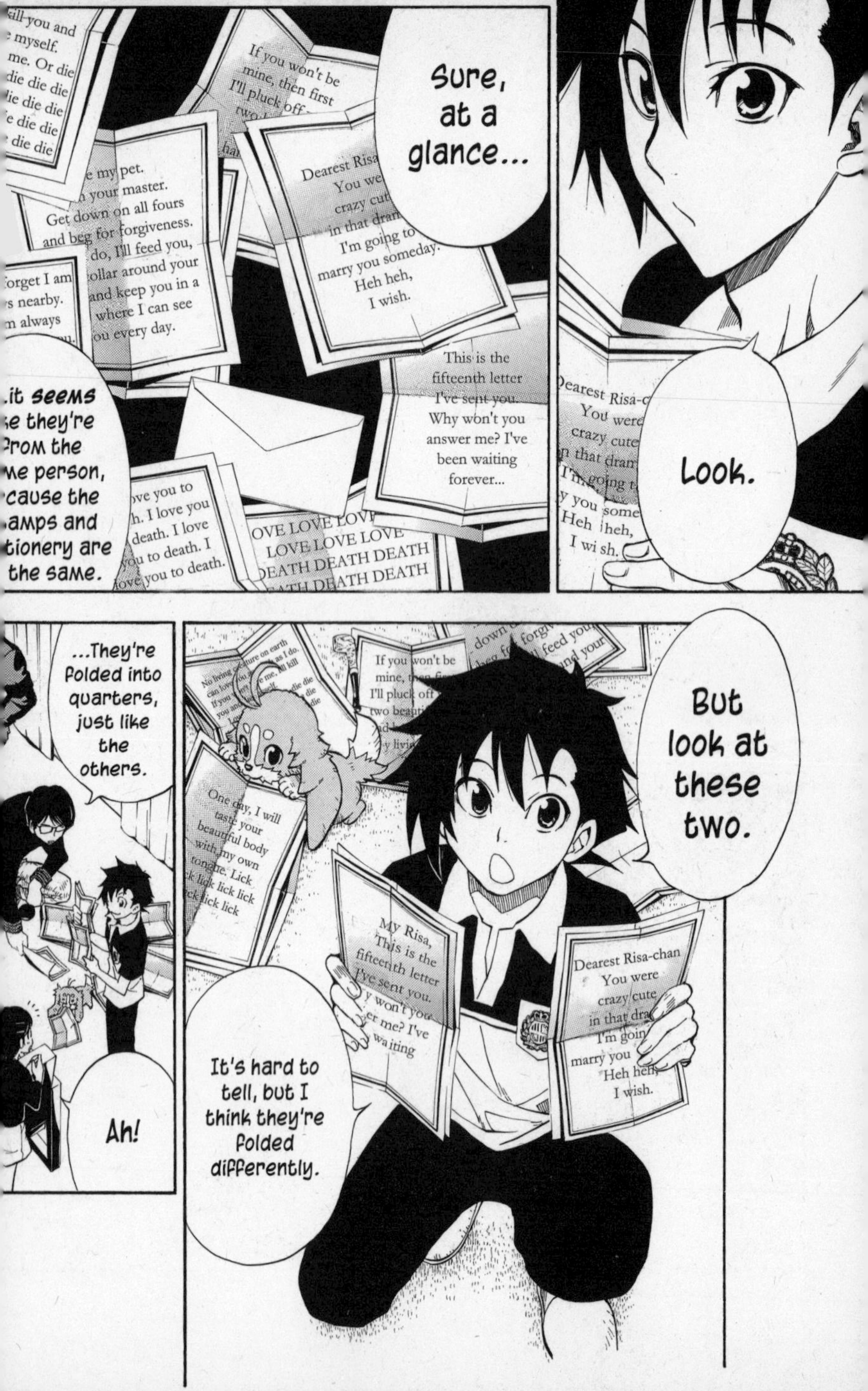

Look.
Sure, at a glance...
..it seems se they're from the me person, cause the amps and tionery are the same.
If you won't be mine, then first I'll pluck off
Get down on all fours and beg for forgiveness.
This is the fifteenth letter I've sent you. Why won't you answer me? I've been waiting forever...
But look at these two.
Dearest Risa-chan
Heh heh, I wish.
One day, I will taste your beautiful body with my own tongue. Lick lick lick lick
It's hard to tell, but I think they're folded differently.
...They're folded into quarters, just like the others.
Ah!

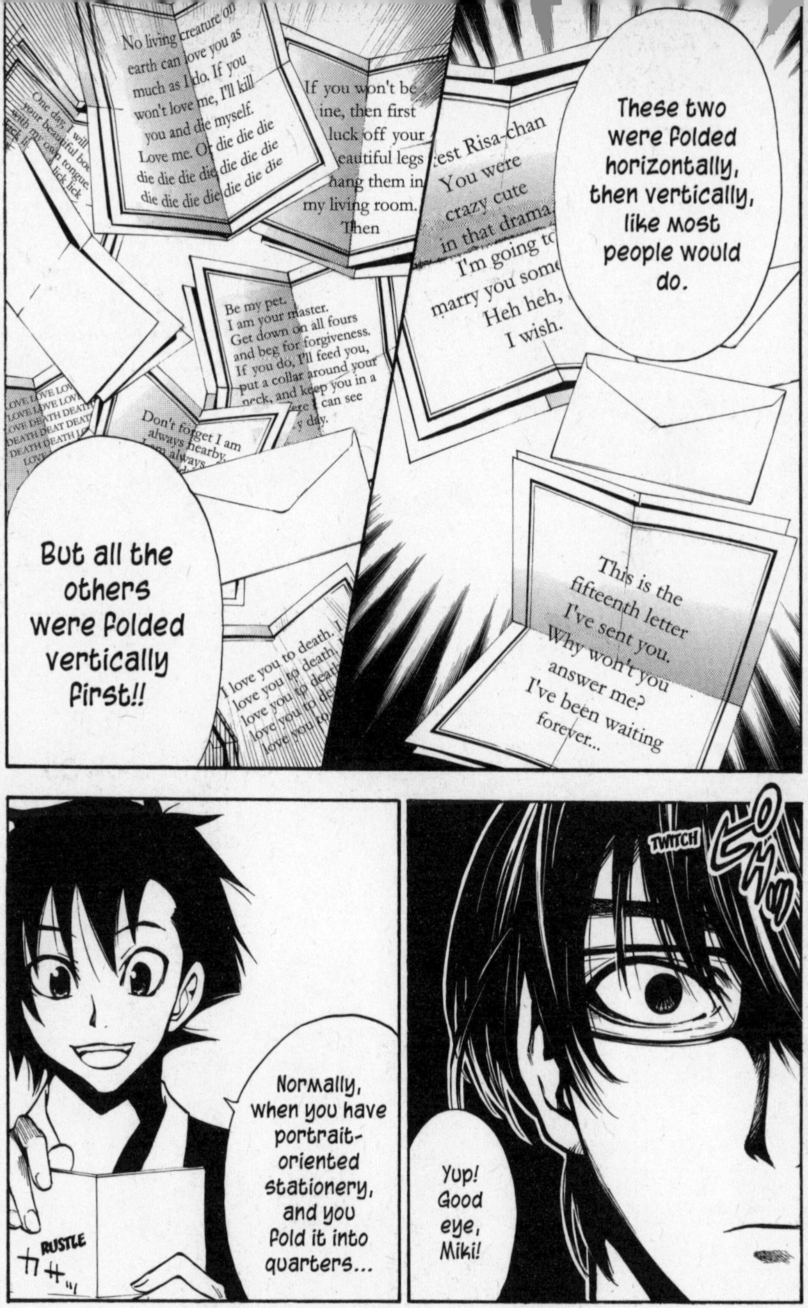
These two were folded horizontally, then vertically, like most people would do.
This is the fifteenth letter I've sent you. Why won't you answer me? I've been waiting forever...
You were crazy cute in that drama
Heh heh, I wish.
If you won't be
then first
my living room.
Then
No living creature on earth can love you as much as I do. If you won't love me, I'll kill you and die myself. Love me. Or die die die
Be my pet. I am your master. Get down on all fours and beg for forgiveness.
But all the others were folded vertically first!!
TWITCH
Yup! Good eye, Miki!
Normally, when you have portrait-oriented stationery, and you fold it into quarters...
RUSTLE

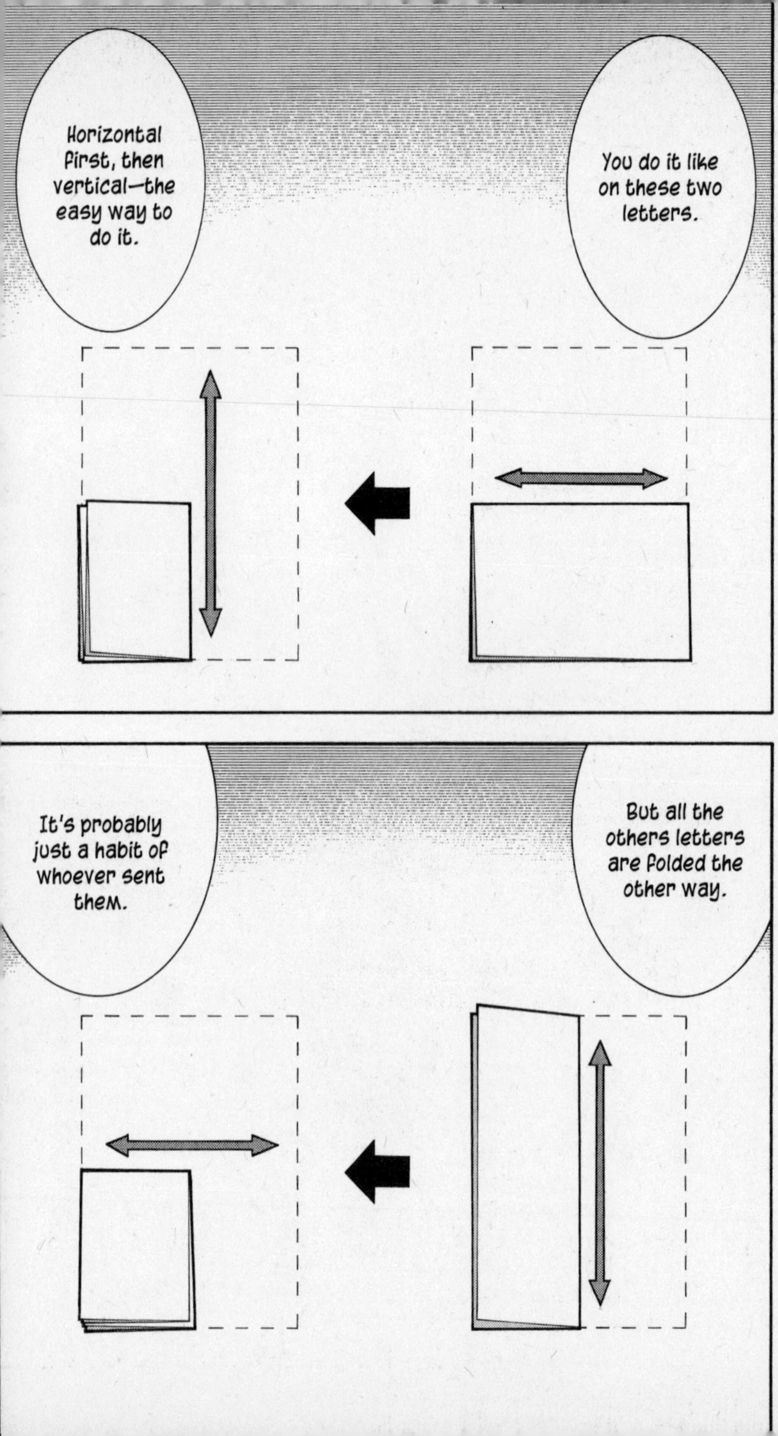
You do it like on these two letters.
Horizontal first, then vertical—the easy way to do it.
But all the others letters are folded the other way.
It's probably just a habit of whoever sent them.

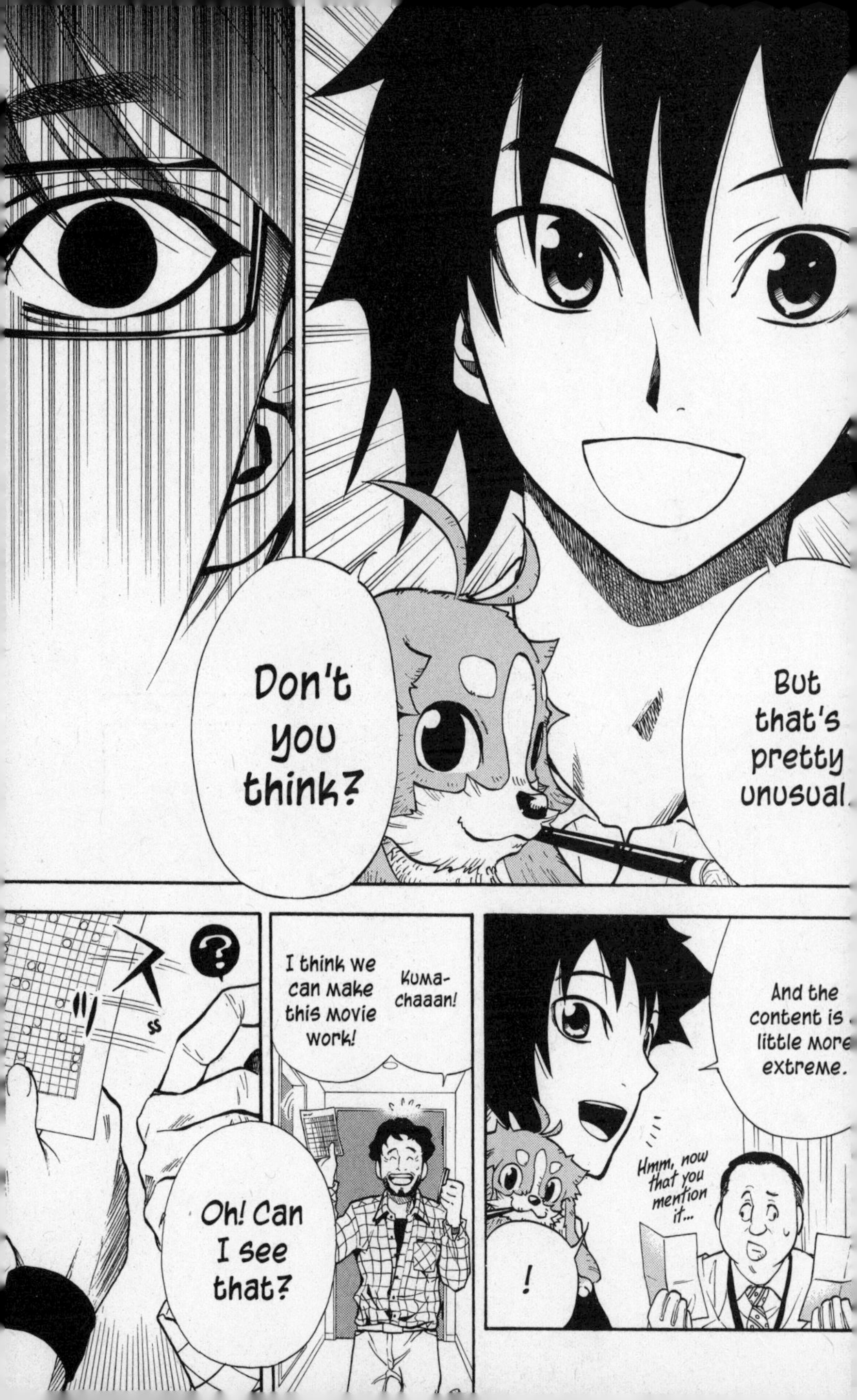
But that's pretty unusual.
Don't you think?
And the content is little more extreme.
Hmm, now that you mention it...
!
Kuma-chaaan!
I think we can make this movie work!
?
Oh! Can I see that?

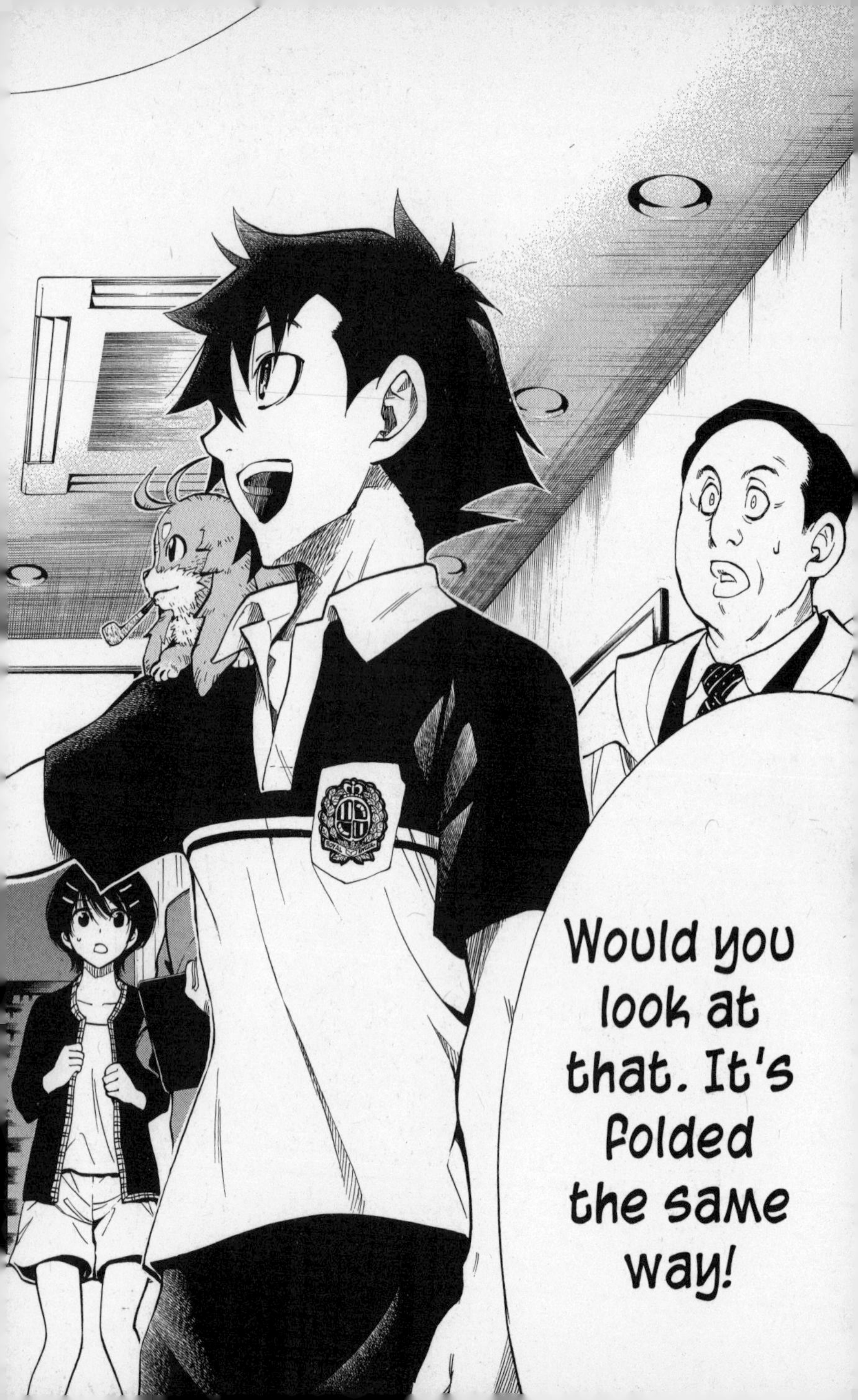
Would you look at that. It's folded the same way!

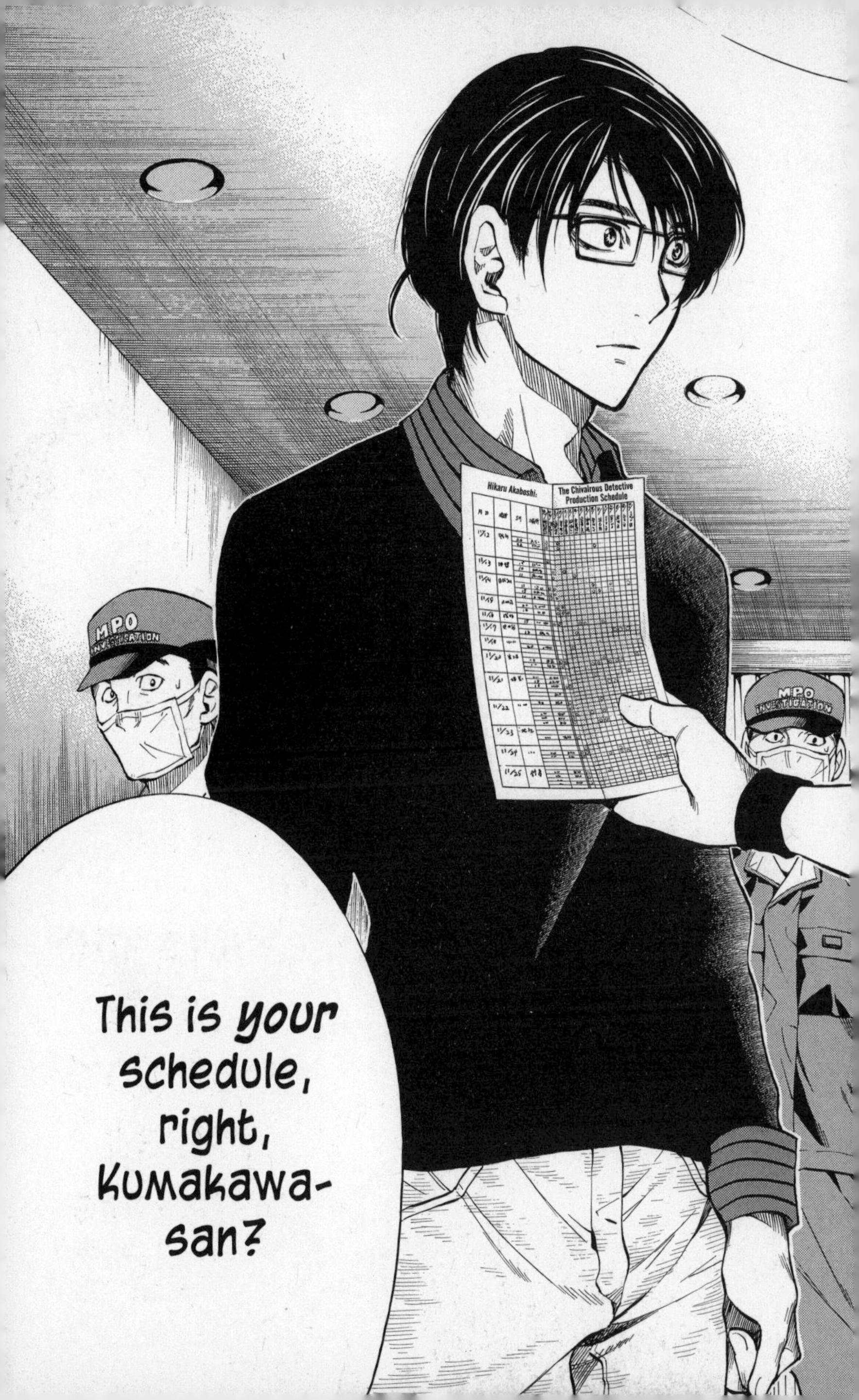
Hikaru Akaboshi:
The Chivalrous Detective Production Schedule
MPO INVESTIGATION
MPO INVESTIGATION
This is your schedule, right, Kumakawa-san?

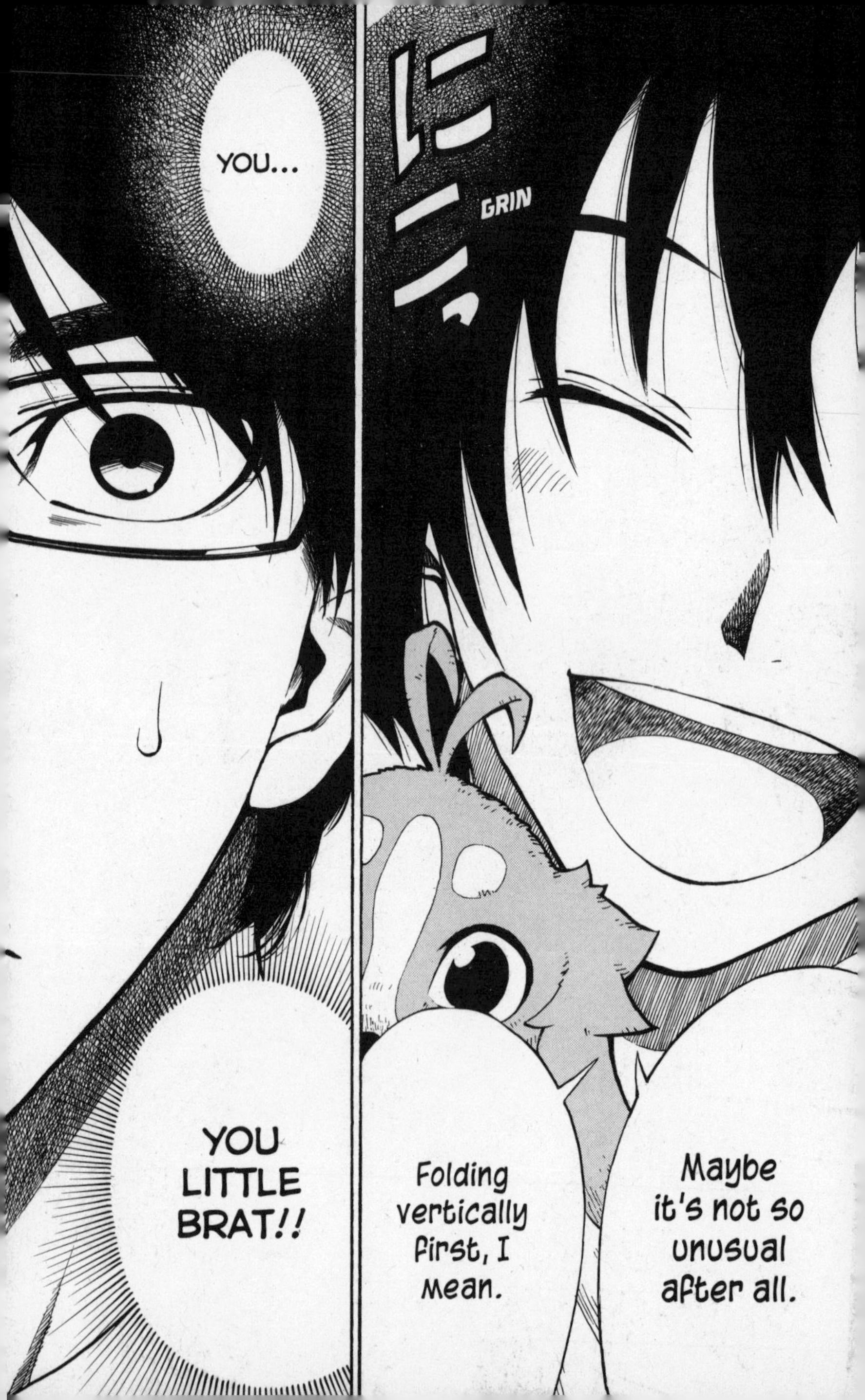
GRIN
Maybe it's not so unusual after all.
Folding vertically first, I mean.
YOU...
YOU LITTLE BRAT!!

Case 2 ⚜ A Script for Death, Part 4

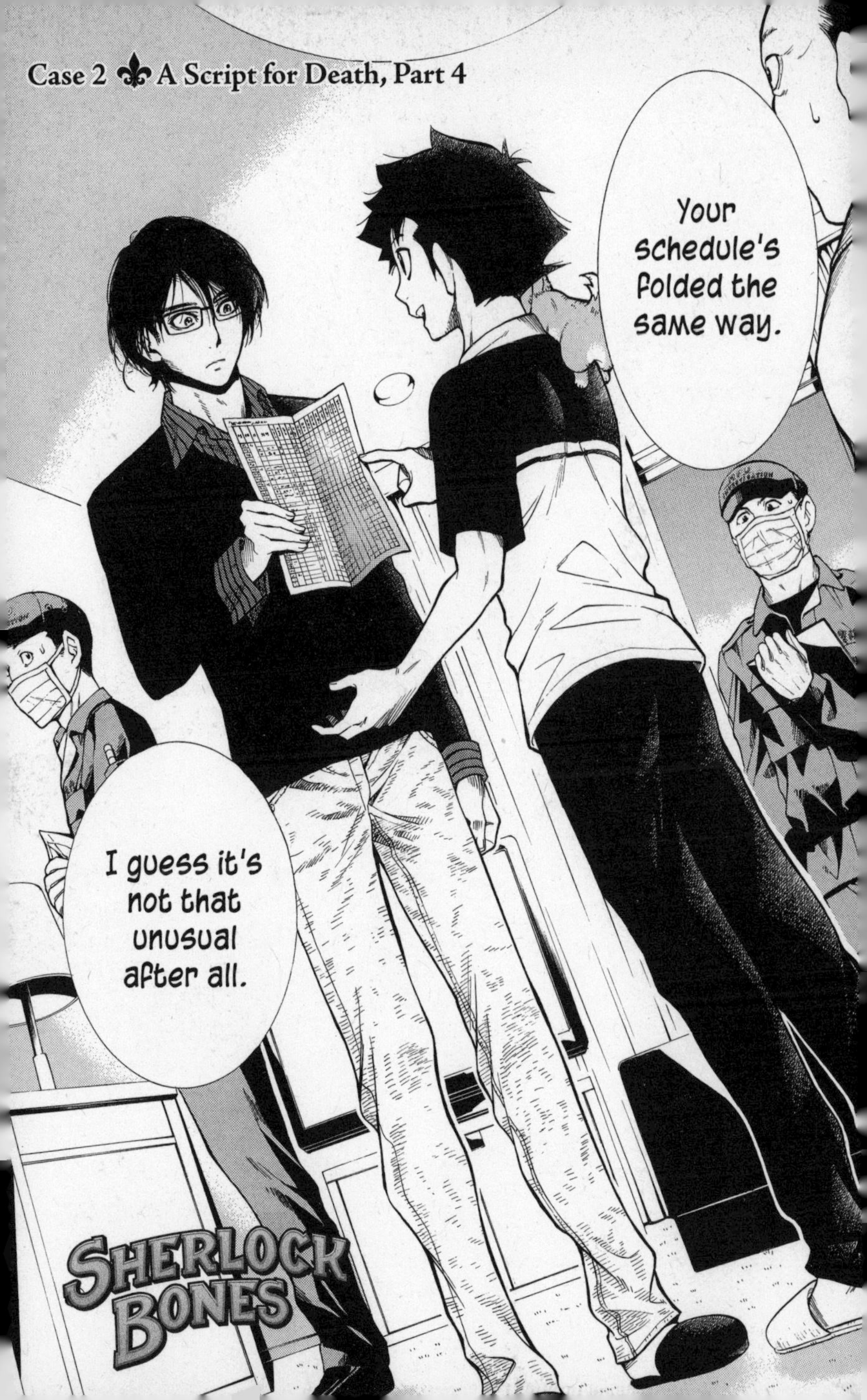
Your schedule's folded the same way.
I guess it's not that unusual after all.
SHERLOCK BONES

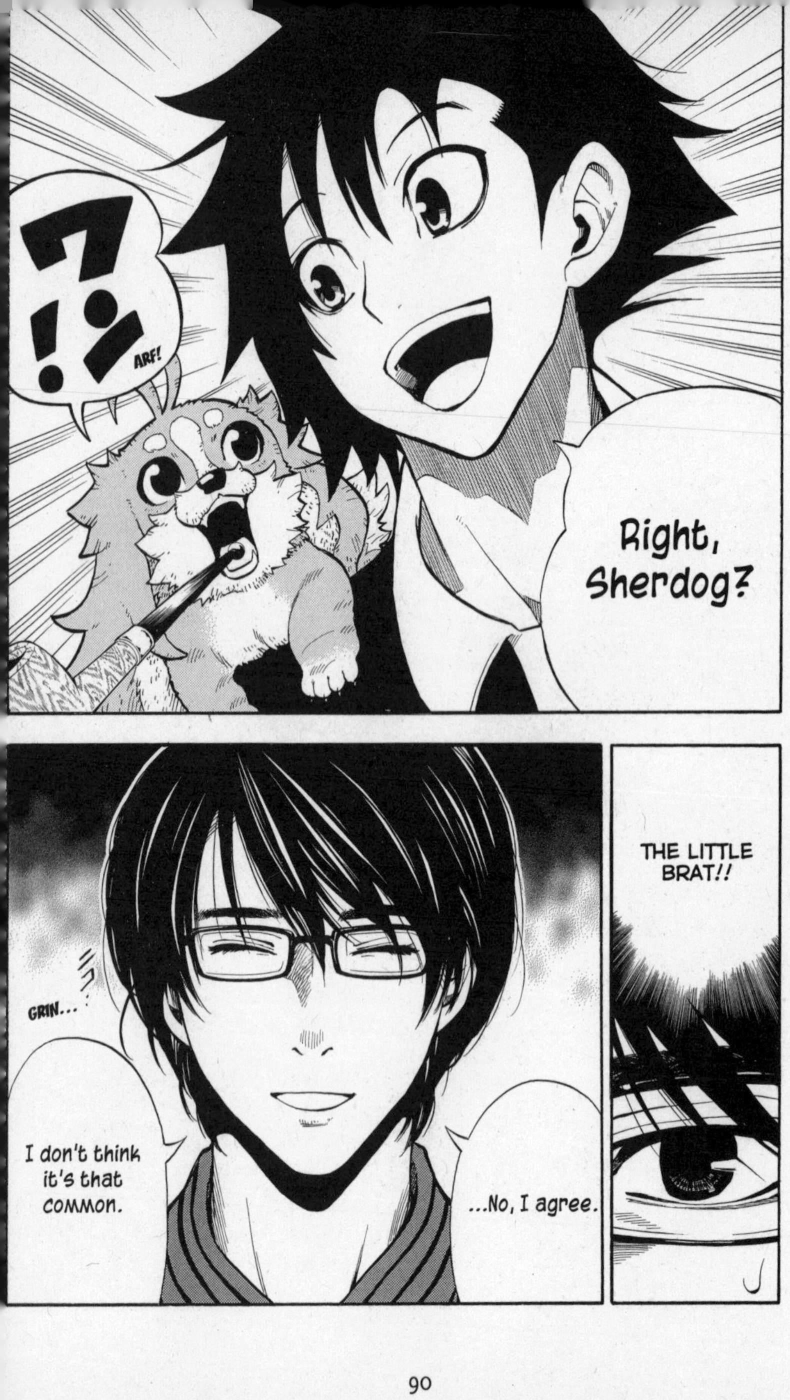
Right, Sherdog?
?!
ARF!
THE LITTLE BRAT!!
...No, I agree.
GRIN...
I don't think it's that common.

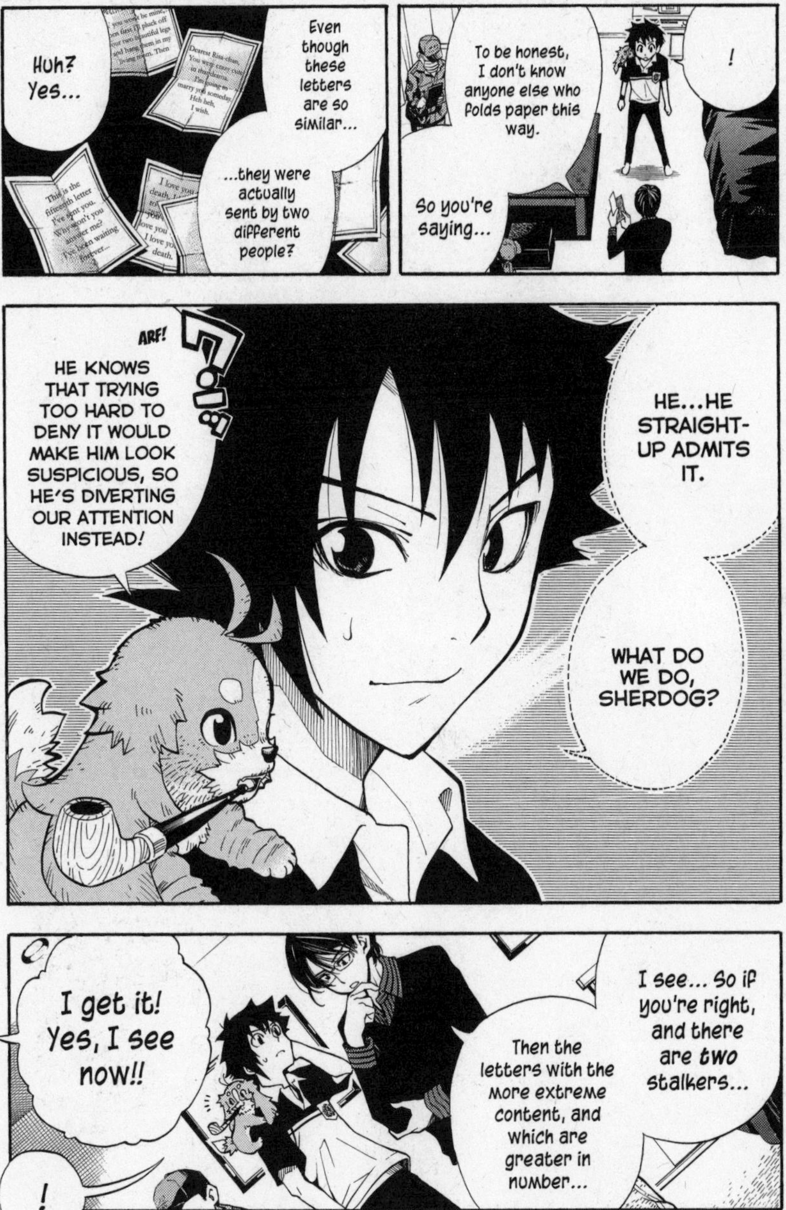
!
To be honest, I don't know anyone else who folds paper this way.
So you're saying...
Even though these letters are so similar...
Huh? Yes...
...they were actually sent by two different people?
HE...HE STRAIGHT-UP ADMITS IT.
WHAT DO WE DO, SHERDOG?
ARF!
HE KNOWS THAT TRYING TOO HARD TO DENY IT WOULD MAKE HIM LOOK SUSPICIOUS, SO HE'S DIVERTING OUR ATTENTION INSTEAD!
I see... So if you're right, and there are *two* stalkers...
Then the letters with the more extreme content, and which are greater in number...
I get it! Yes, I see now!!
!

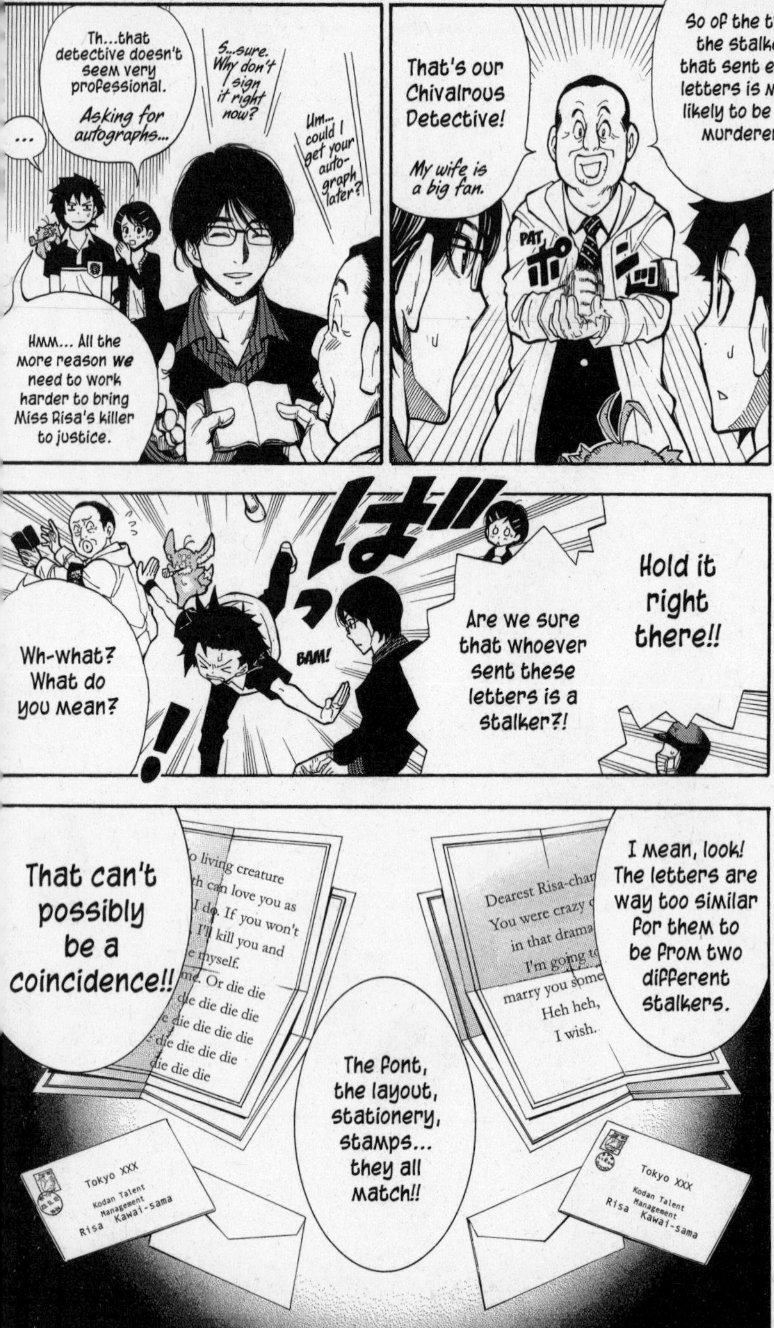
So of the two, the stalker that sent eight letters is more likely to be the murderer!
That's our Chivalrous Detective!
My wife is a big fan.
PAT
Um... could I get your autograph later?
S...sure. Why don't I sign it right now?
Th...that detective doesn't seem very professional.
Asking for autographs...
...
Hmm... All the more reason we need to work harder to bring Miss Risa's killer to justice.
Hold it right there!!
Are we sure that whoever sent these letters is a stalker?!
BAM!
Wh-what? What do you mean?
I mean, look! The letters are way too similar for them to be from two different stalkers.
Dearest Risa-chan
You were crazy
in that drama
I'm going to
marry you some
Heh heh,
I wish.
Tokyo XXX
Kodan Talent Management
Risa Kawai-sama
The font, the layout, stationery, stamps... they all match!!
That can't possibly be a coincidence!!
living creature
can love you as
I do. If you won't
I'll kill you and
myself.
Or die die die
die die die
die die die
die die die
die die die
Tokyo XXX
Kodan Talent Management
Risa Kawai-sama

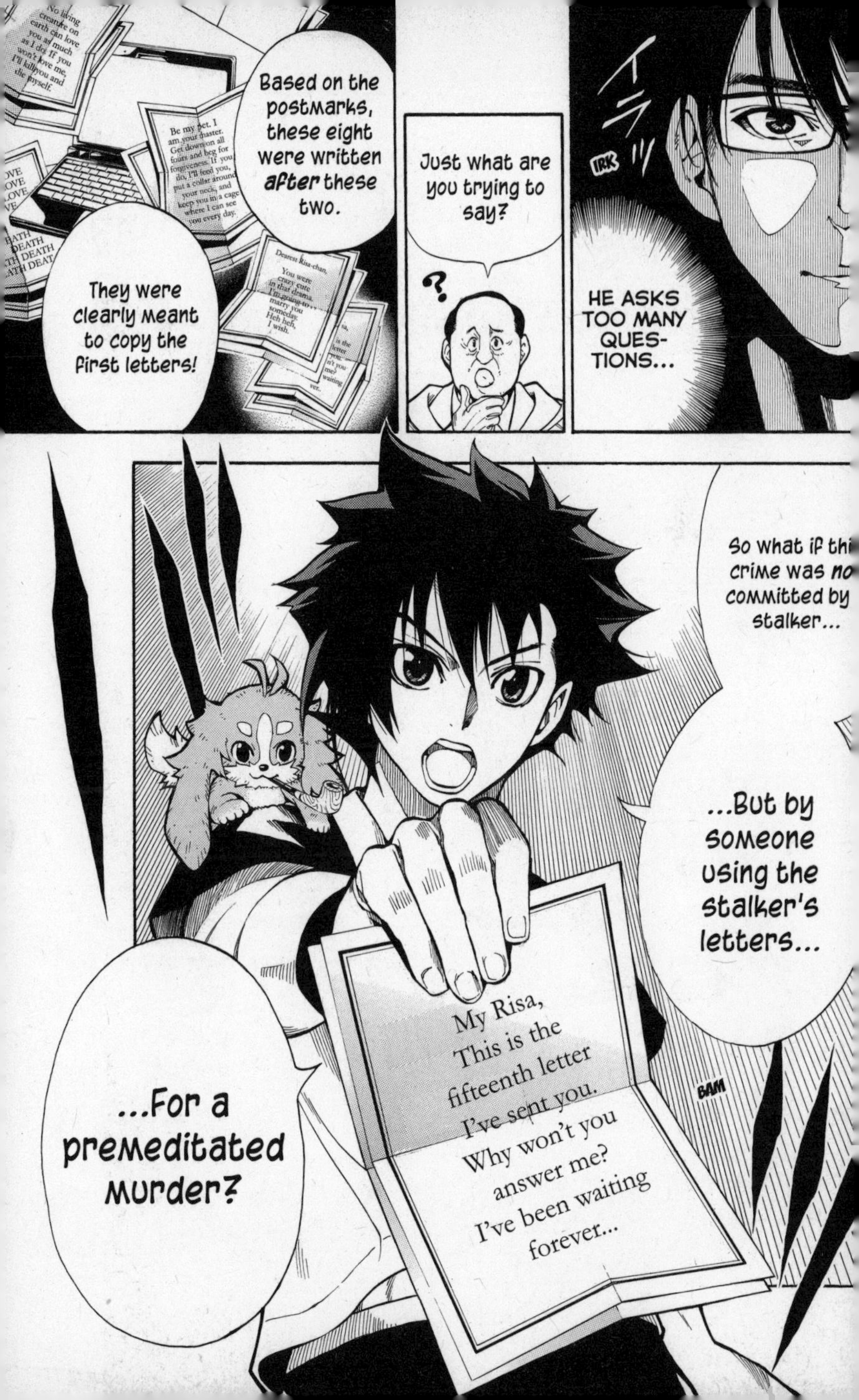
IRK
HE ASKS TOO MANY QUES-TIONS...
Just what are you trying to say?
?
Based on the postmarks, these eight were written *after* these two.
No living creature on earth can love you as much as I do. If you won't love me, I'll kill you and then myself.
Be my pet. I am your master. Get down on all fours and beg for forgiveness. If you do, I'll feed you, put a collar around your neck, and keep you in a cage where I can see you every day.
Dearest Risa-chan, You were crazy cute in that drama. I'm going to... marry you someday. Heh heh, I wish.
They were clearly meant to copy the first letters!
So what if thi crime was no committed by stalker...
...But by someone using the stalker's letters...
BAM
My Risa, This is the fifteenth letter I've sent you. Why won't you answer me? I've been waiting forever...
...For a premeditated murder?

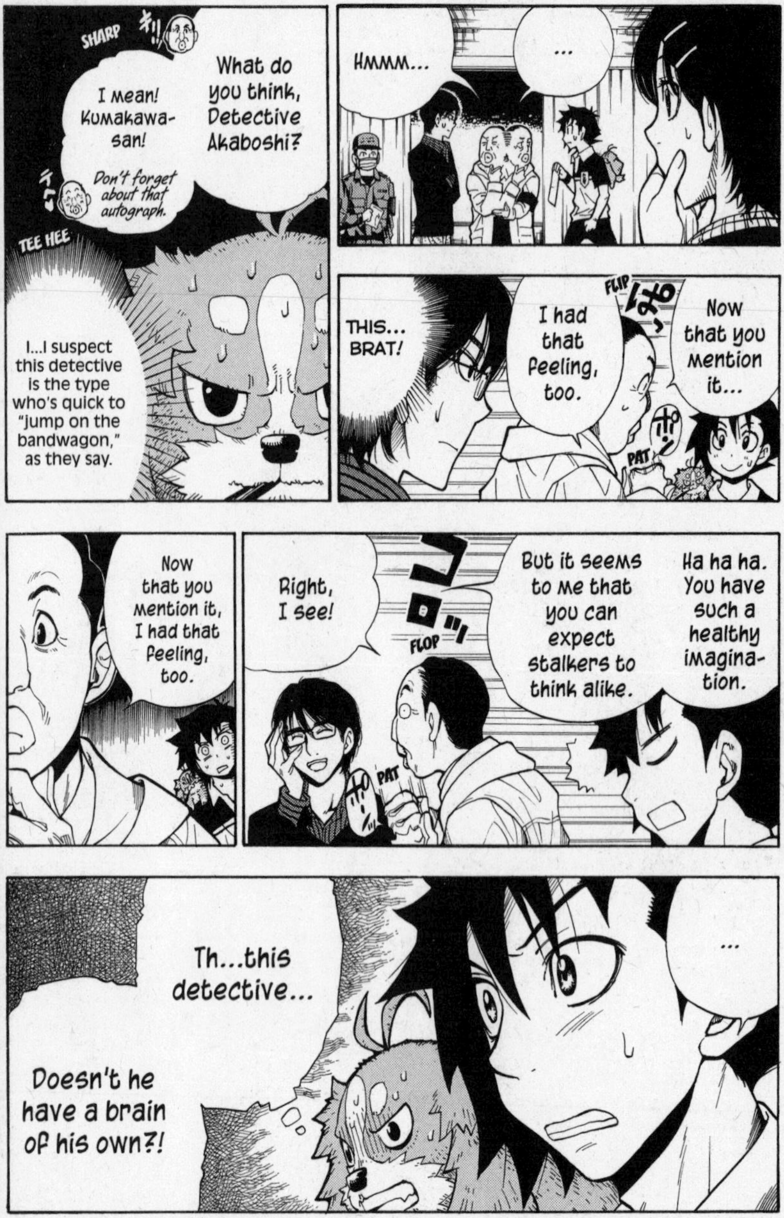
...
HMMM...
Now that you mention it...
PAT
I had that feeling, too.
FLIP
THIS... BRAT!
SHARP
What do you think, Detective Akaboshi?
I mean! Kumakawa-san!
Don't forget about that autograph.
TEE HEE
I...I suspect this detective is the type who's quick to "jump on the bandwagon," as they say.
Ha ha ha. You have such a healthy imagination.
But it seems to me that you can expect stalkers to think alike.
FLOP
Right, I see!
PAT
Now that you mention it, I had that feeling, too.
...
Th...this detective...
Doesn't he have a brain of his own?!

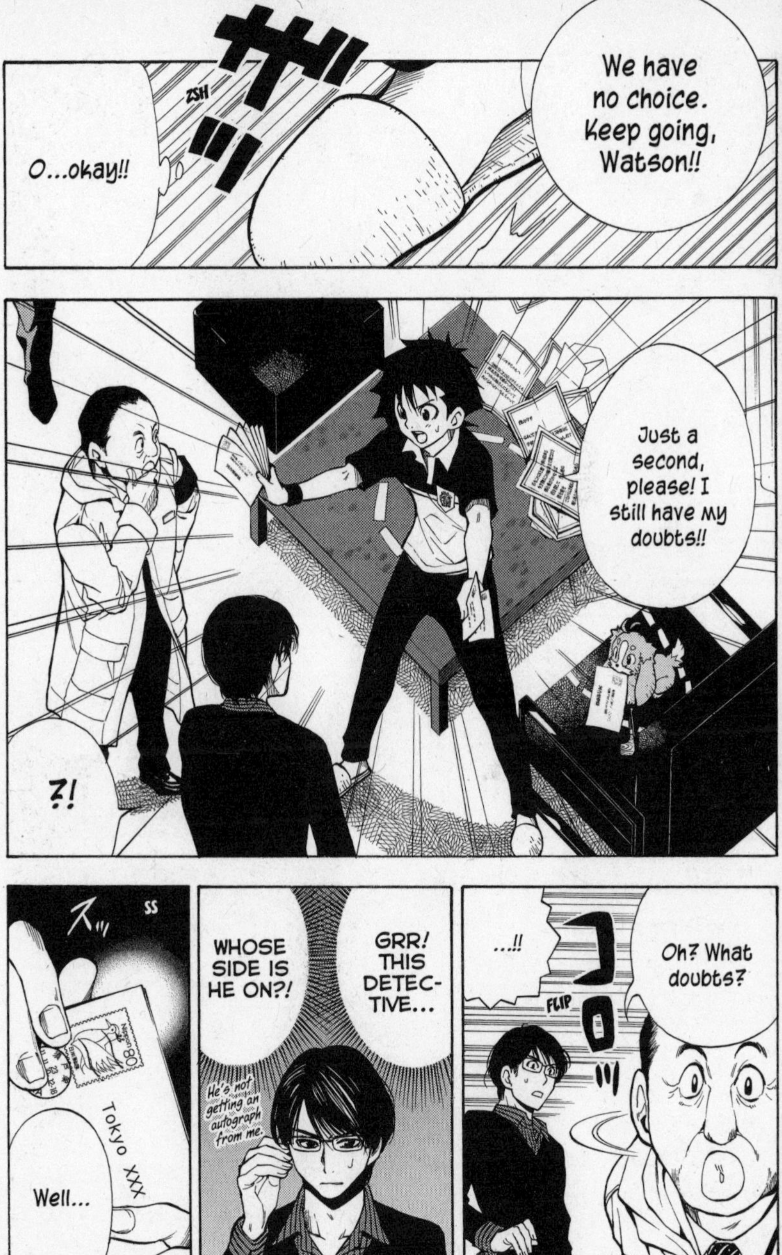
We have no choice. Keep going, Watson!!
ZSH
O...okay!!
Just a second, please! I still have my doubts!!
?!
Oh? What doubts?
FLIP
...!!
GRR! THIS DETECTIVE...
WHOSE SIDE IS HE ON?!
He's not getting an autograph from me.
SS
Tokyo XXX
Well...

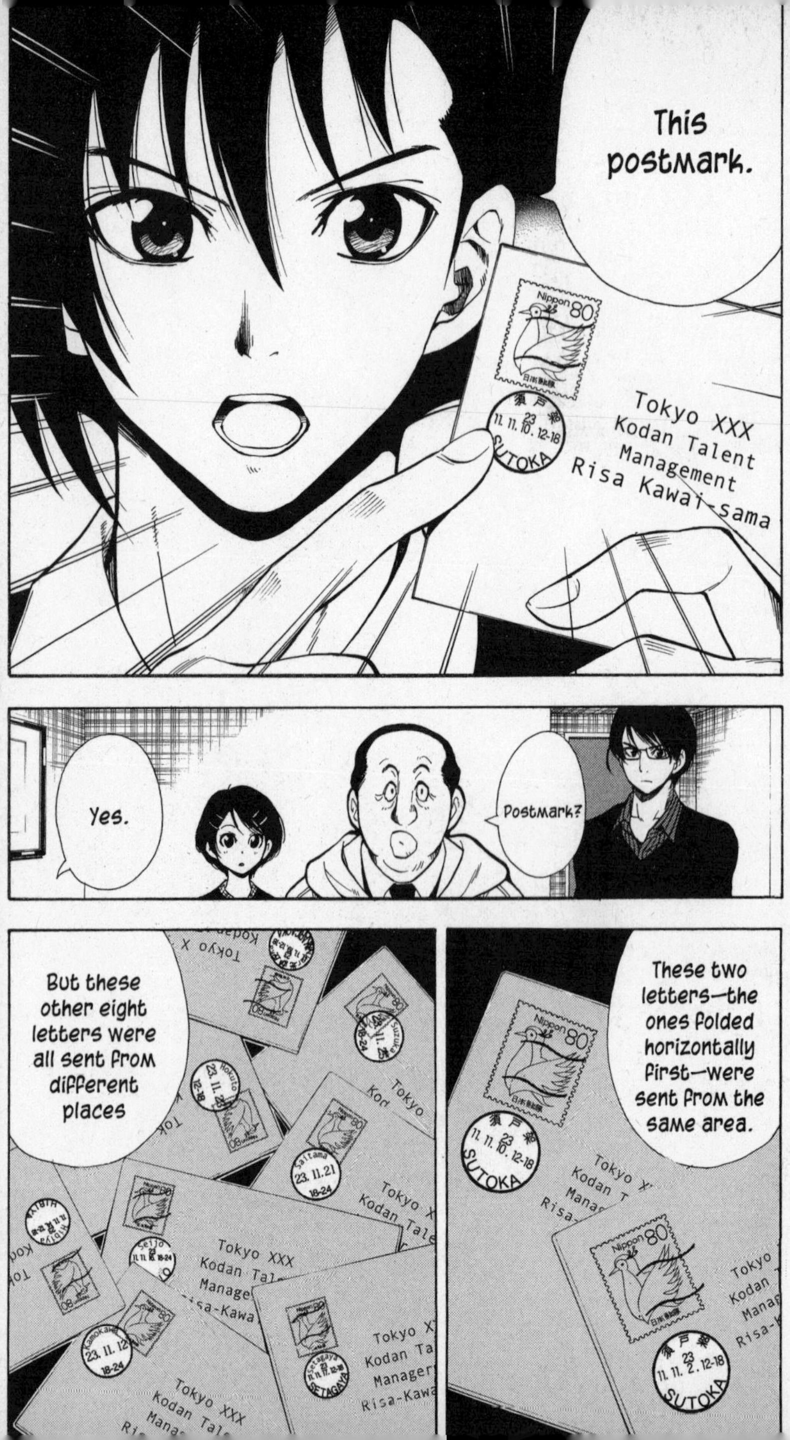
This postmark.
Nippon 80
23 11. 11. 10. 12-18 SUTOKA
Tokyo XXX
Kodan Talent
Management
Risa Kawai-sama
Postmark?
Yes.
These two letters—the ones folded horizontally first—were sent from the same area.
But these other eight letters were all sent from different places

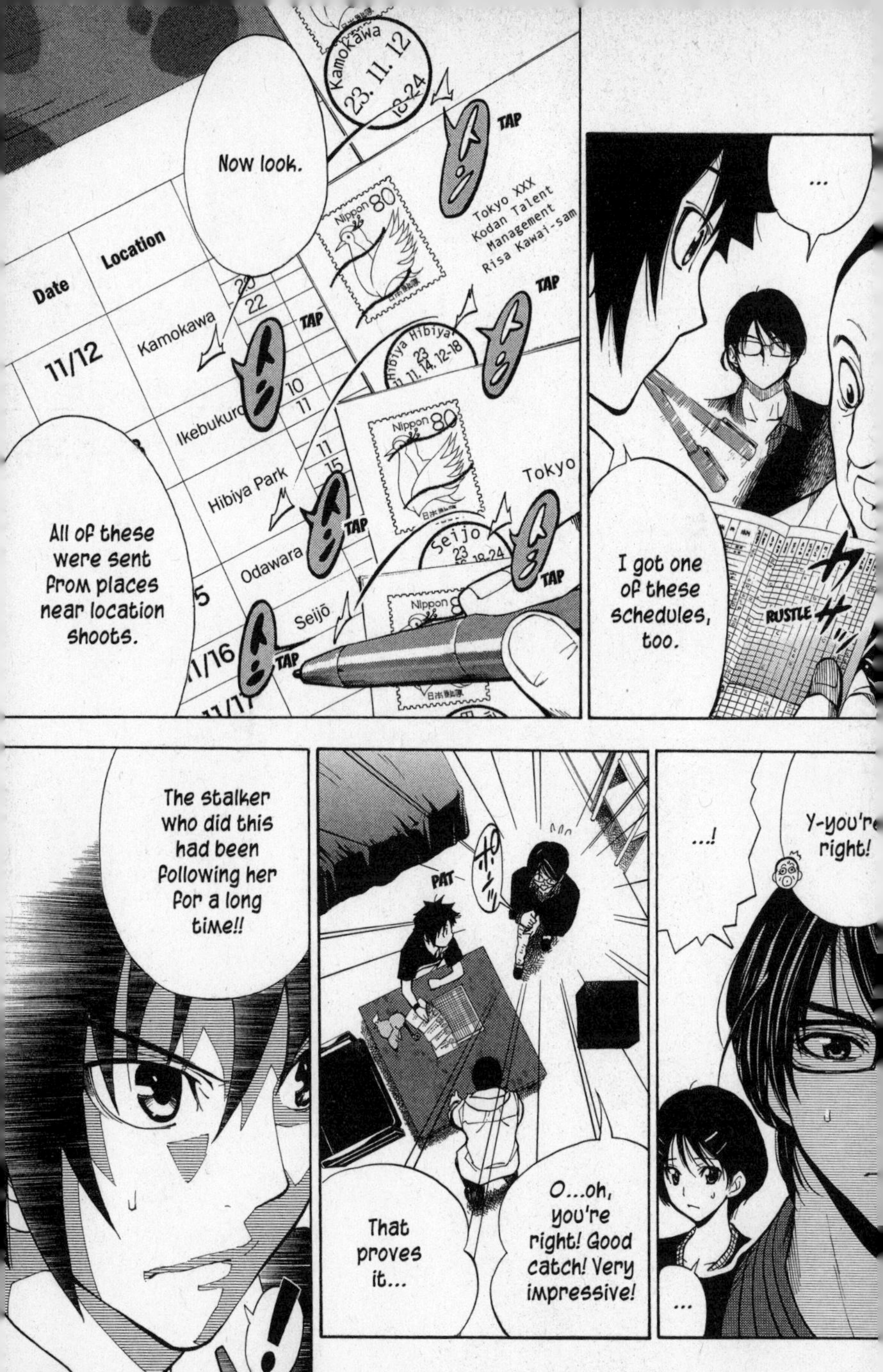
...
I got one of these schedules, too.
RUSTLE
Now look.
Kamokawa 23. 11. 12
Tokyo XXX Kodan Talent Management Risa Kawai-sam
TAP
TAP
Hibiya Hibiya 23 11. 14. 12-18
Date
Location
11/12
Kamokawa
Ikebukuro
Hibiya Park
Odawara
Seijō
11/16
TAP
TAP
Tokyo
Seijo
TAP
TAP
All of these were sent from places near location shoots.
Y-you're right!
...!
...
PAT
O...oh, you're right! Good catch! Very impressive!
That proves it...
The stalker who did this had been following her for a long time!!

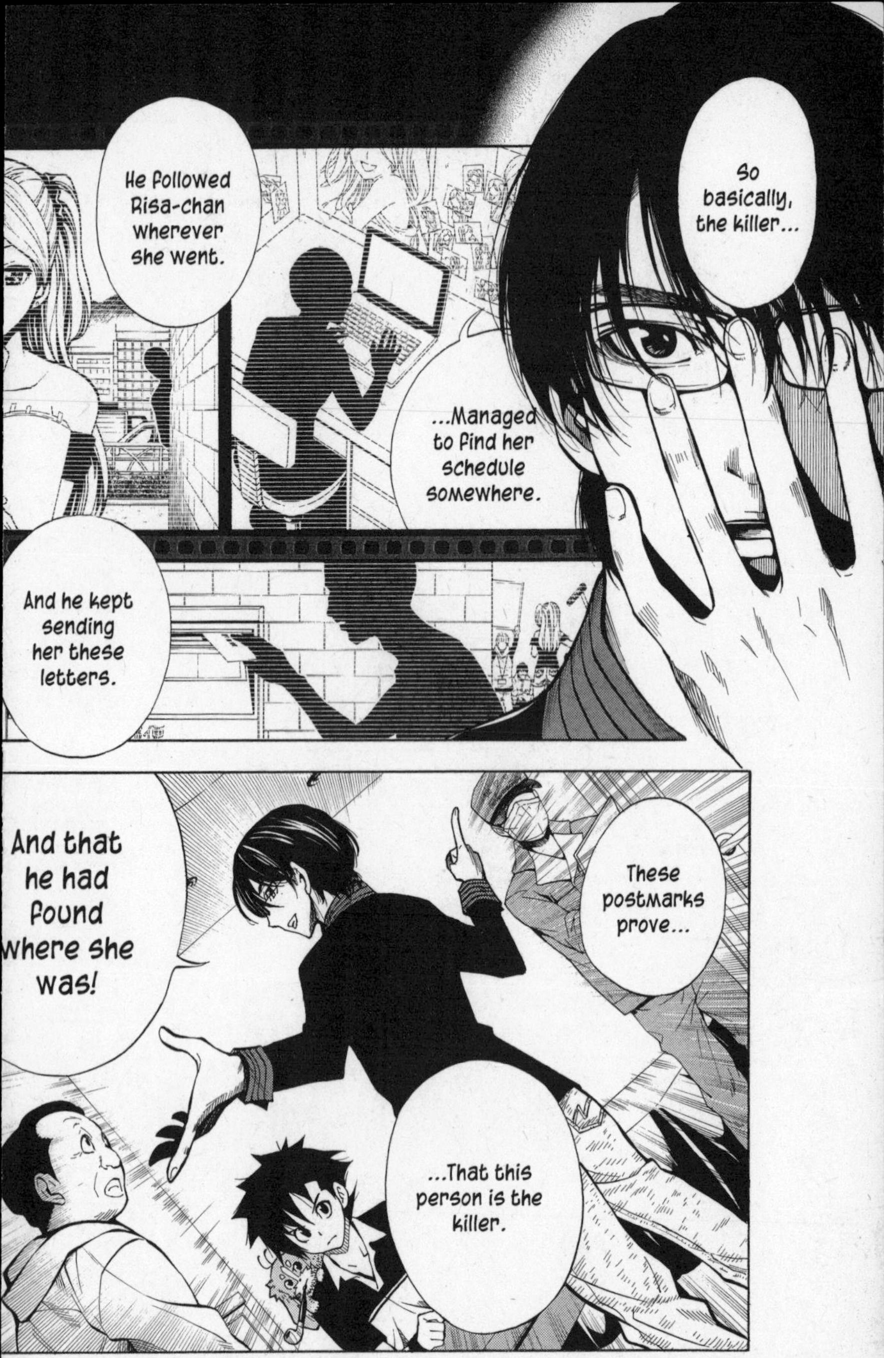
So basically, the killer...
...Managed to find her schedule somewhere.
He followed Risa-chan wherever she went.
And he kept sending her these letters.
These postmarks prove...
And that he had found where she was!
...That this person is the killer.

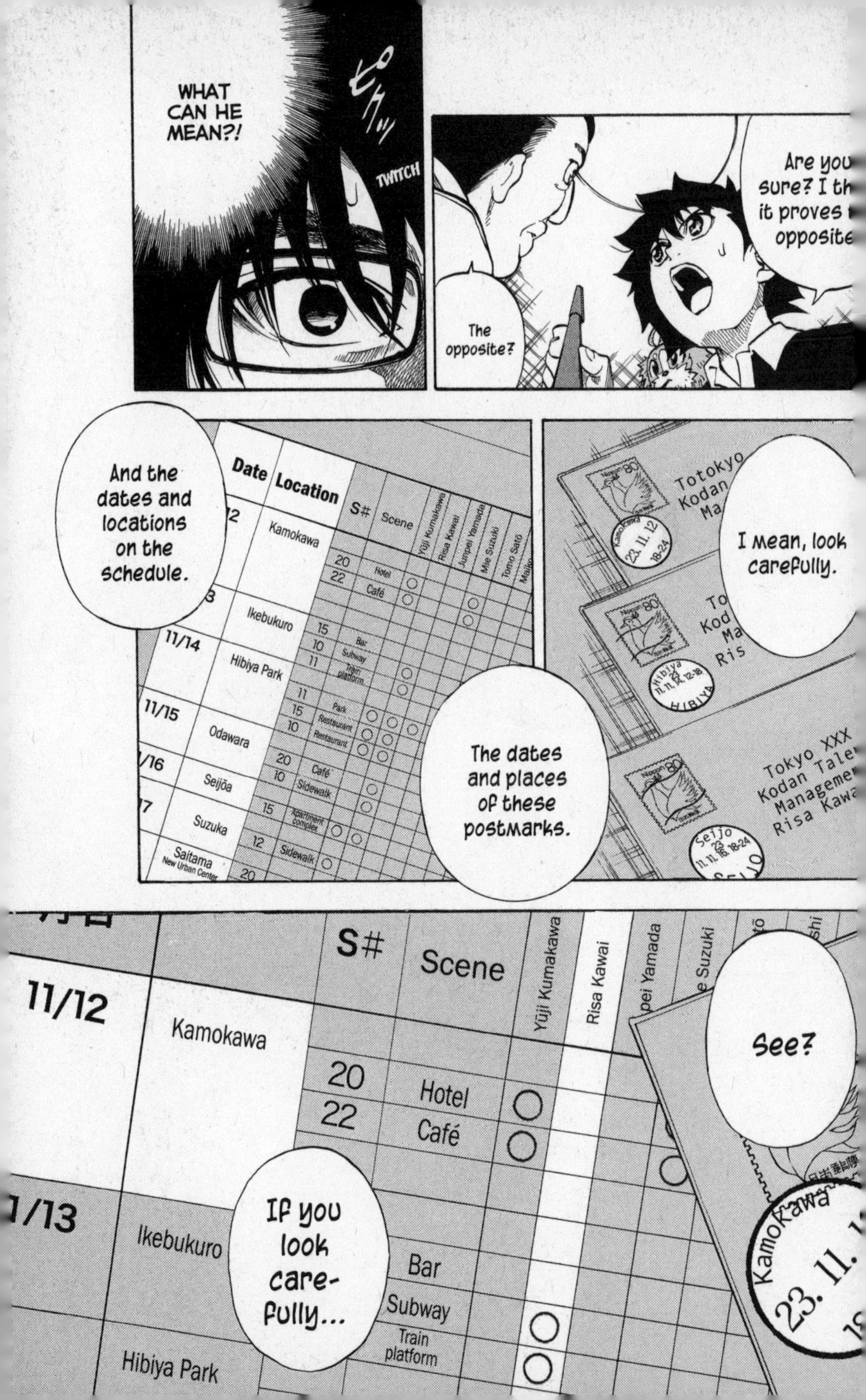

Are you sure? I th it proves t opposite
The opposite?
WHAT CAN HE MEAN?!
TWITCH
I mean, look carefully.
The dates and places of these postmarks.
And the dates and locations on the schedule.
Date
Location
S#
Scene
See?
If you look care-fully...

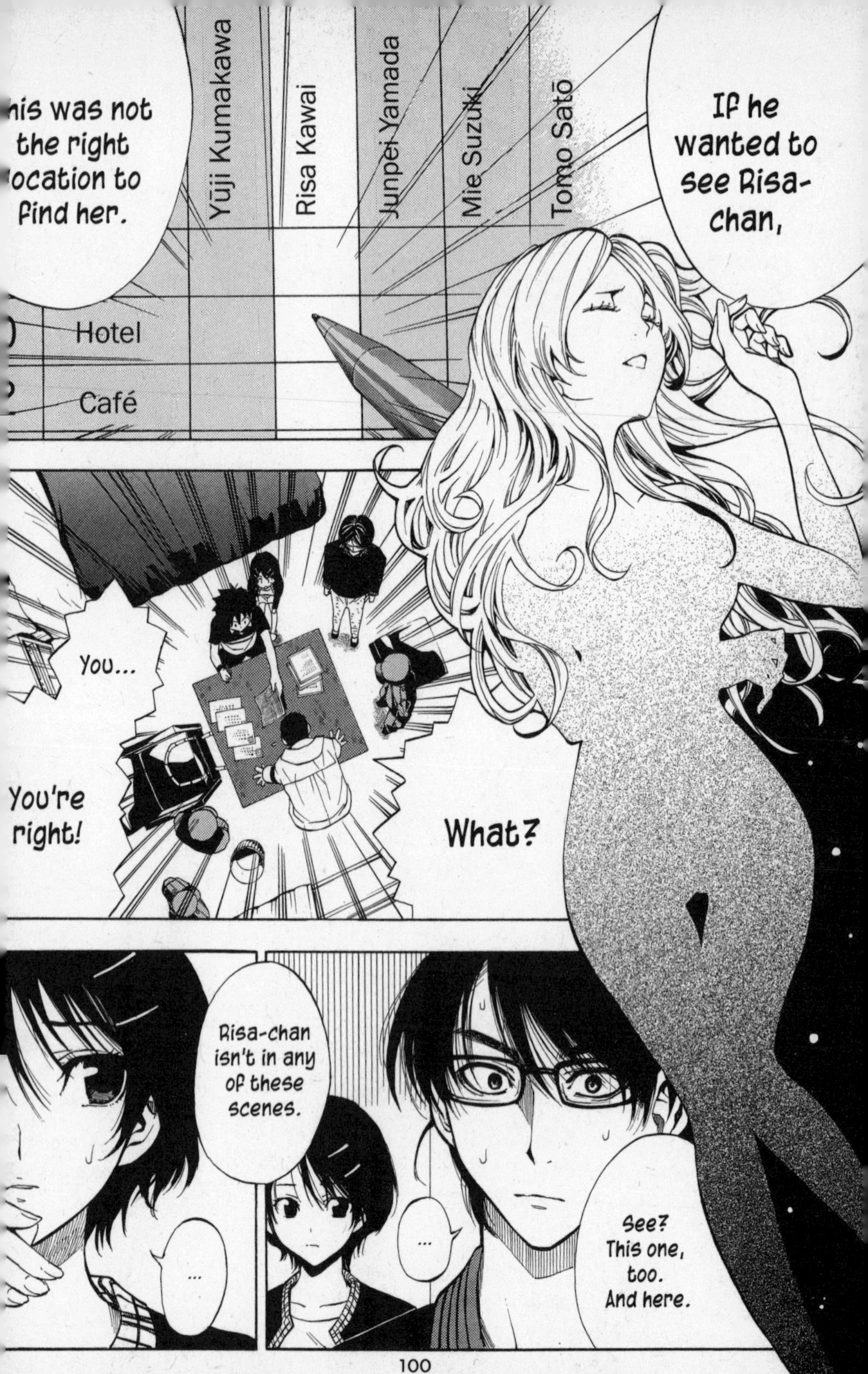

If he wanted to see Risa-chan,
his was not the right ocation to find her.
Yūji Kumakawa
Risa Kawai
Junpei Yamada
Mie Suzuki
Tomo Satō
Hotel
Café
What?
You...
You're right!
Risa-chan isn't in any of these scenes.
See? This one, too. And here.
...
...

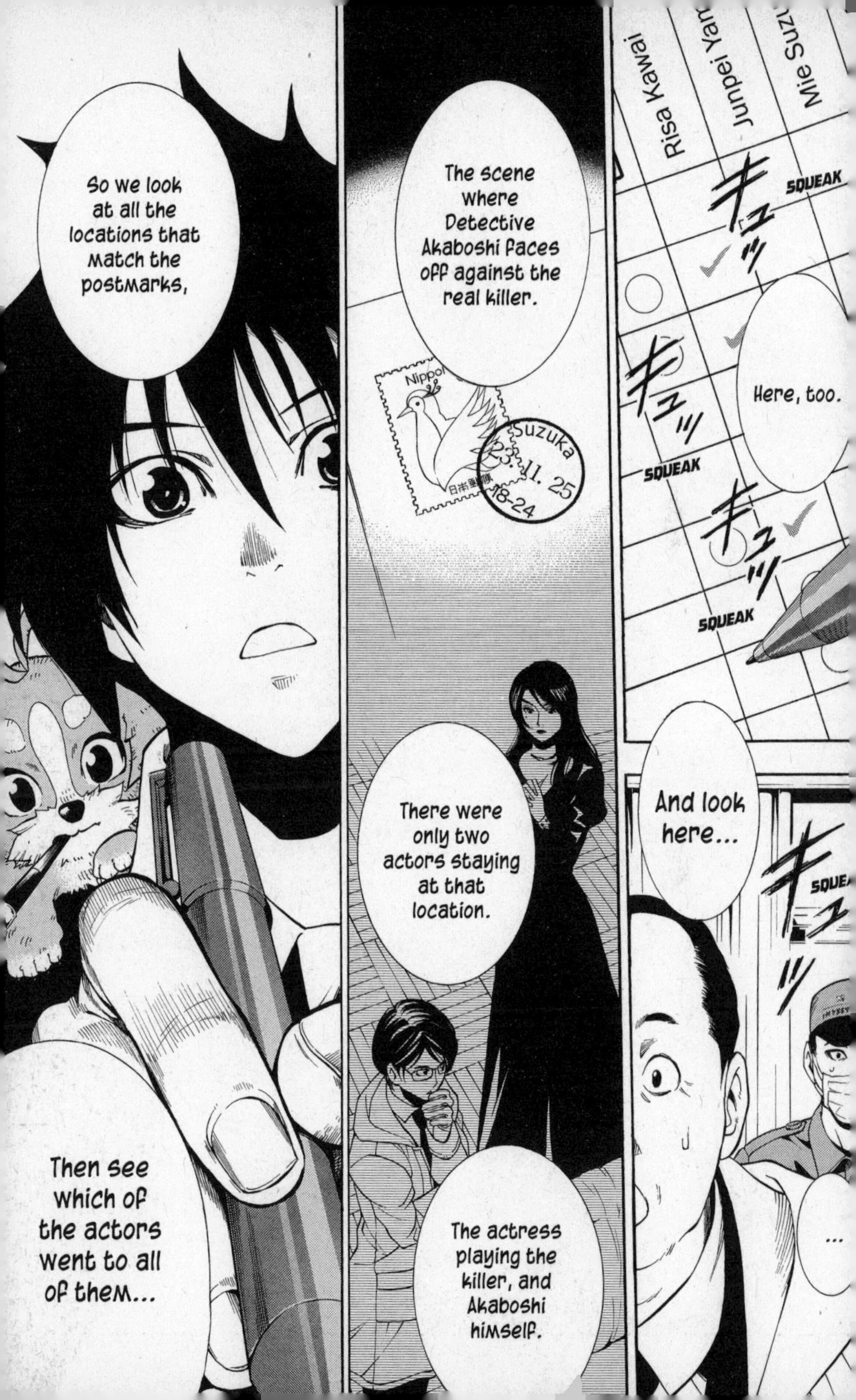

Risa Kawai
SQUEAK
SQUEAK
Here, too.
SQUEAK
And look here...
...
The scene where Detective Akaboshi faces off against the real killer.
Nippon
Suzuka
23. 11. 25
18-24
There were only two actors staying at that location.
The actress playing the killer, and Akaboshi himself.
So we look at all the locations that match the postmarks,
Then see which of the actors went to all of them...

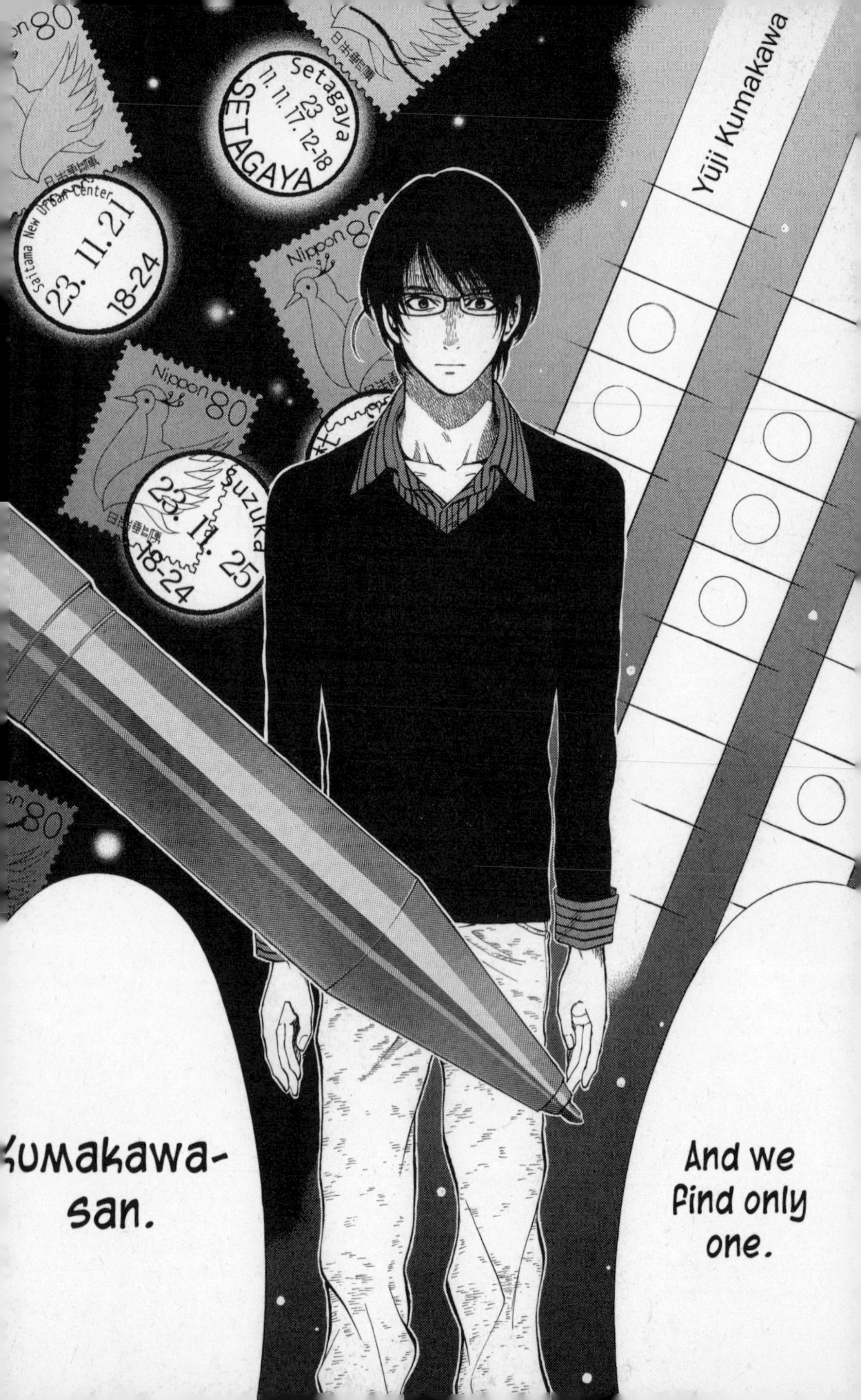
Yūji Kumakawa
Setagaya
23
11.11.17.12-18
SETAGAYA
Nippon 80
Saitama New Urban Center
23. 11.21
18-24
Nippon 80
Suzuka
23. 11. 25
18-24
And we find only one.
Kumakawa-san.

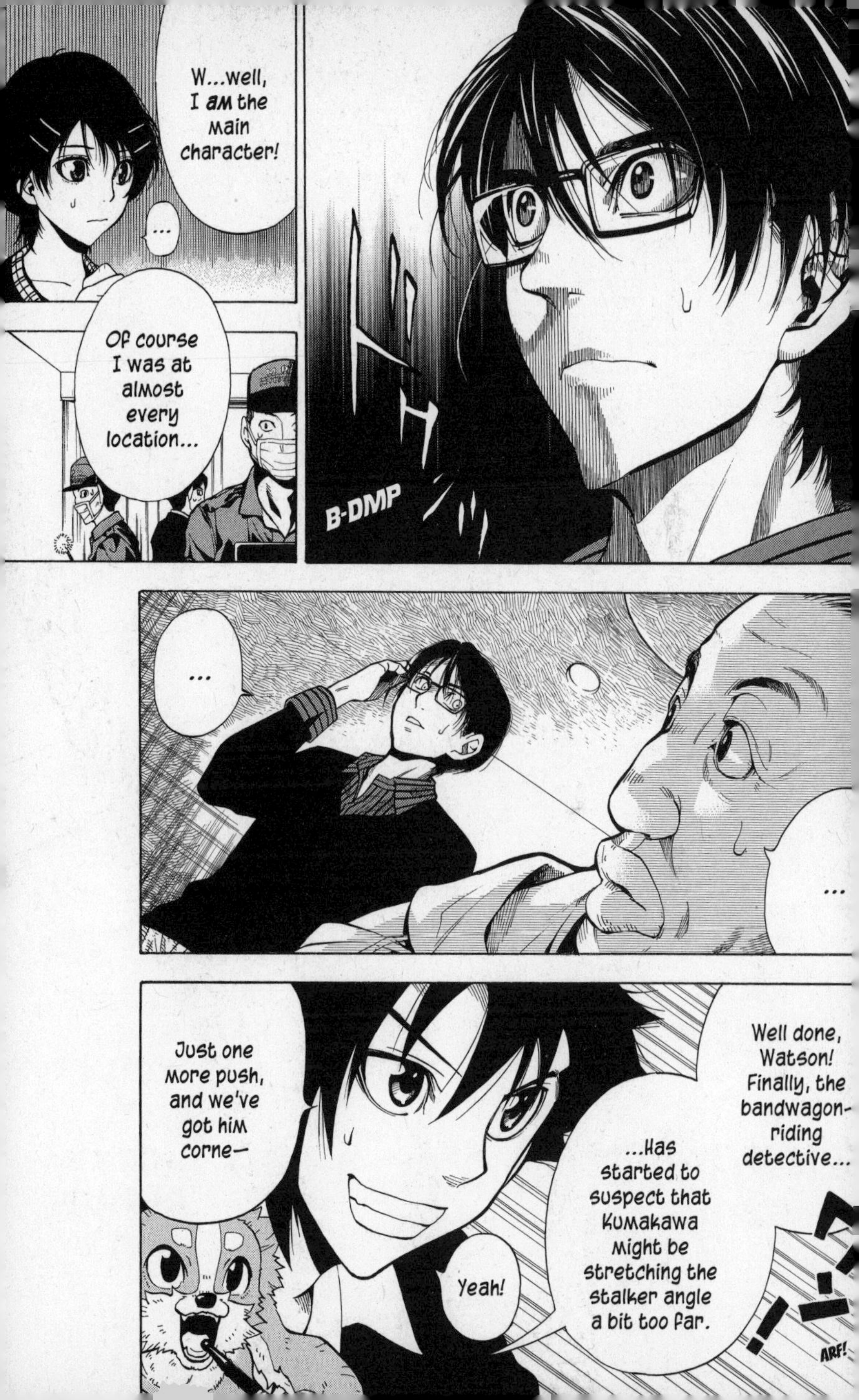
B-DMP
W...well, I am the main character!
...
Of course I was at almost every location...
...
...
Well done, Watson! Finally, the bandwagon-riding detective...
...Has started to suspect that Kumakawa might be stretching the stalker angle a bit too far.
Yeah!
Just one more push, and we've got him corne—
!!
ARF!

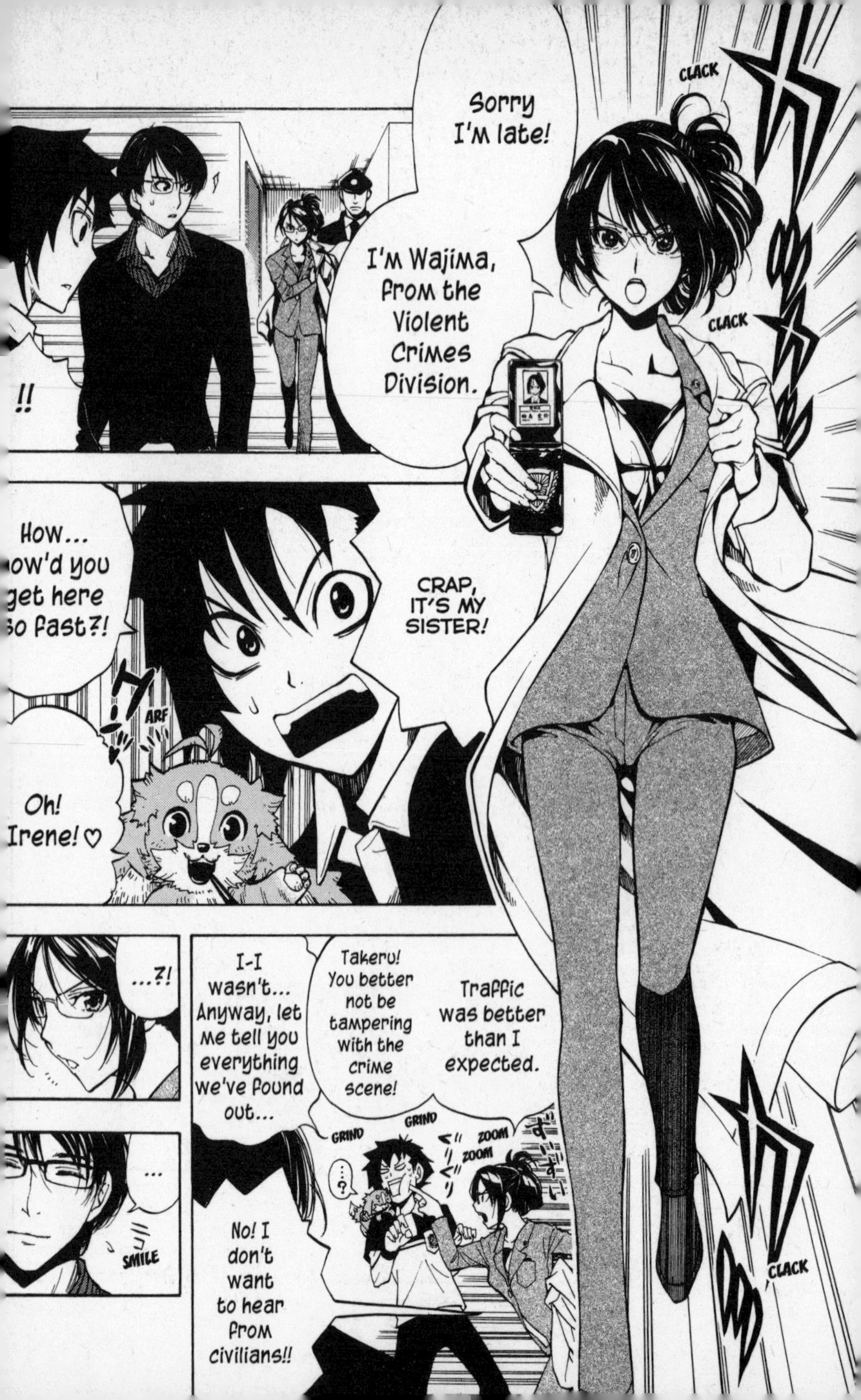
CLACK
Sorry I'm late!
I'm Wajima, from the Violent Crimes Division.
CLACK
CLACK
!!
CRAP, IT'S MY SISTER!
How... ow'd you get here so fast?!
ARF
Oh! Irene! ♡
Traffic was better than I expected.
Takeru! You better not be tampering with the crime scene!
I-I wasn't... Anyway, let me tell you everything we've found out...
GRIND
GRIND
ZOOM
ZOOM
...?
No! I don't want to hear from civilians!!
...?!
...
SMILE

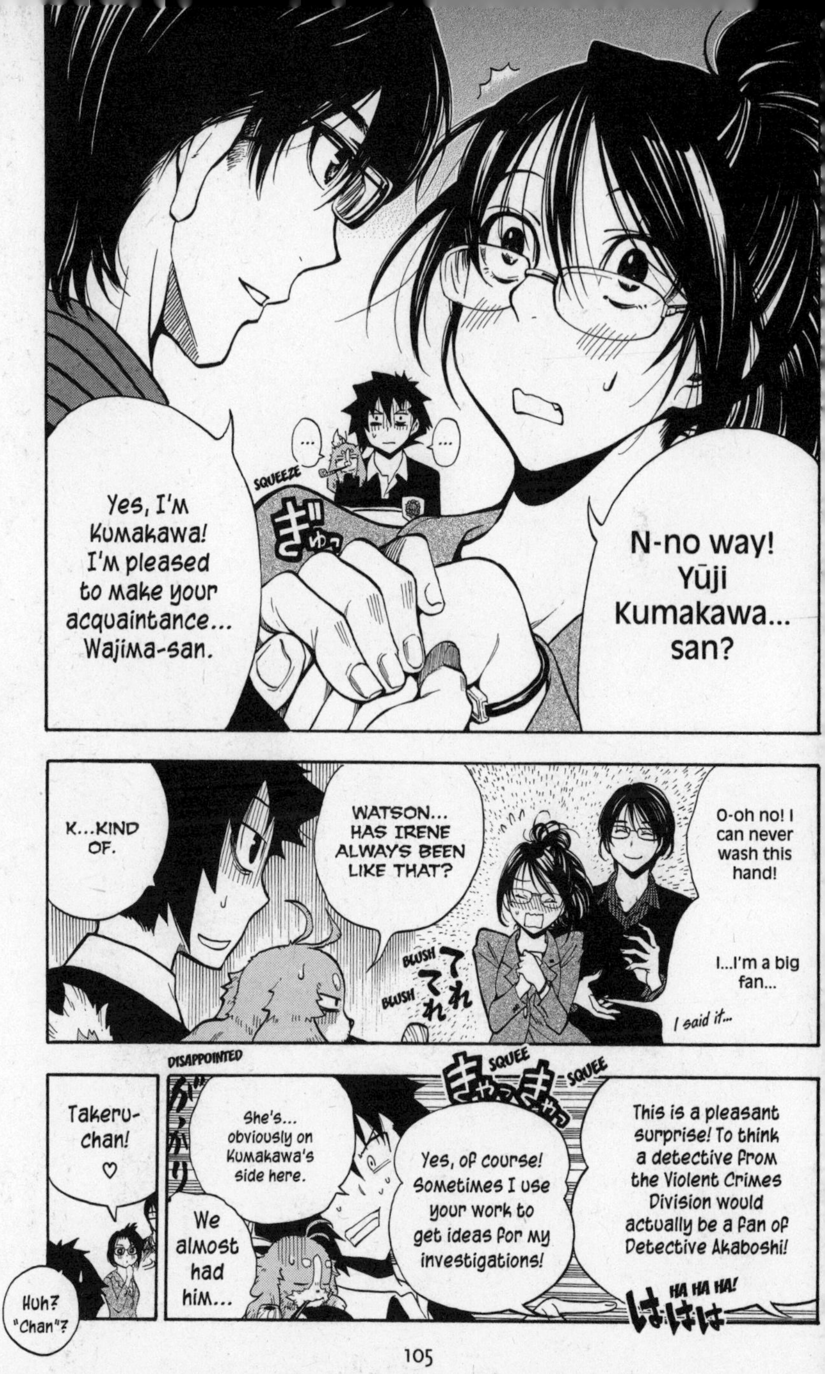

N-no way! Yūji Kumakawa... san?
...
...
SQUEEZE
ぎゅっ
Yes, I'm Kumakawa! I'm pleased to make your acquaintance... Wajima-san.
O-oh no! I can never wash this hand!
I...I'm a big fan...
I said it...
BLUSH
てれ
BLUSH
てれ
WATSON... HAS IRENE ALWAYS BEEN LIKE THAT?
K...KIND OF.
SQUEE
きゃっきゃっ
SQUEE
This is a pleasant surprise! To think a detective from the Violent Crimes Division would actually be a fan of Detective Akaboshi!
Yes, of course! Sometimes I use your work to get ideas for my investigations!
HA HA HA!
ははは
DISAPPOINTED
がっかり
She's... obviously on Kumakawa's side here.
We almost had him...
Takeru-chan! ♡
Huh? "Chan"?

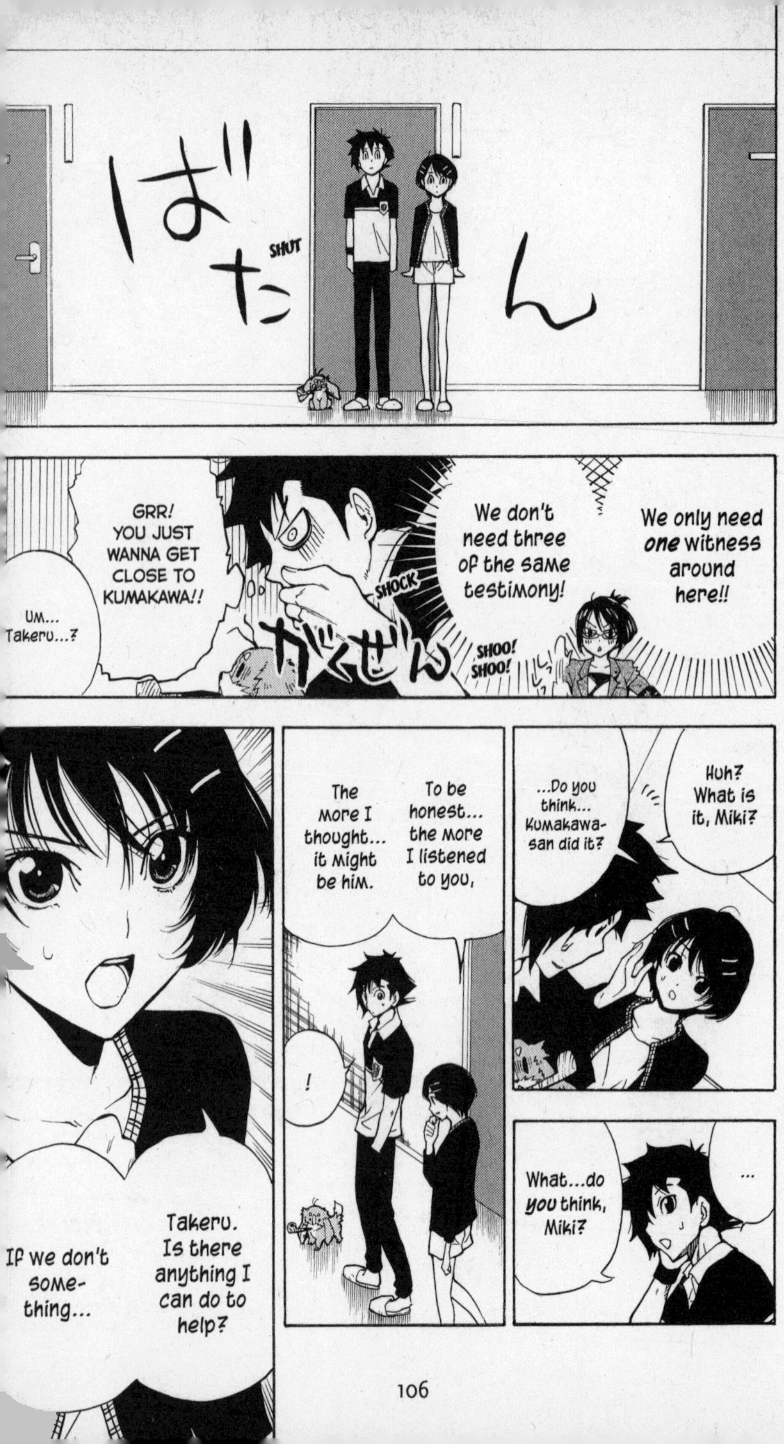
ばたん
SHUT
We only need *one* witness around here!!
We don't need three of the same testimony!
SHOO! SHOO!
SHOCK
がくぜん
GRR! YOU JUST WANNA GET CLOSE TO KUMAKAWA!!
Um... Takeru...?
Huh? What is it, Miki?
...Do you think... Kumakawa-san did it?
...
What...do *you* think, Miki?
To be honest... the more I listened to you,
The more I thought... it might be him.
!
Takeru. Is there anything I can do to help?
If we don't some-thing...

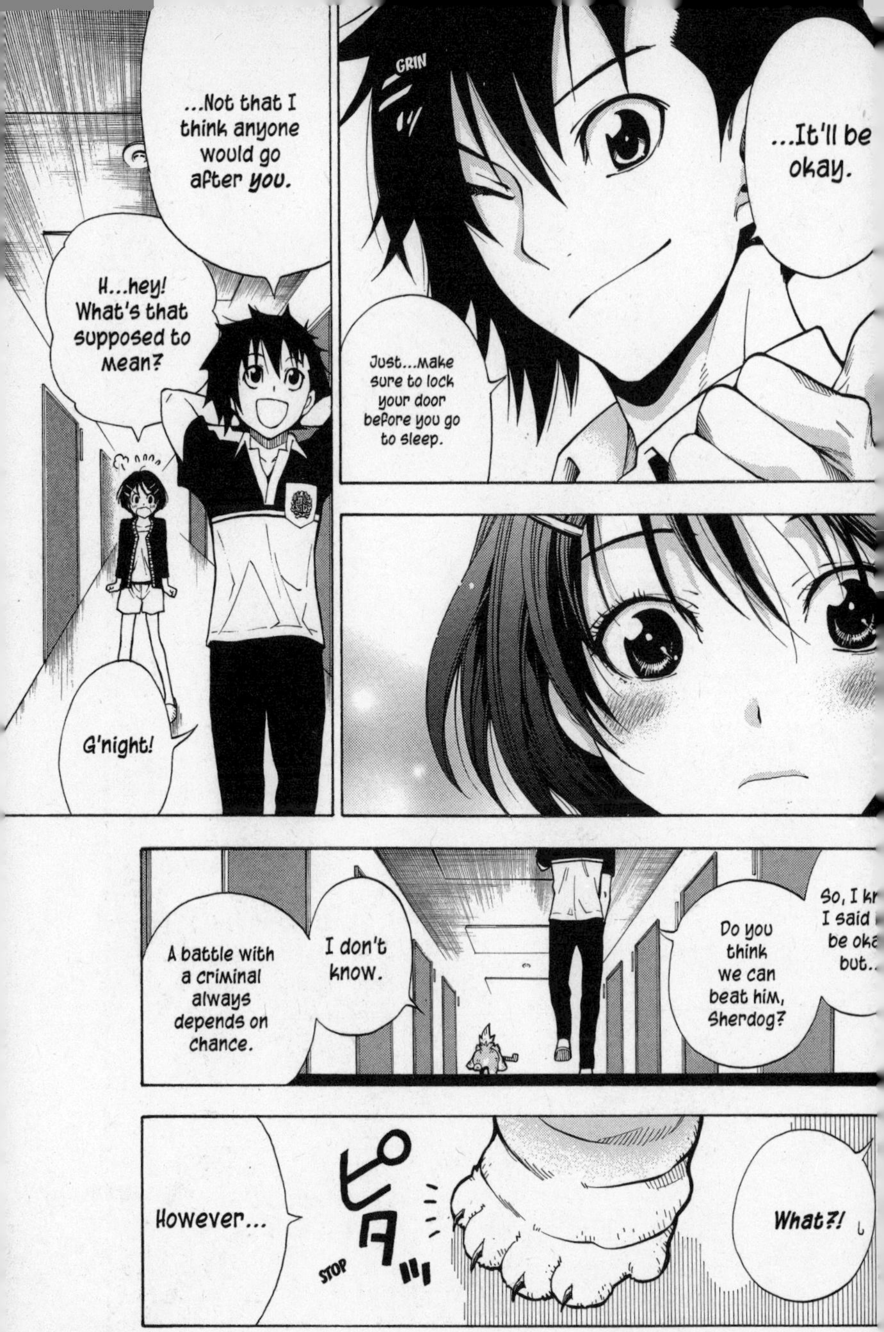
...It'll be okay.
GRIN
Just...make sure to lock your door before you go to sleep.
...Not that I think anyone would go after you.
H...hey! What's that supposed to mean?
G'night!
So, I kn
I said
be oka
but..
Do you think we can beat him, Sherdog?
I don't know.
A battle with a criminal always depends on chance.
What?!
ピタッ
STOP
However...

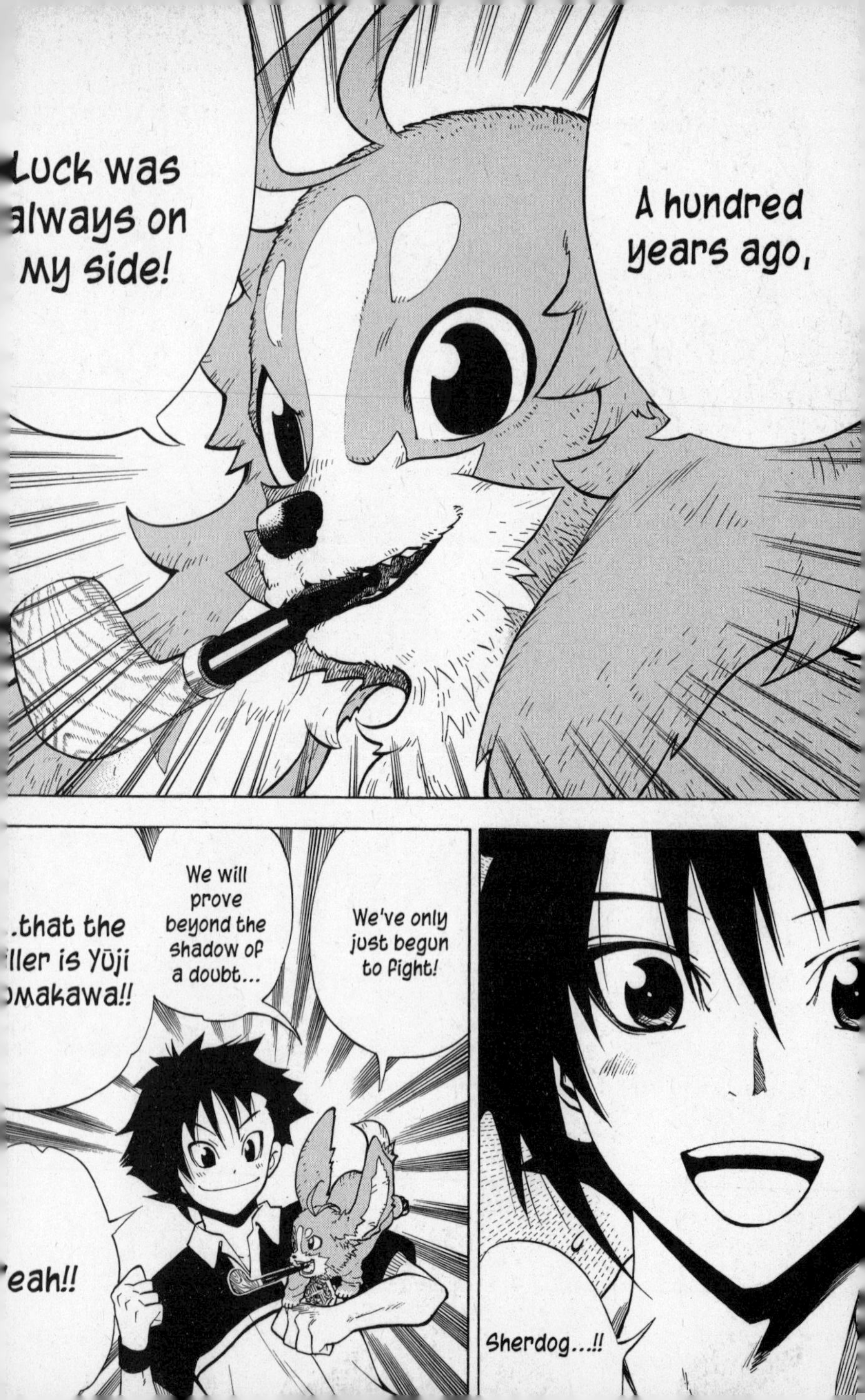
A hundred years ago,
Luck was always on my side!
Sherdog...!!
We've only just begun to fight!
We will prove beyond the shadow of a doubt...
..that the
ller is Yūji
makawa!!
eah!!

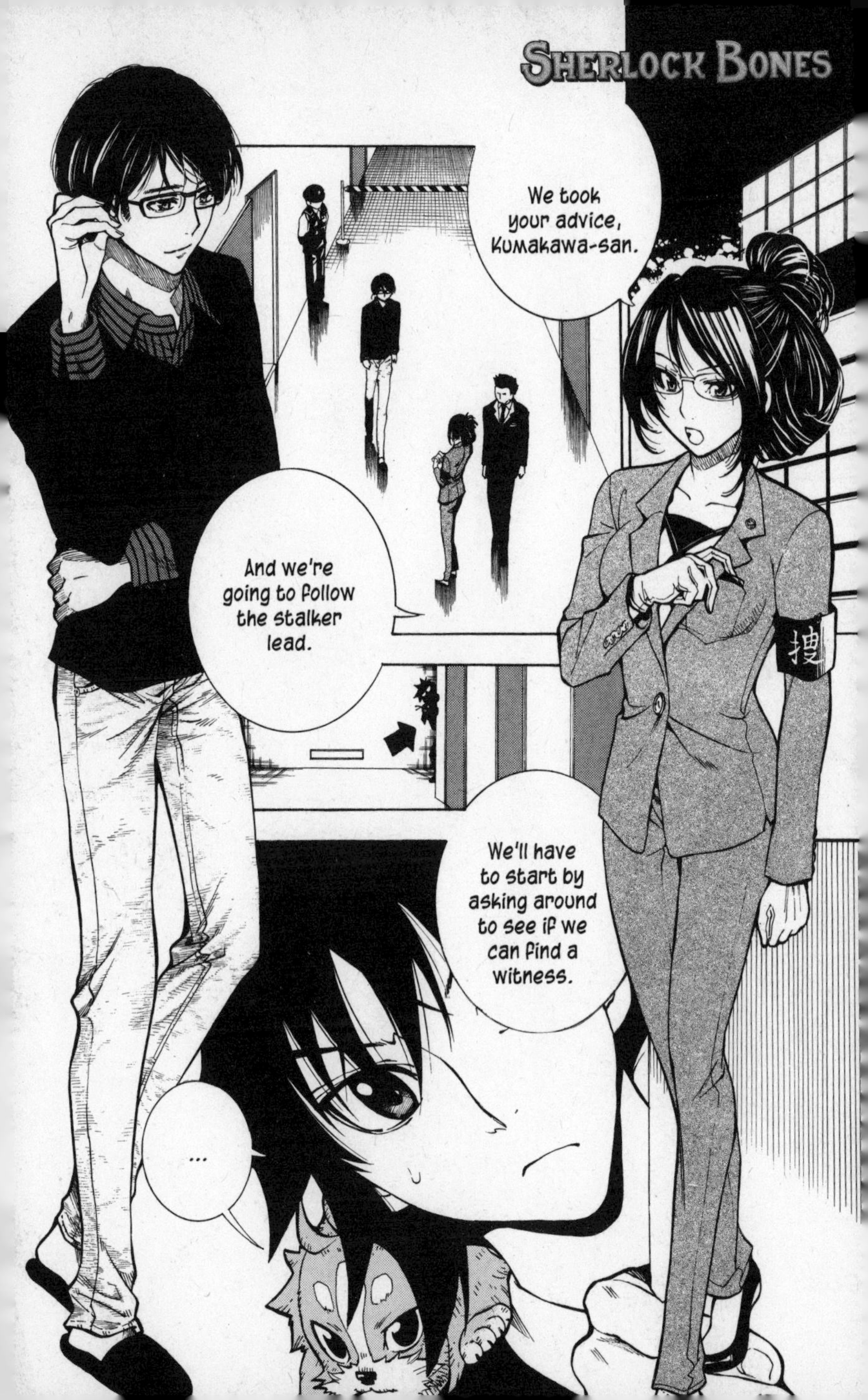
We took your advice, Kumakawa-san.
And we're going to follow the stalker lead.
We'll have to start by asking around to see if we can find a witness.
...
捜

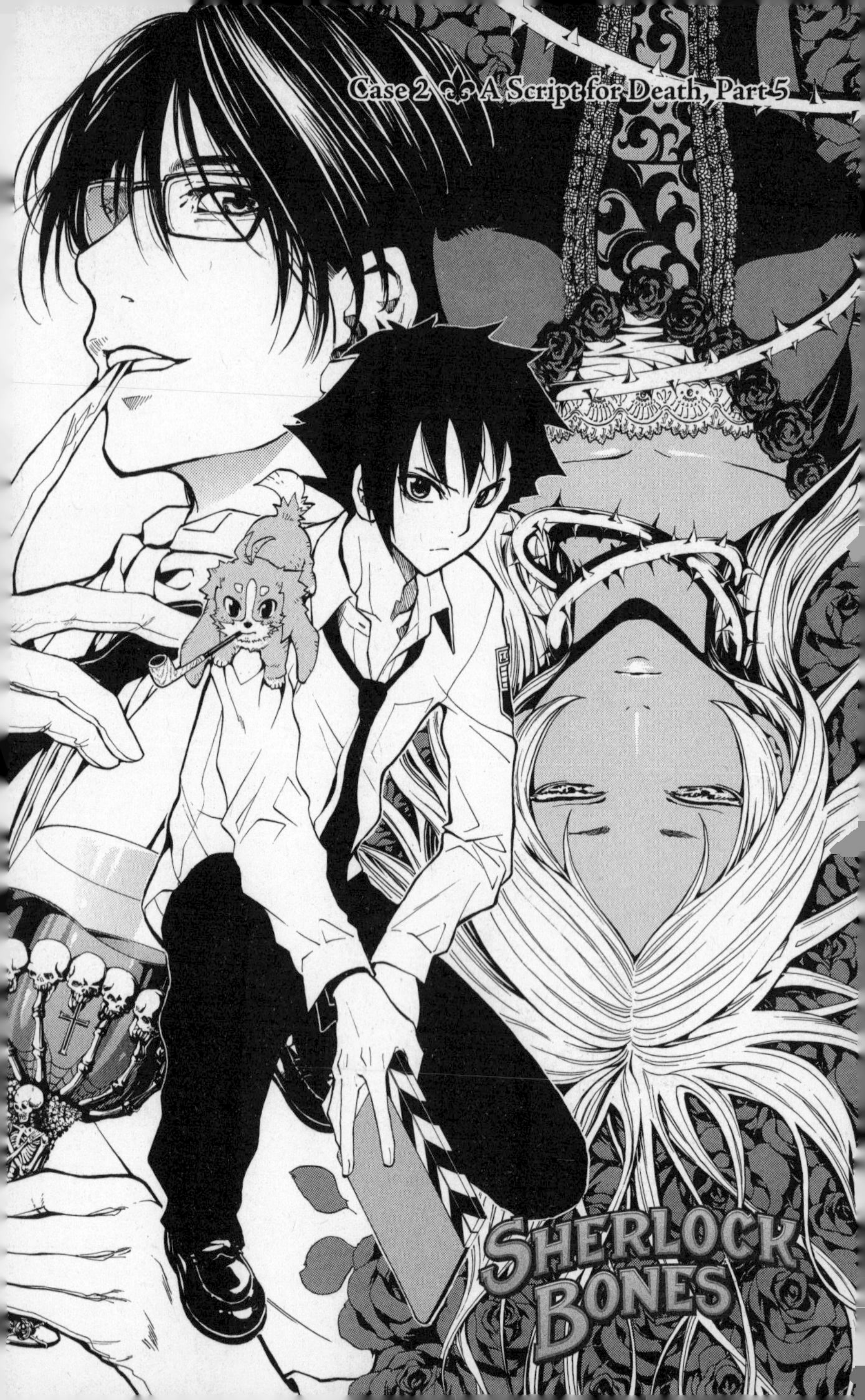
Case 2 ⚜ A Script for Death, Part 5
SHERLOCK BONES

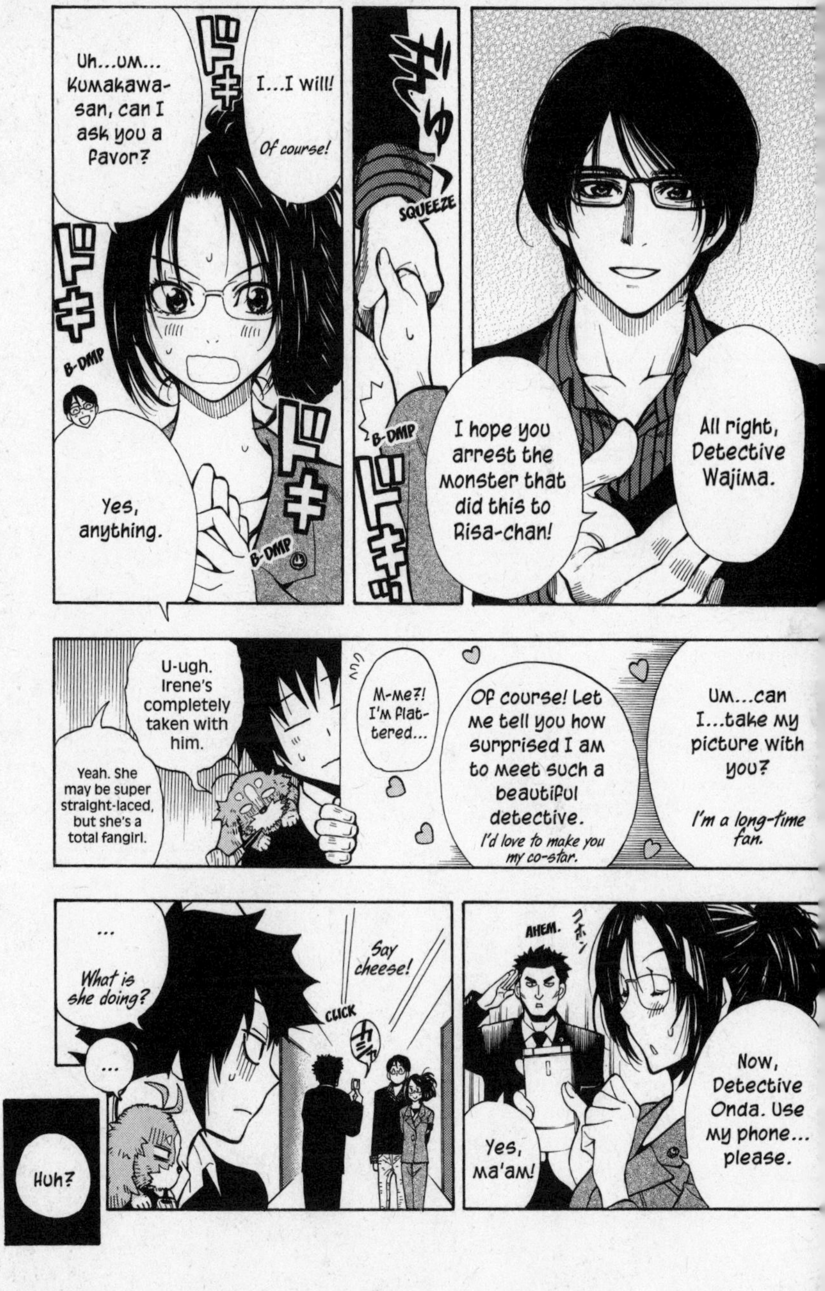
All right, Detective Wajima.
I hope you arrest the monster that did this to Risa-chan!
SQUEEZE
B-DMP
I...I will!
Of course!
Uh...um... Kumakawa-san, can I ask you a favor?
B-DMP
B-DMP
Yes, anything.
Um...can I...take my picture with you?
I'm a long-time fan.
Of course! Let me tell you how surprised I am to meet such a beautiful detective.
I'd love to make you my co-star.
M-me?! I'm flat-tered...
U-ugh. Irene's completely taken with him.
Yeah. She may be super straight-laced, but she's a total fangirl.
AHEM.
Now, Detective Onda. Use my phone... please.
Yes, ma'am!
Say cheese!
CLICK
...
What is she doing?
...
Huh?

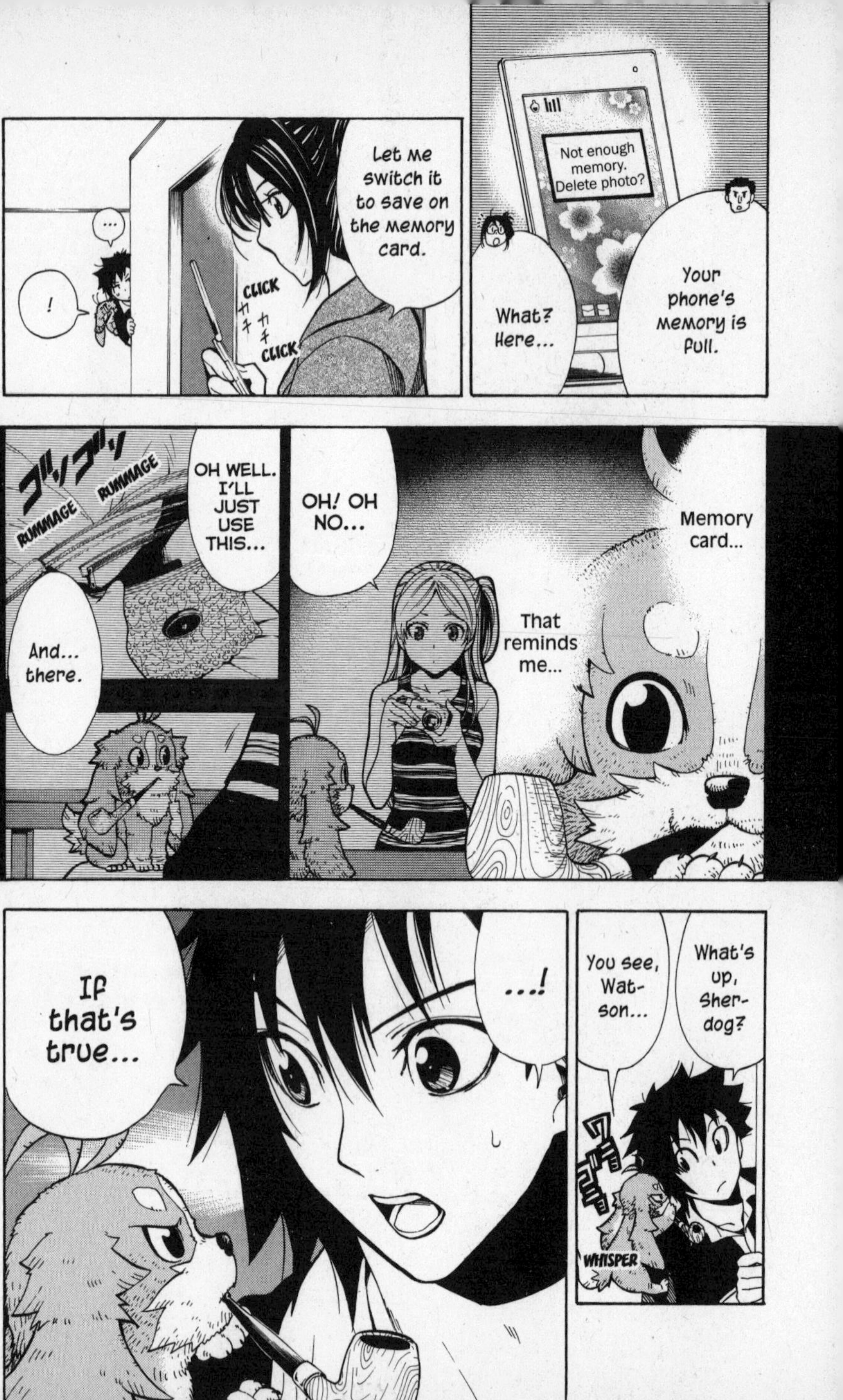
Not enough memory. Delete photo?
Your phone's memory is full.
What? Here...
Let me switch it to save on the memory card.
CLICK
CLICK
...
!
Memory card...
That reminds me...
OH! OH NO...
OH WELL. I'LL JUST USE THIS...
RUMMAGE
RUMMAGE
And... there.
What's up, Sher-dog?
You see, Wat-son...
WHISPER
...!
If that's true...

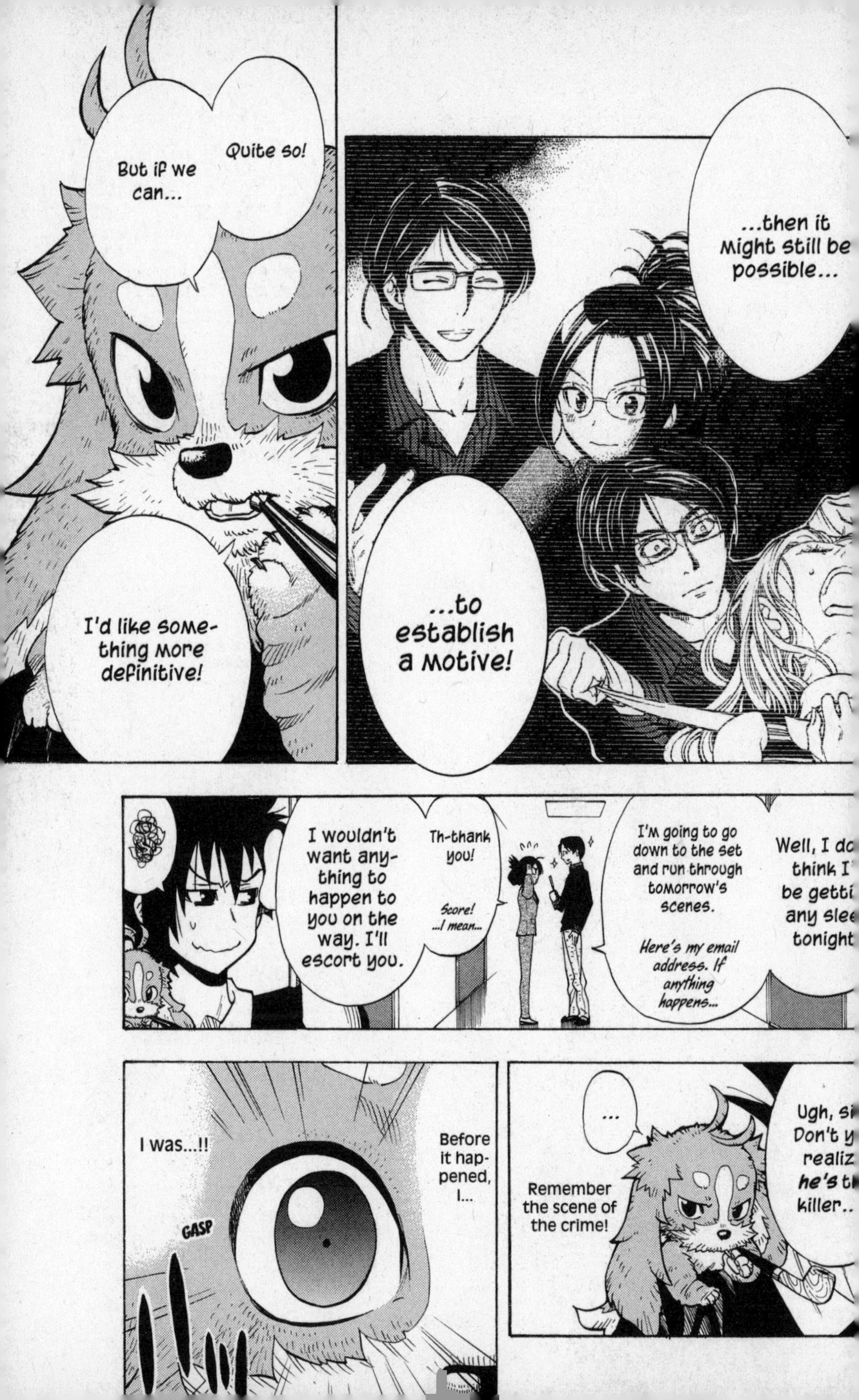
...then it might still be possible...
...to establish a motive!
Quite so!
But if we can...
I'd like some-thing more definitive!
Well, I do think I be getti any slee tonight
I'm going to go down to the set and run through tomorrow's scenes.
Here's my email address. If anything happens...
Th-thank you!
Score! ...I mean...
I wouldn't want any-thing to happen to you on the way. I'll escort you.
Ugh, si Don't y realiz he's t killer..
...
Remember the scene of the crime!
Before it hap-pened, I...
I was...!!
GASP

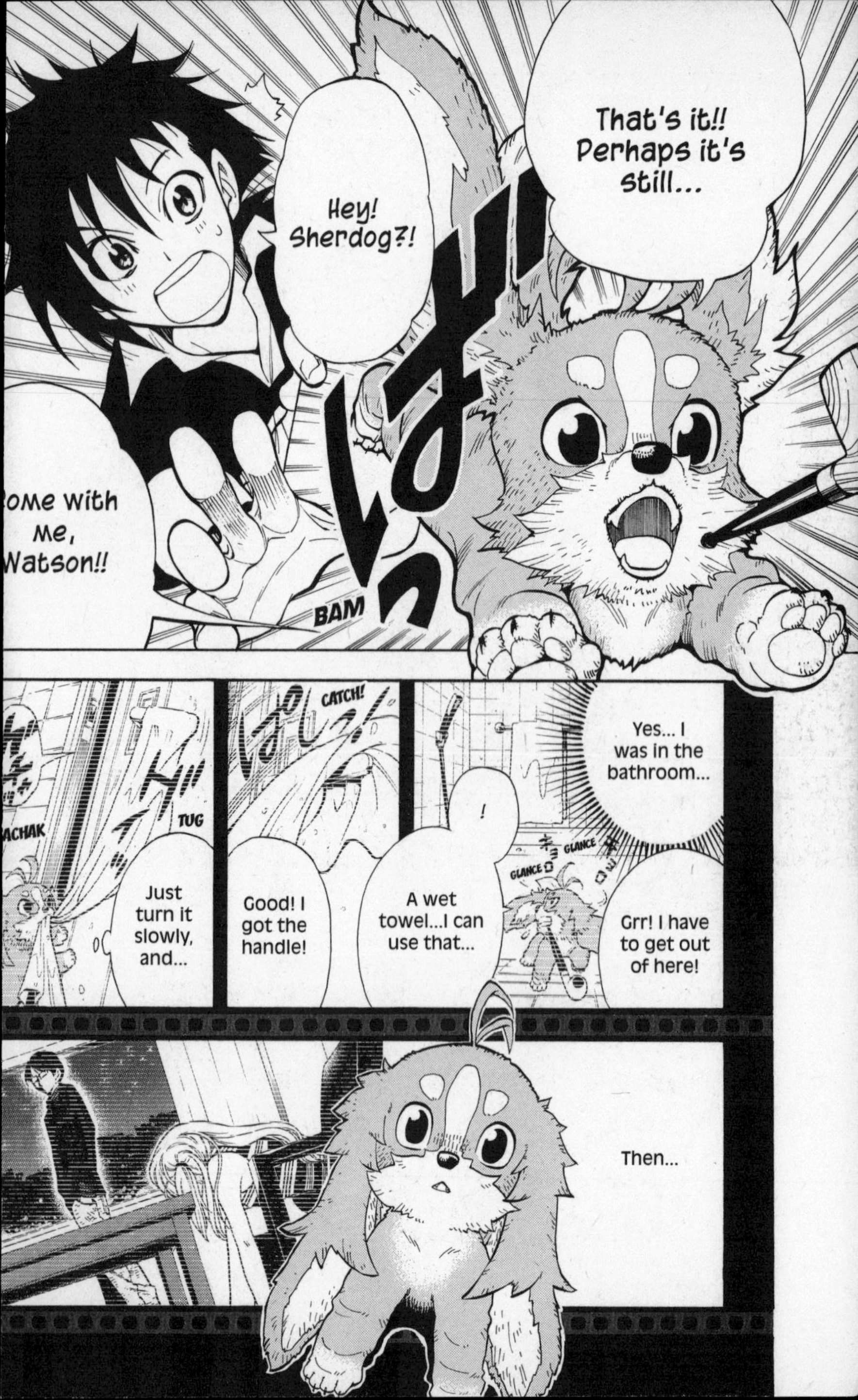
That's it!! Perhaps it's still...
Hey! Sherdog?!
ome with me, Watson!!
BAM
Yes... I was in the bathroom...
Grr! I have to get out of here!
GLANCE
GLANCE
!
A wet towel...I can use that...
CATCH!
Good! I got the handle!
TUG
Just turn it slowly, and...
ACHAK
Then...

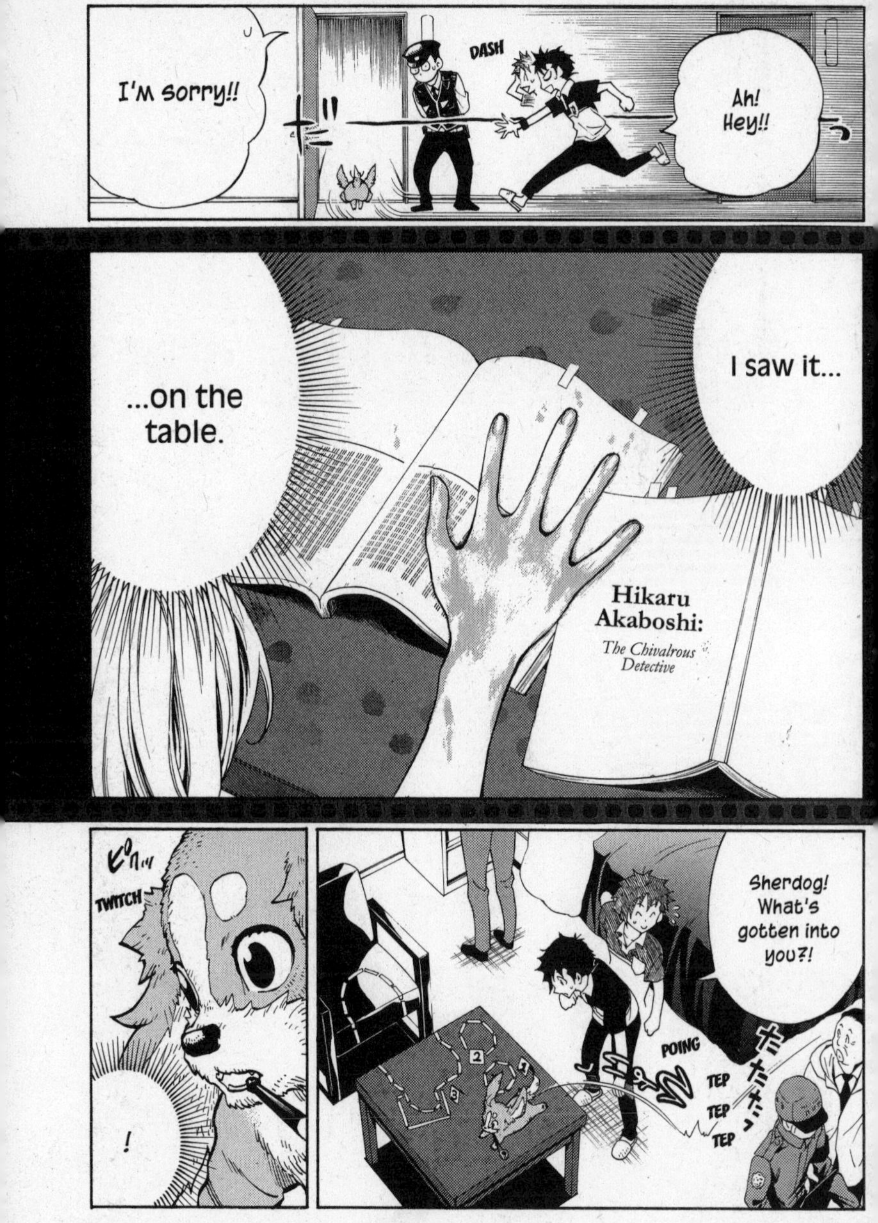
Ah! Hey!!
DASH
I'm sorry!!
I saw it...
...on the table.
Hikaru Akaboshi:
The Chivalrous Detective
Sherdog! What's gotten into you?!
POING
TEP
TEP
TEP
TWITCH
!

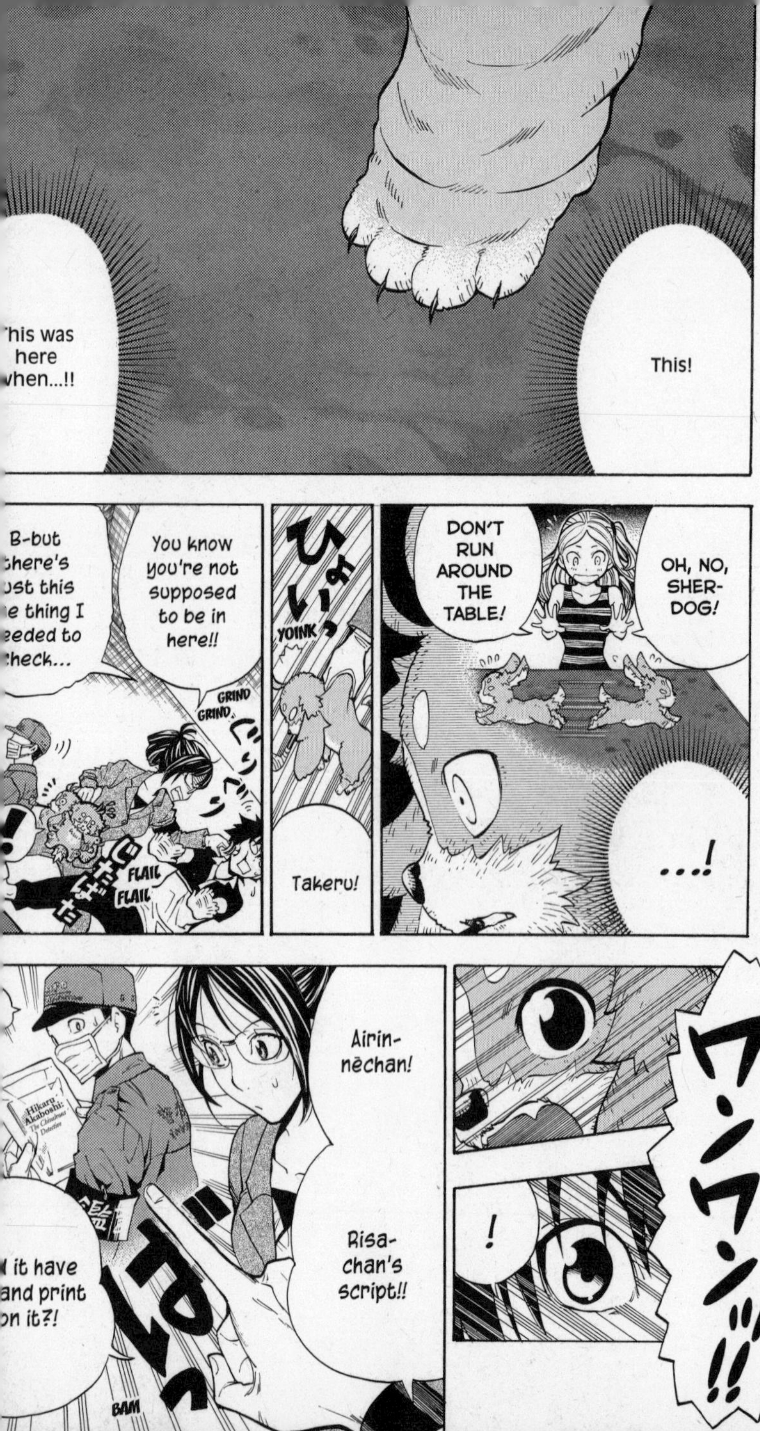
This!
his was here vhen...!!
OH, NO, SHER-DOG!
DON'T RUN AROUND THE TABLE!
...!
YOINK
Takeru!
You know you're not supposed to be in here!!
B-but here's ust this e thing I eeded to check...
GRIND GRIND
FLAIL FLAIL
ARF!!
ARF!!
!
Airin-nēchan!
Risa-chan's script!!
it have and print on it?!
Hikaru Akaboshi: The Chihuahua Detective
BAM

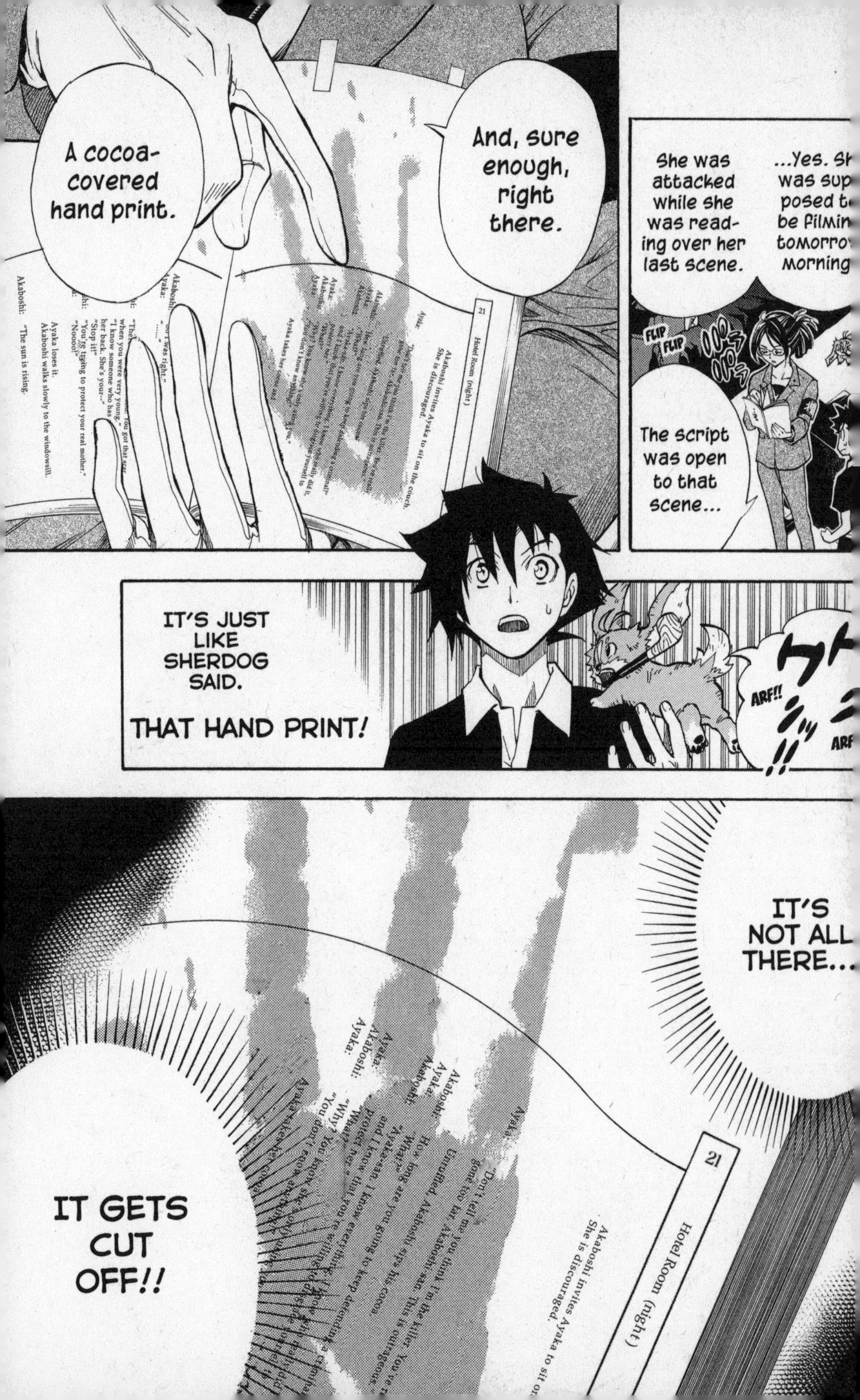
...Yes. Sh was sup posed t be filmin tomorro morning
She was attacked while she was reading over her last scene.
FLIP FLIP
The script was open to that scene...
And, sure enough, right there.
A cocoa-covered hand print.
21
Hotel Room (night)
Akaboshi invites Ayaka to sit on the couch.
She is discouraged.
ARF!!
ARF
IT'S JUST LIKE SHERDOG SAID.
THAT HAND PRINT!
IT'S NOT ALL THERE...
IT GETS CUT OFF!!

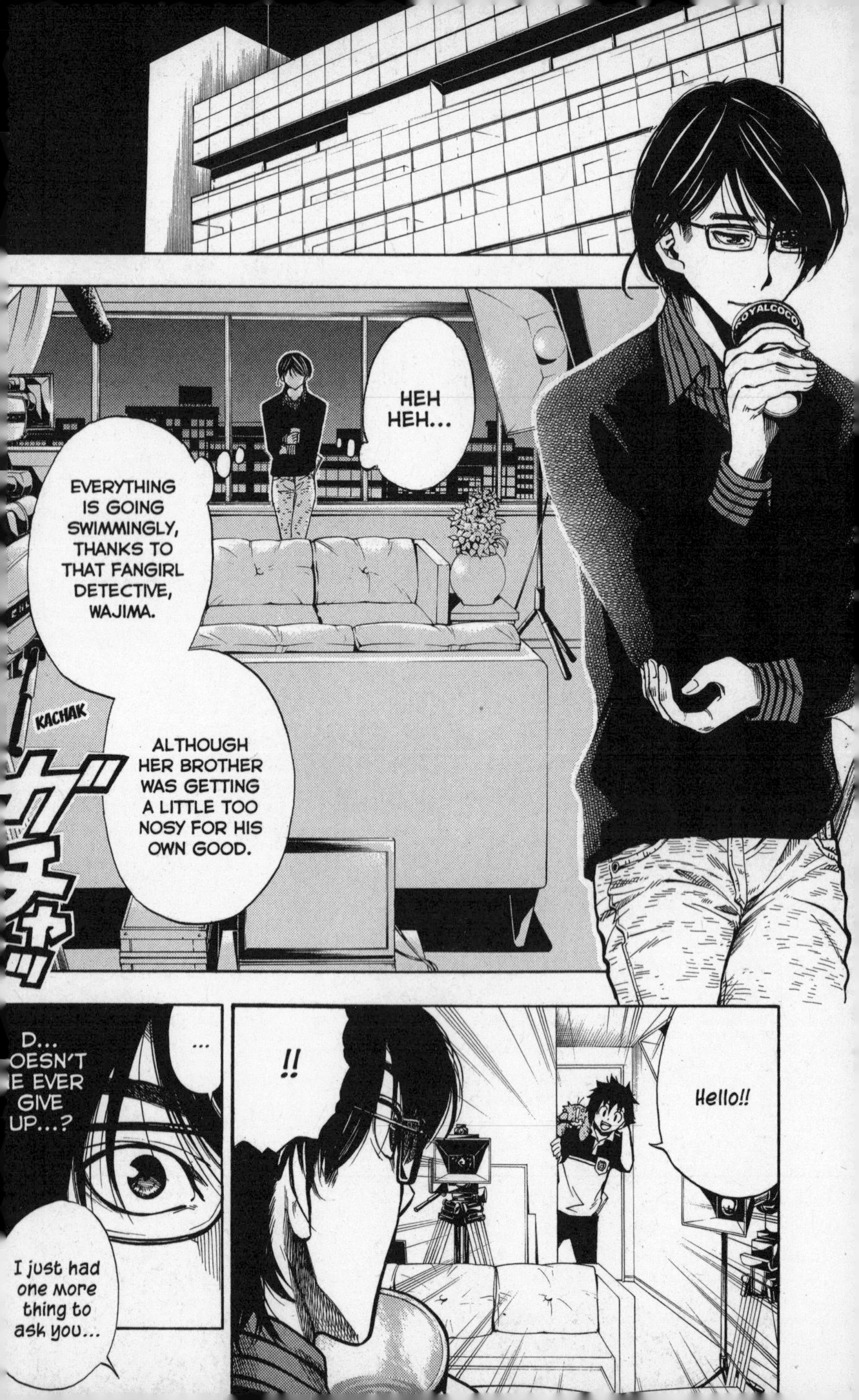
HEH HEH...
EVERYTHING IS GOING SWIMMINGLY, THANKS TO THAT FANGIRL DETECTIVE, WAJIMA.
ALTHOUGH HER BROTHER WAS GETTING A LITTLE TOO NOSY FOR HIS OWN GOOD.
KACHAK
ガチャッ
Hello!!
!!
...
D... OESN'T E EVER GIVE UP...?
I just had one more thing to ask you...

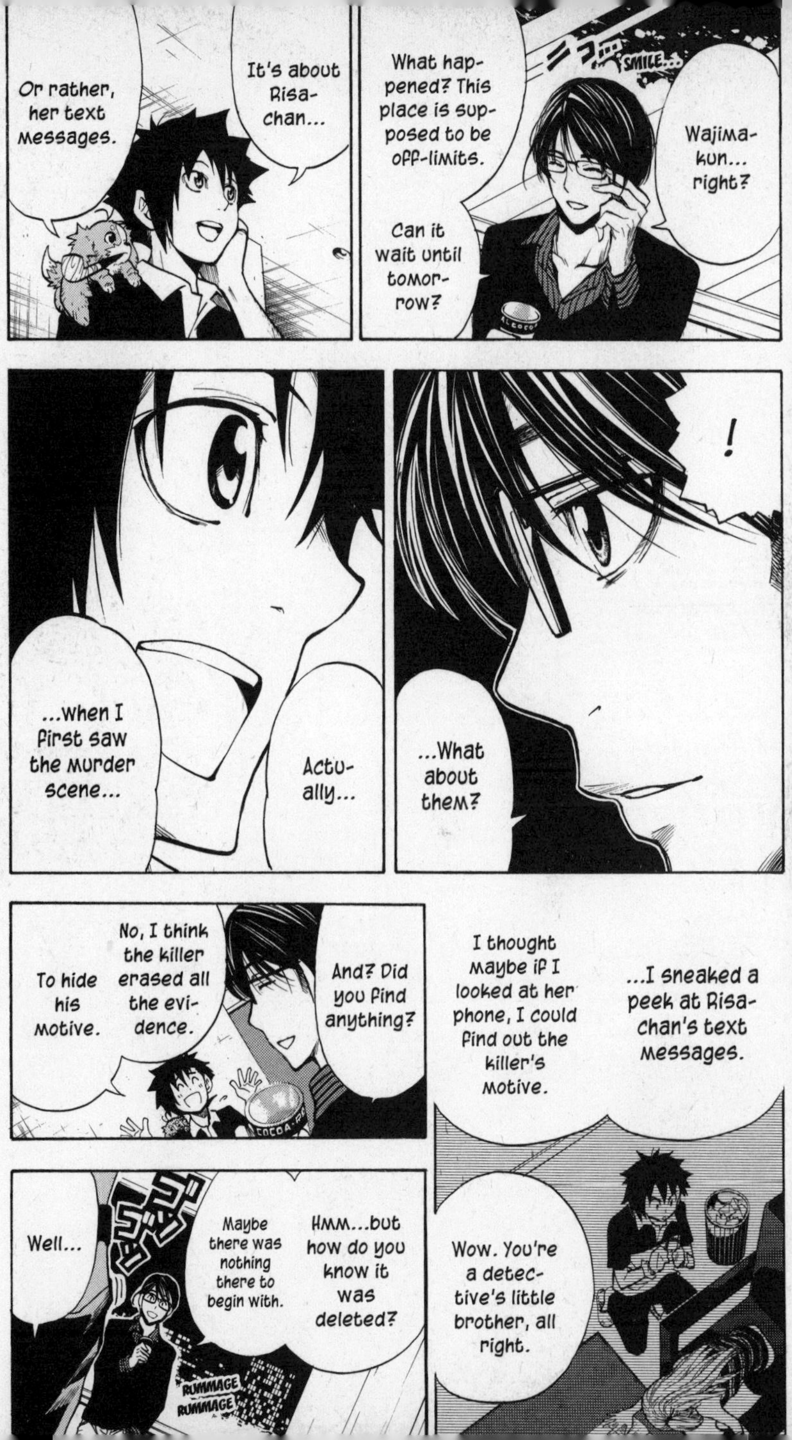
SMILE...
Wajima-kun... right?
What happened? This place is supposed to be off-limits.
Can it wait until tomorrow?
It's about Risa-chan...
Or rather, her text messages.
!
...What about them?
Actually...
...when I first saw the murder scene...
...I sneaked a peek at Risa-chan's text messages.
I thought maybe if I looked at her phone, I could find out the killer's motive.
Wow. You're a detective's little brother, all right.
And? Did you find anything?
No, I think the killer erased all the evidence.
To hide his motive.
HMM...but how do you know it was deleted?
Maybe there was nothing there to begin with.
Well...
RUMMAGE
RUMMAGE

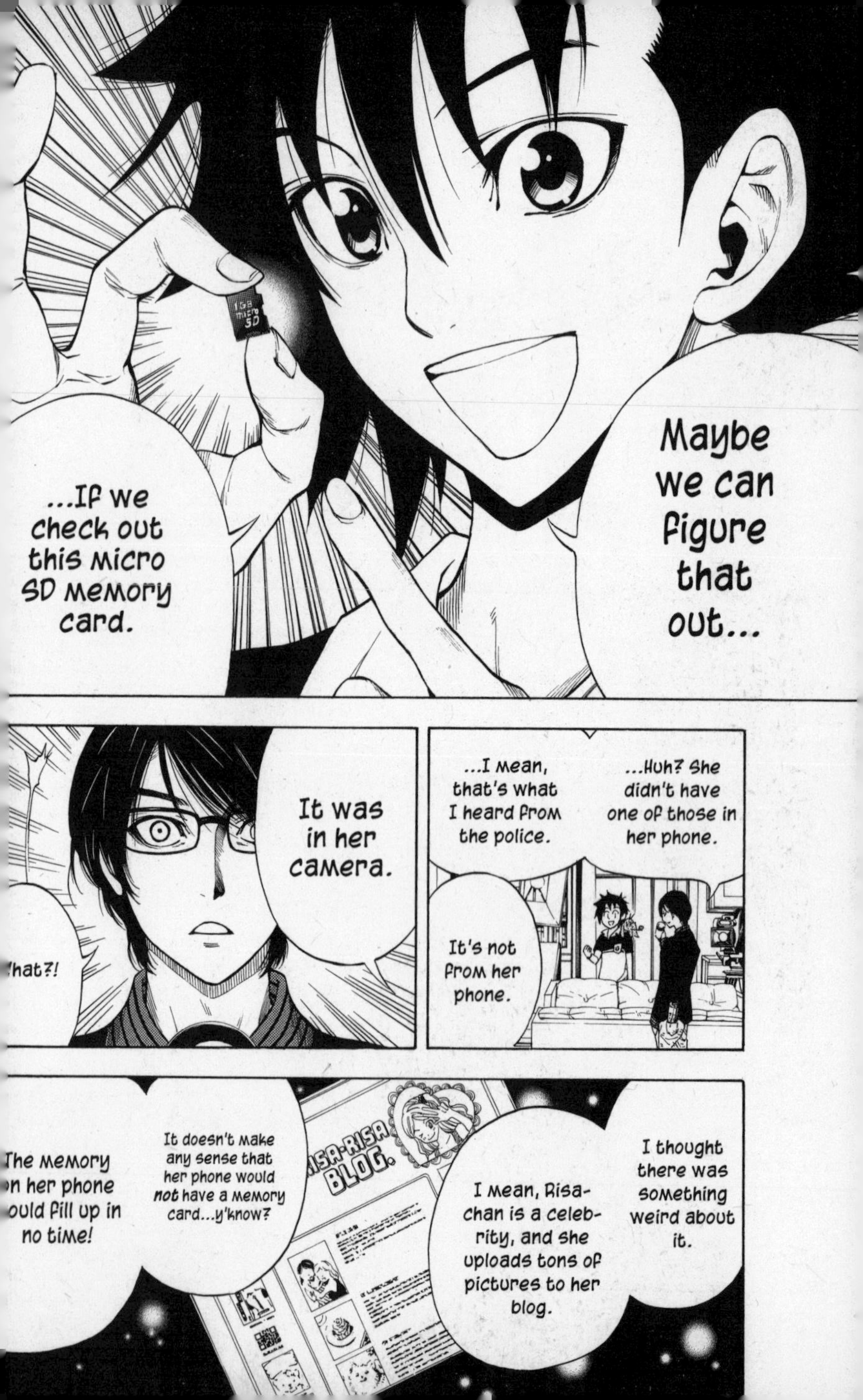
Maybe we can figure that out...
...If we check out this micro SD memory card.
...Huh? She didn't have one of those in her phone.
...I mean, that's what I heard from the police.
It's not from her phone.
It was in her camera.
hat?!
I thought there was something weird about it.
I mean, Risa-chan is a celebrity, and she uploads tons of pictures to her blog.
ISA-RISA BLOG.
It doesn't make any sense that her phone would *not* have a memory card...y'know?
The memory on her phone ould fill up in no time!

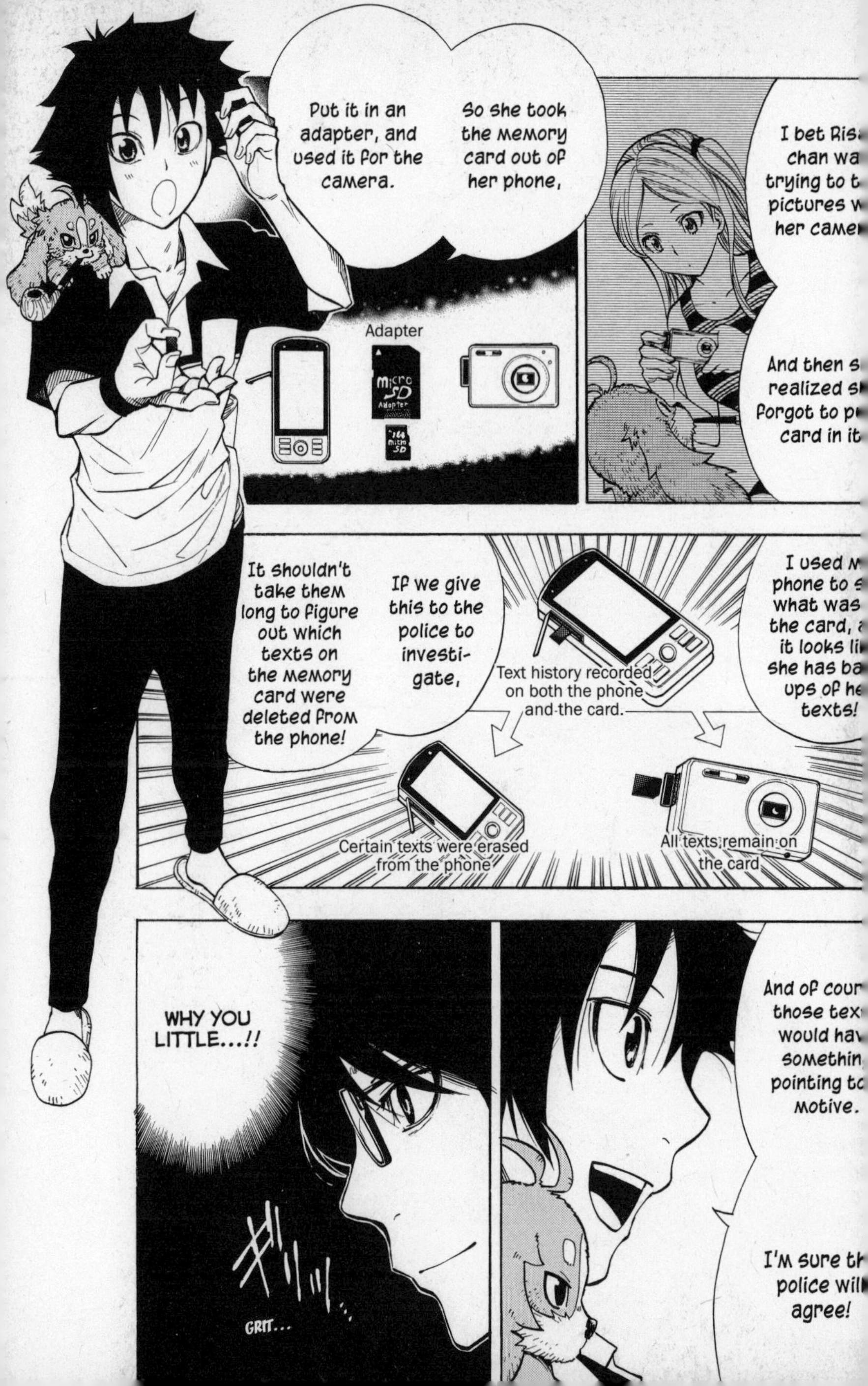
I bet Risa chan wa trying to t pictures w her camer
And then s realized s forgot to p card in it
So she took the memory card out of her phone,
Put it in an adapter, and used it for the camera.
Adapter
micro SD Adapter
1GB micro SD
I used m phone to s what was the card, it looks li she has ba ups of he texts!
Text history recorded on both the phone and the card.
All texts remain on the card
Certain texts were erased from the phone
If we give this to the police to investi-gate,
It shouldn't take them long to figure out which texts on the memory card were deleted from the phone!
And of cour those tex would hav somethin pointing to motive.
I'm sure th police wil agree!
WHY YOU LITTLE...!!
GRIT...

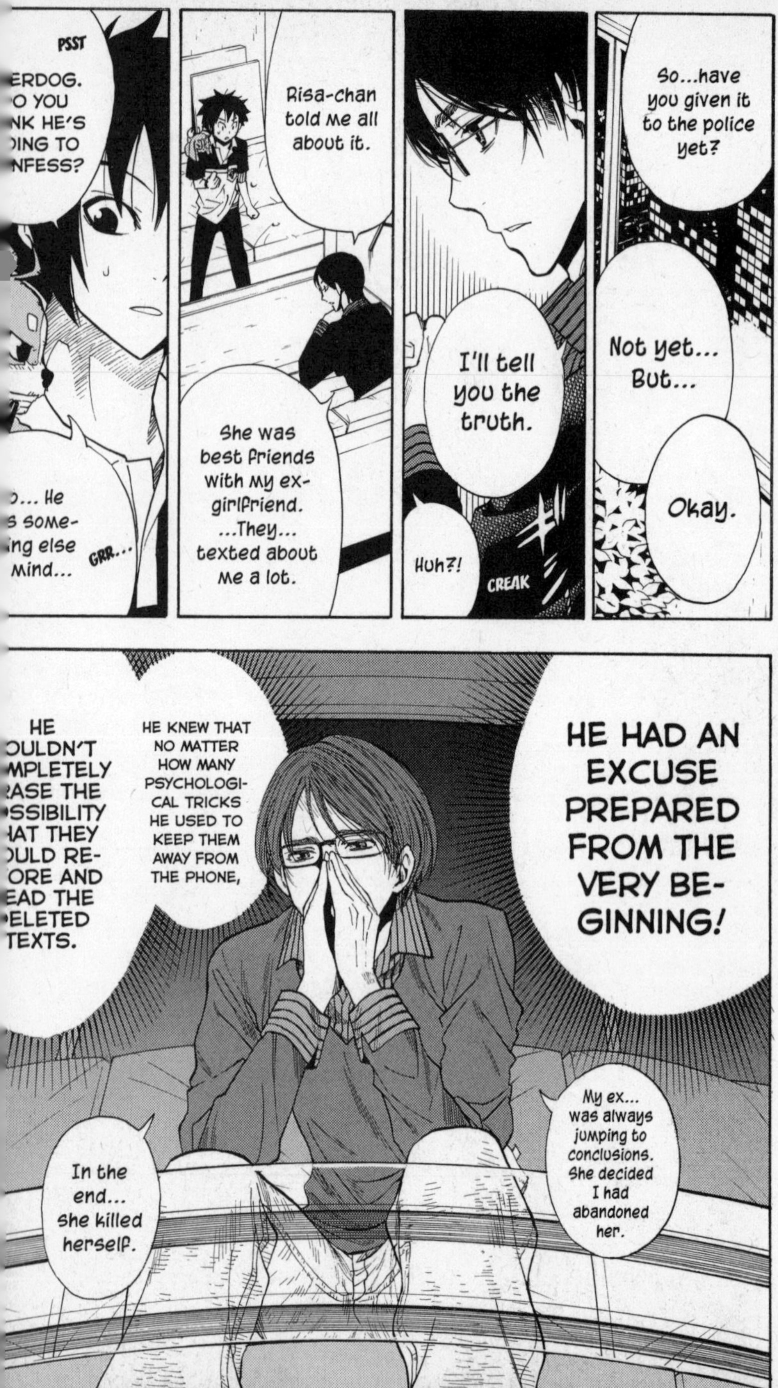
So...have you given it to the police yet?
Not yet... But...
Okay.
I'll tell you the truth.
CREAK
Huh?!
Risa-chan told me all about it.
She was best friends with my ex-girlfriend. ...They... texted about me a lot.
PSST
ERDOG. O YOU NK HE'S ING TO NFESS?
o... He s some- ing else mind...
GRR...
HE HAD AN EXCUSE PREPARED FROM THE VERY BE-GINNING!
HE KNEW THAT NO MATTER HOW MANY PSYCHOLOGI-CAL TRICKS HE USED TO KEEP THEM AWAY FROM THE PHONE,
HE OULDN'T MPLETELY ASE THE SSIBILITY HAT THEY OULD RE- ORE AND EAD THE ELETED TEXTS.
My ex... was always jumping to conclusions. She decided I had abandoned her.
In the end... she killed herself.

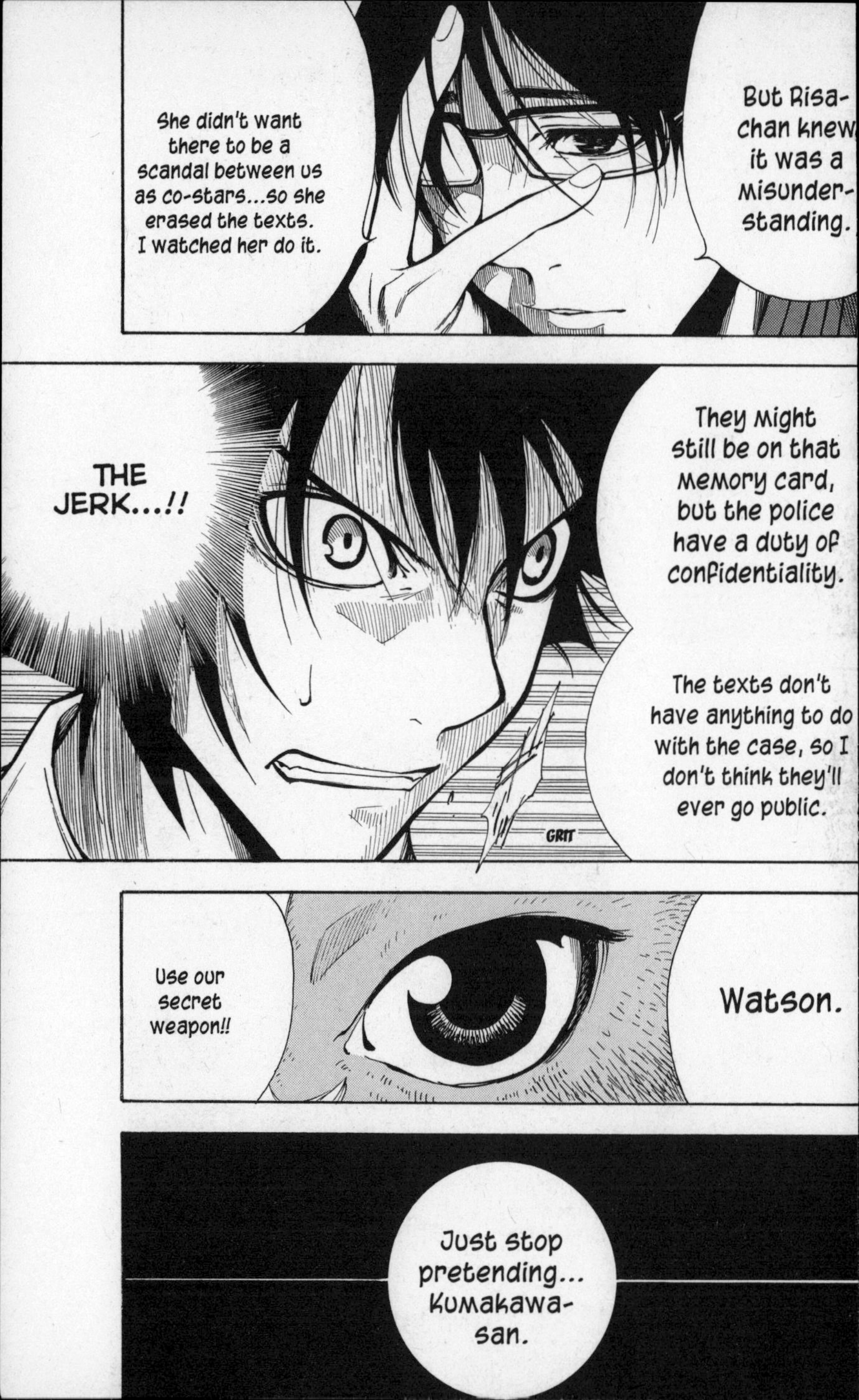
But Risa-chan knew it was a misunderstanding.
She didn't want there to be a scandal between us as co-stars...so she erased the texts. I watched her do it.
They might still be on that memory card, but the police have a duty of confidentiality.
The texts don't have anything to do with the case, so I don't think they'll ever go public.
GRIT
THE JERK...!!
Watson.
Use our secret weapon!!
Just stop pretending... Kumakawa-san.

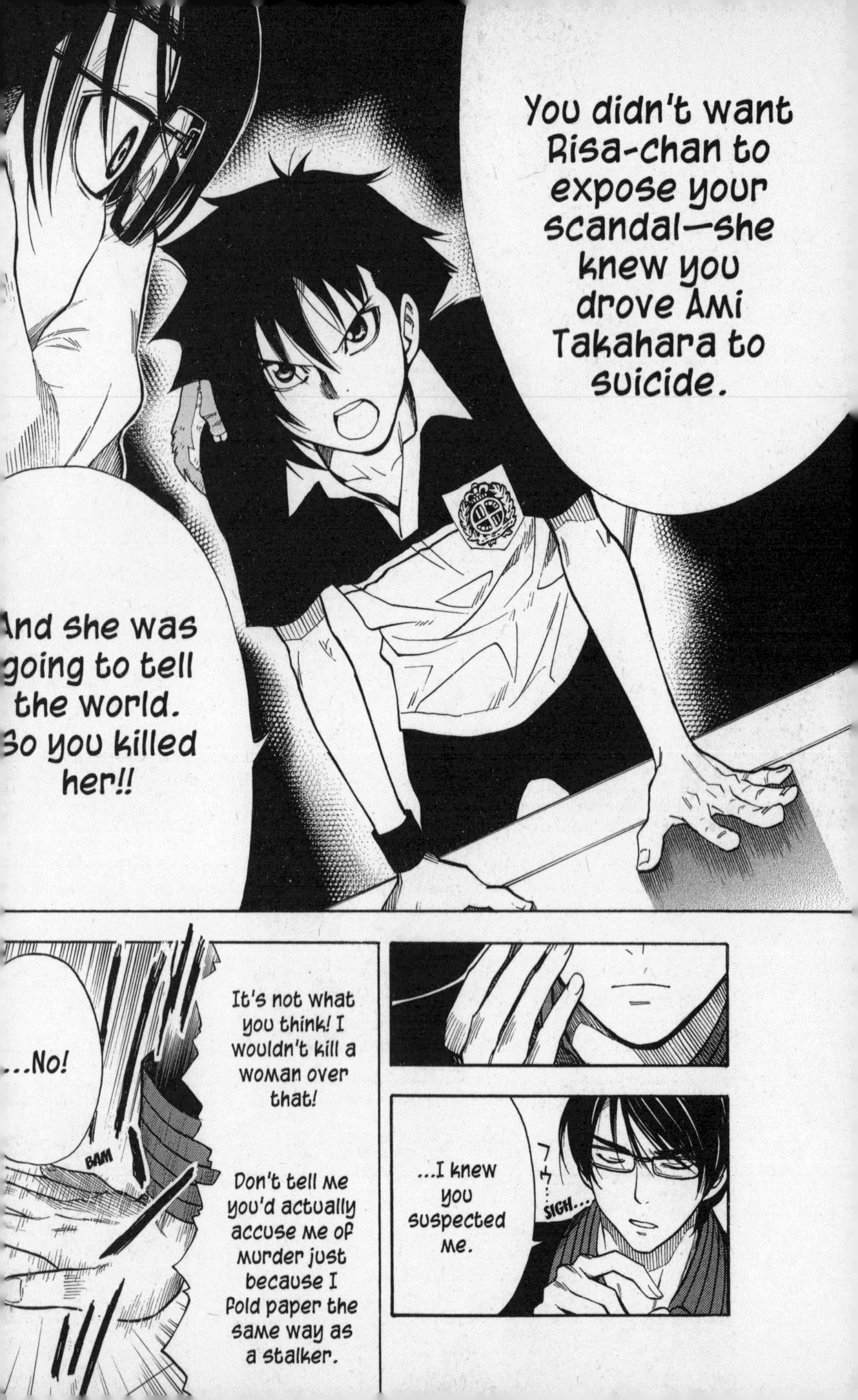
You didn't want Risa-chan to expose your scandal—she knew you drove Ami Takahara to suicide.
And she was going to tell the world. So you killed her!!
...I knew you suspected me.
SIGH...
It's not what you think! I wouldn't kill a woman over that!
...No!
BAM
Don't tell me you'd actually accuse me of murder just because I fold paper the same way as a stalker.

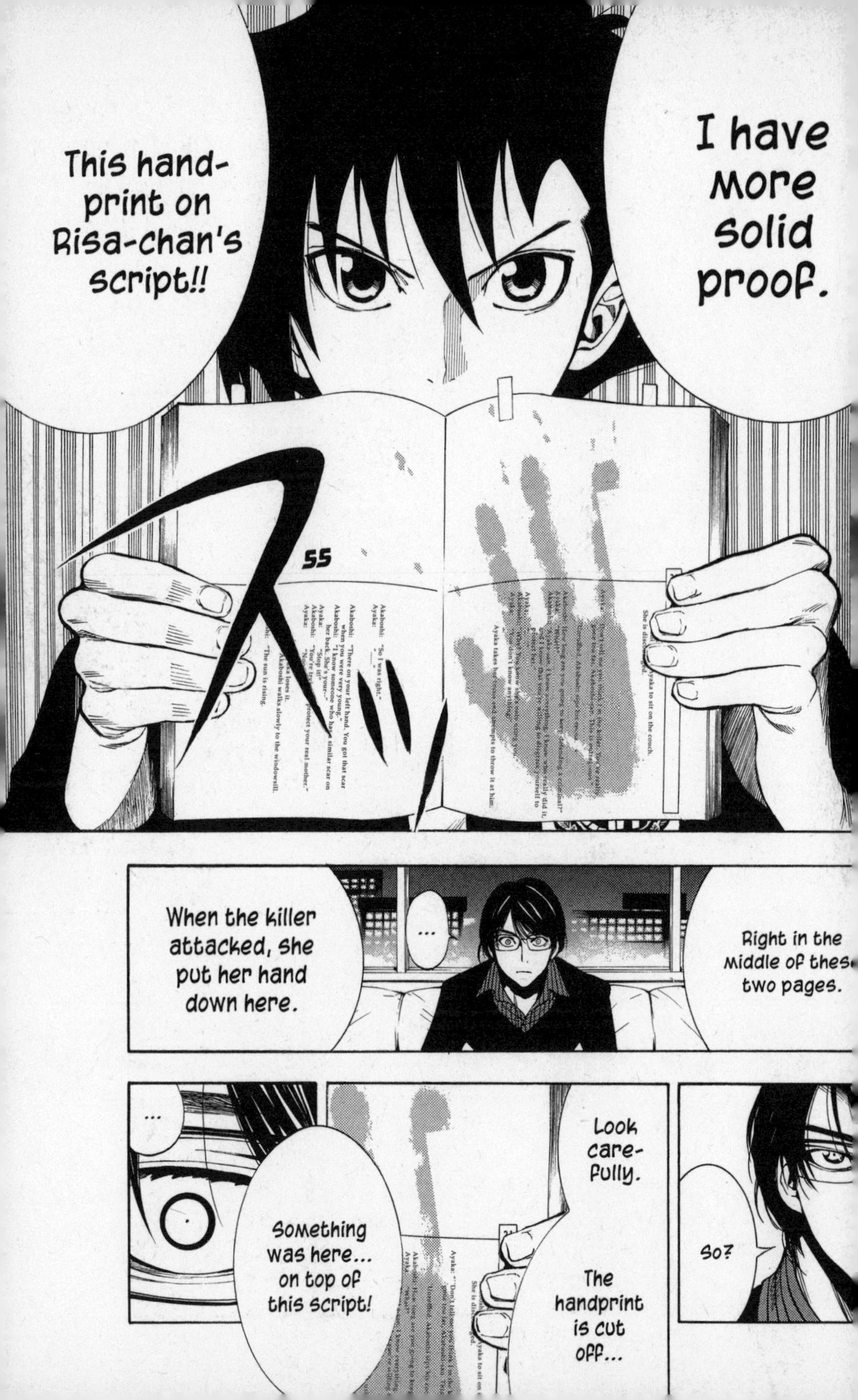
I have more solid proof.
This hand-print on Risa-chan's script!!
55
Right in the middle of thes two pages.
...
When the killer attacked, she put her hand down here.
So?
Look care-fully.
The handprint is cut off...
Something was here... on top of this script!
...

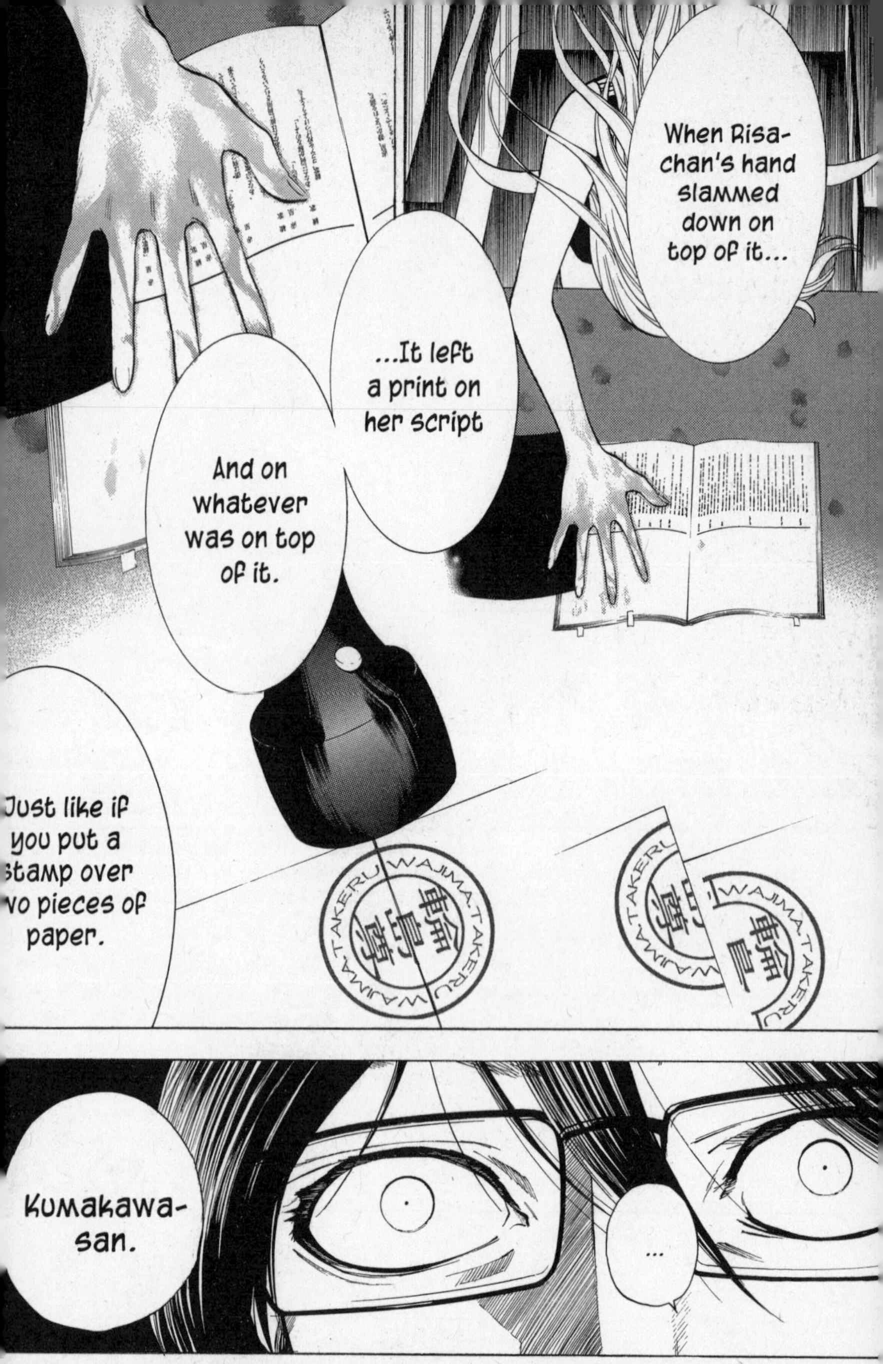
When Risa-chan's hand slammed down on top of it...
...It left a print on her script
And on whatever was on top of it.
WAJIMA.TAKERU 輪島尊
WAJIMA.TAKERU 輪島尊
Just like if you put a stamp over two pieces of paper.
...
Kumakawa-san.

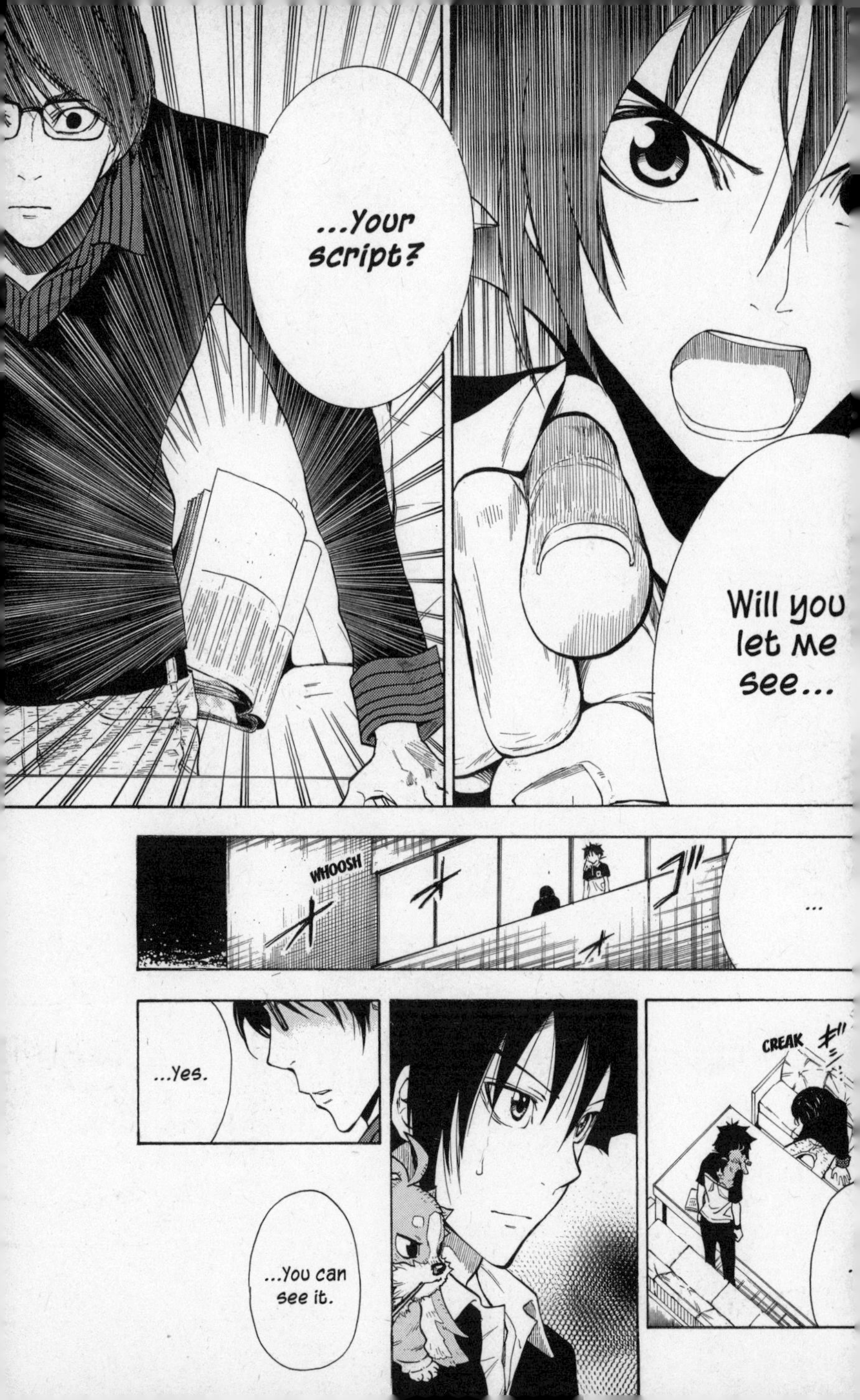
Will you let me see...
...Your script?
...
WHOOSH
CREAK
...You can see it.
...Yes.

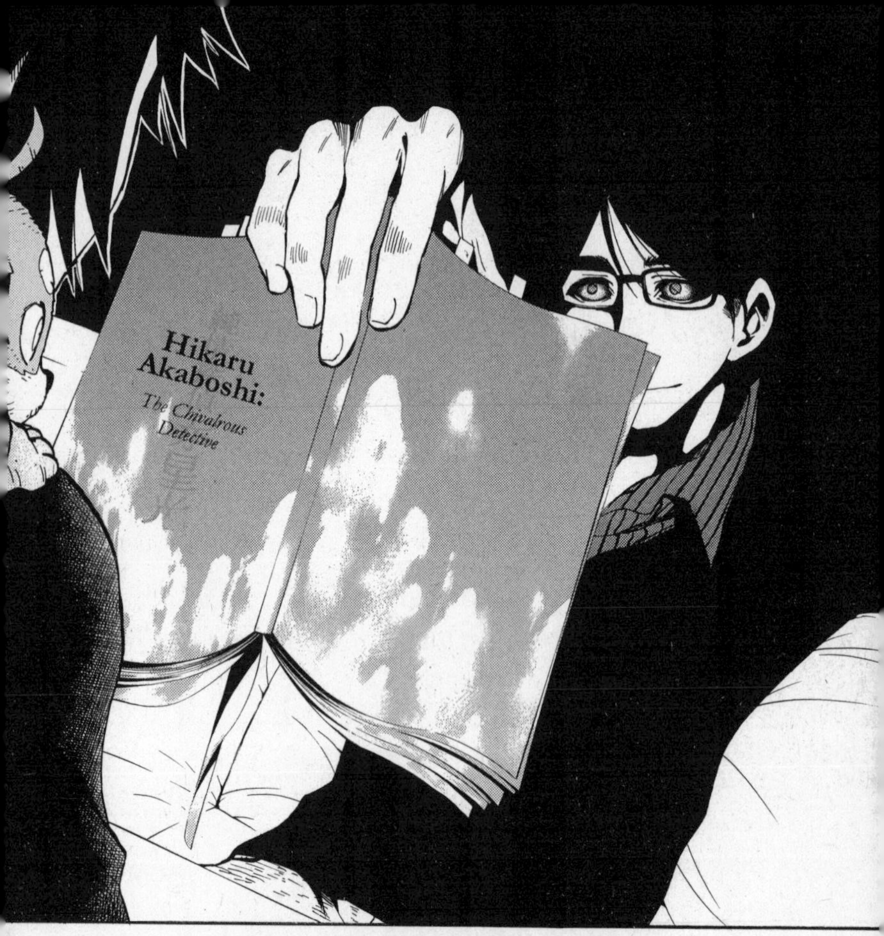
Hikaru Akaboshi:
The Chivalrous Detective

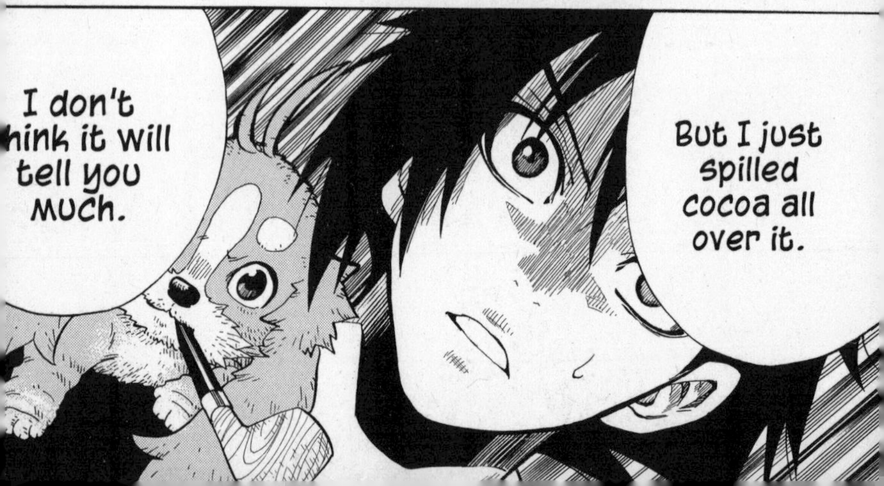
But I just spilled cocoa all over it.
I don't hink it will tell you much.

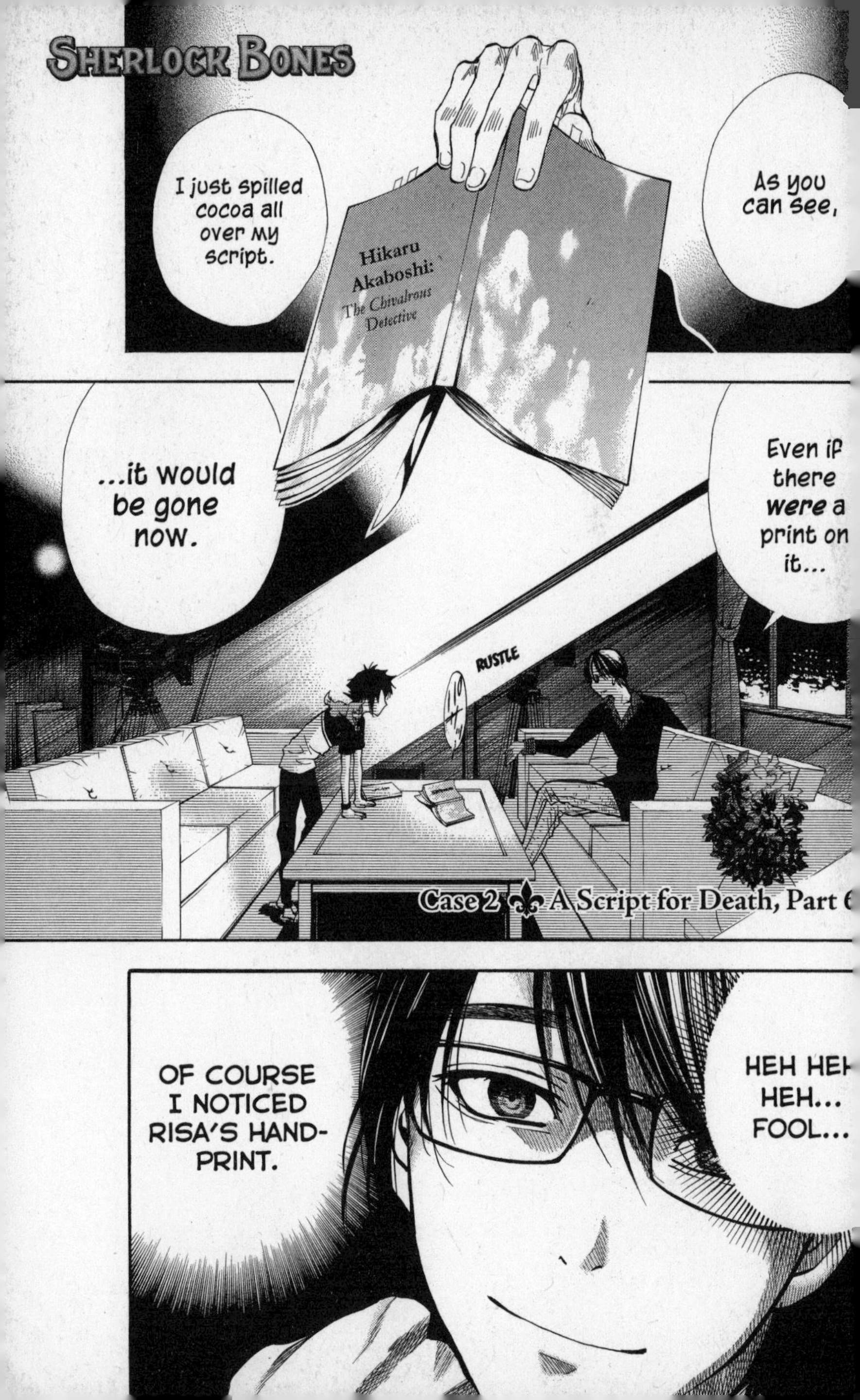
SHERLOCK BONES
As you can see,
I just spilled cocoa all over my script.
Hikaru Akaboshi: The Chivalrous Detective
Even if there *were* a print on it...
...it would be gone now.
RUSTLE
Case 2 A Script for Death, Part 6
HEH HEH HEH... FOOL...
OF COURSE I NOTICED RISA'S HAND-PRINT.

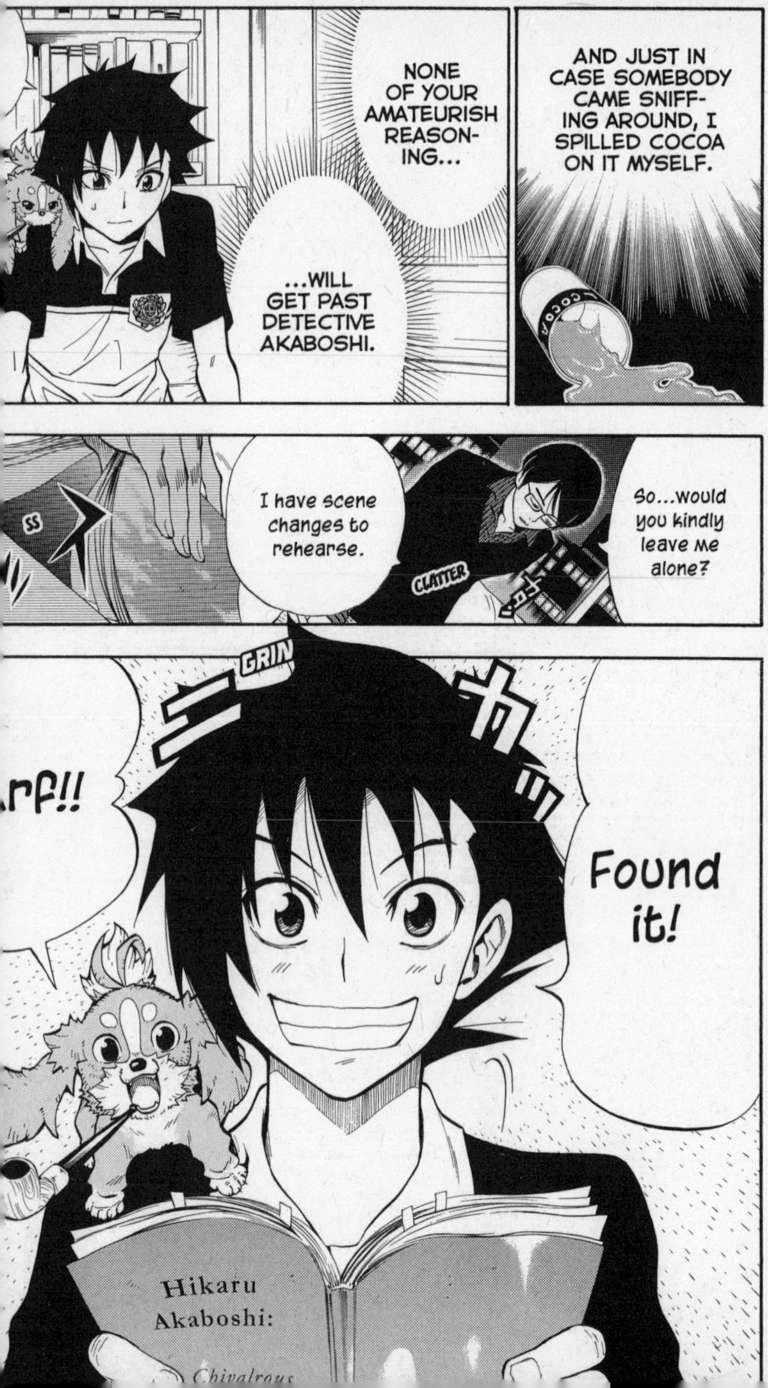
AND JUST IN CASE SOMEBODY CAME SNIFF-ING AROUND, I SPILLED COCOA ON IT MYSELF.
COCOA
NONE OF YOUR AMATEURISH REASON-ING...
...WILL GET PAST DETECTIVE AKABOSHI.
So...would you kindly leave me alone?
I have scene changes to rehearse.
CLATTER
SS
GRIN
Found it!
rf!!
Hikaru Akaboshi:
Chivalrous

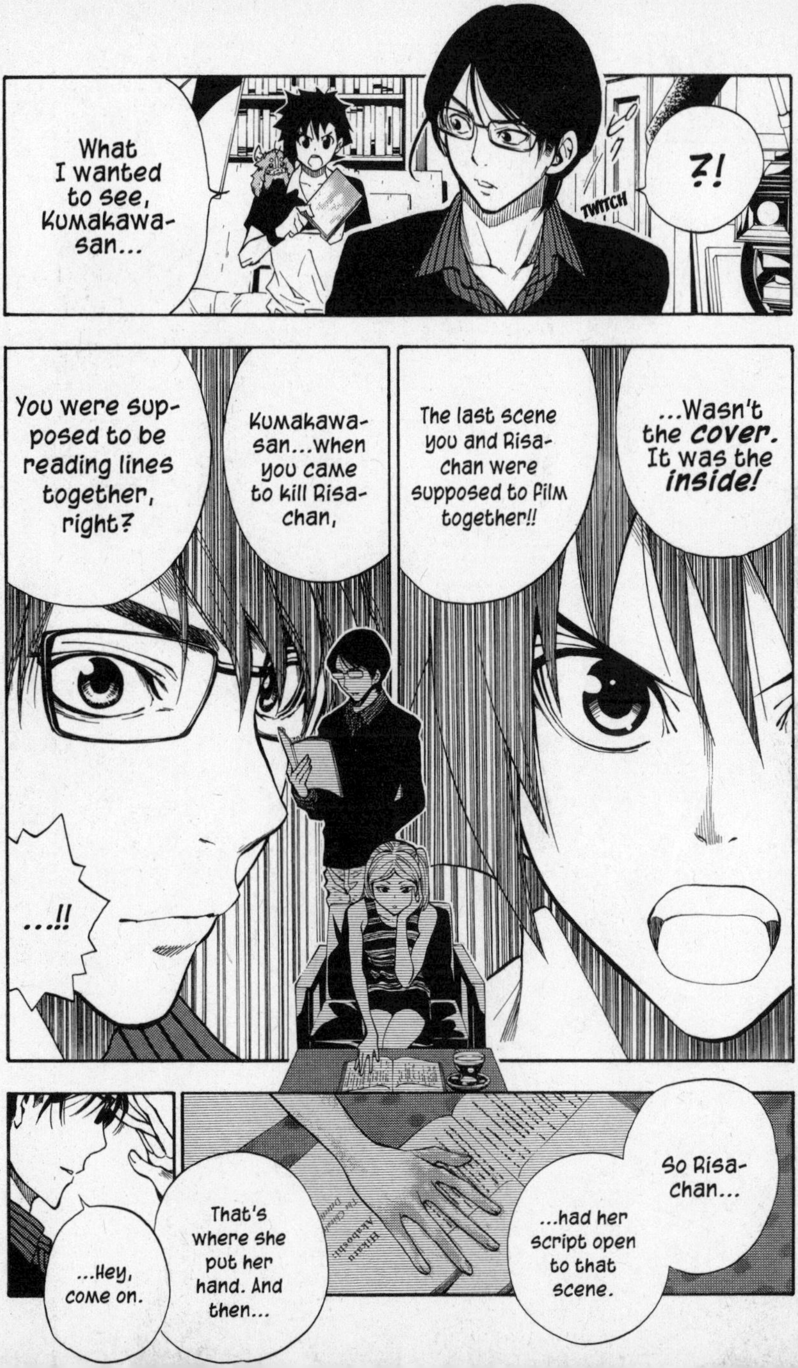
?!
TWITCH
What I wanted to see, Kumakawa-san...
...Wasn't the *cover*. It was the *inside!*
The last scene you and Risa-chan were supposed to film together!!
Kumakawa-san...when you came to kill Risa-chan,
You were supposed to be reading lines together, right?
...!!
So Risa-chan...
...had her script open to that scene.
That's where she put her hand. And then...
...Hey, come on.

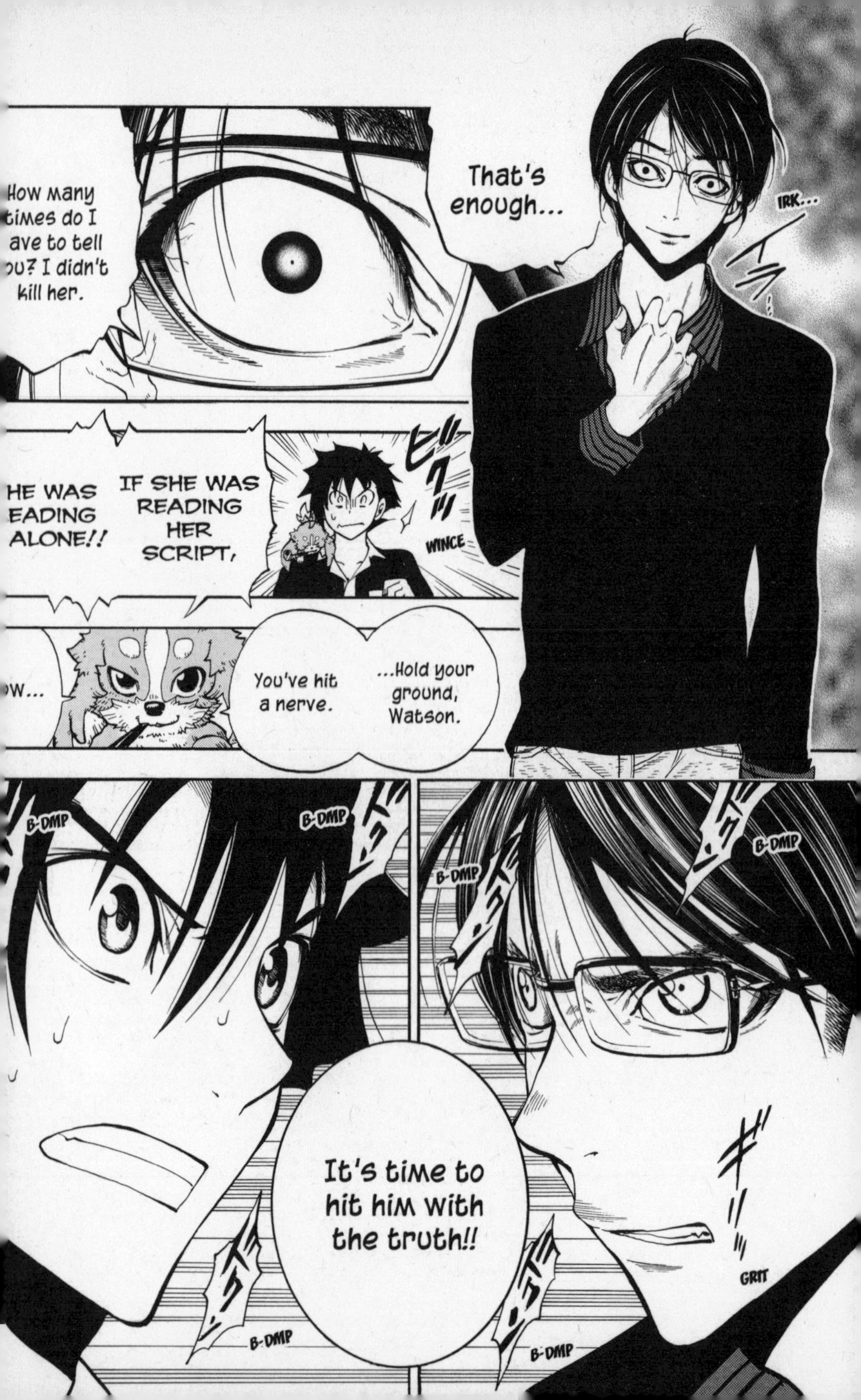

That's enough...
IRK...
How many times do I ave to tell ou? I didn't kill her.
WINCE
IF SHE WAS READING HER SCRIPT,
HE WAS EADING ALONE!!
...Hold your ground, Watson.
You've hit a nerve.
W...
B-DMP
B-DMP
GRIT
It's time to hit him with the truth!!
B-DMP
B-DMP
B-DMP
B-DMP
B-DMP

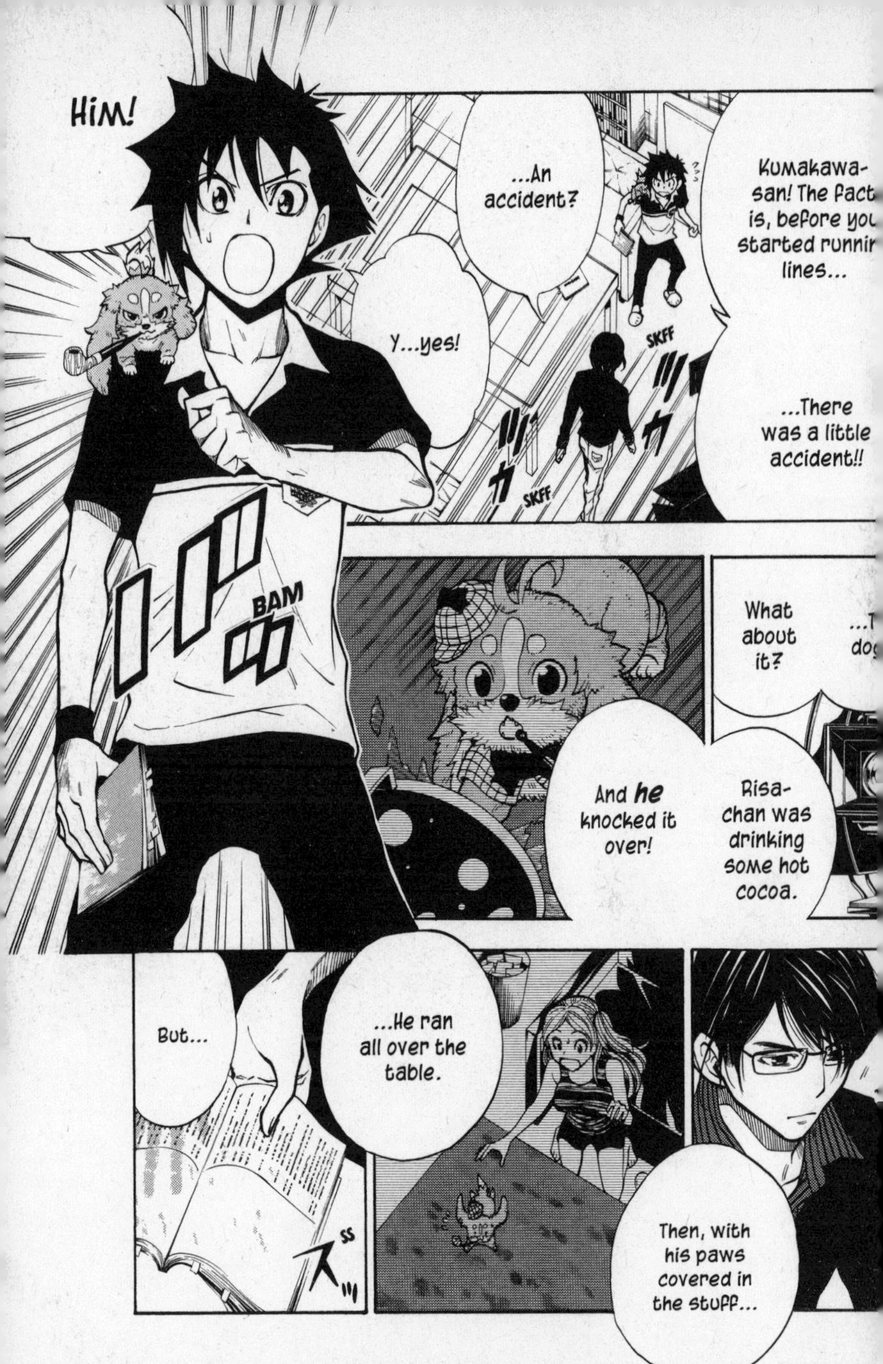
Kumakawa-san! The fact is, before you started runnin lines...
...An accident?
Y...yes!
SKFF
SKFF
...There was a little accident!!
What about it?
Risa-chan was drinking some hot cocoa.
And he knocked it over!
HIM!
BAM
Then, with his paws covered in the stuff...
...He ran all over the table.
But...
SS

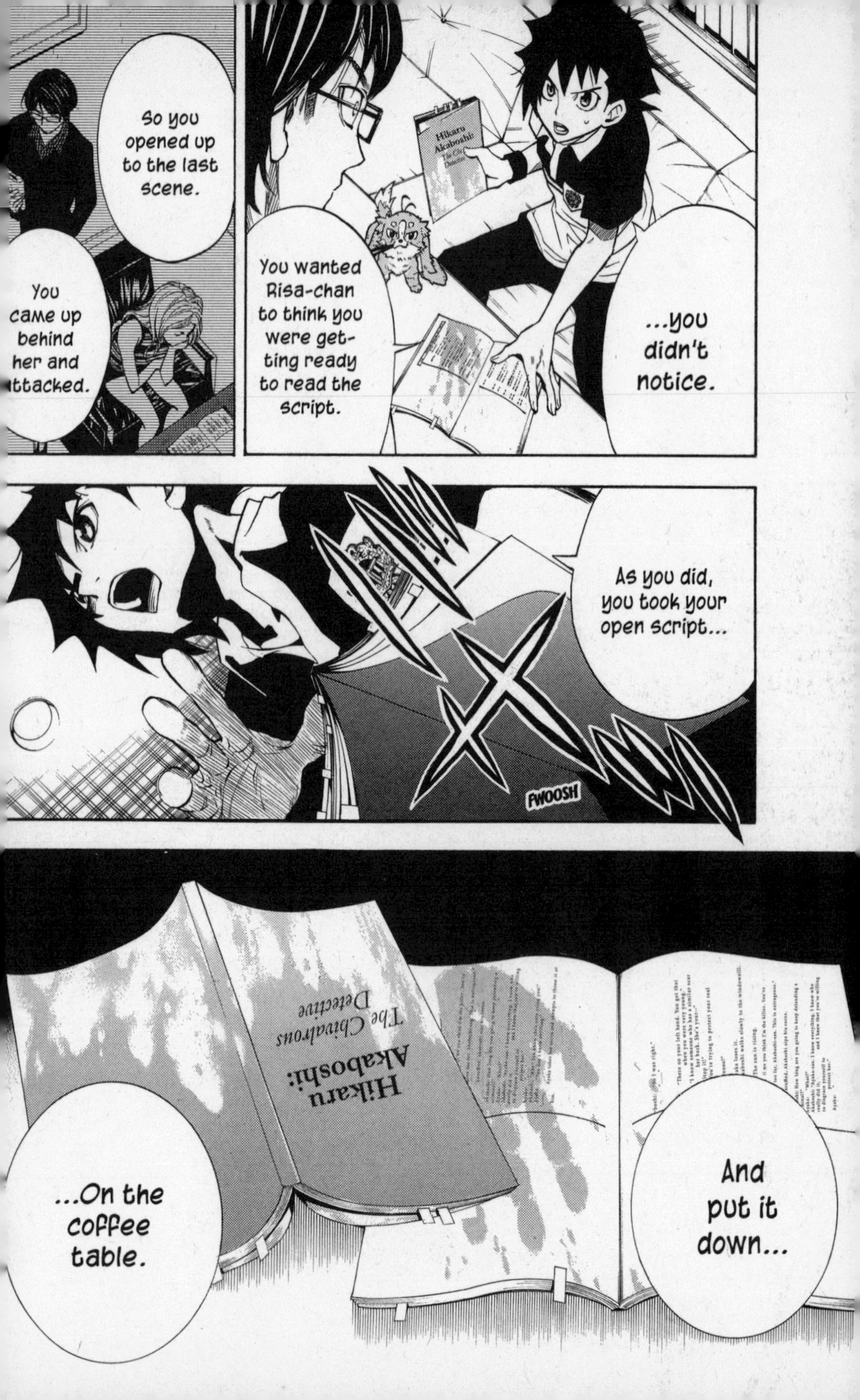
...you didn't notice.
You wanted Risa-chan to think you were get-ting ready to read the script.
So you opened up to the last scene.
You came up behind her and attacked.
As you did, you took your open script...
FWOOSH
And put it down...
Hikaru Akaboshi: The Chivalrous Detective
...On the coffee table.

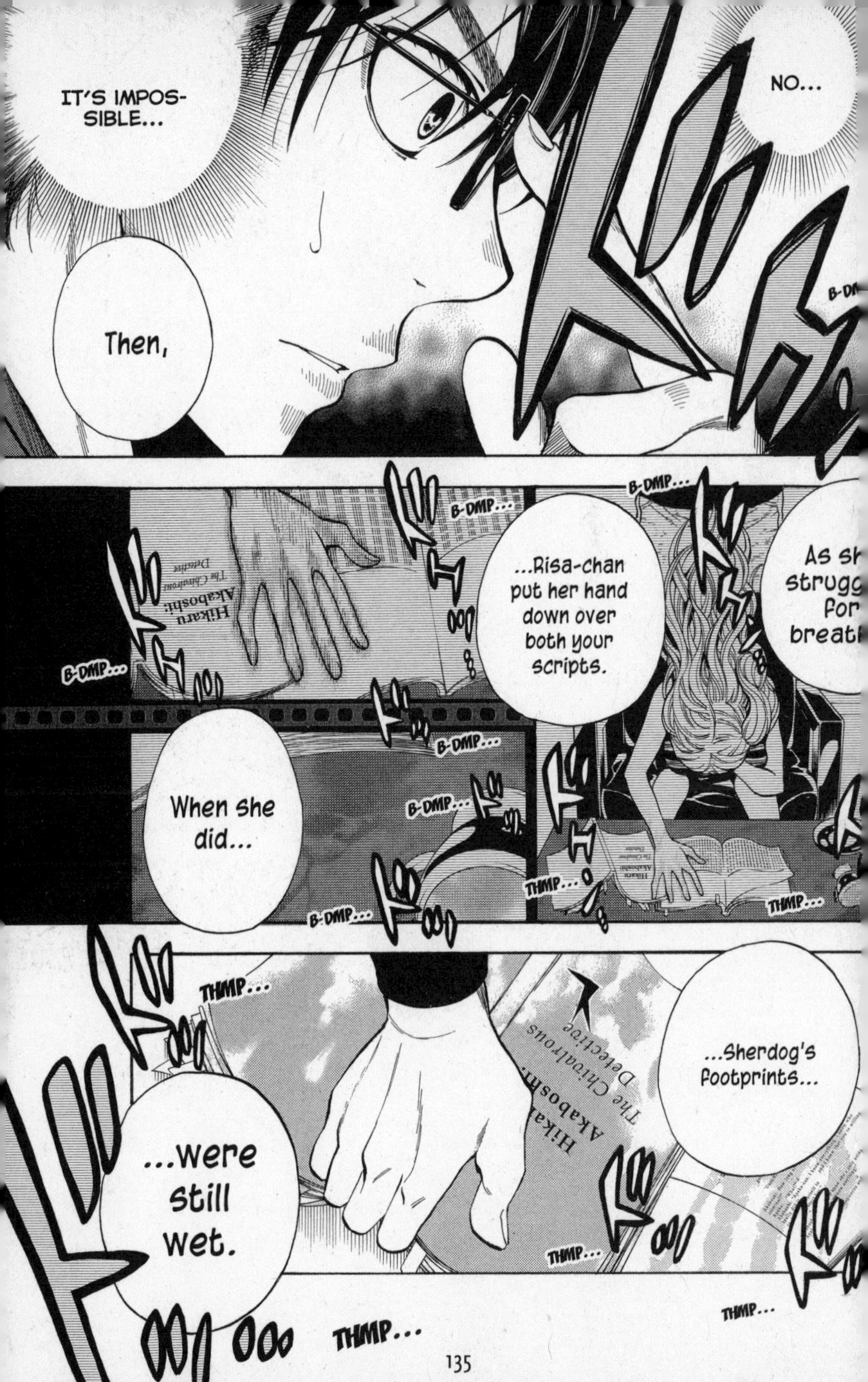
NO...
IT'S IMPOSSIBLE...
Then,
B-DMP...
...Risa-chan put her hand down over both your scripts.
B-DMP...
Hikaru Akaboshi: The Chivalrous Detective
B-DMP...
B-DMP...
When she did...
B-DMP...
B-DMP...
THMP...
THMP...
...Sherdog's footprints...
Hikaru Akaboshi: The Chivalrous Detective
THMP...
...were still wet.
THMP...
THMP...

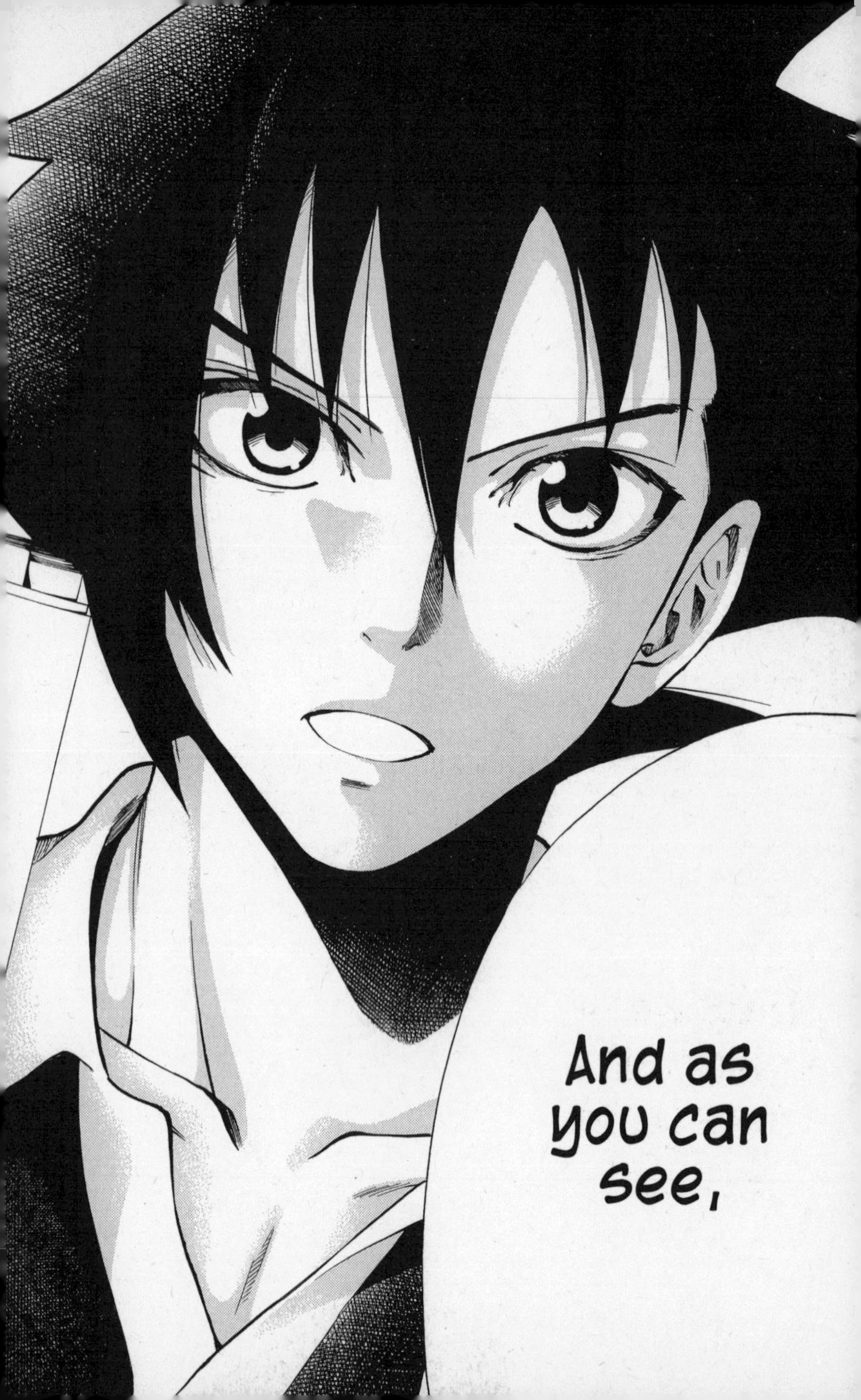
And as you can see,

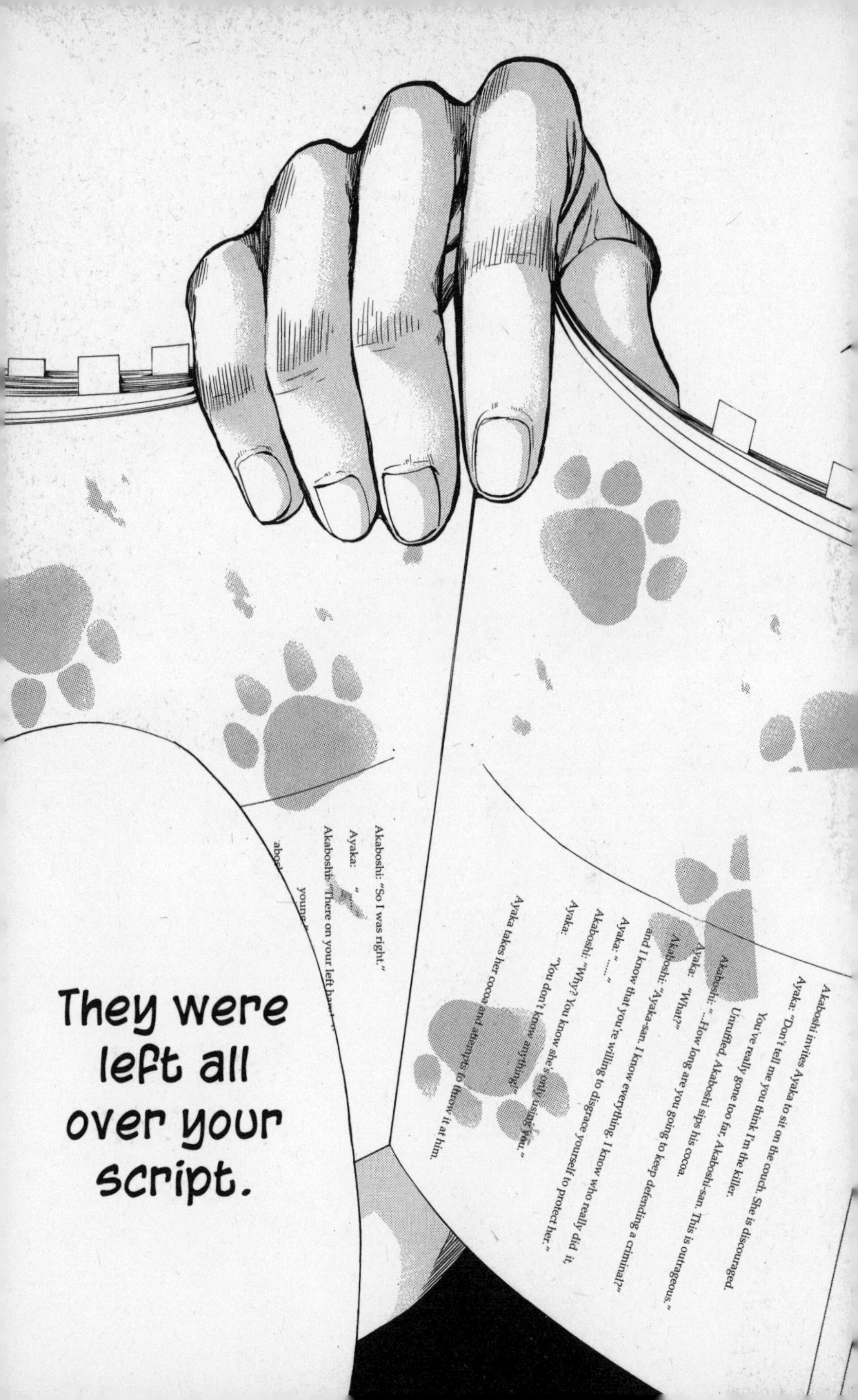
Akaboshi invites Ayaka to sit on the couch. She is discouraged.
Ayaka: "Don't tell me you think I'm the killer.
You've really gone too far, Akaboshi-san. This is outrageous."
Unruffled, Akaboshi sips his cocoa.
Akaboshi: "...How long are you going to keep defending a criminal?"
Ayaka: "What?"
Akaboshi: "Ayaka-san. I know everything. I know who really did it,
and I know that you're willing to disgrace yourself to protect her."
Ayaka: "......"
Akaboshi: "Why? You know she's only using you."
Ayaka: "You don't know anything!"
Ayaka takes her cocoa and attempts to throw it at him.
Akaboshi: "So I was right."
They were left all over your script.

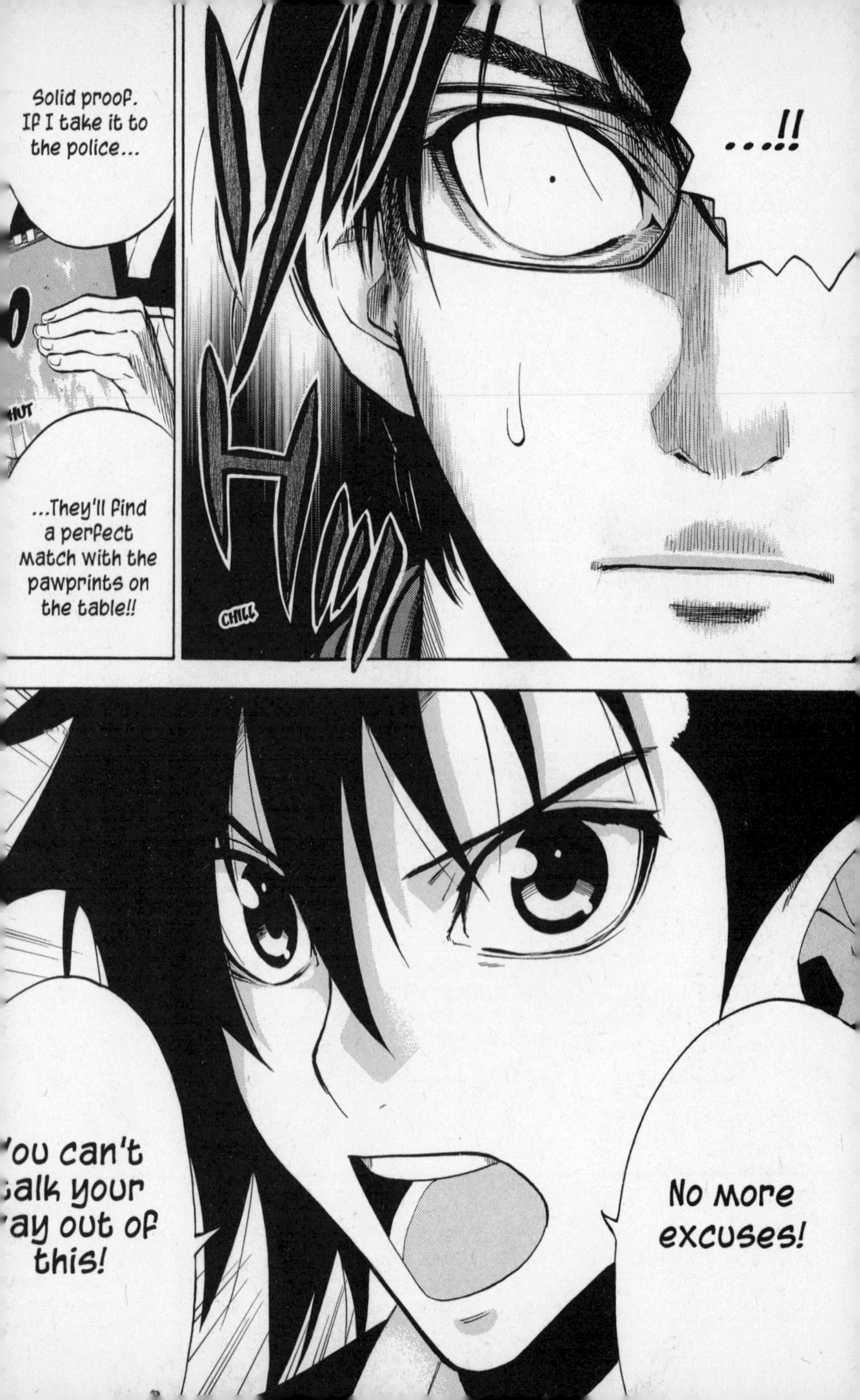
....!!
CHILL
Solid proof. If I take it to the police...
HUT
...They'll find a perfect match with the pawprints on the table!!
No more excuses!
ou can't alk your ay out of this!

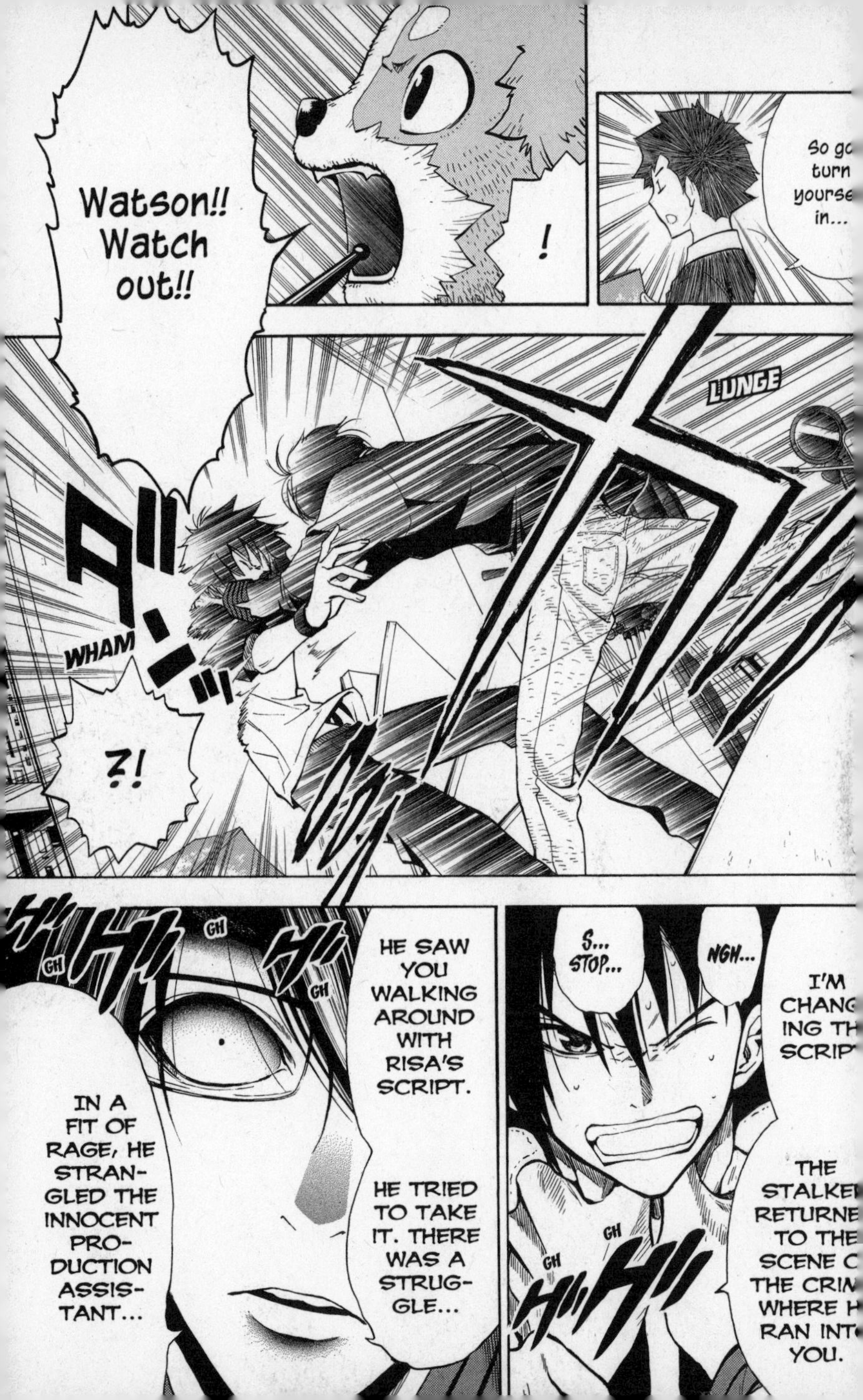
So go turn yourse in...
Watson!! Watch out!!
!
LUNGE
WHAM
?!
S... STOP...
NGH...
I'M CHANG ING TH SCRIPT
THE STALKE RETURNE TO THE SCENE O THE CRIM WHERE H RAN INTO YOU.
GH
GH
HE SAW YOU WALKING AROUND WITH RISA'S SCRIPT.
HE TRIED TO TAKE IT. THERE WAS A STRUG- GLE...
IN A FIT OF RAGE, HE STRAN- GLED THE INNOCENT PRO- DUCTION ASSIS- TANT...
GH
GH
GH

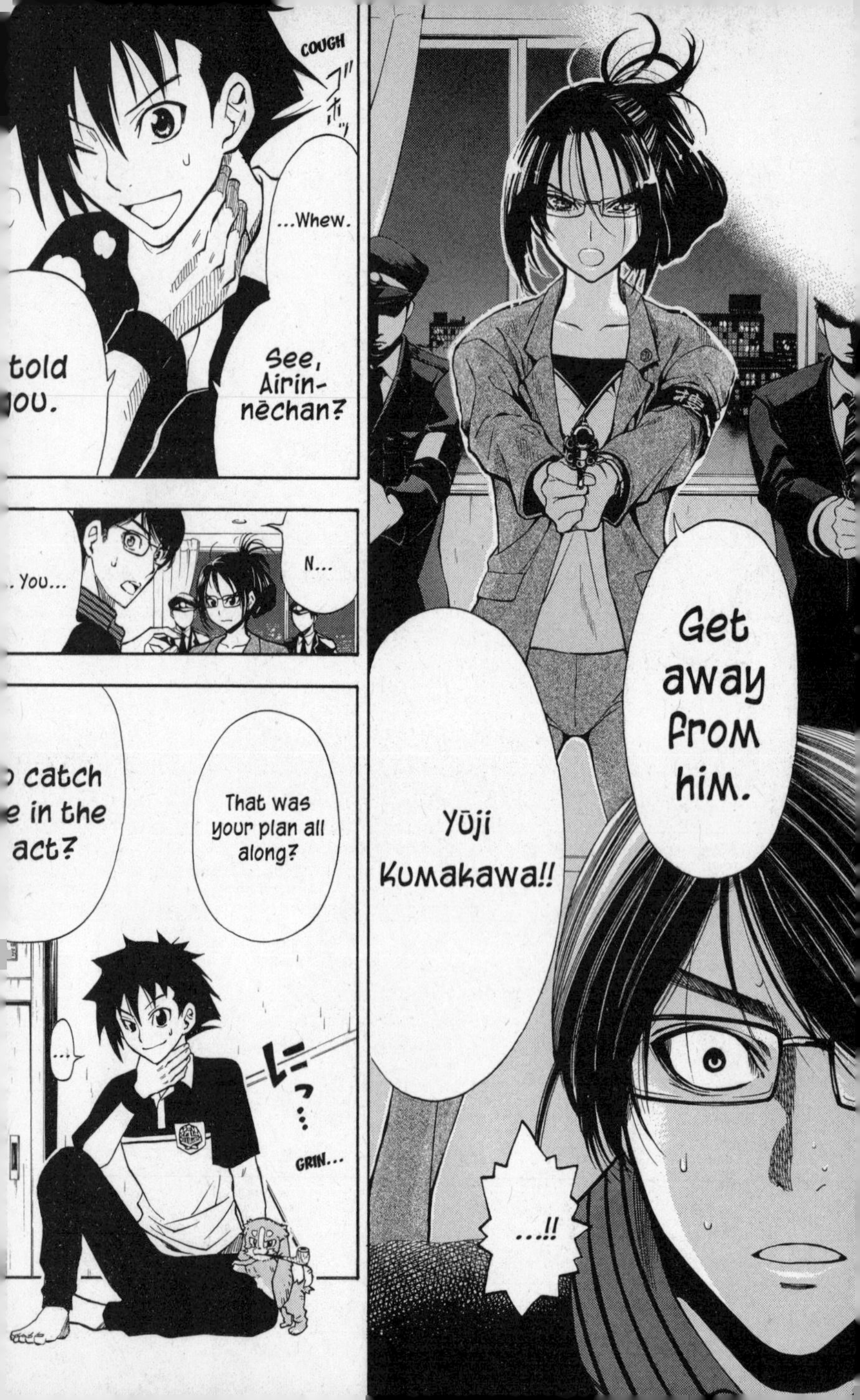
Get away from him.
Yūji Kumakawa!!
...!!
COUGH
ゴホッ
...Whew.
See, Airin-nēchan?
told you.
N...
. You...
catch e in the act?
That was your plan all along?
...
ニッ
GRIN...

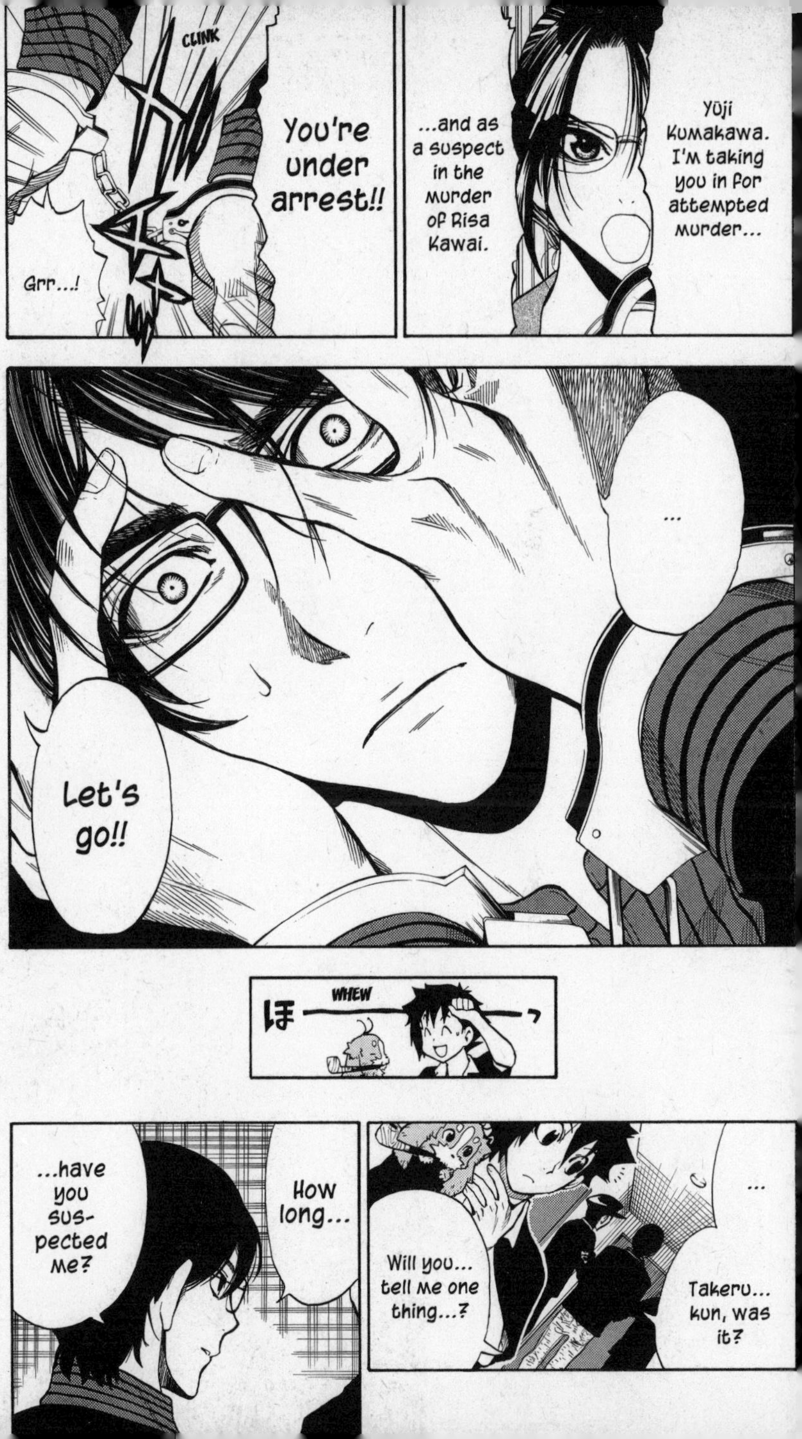
Yūji Kumakawa. I'm taking you in for attempted murder...
...and as a suspect in the murder of Risa Kawai.
CLINK
You're under arrest!!
Grr...!
...
Let's go!!
ほ
WHEW
...
Takeru... kun, was it?
Will you... tell me one thing...?
How long...
...have you sus-pected me?

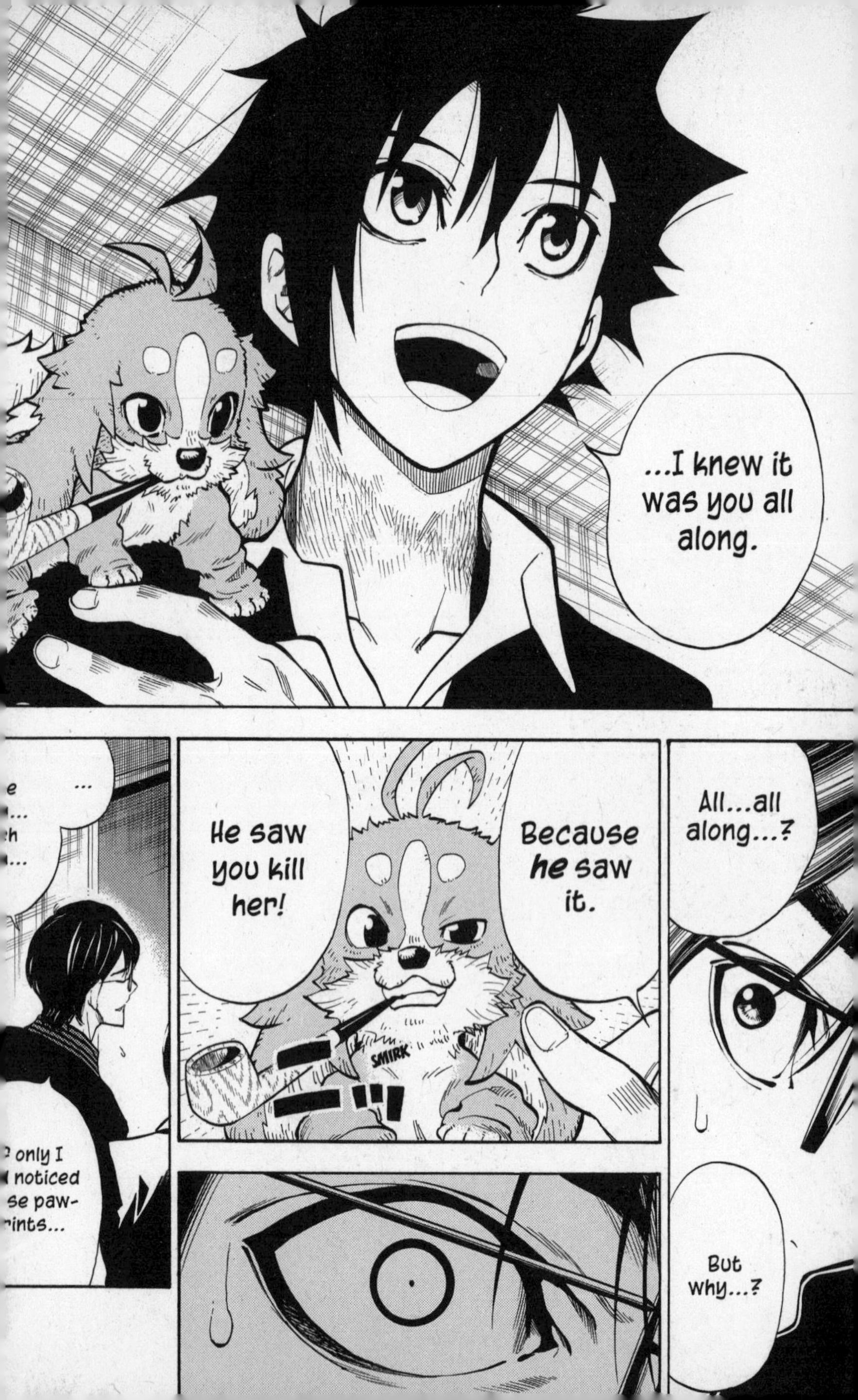
...I knew it was you all along.
All...all along...?
But why...?
Because he saw it.
He saw you kill her!
SMIRK
only I noticed se paw-rints...

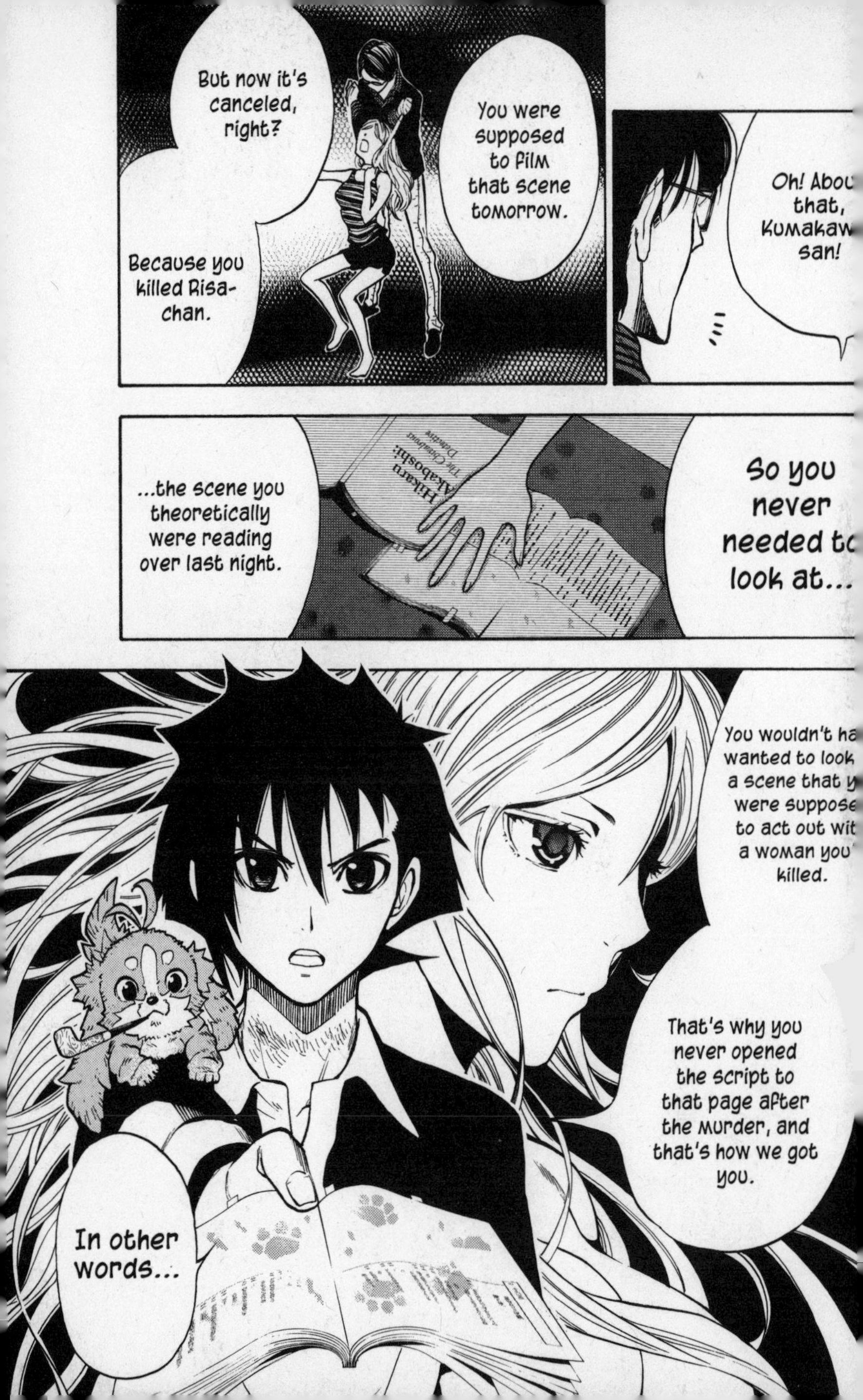

Oh! Abou that, Kumakaw san!
You were supposed to film that scene tomorrow.
But now it's canceled, right?
Because you killed Risa-chan.
So you never needed to look at...
...the scene you theoretically were reading over last night.
You wouldn't ha wanted to look a scene that y were suppose to act out wit a woman you' killed.
That's why you never opened the script to that page after the murder, and that's how we got you.
In other words...

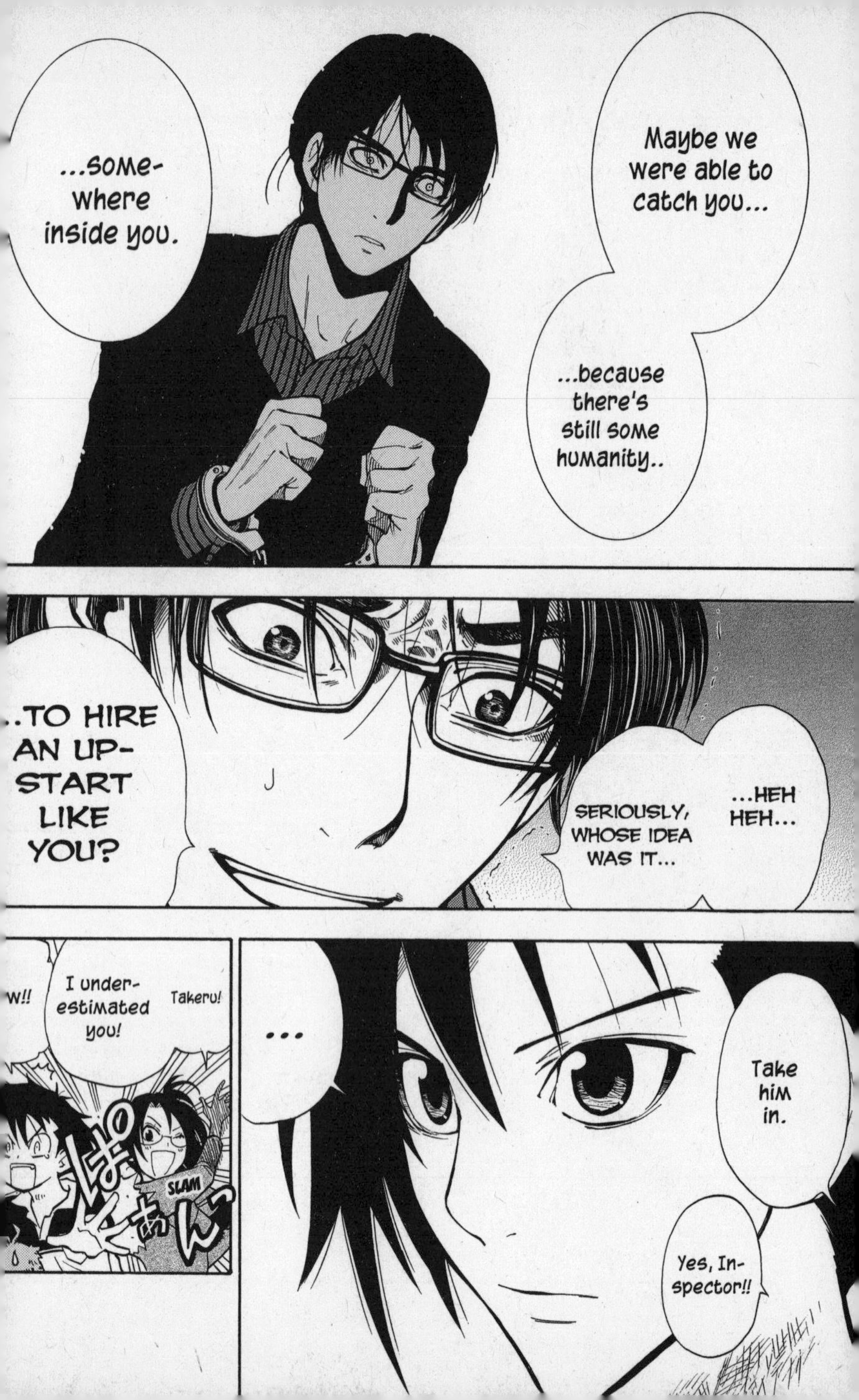
Maybe we were able to catch you...
...because there's still some humanity..
...some-where inside you.
...HEH HEH...
SERIOUSLY, WHOSE IDEA WAS IT...
..TO HIRE AN UP-START LIKE YOU?
Take him in.
Yes, In-spector!!
...
Takeru!
I under-estimated you!
SLAM

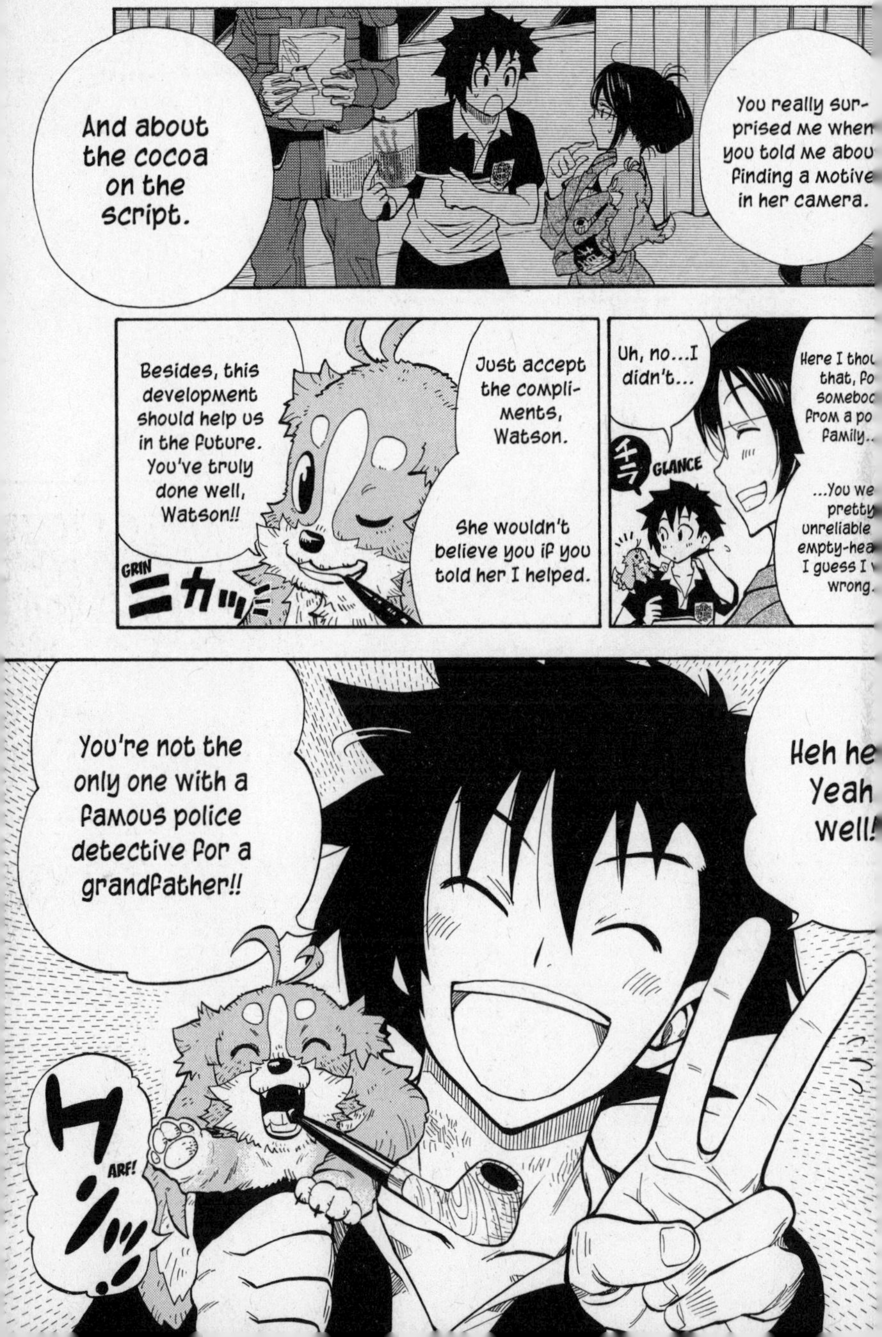
You really sur-prised me when you told me abou finding a motive in her camera.
And about the cocoa on the script.
Here I thou that, fo somebod from a po family..
...You we pretty unreliable empty-hea I guess I wrong.
Uh, no...I didn't...
GLANCE
Just accept the compli-ments, Watson.
She wouldn't believe you if you told her I helped.
Besides, this development should help us in the future. You've truly done well, Watson!!
GRIN
Heh he Yeah well!
You're not the only one with a famous police detective for a grandfather!!
ARF!

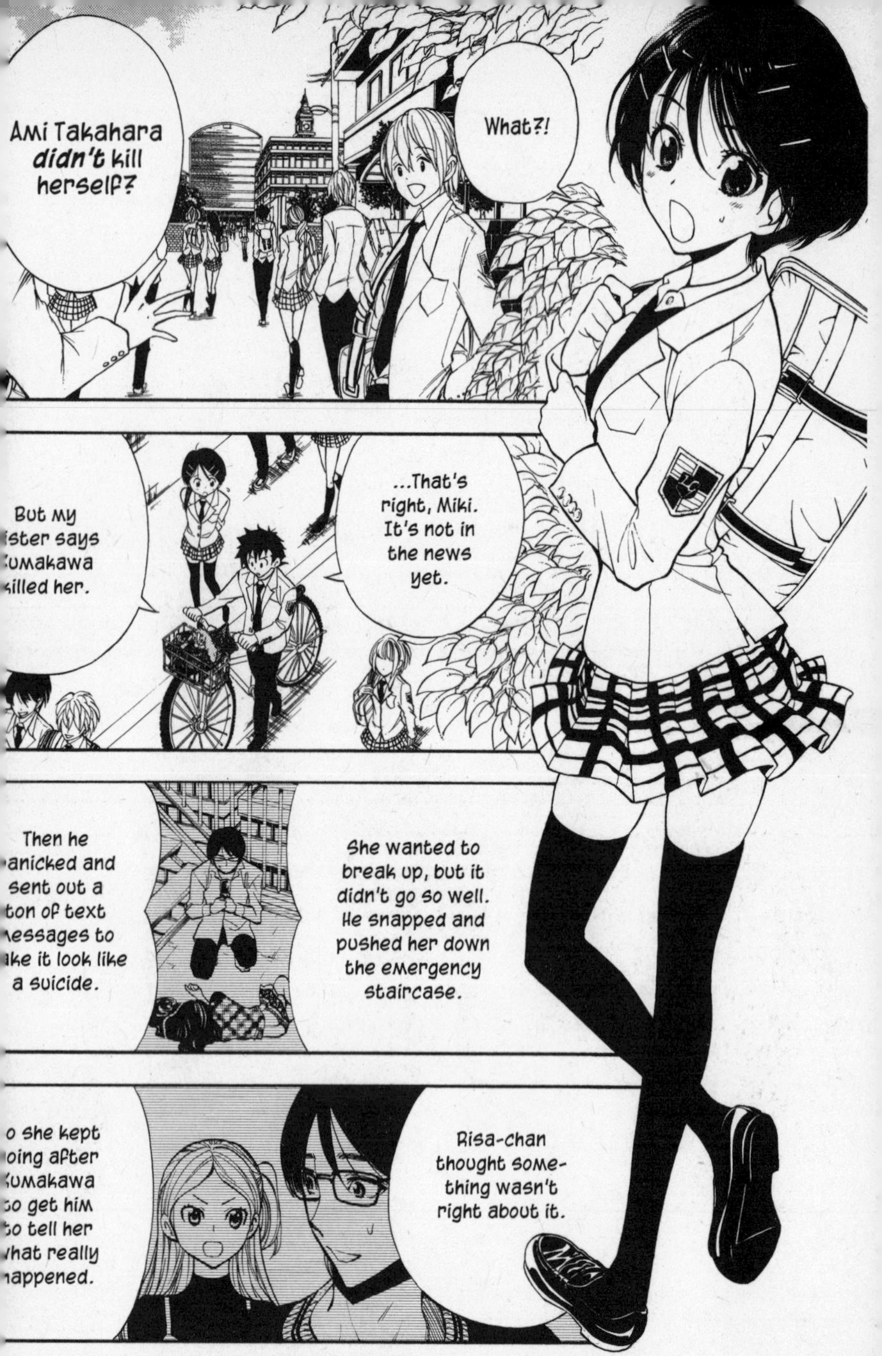
What?!
Ami Takahara didn't kill herself?
...That's right, Miki. It's not in the news yet.
But my ister says umakawa illed her.
She wanted to break up, but it didn't go so well. He snapped and pushed her down the emergency staircase.
Then he anicked and sent out a ton of text essages to ake it look like a suicide.
Risa-chan thought some-thing wasn't right about it.
o she kept oing after umakawa o get him o tell her hat really appened.

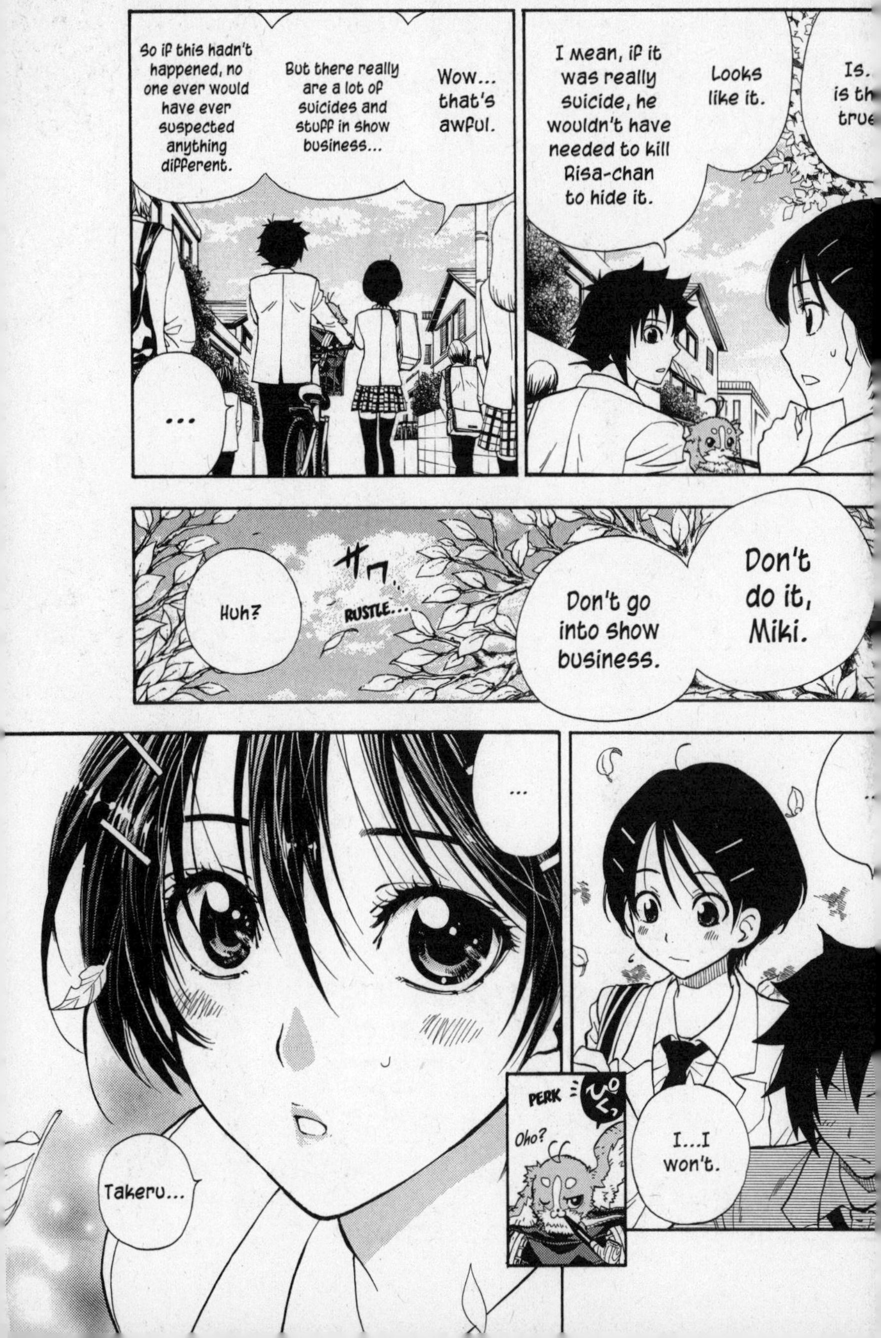

Is.
is th
true
Looks like it.
I mean, if it was really suicide, he wouldn't have needed to kill Risa-chan to hide it.
Wow... that's awful.
But there really are a lot of suicides and stuff in show business...
So if this hadn't happened, no one ever would have ever suspected anything different.
...
Don't do it, Miki.
Don't go into show business.
RUSTLE...
Huh?
I...I won't.
PERK
Oho?
...
Takeru...

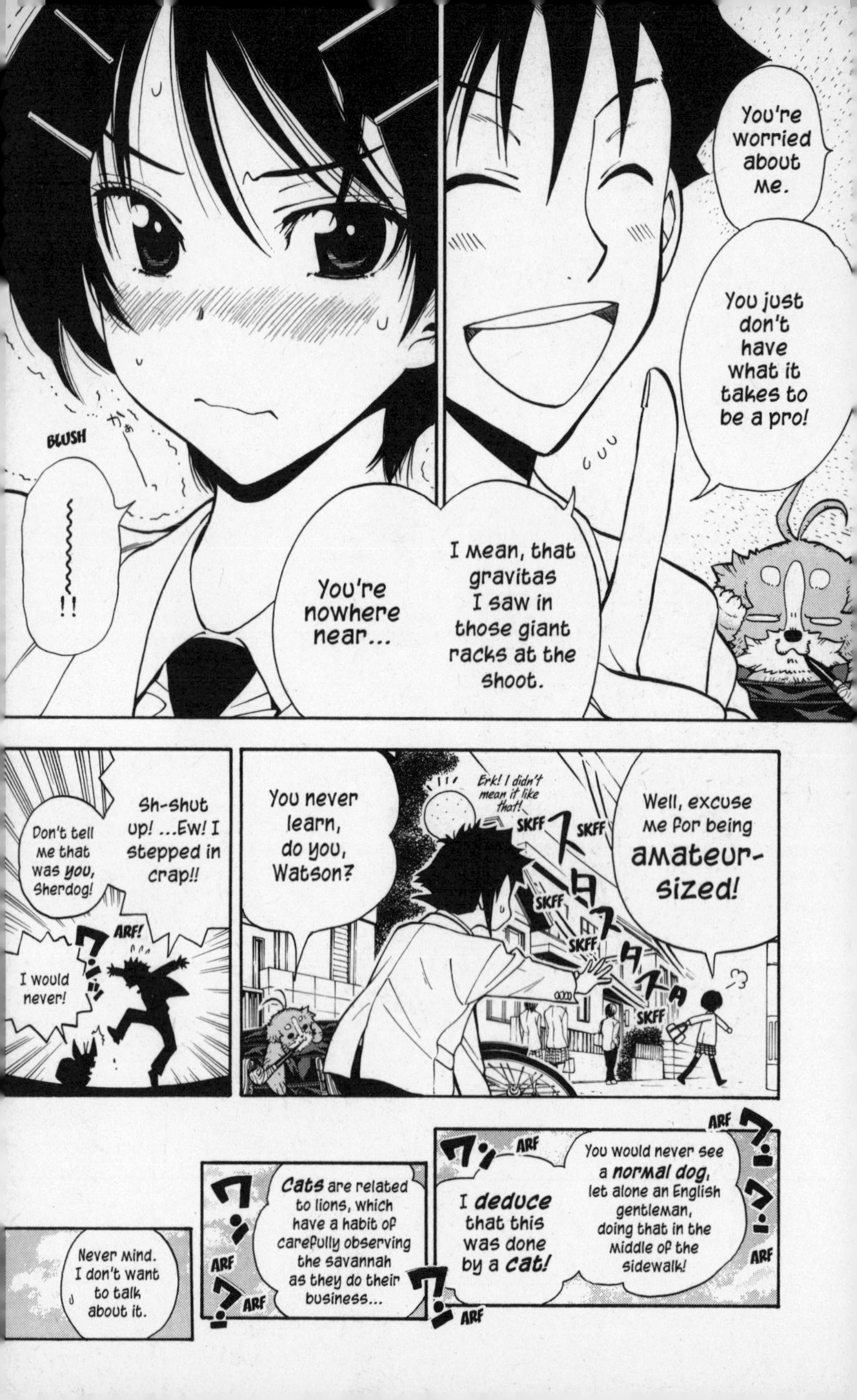

You're worried about me.
You just don't have what it takes to be a pro!
I mean, that gravitas I saw in those giant racks at the shoot.
You're nowhere near...
BLUSH
~~~~!!
Well, excuse me for being amateur-sized!
Erk! I didn't mean it like that!
SKFF
SKFF
SKFF
SKFF
SKFF
You never learn, do you, Watson?
Sh-shut up! ...Ew! I stepped in crap!!
Don't tell me that was you, Sherdog!
ARF!
I would never!
ARF
You would never see a normal dog, let alone an English gentleman, doing that in the middle of the sidewalk!
ARF
I deduce that this was done by a cat!
ARF
Cats are related to lions, which have a habit of carefully observing the savannah as they do their business...
ARF
ARF
ARF
Never mind. I don't want to talk about it.
~~~~

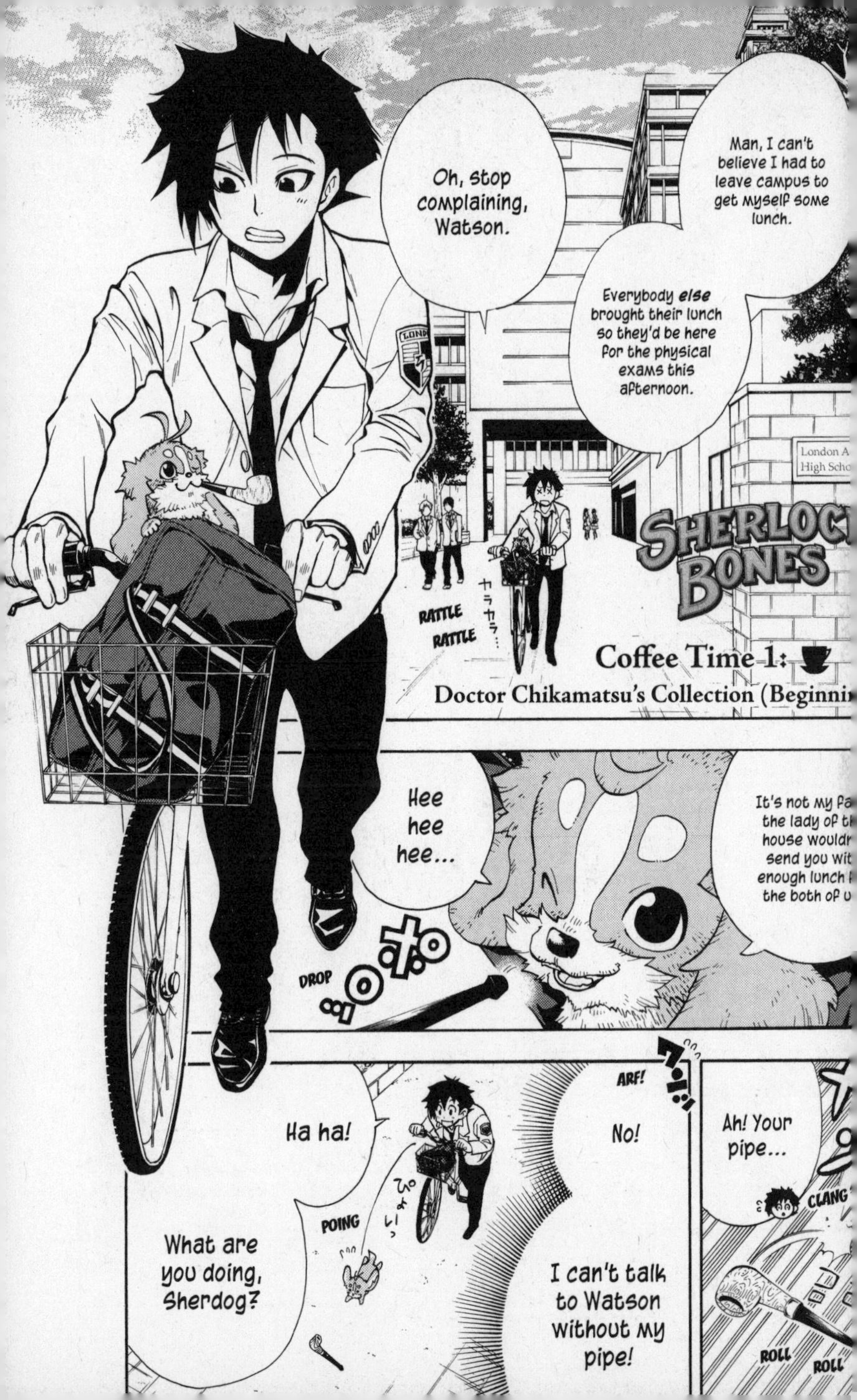
Man, I can't believe I had to leave campus to get myself some lunch.
Everybody else brought their lunch so they'd be here for the physical exams this afternoon.
Oh, stop complaining, Watson.
London A
High Scho
SHERLOC
BONES
Coffee Time 1:
Doctor Chikamatsu's Collection (Beginni
RATTLE RATTLE
カラカラ…
It's not my fa the lady of th house wouldr send you wit enough lunch f the both of u
Hee hee hee...
DROP
Ah! Your pipe...
CLANG
ROLL
ROLL
ARF!
No!
I can't talk to Watson without my pipe!
Ha ha!
POING
What are you doing, Sherdog?

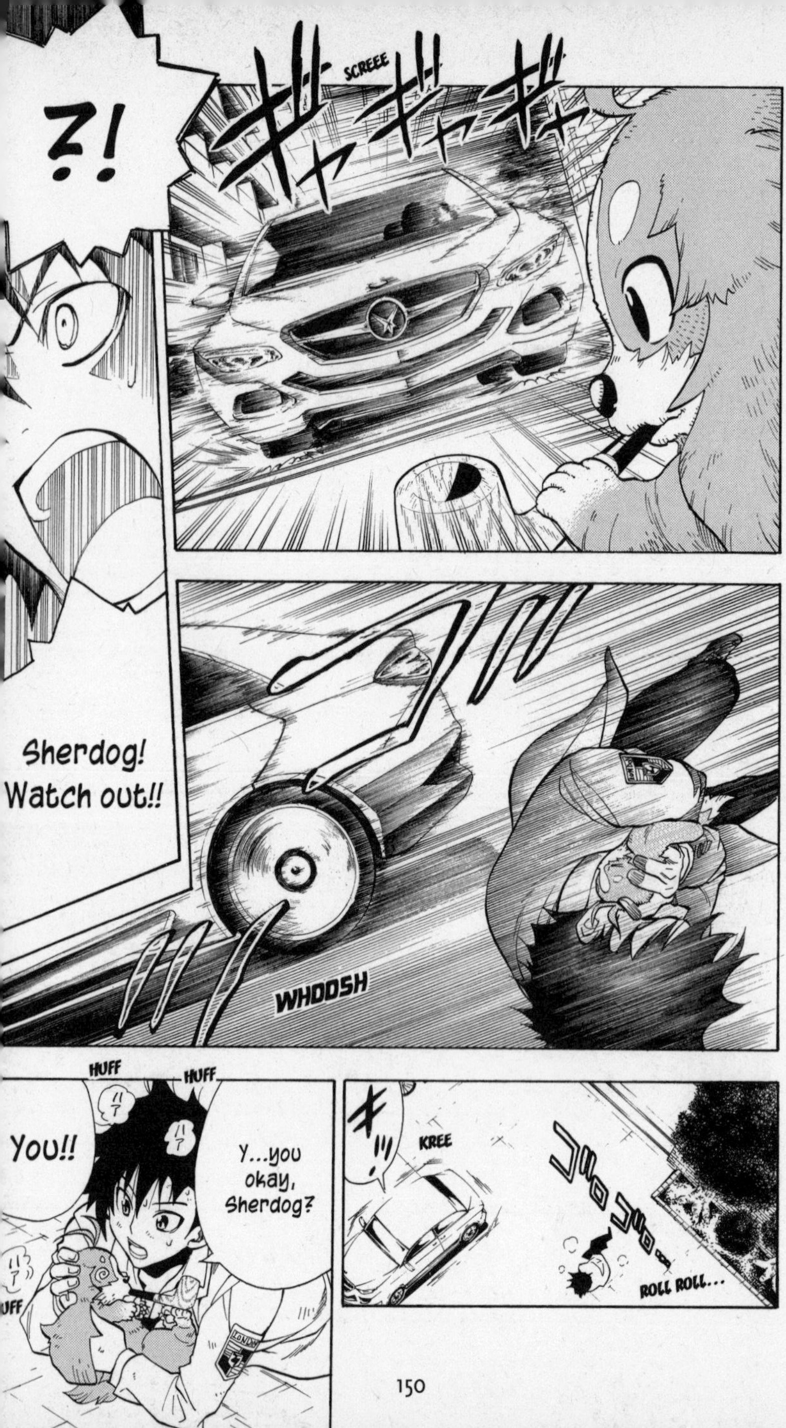
SCREEE
WHOOSH
?!
Sherdog! Watch out!!
KREE
ROLL ROLL...
HUFF
HUFF
Y...you okay, Sherdog?
YOU!!
UFF

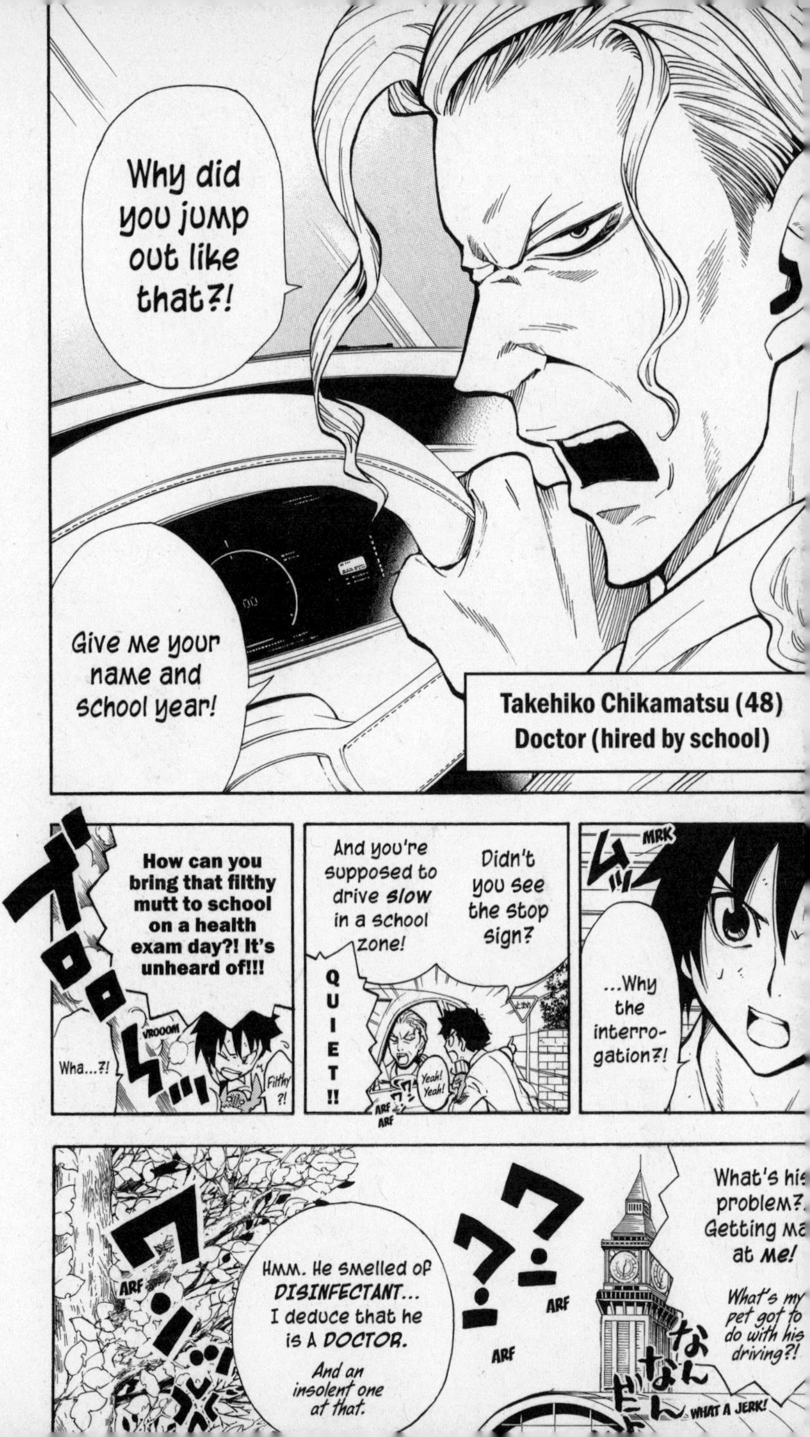

Why did you jump out like that?!
Give me your name and school year!
Takehiko Chikamatsu (48)
Doctor (hired by school)
MRK
...Why the interro-gation?!
Didn't you see the stop sign?
And you're supposed to drive *slow* in a school zone!
QUIET!!
Yeah! Yeah!
ARF ARF
How can you bring that filthy mutt to school on a health exam day?! It's unheard of!!!
VROOOM
Filthy?!
Wha...?!
What's his problem?! Getting ma at me!
What's my pet got to do with his driving?!
WHAT A JERK!
ARF
ARF
Hmm. He smelled of *DISINFECTANT*... I deduce that he is a *DOCTOR.*
And an insolent one at that.
ARF

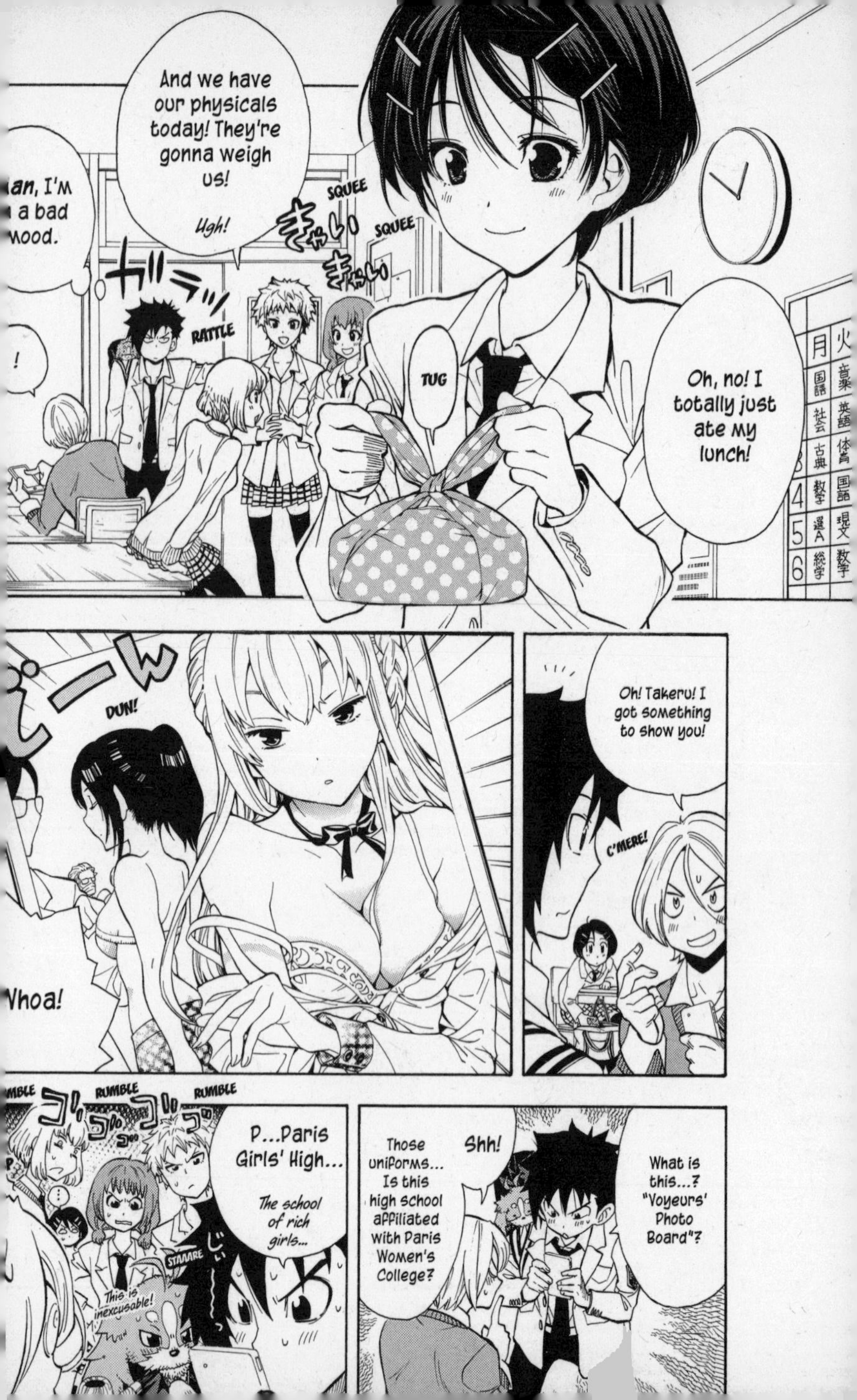

Oh, no! I totally just ate my lunch!
TUG
SQUEE
SQUEE
And we have our physicals today! They're gonna weigh us!
Ugh!
RATTLE
an, I'M a bad mood.
!
Oh! Takeru! I got something to show you!
C'MERE!
DUN!
Whoa!
What is this...? "Voyeurs' Photo Board"?
Shh!
Those uniforms... Is this high school affiliated with Paris Women's College?
P...Paris Girls' High...
The school of rich girls...
RUMBLE
RUMBLE
RUMBLE
STAAARE
This is inexcusable!

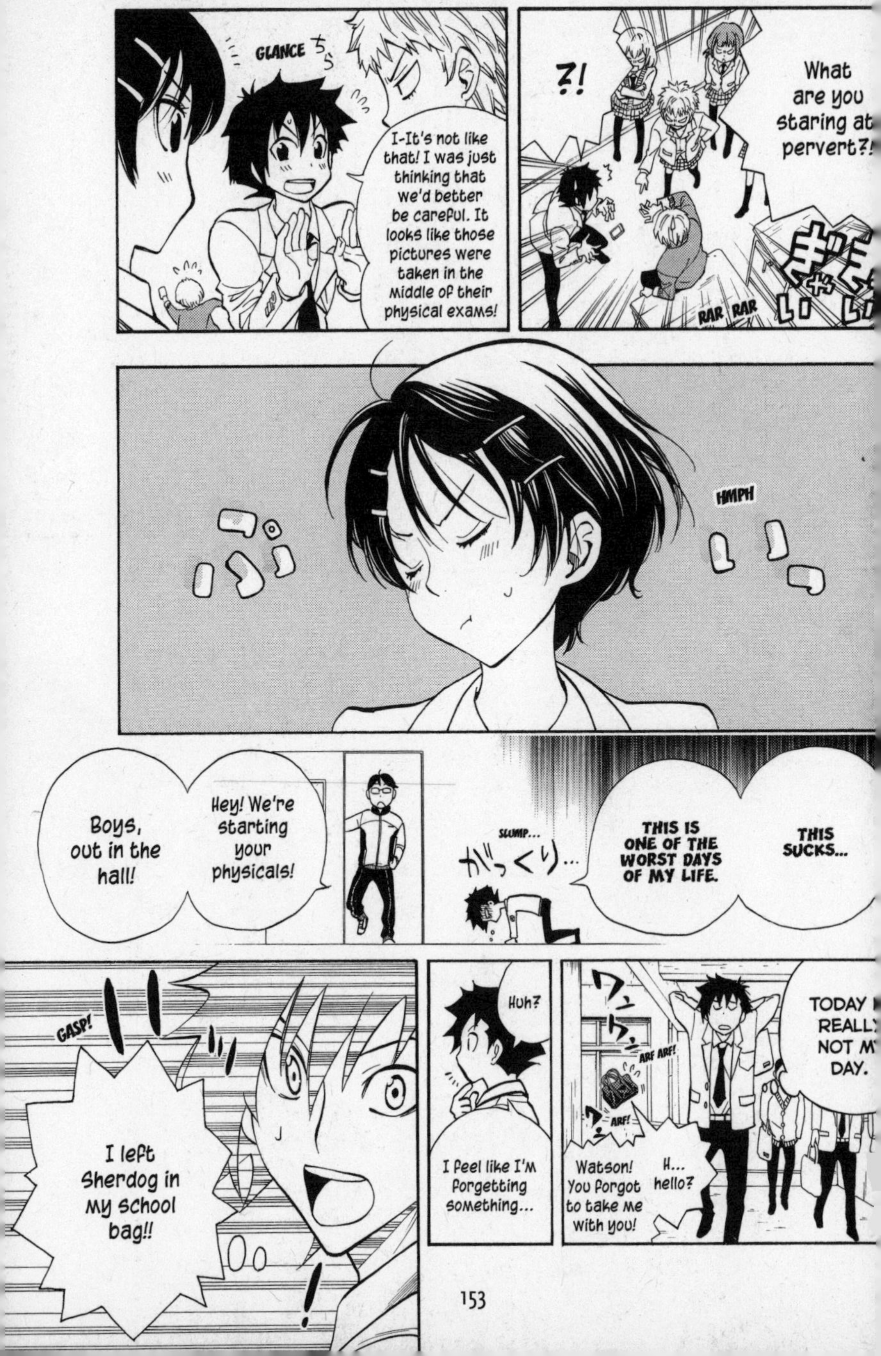
What are you staring at pervert?!
?!
RAR RAR
GLANCE ちら
I-It's not like that! I was just thinking that we'd better be careful. It looks like those pictures were taken in the middle of their physical exams!
HMPH
THIS SUCKS...
THIS IS ONE OF THE WORST DAYS OF MY LIFE.
SLUMP...
がっくり...
Hey! We're starting your physicals!
Boys, out in the hall!
TODAY
REALL
NOT M
DAY.
H... hello?
Watson! You forgot to take me with you!
ARF ARF!
ARF!
Huh?
I feel like I'm forgetting something...
GASP!
I left Sherdog in my school bag!!

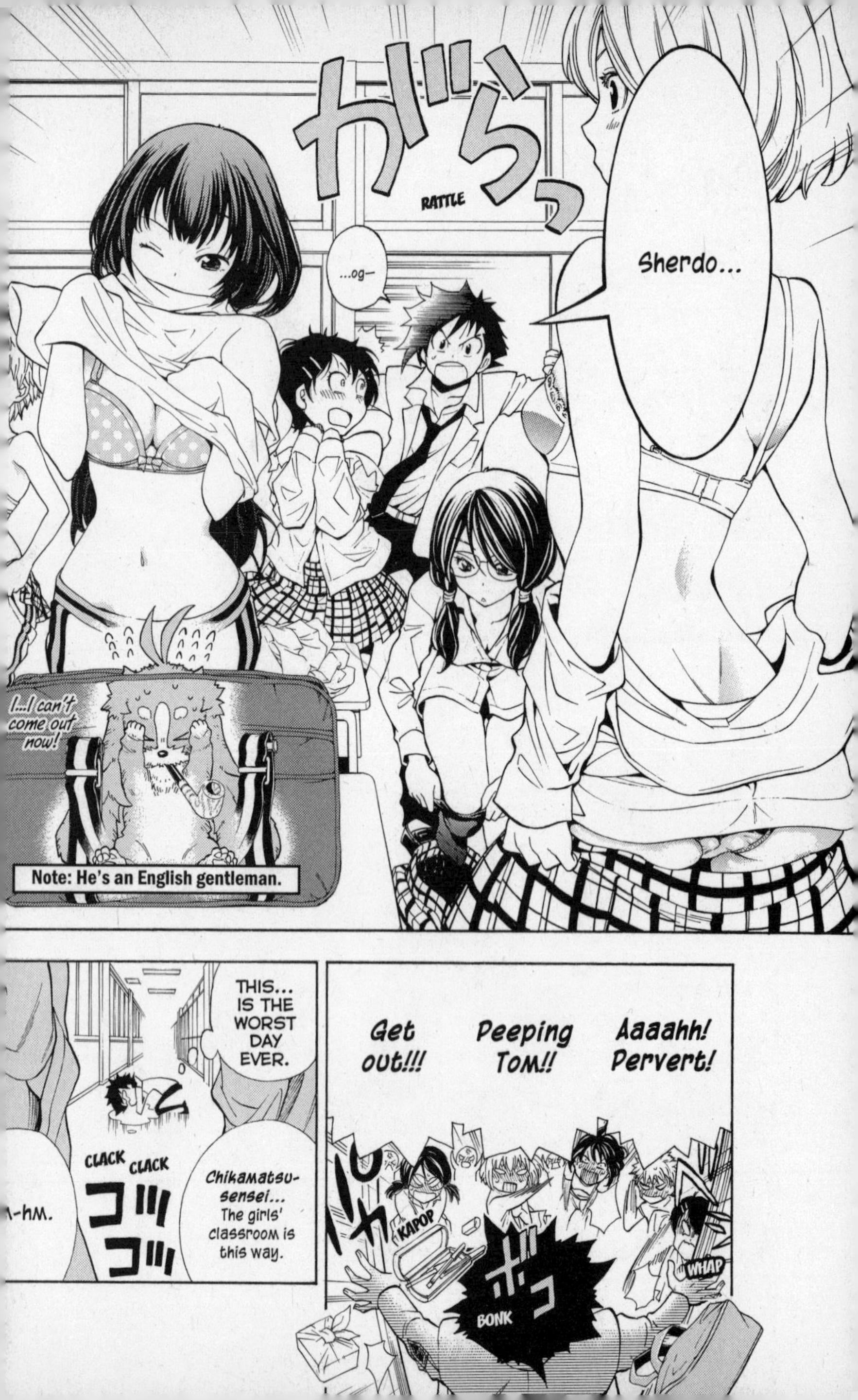
がらっ
RATTLE
Sherdo...
...og—
I...I can't come out now!
Note: He's an English gentleman.
Aaaahh! Pervert!
Peeping Tom!!
Get out!!!
WHAP
ボコ
BONK
KAPOP
THIS... IS THE WORST DAY EVER.
Chikamatsu-sensei... The girls' classroom is this way.
コツコツ
CLACK CLACK

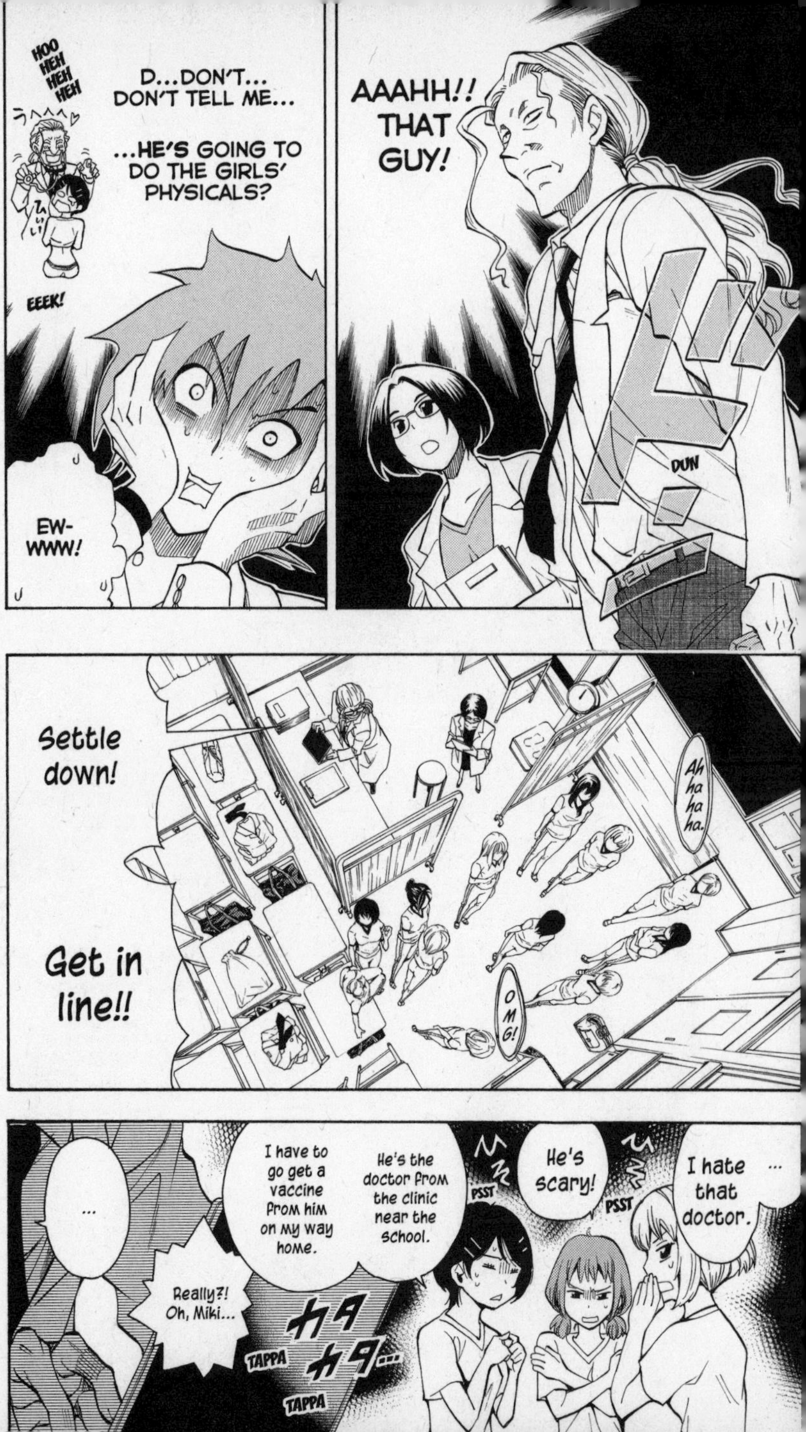
AAAHH!! THAT GUY!
DUN
D...DON'T... DON'T TELL ME...
...HE'S GOING TO DO THE GIRLS' PHYSICALS?
HOO HEH HEH HEH
EEEK!
EW-WWW!
Ah ha ha ha.
OMG!
Settle down!
Get in line!!
...
I hate that doctor.
PSST
He's scary!
PSST
He's the doctor from the clinic near the school.
I have to go get a vaccine from him on my way home.
...
Really?! Oh, Miki...
TAPPA
TAPPA

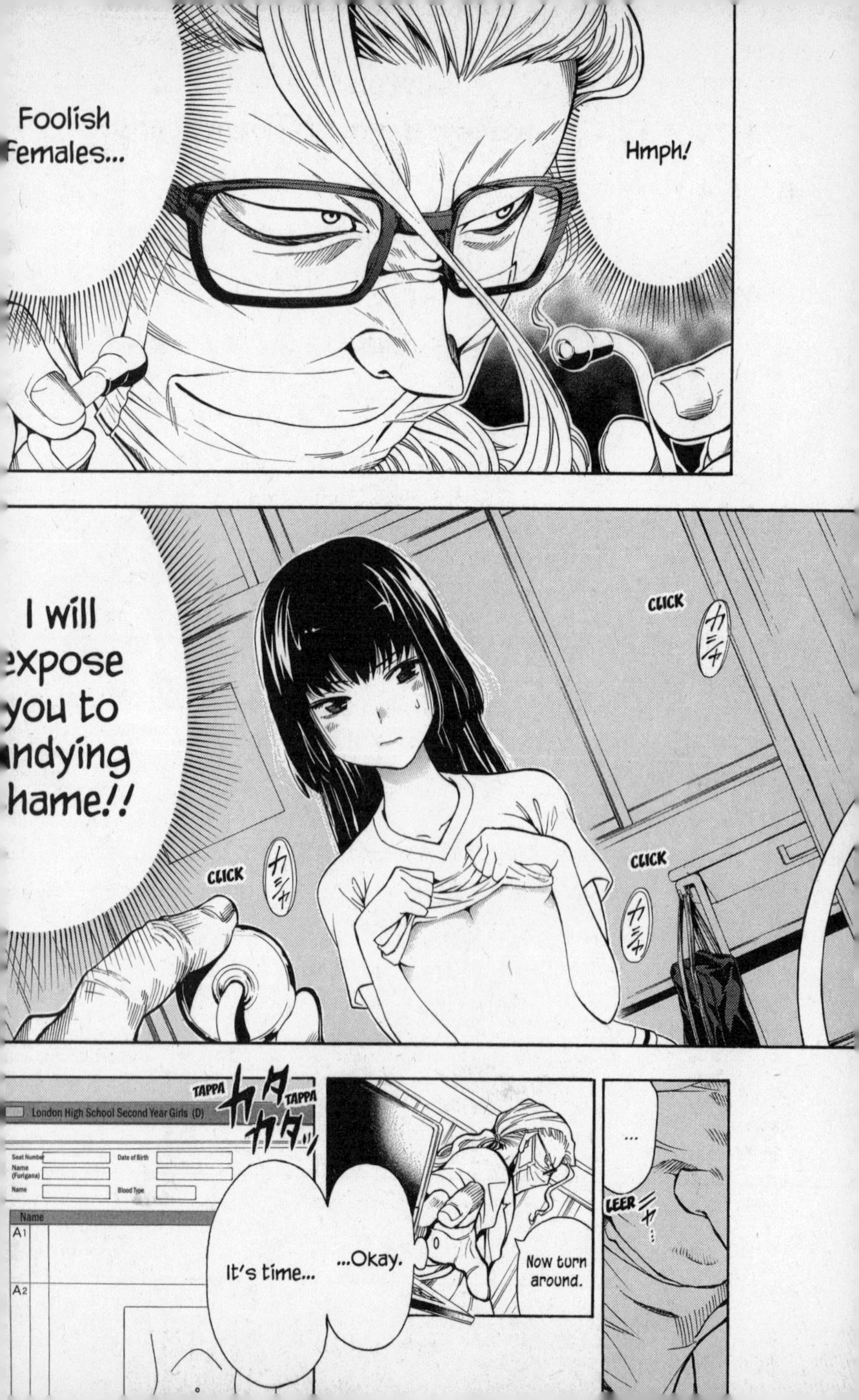
Hmph!
Foolish females...
CLICK
カシャ
I will xpose you to ndying hame!!
CLICK
カシャ
CLICK
カシャ
...
LEER
ニヤ…
Now turn around.
...Okay.
TAPPA
カタ
TAPPA
カタッ
London High School Second Year Girls (D)
Seat Number
Date of Birth
Name (Furigana)
Name
Blood Type
Name
A1
A2
It's time...

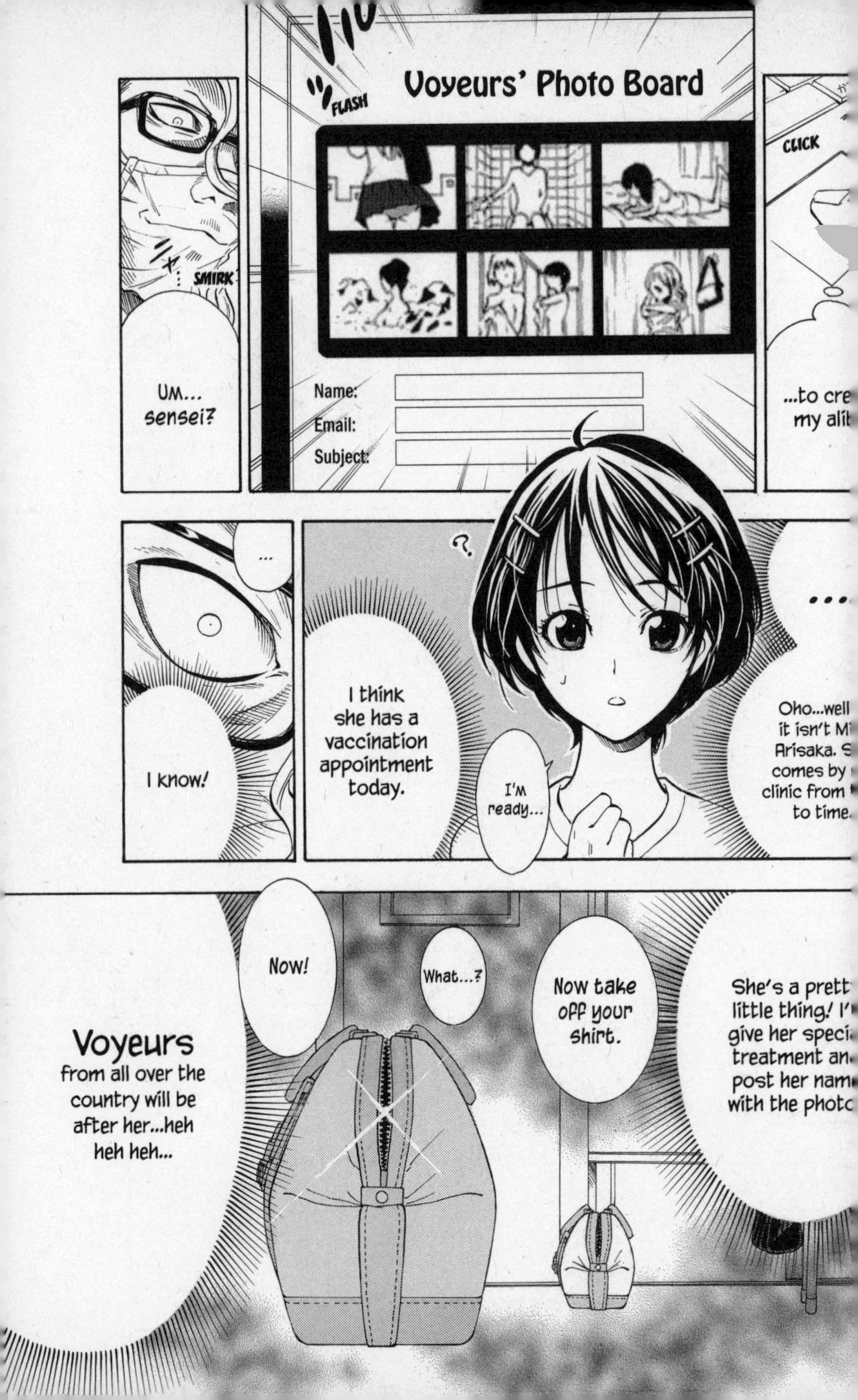

CLICK
...to cre
my alib
FLASH
Voyeurs' Photo Board
Name:
Email:
Subject:
SMIRK
Um... sensei?
...
Oho...well
it isn't Mi
Arisaka. S
comes by
clinic from
to time.
?
I'm ready...
I think she has a vaccination appointment today.
...
I know!
She's a prett
little thing! I'
give her speci
treatment an
post her nam
with the photo
Now take off your shirt.
What...?
Now!
Voyeurs from all over the country will be after her...heh heh heh...

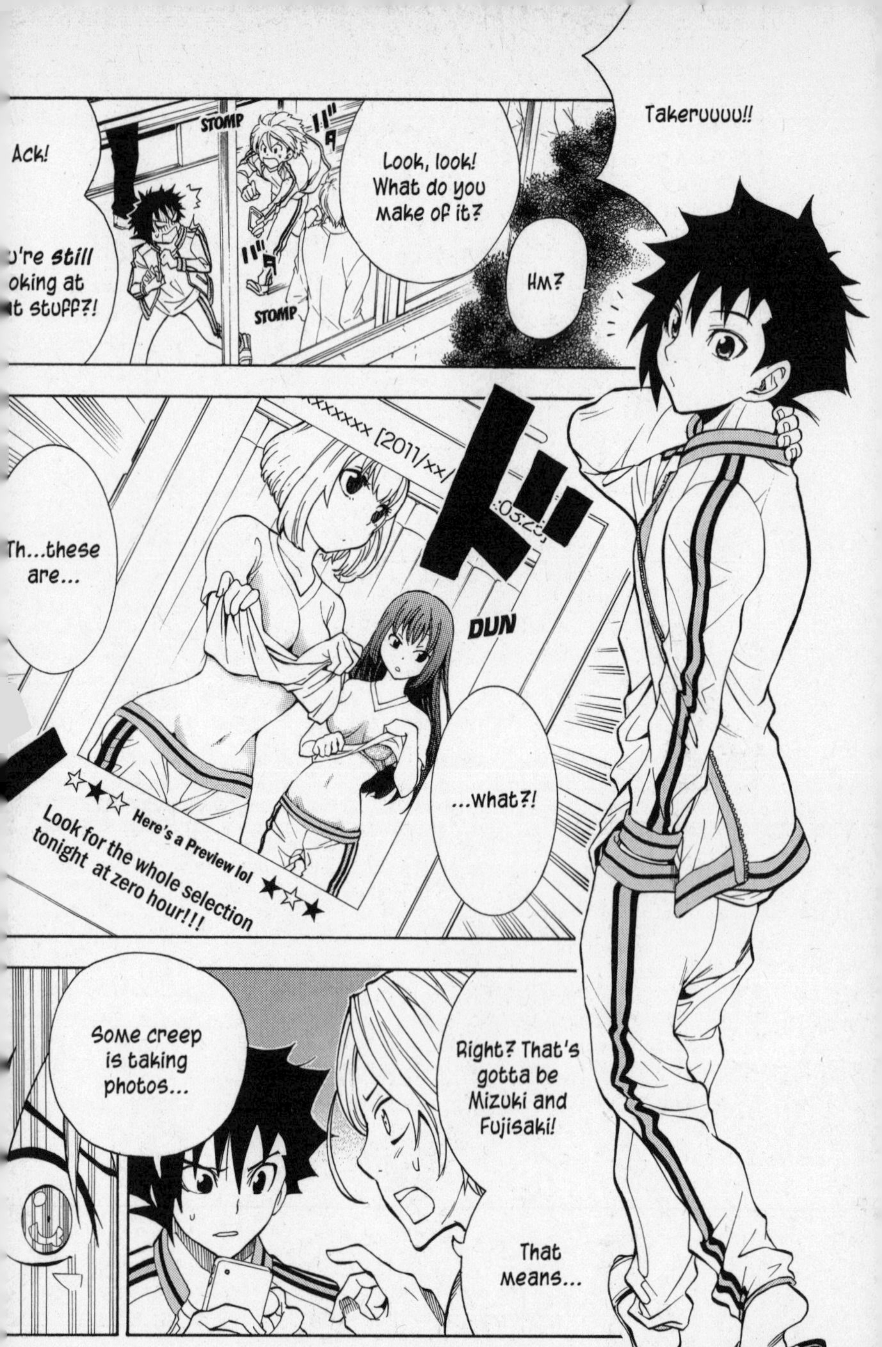

Takeruuuu!!
Hm?
Look, look! What do you make of it?
STOMP
STOMP
Ack!
u're still oking at t stuff?!
DUN
...what?!
xxxxxxx [2011/xx/ :03:25]
Th...these are...
Here's a Preview lol
Look for the whole selection tonight at zero hour!!!
That means...
Right? That's gotta be Mizuki and Fujisaki!
Some creep is taking photos...

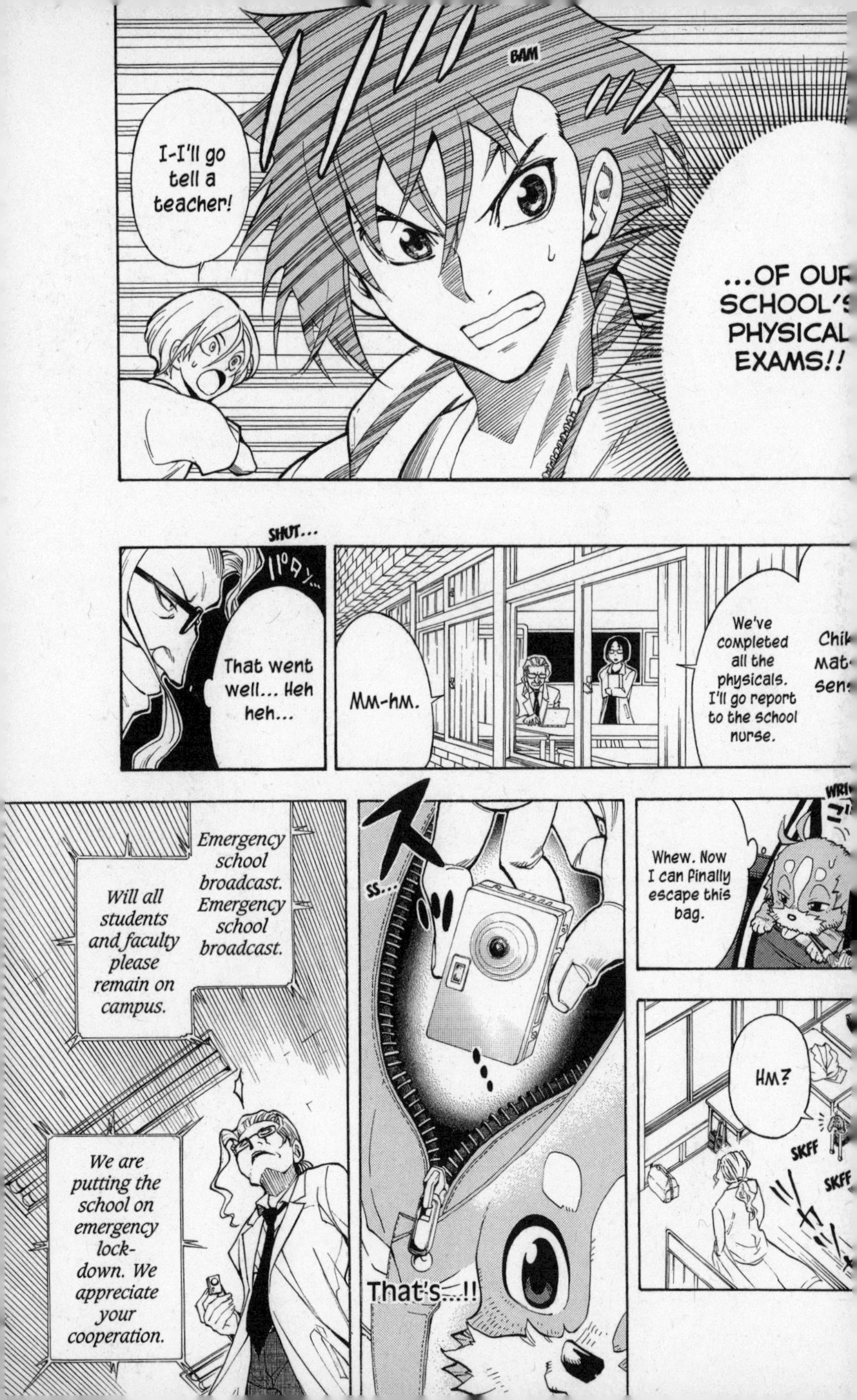
BAM
...OF OUR SCHOOL'S PHYSICAL EXAMS!!
I-I'll go tell a teacher!
We've completed all the physicals. I'll go report to the school nurse.
Mm-hm.
SHUT...
That went well... Heh heh...
Whew. Now I can finally escape this bag.
HM?
SKFF
SKFF
SS...
That's...!!
Emergency school broadcast. Emergency school broadcast.
Will all students and faculty please remain on campus.
We are putting the school on emergency lock-down. We appreciate your cooperation.

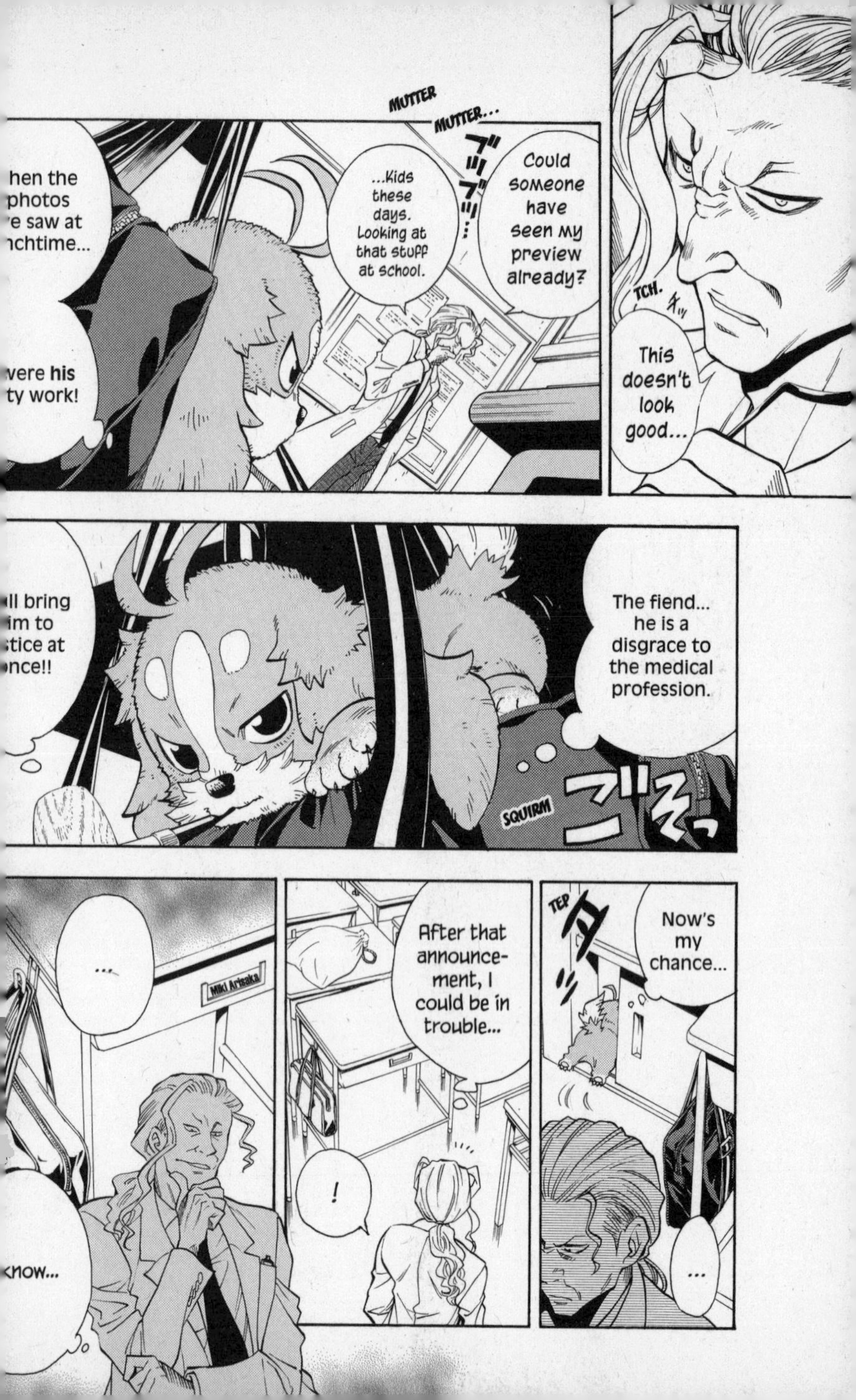
TCH.
This doesn't look good...
MUTTER
MUTTER...
ブツブツ...
Could someone have seen my preview already?
...Kids these days. Looking at that stuff at school.
hen the photos
e saw at
nchtime...
vere his
ty work!
The fiend... he is a disgrace to the medical profession.
SQUIRM
ll bring
im to
stice at
nce!!
TEP
Now's my chance...
...
After that announcement, I could be in trouble...
!
...
Miki Arisaka
know...

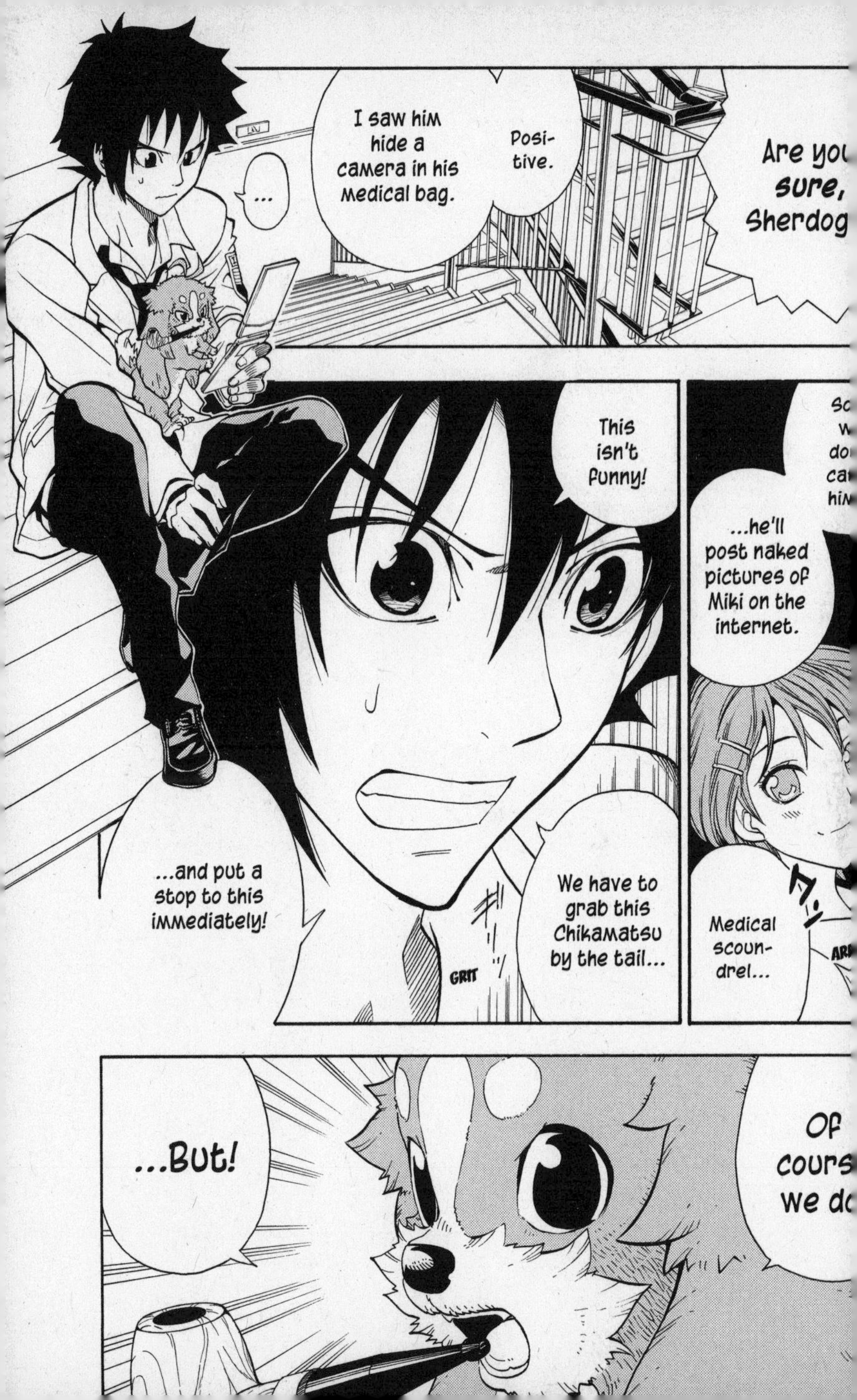

Are you sure, Sherdog
Positive.
I saw him hide a camera in his medical bag.
...
...he'll post naked pictures of Miki on the internet.
Medical scoundrel...
This isn't funny!
We have to grab this Chikamatsu by the tail...
GRIT
...and put a stop to this immediately!
Of
...But!

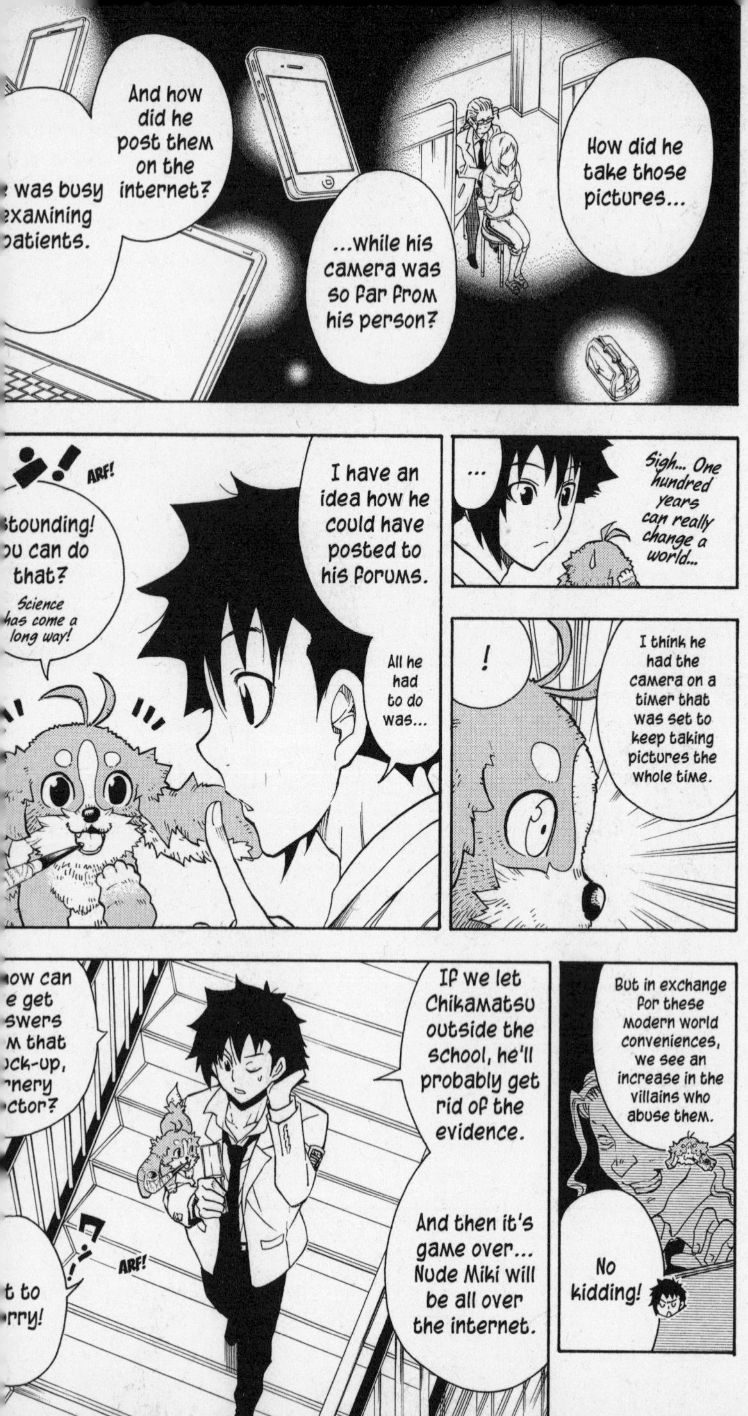
How did he take those pictures...
...while his camera was so far from his person?
And how did he post them on the internet?
e was busy xamining atients.
...
Sigh... One hundred years can really change a world...
!
I think he had the camera on a timer that was set to keep taking pictures the whole time.
I have an idea how he could have posted to his forums.
All he had to do was...
ARF!
stounding! ou can do that?
Science has come a long way!
But in exchange for these modern world conveniences, we see an increase in the villains who abuse them.
No kidding!
If we let Chikamatsu outside the school, he'll probably get rid of the evidence.
And then it's game over... Nude Miki will be all over the internet.
ow can e get swers M that ock-up, rnery ctor?
ARF!
t to rry!

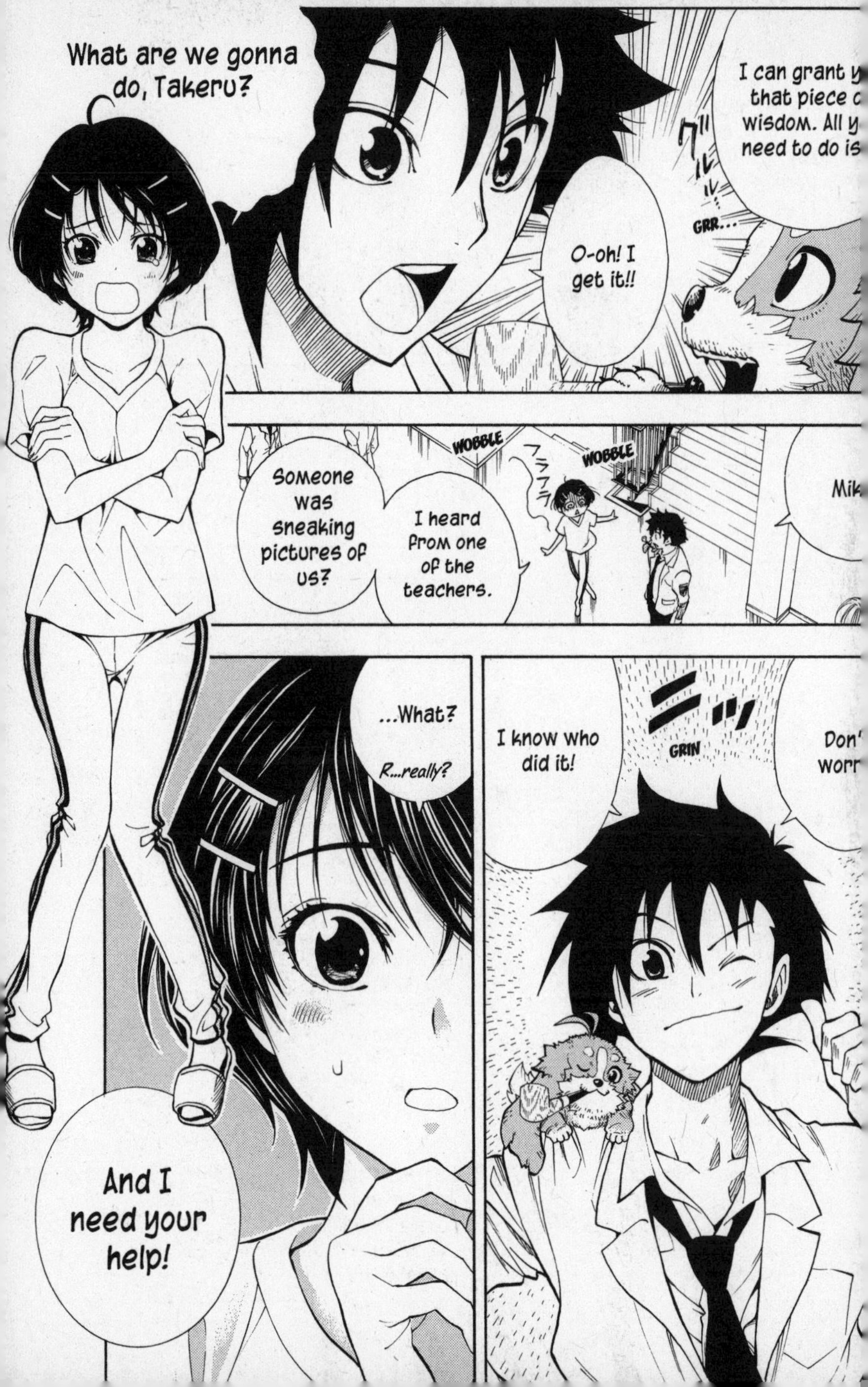
I can grant y
that piece c
wisdom. All y
need to do is
GRR...
O-oh! I get it!!
Mik
WOBBLE
WOBBLE
I heard from one of the teachers.
Someone was sneaking pictures of us?
Don'
worr
GRIN
I know who did it!
...What?
R...really?
What are we gonna do, Takeru?
And I need your help!

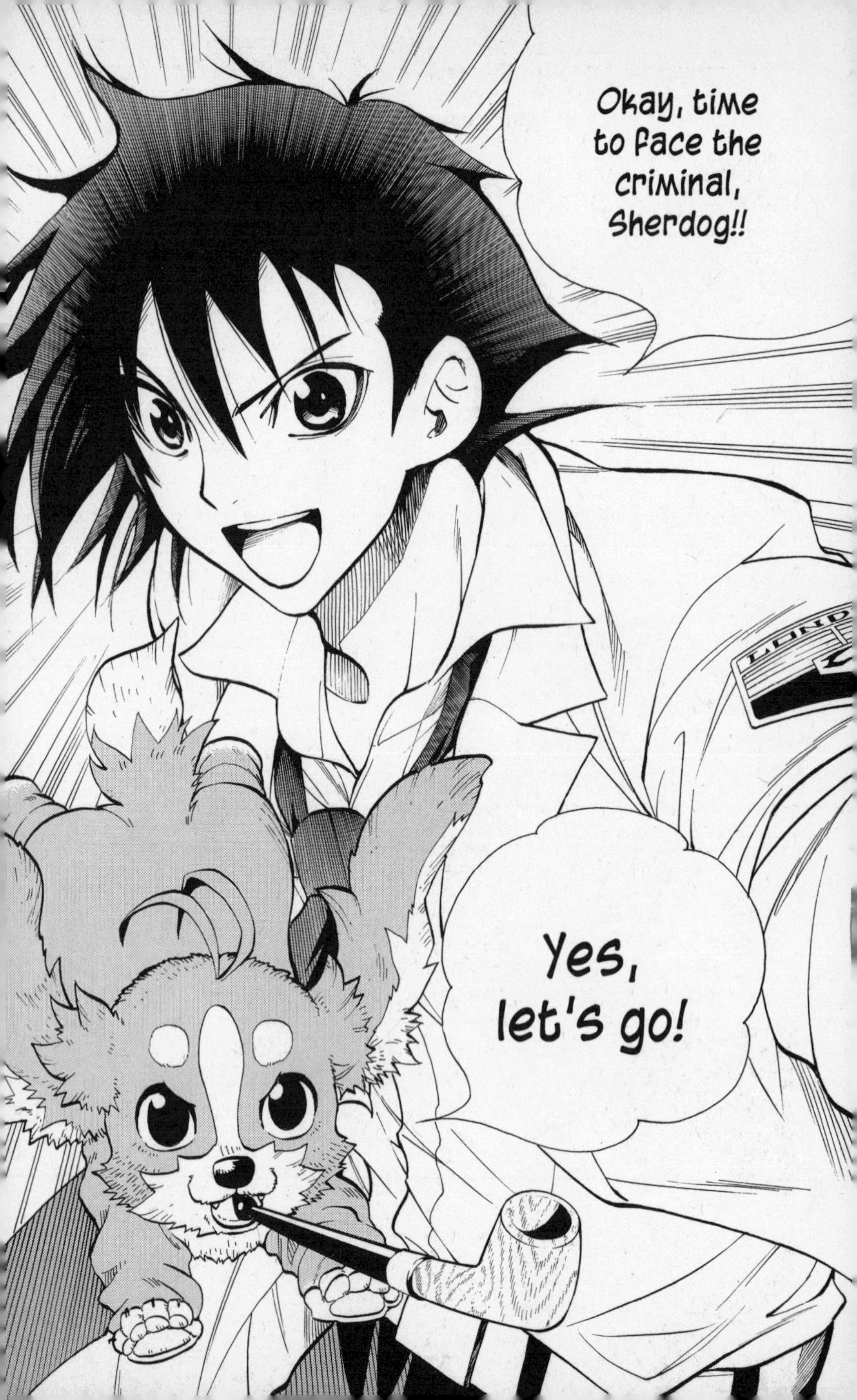
Okay, time to face the criminal, Sherdog!!
Yes, let's go!

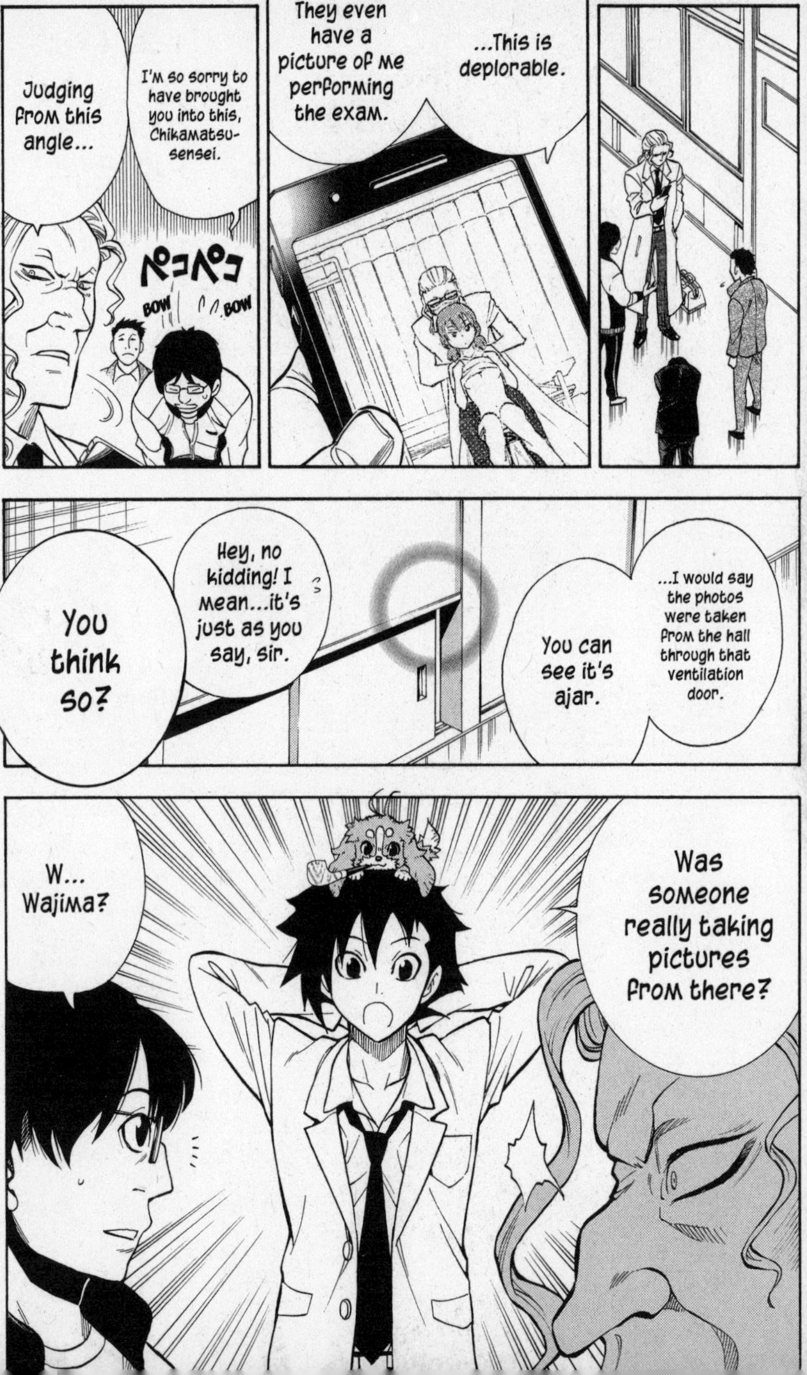
...This is deplorable.
They even have a picture of me performing the exam.
I'm so sorry to have brought you into this, Chikamatsu-sensei.
Judging from this angle...
ペコペコ
BOW
BOW
...I would say the photos were taken from the hall through that ventilation door.
You can see it's ajar.
Hey, no kidding! I mean...it's just as you say, sir.
You think so?
Was someone really taking pictures from there?
W... Wajima?

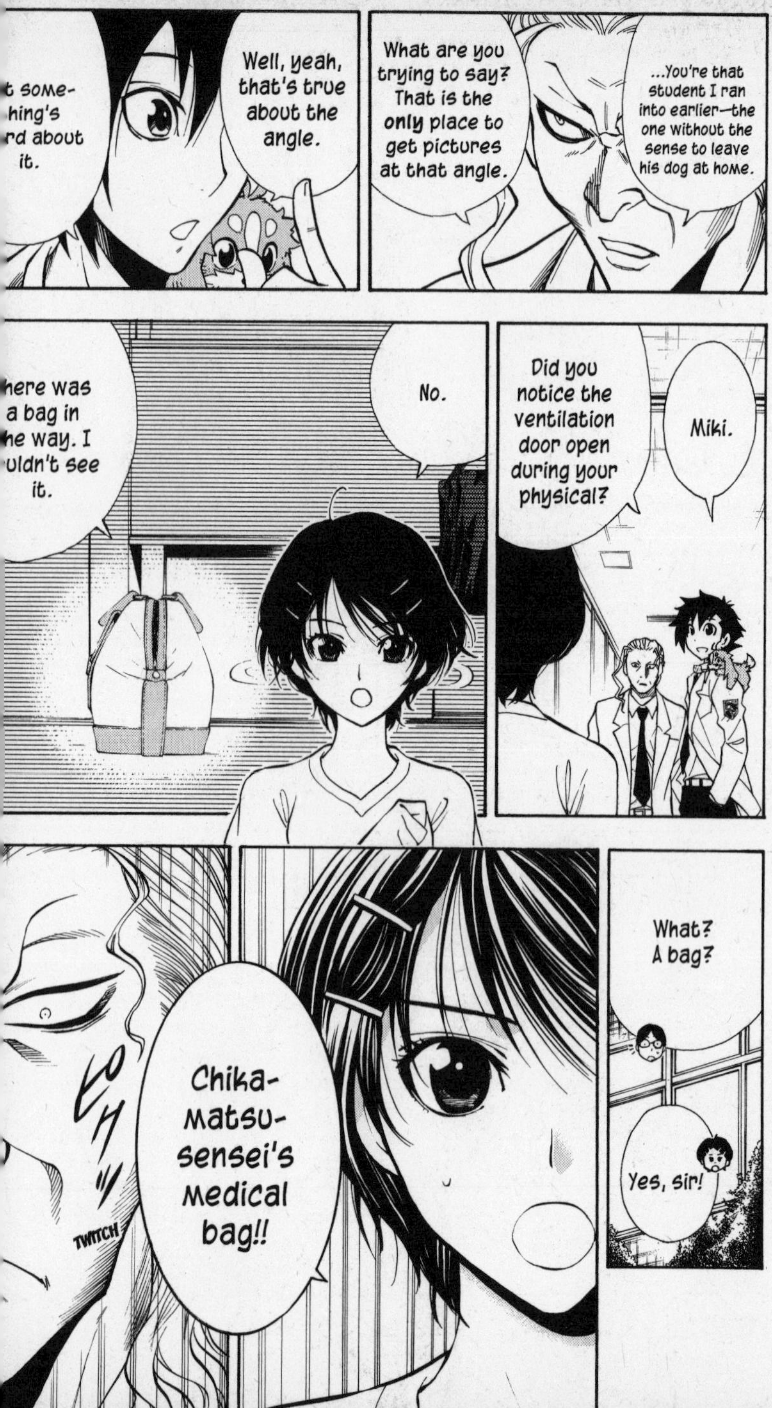
...You're that student I ran into earlier—the one without the sense to leave his dog at home.
What are you trying to say? That is the only place to get pictures at that angle.
Well, yeah, that's true about the angle.
t some- hing's rd about it.
Miki.
Did you notice the ventilation door open during your physical?
No.
here was a bag in he way. I uldn't see it.
What? A bag?
Yes, sir!
Chika-matsu-sensei's medical bag!!
TWITCH

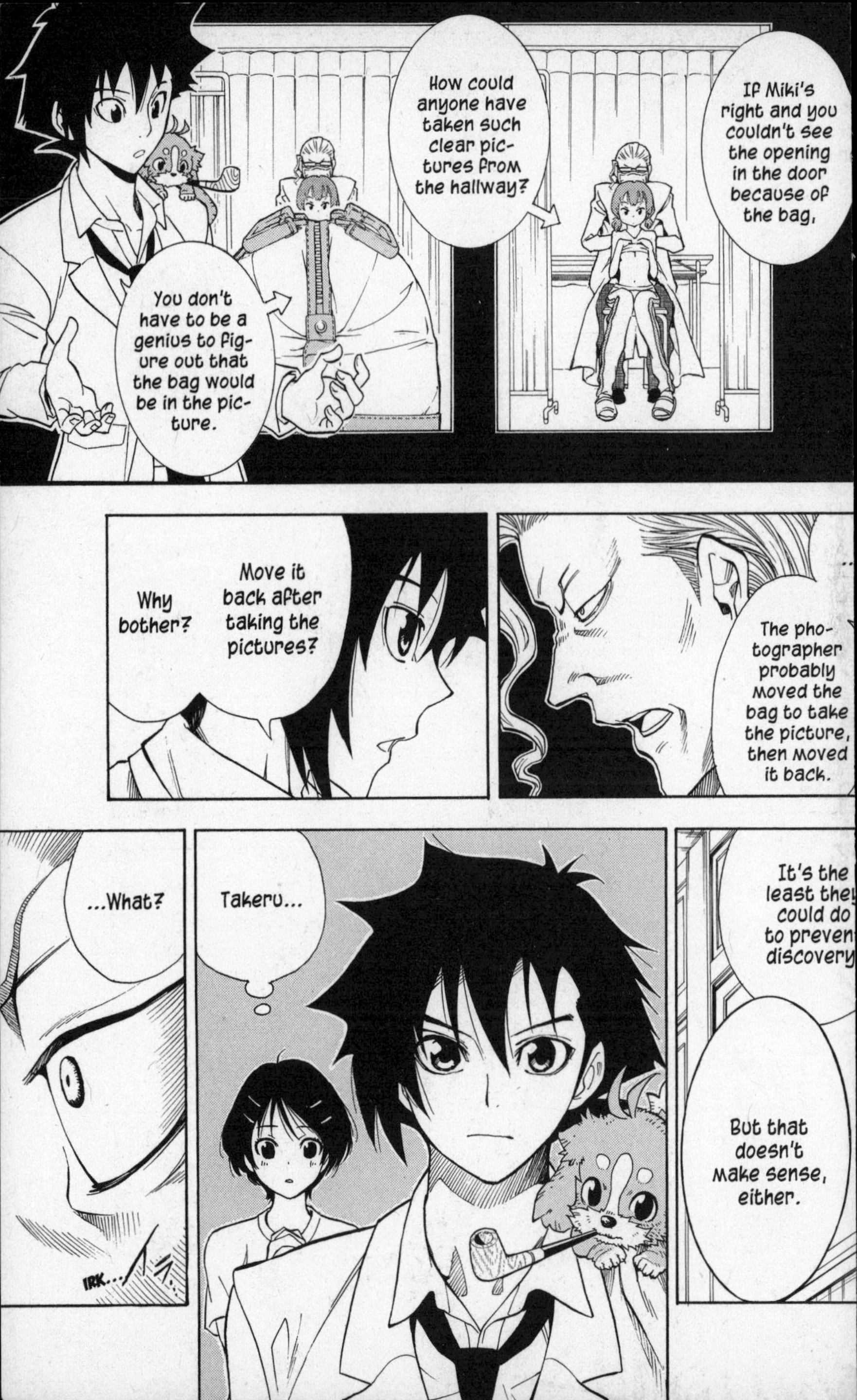

If Miki's right and you couldn't see the opening in the door because of the bag,
How could anyone have taken such clear pictures from the hallway?
You don't have to be a genius to figure out that the bag would be in the picture.
...
The photographer probably moved the bag to take the picture, then moved it back.
Move it back after taking the pictures?
Why bother?
It's the least the could do to preven discovery
But that doesn't make sense, either.
Takeru...
...What?
IRK...

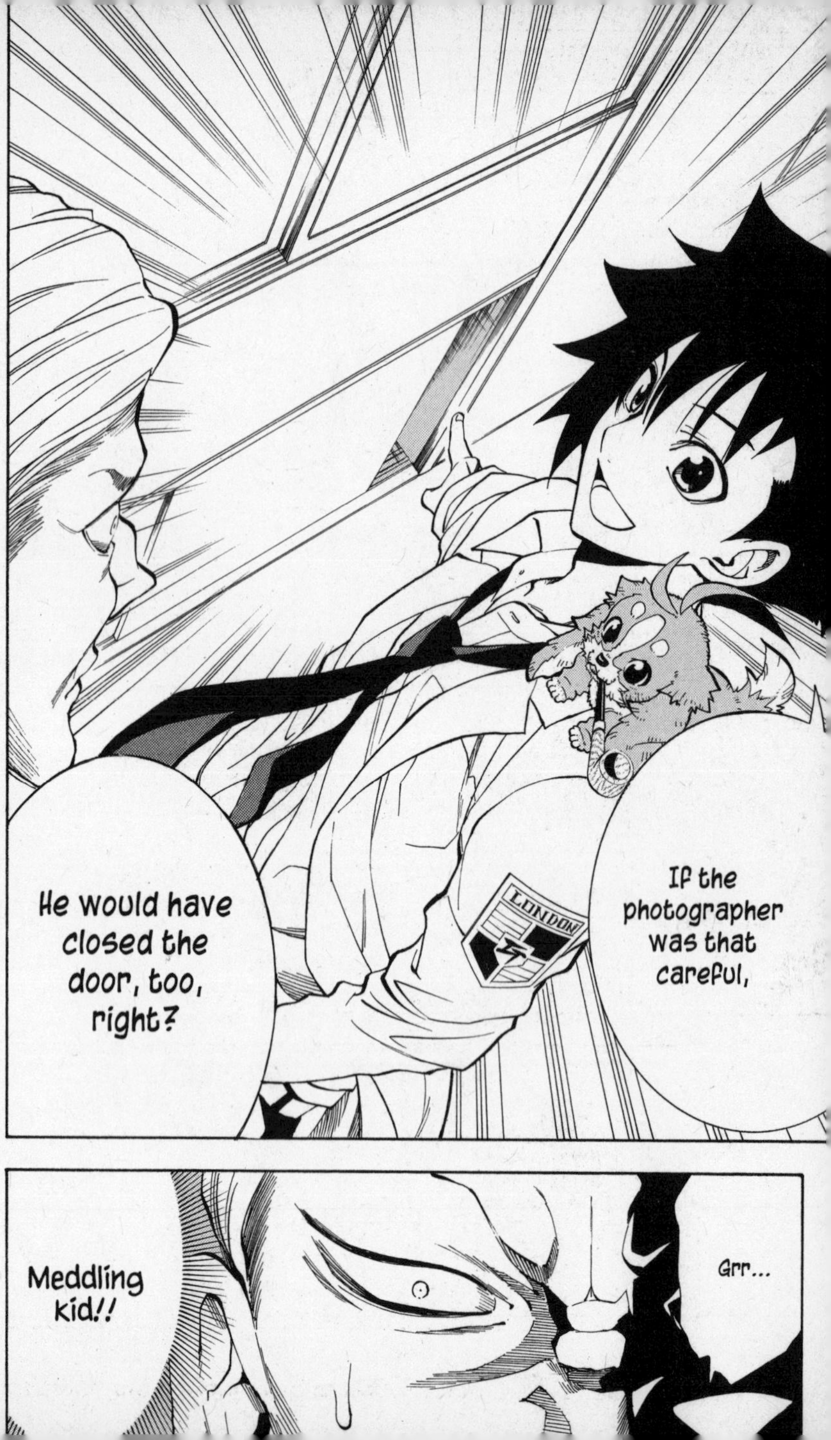
If the photographer was that careful,
He would have closed the door, too, right?
Grr...
Meddling kid!!

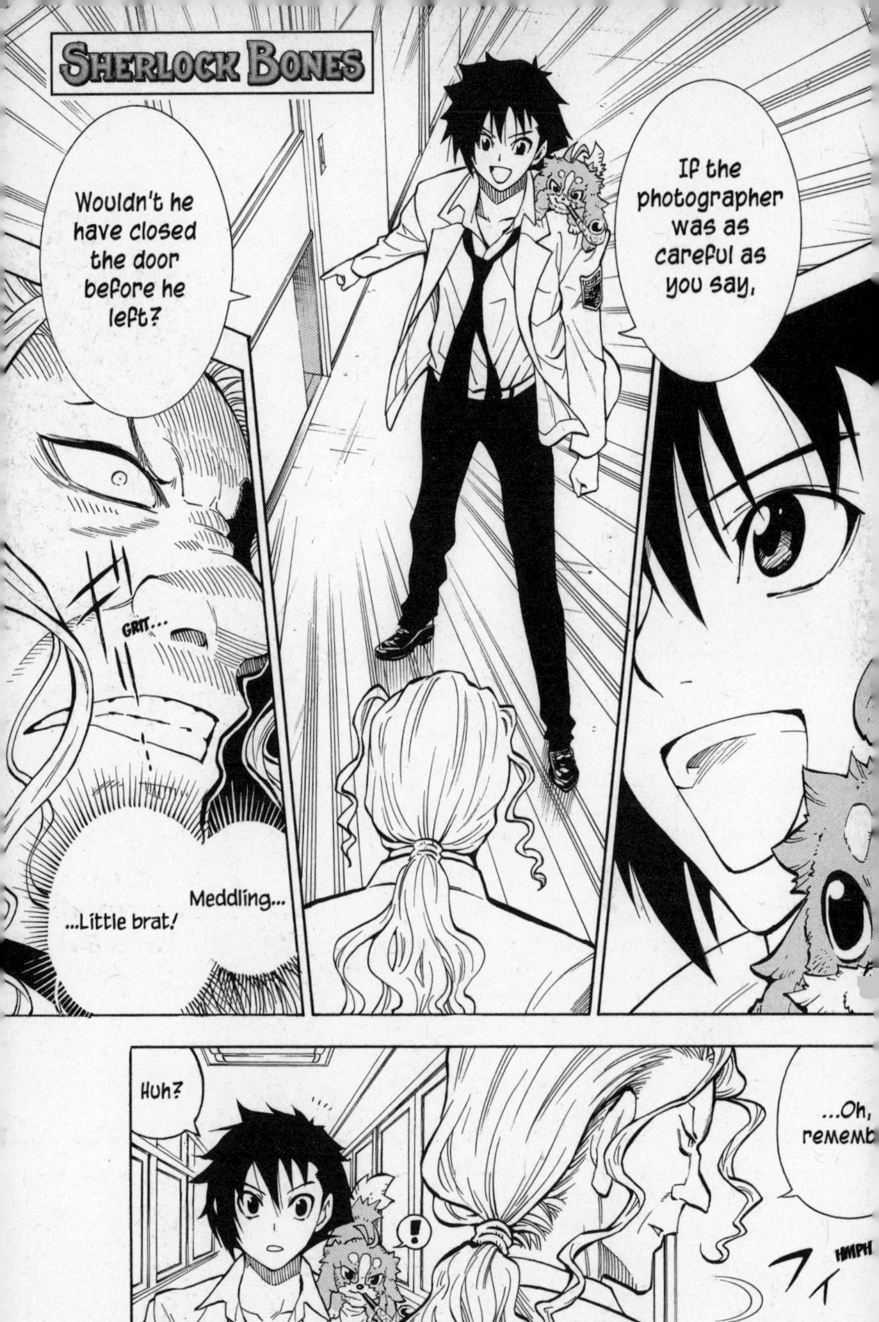
If the photographer was as careful as you say,
Wouldn't he have closed the door before he left?
GRIT...
Meddling...
...Little brat!
...Oh, rememb
HMPH
!
Huh?

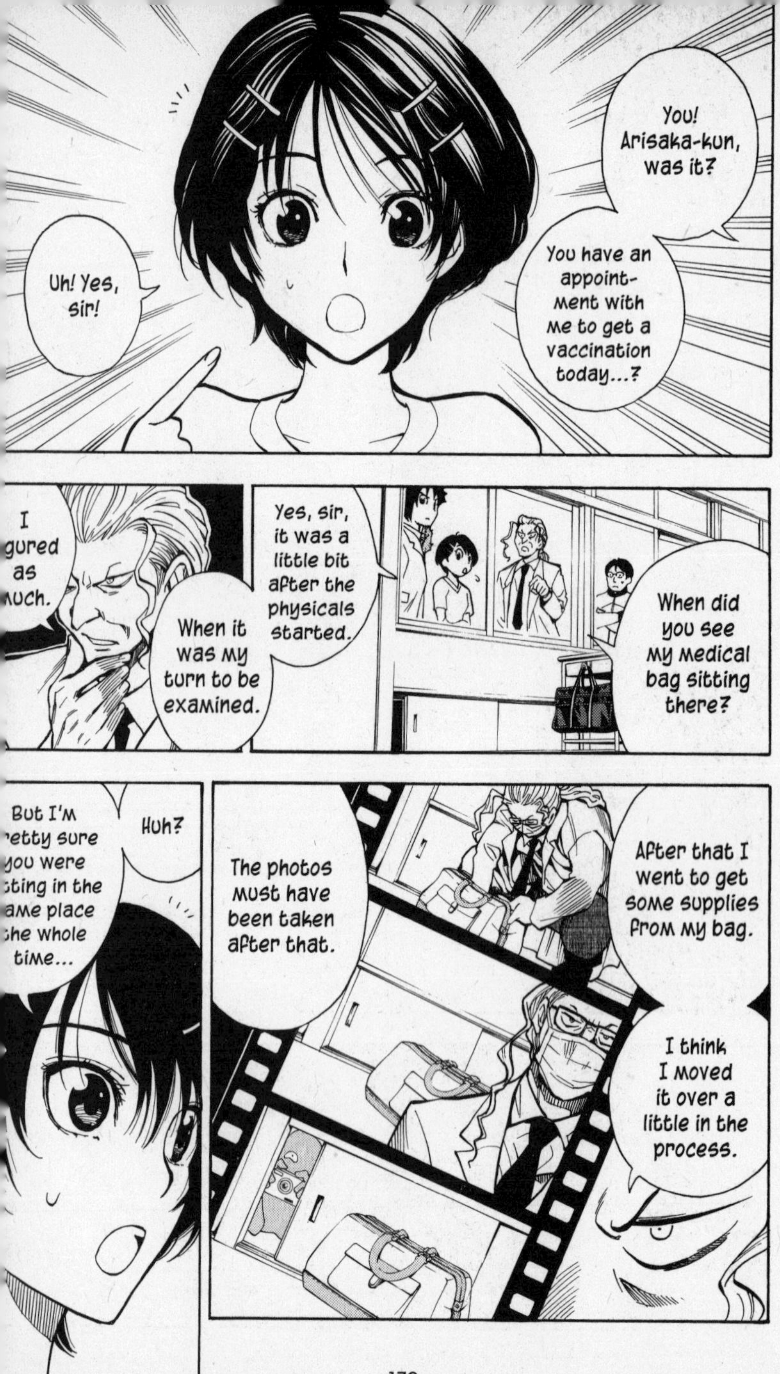
You! Arisaka-kun, was it?
You have an appoint-ment with me to get a vaccination today...?
Uh! Yes, sir!
When did you see my medical bag sitting there?
Yes, sir, it was a little bit after the physicals started.
When it was my turn to be examined.
I gured as uch.
After that I went to get some supplies from my bag.
I think I moved it over a little in the process.
The photos must have been taken after that.
Huh?
But I'm retty sure you were tting in the ame place he whole time...

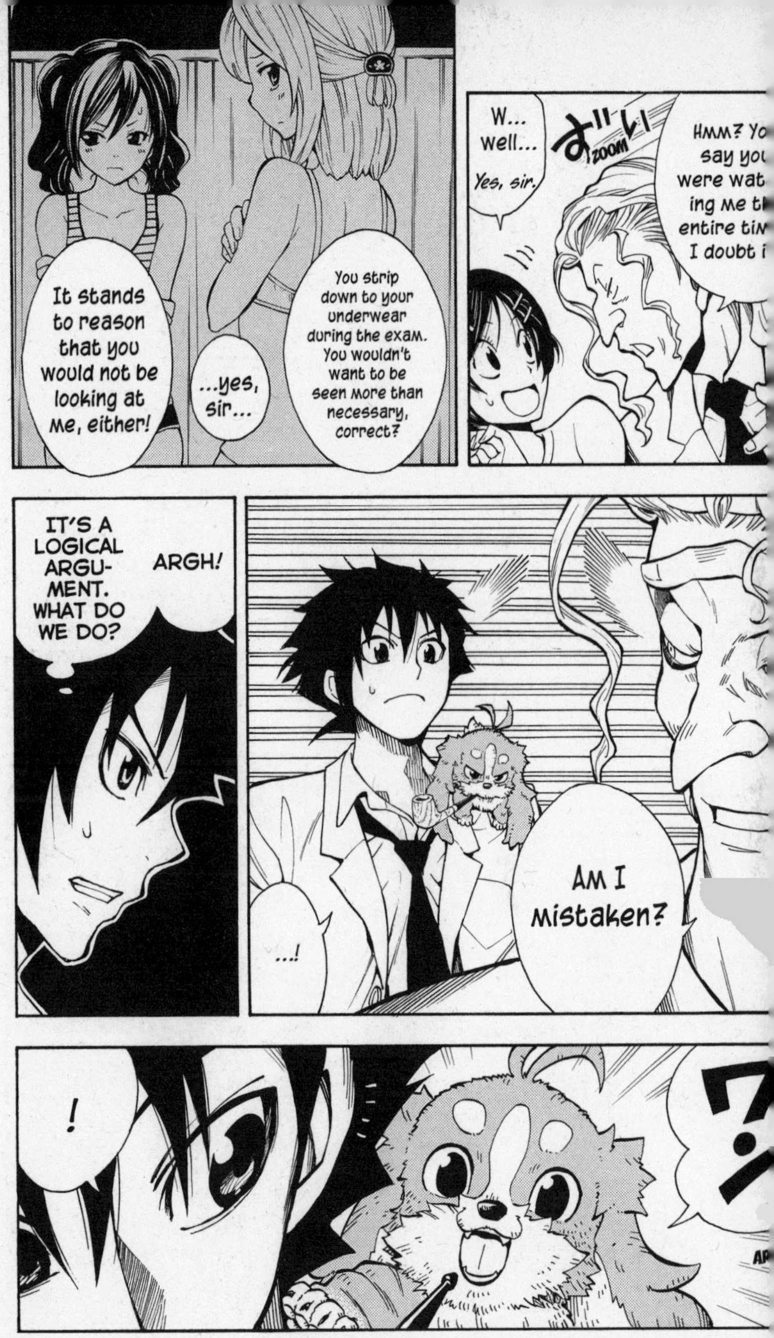
HMM? Yo say you were wat ing me t entire tim I doubt i
ZOOM
W... well... Yes, sir.
You strip down to your underwear during the exam. You wouldn't want to be seen more than necessary, correct?
...yes, sir...
It stands to reason that you would not be looking at me, either!
Am I mistaken?
...!
IT'S A LOGICAL ARGUMENT. WHAT DO WE DO?
ARGH!
?!
!

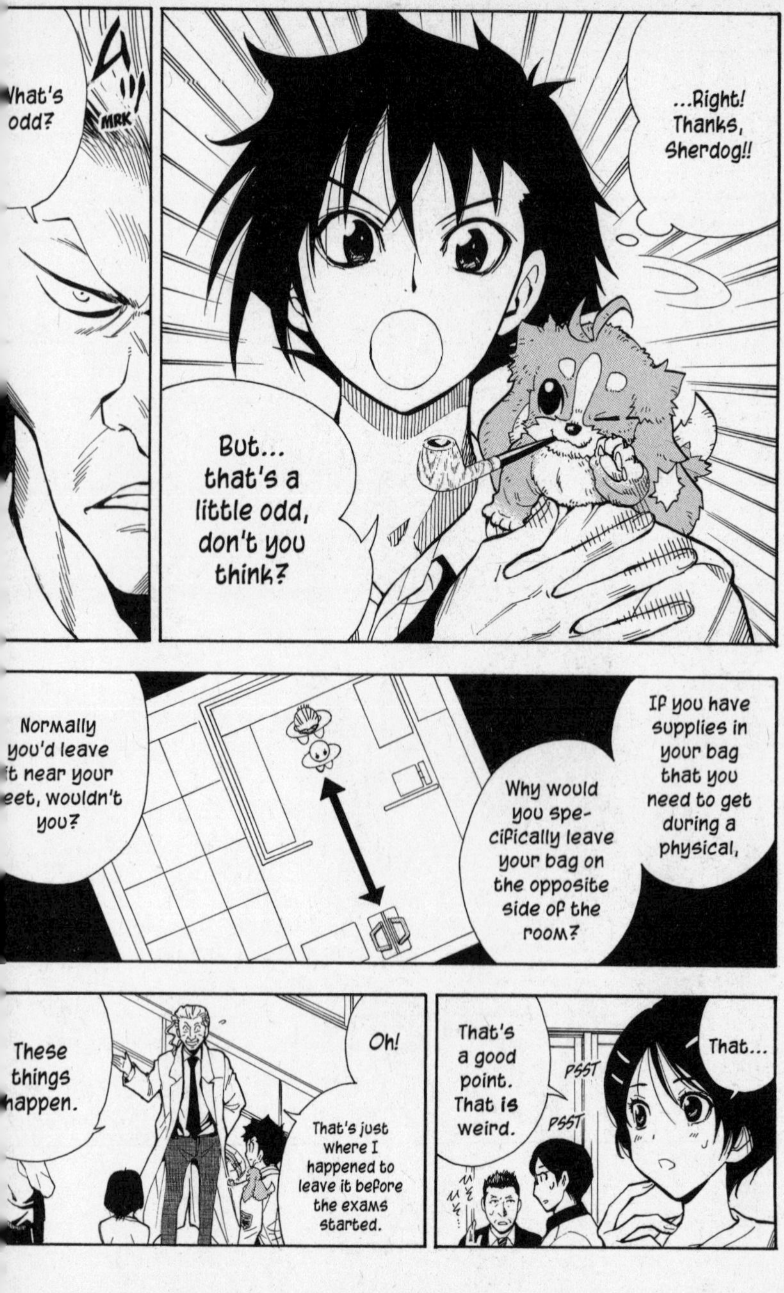

...Right! Thanks, Sherdog!!
But... that's a little odd, don't you think?
Vhat's odd?
MRK
If you have supplies in your bag that you need to get during a physical,
Why would you spe-cifically leave your bag on the opposite side of the room?
Normally you'd leave t near your eet, wouldn't you?
That...
That's a good point. That is weird.
PSST
PSST
Oh!
That's just where I happened to leave it before the exams started.
These things happen.

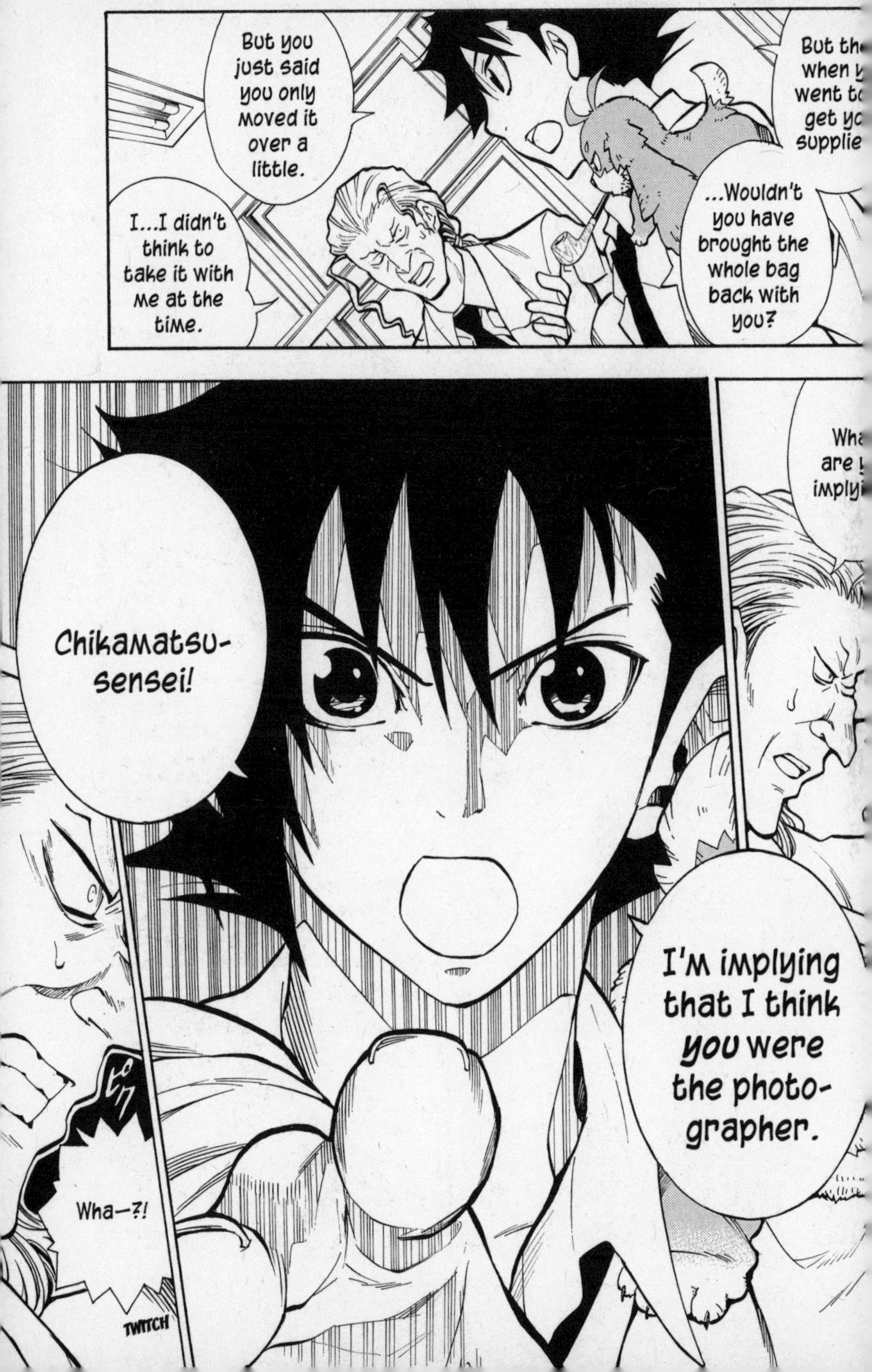
But th when y went t get yo supplie
...Wouldn't you have brought the whole bag back with you?
But you just said you only moved it over a little.
I...I didn't think to take it with me at the time.
Wha are y implyi
I'm implying that I think *you* were the photo-grapher.
Chikamatsu-sensei!
Wha—?!
TWITCH

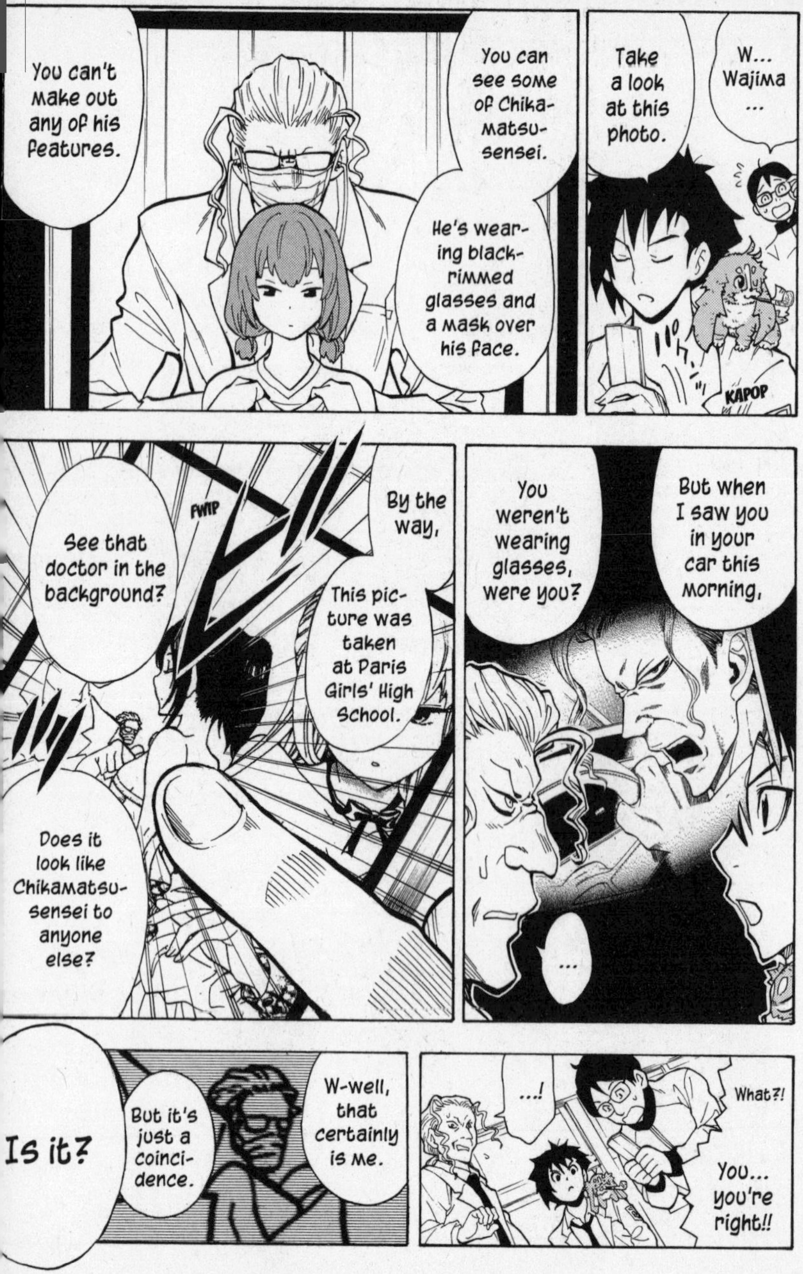
W... Wajima ...
Take a look at this photo.
KAPOP
You can see some of Chika-matsu-sensei.
He's wear-ing black-rimmed glasses and a mask over his face.
You can't make out any of his features.
But when I saw you in your car this morning,
You weren't wearing glasses, were you?
...
By the way,
This pic-ture was taken at Paris Girls' High School.
FWIP
See that doctor in the background?
Does it look like Chikamatsu-sensei to anyone else?
What?!
...!
You... you're right!!
W-well, that certainly is me.
But it's just a coinci-dence.
Is it?

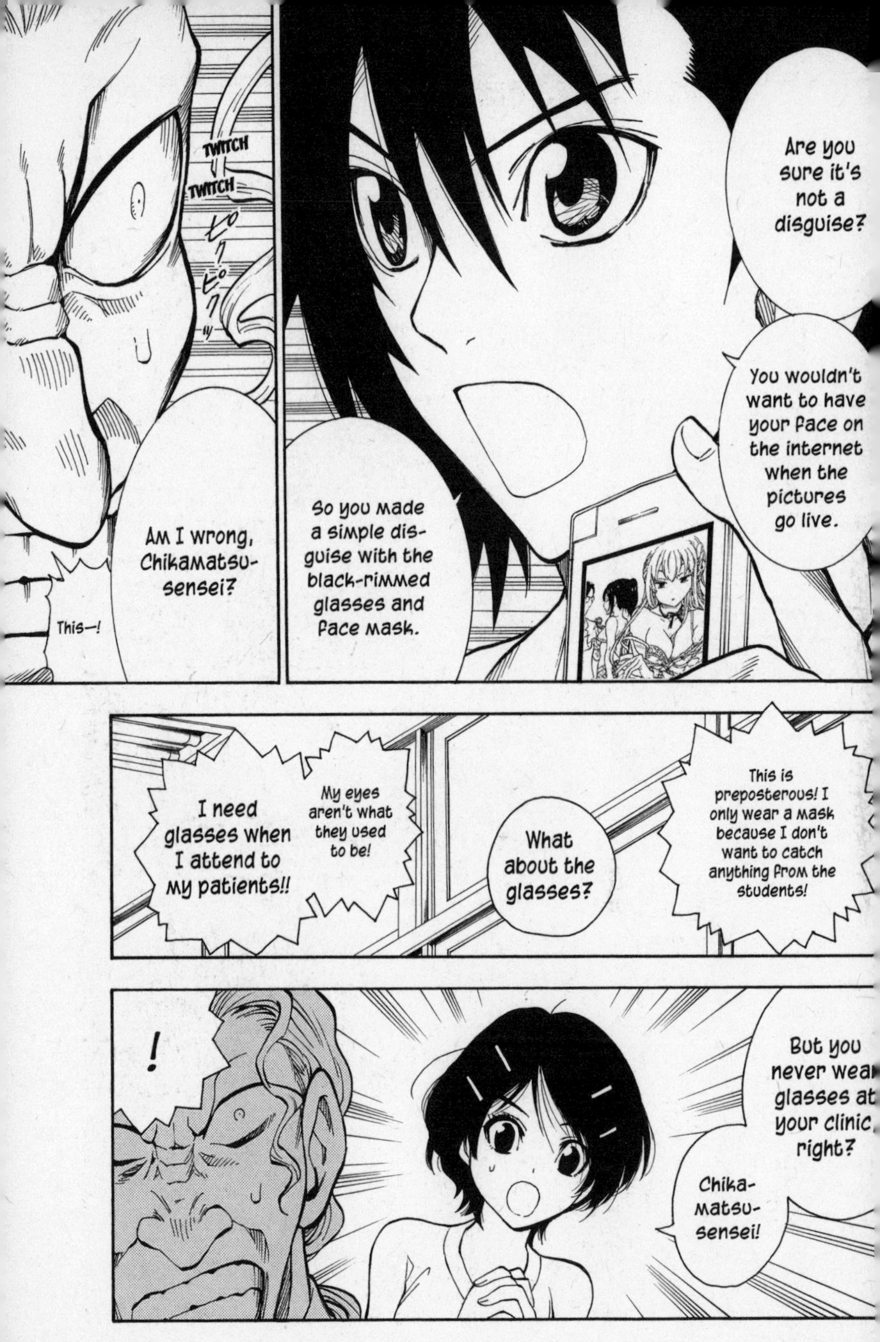
Are you sure it's not a disguise?
You wouldn't want to have your face on the internet when the pictures go live.
So you made a simple disguise with the black-rimmed glasses and face mask.
Am I wrong, Chikamatsu-sensei?
TWITCH
TWITCH
This—!
This is preposterous! I only wear a mask because I don't want to catch anything from the students!
What about the glasses?
My eyes aren't what they used to be!
I need glasses when I attend to my patients!!
But you never wear glasses at your clinic, right?
Chika-matsu-sensei!
!

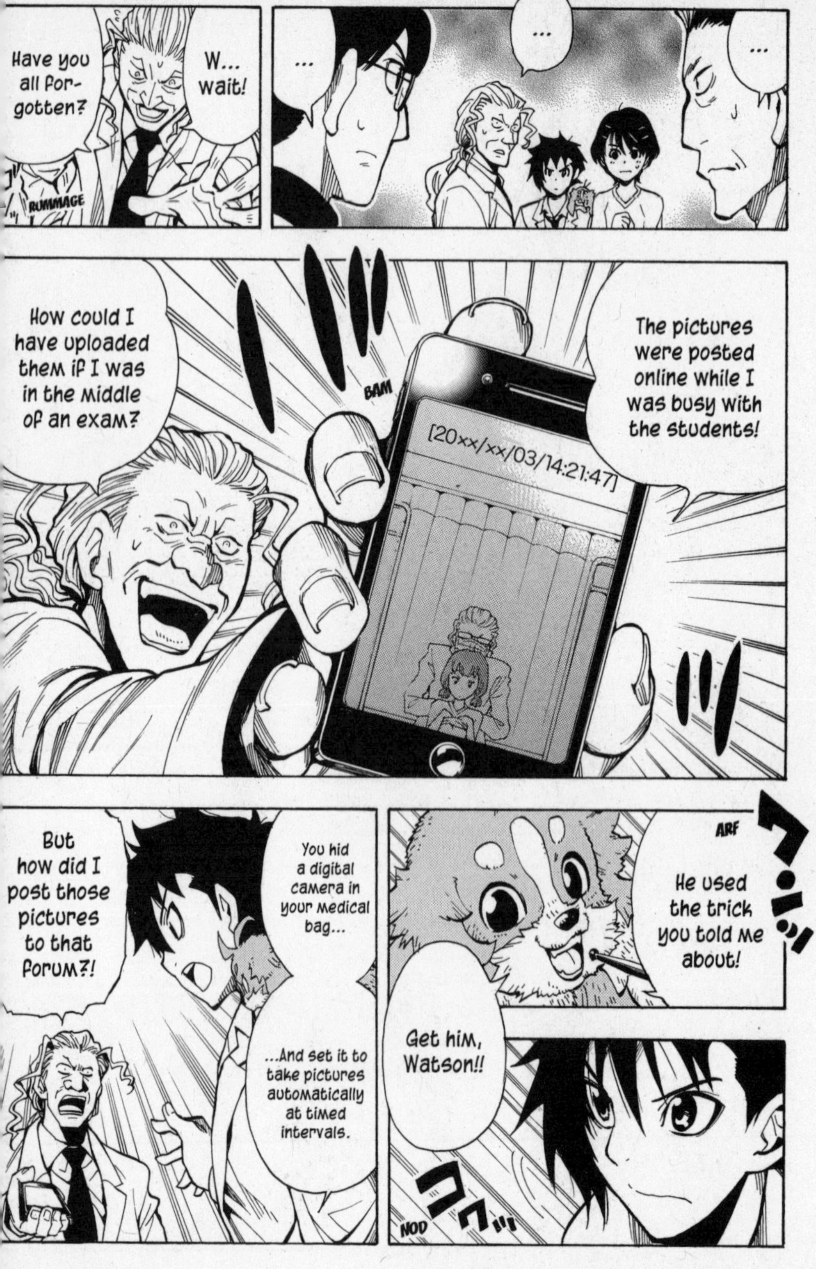
...
...
...
W... wait!
Have you all forgotten?
RUMMAGE
The pictures were posted online while I was busy with the students!
BAM
[20xx/xx/03/14:21:47]
How could I have uploaded them if I was in the middle of an exam?
ARF
He used the trick you told me about!
Get him, Watson!!
NOD
You hid a digital camera in your medical bag...
But how did I post those pictures to that forum?!
...And set it to take pictures automatically at timed intervals.

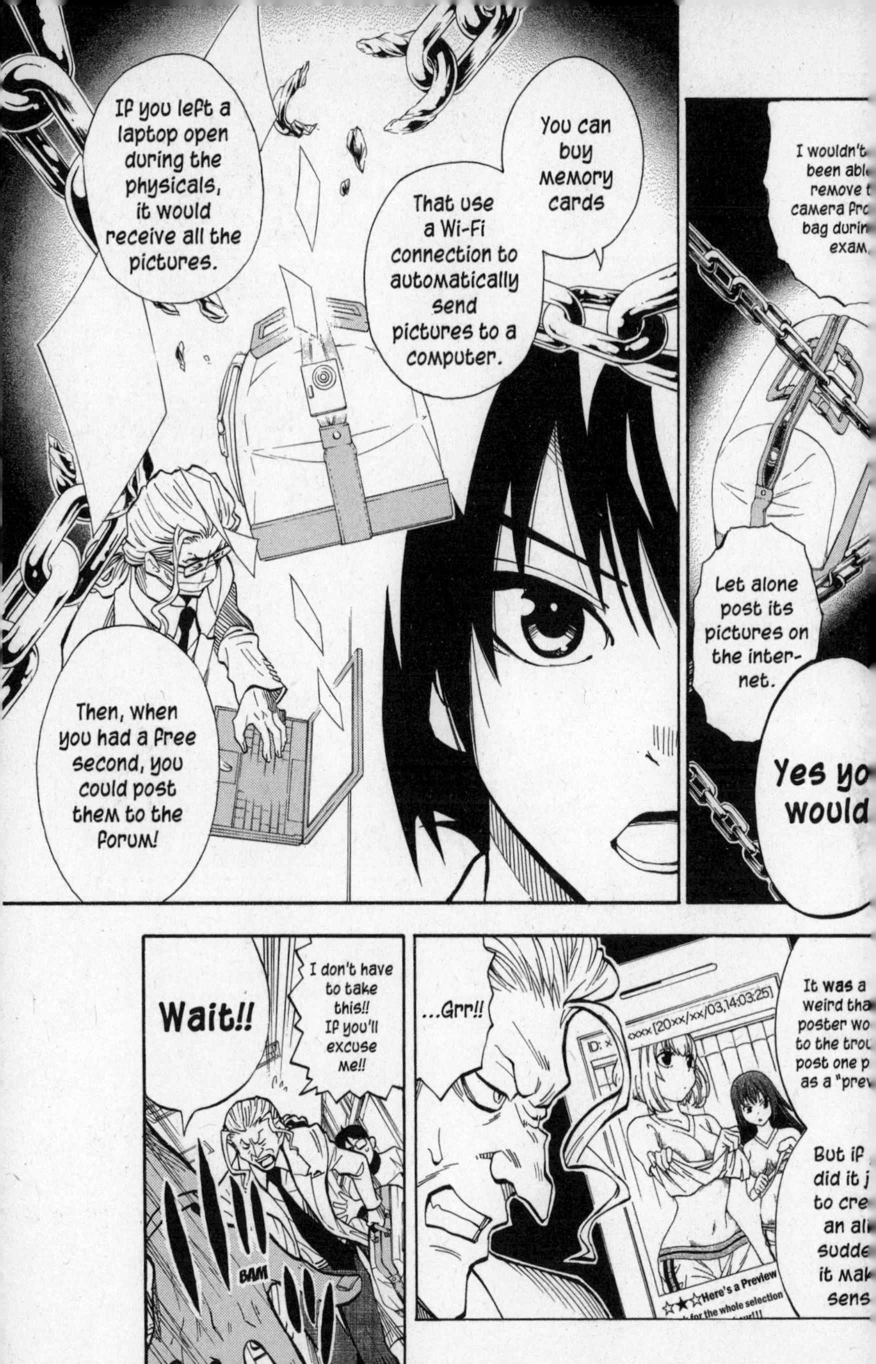
I wouldn't been abl remove t camera fro bag durin exam.
Let alone post its pictures on the inter-net.
Yes yo would
You can buy memory cards
That use a Wi-Fi connection to automatically send pictures to a computer.
If you left a laptop open during the physicals, it would receive all the pictures.
Then, when you had a free second, you could post them to the forum!
It was a weird tha poster wo to the trou post one p as a "prev
But if did it j to cre an al sudde it mak sens
xxxx [20xx/xx/03,14:03:25]
ID: x
☆★☆Here's a Preview
for the whole selection
...Grr!!
I don't have to take this!! If you'll excuse me!!
Wait!!
BAM

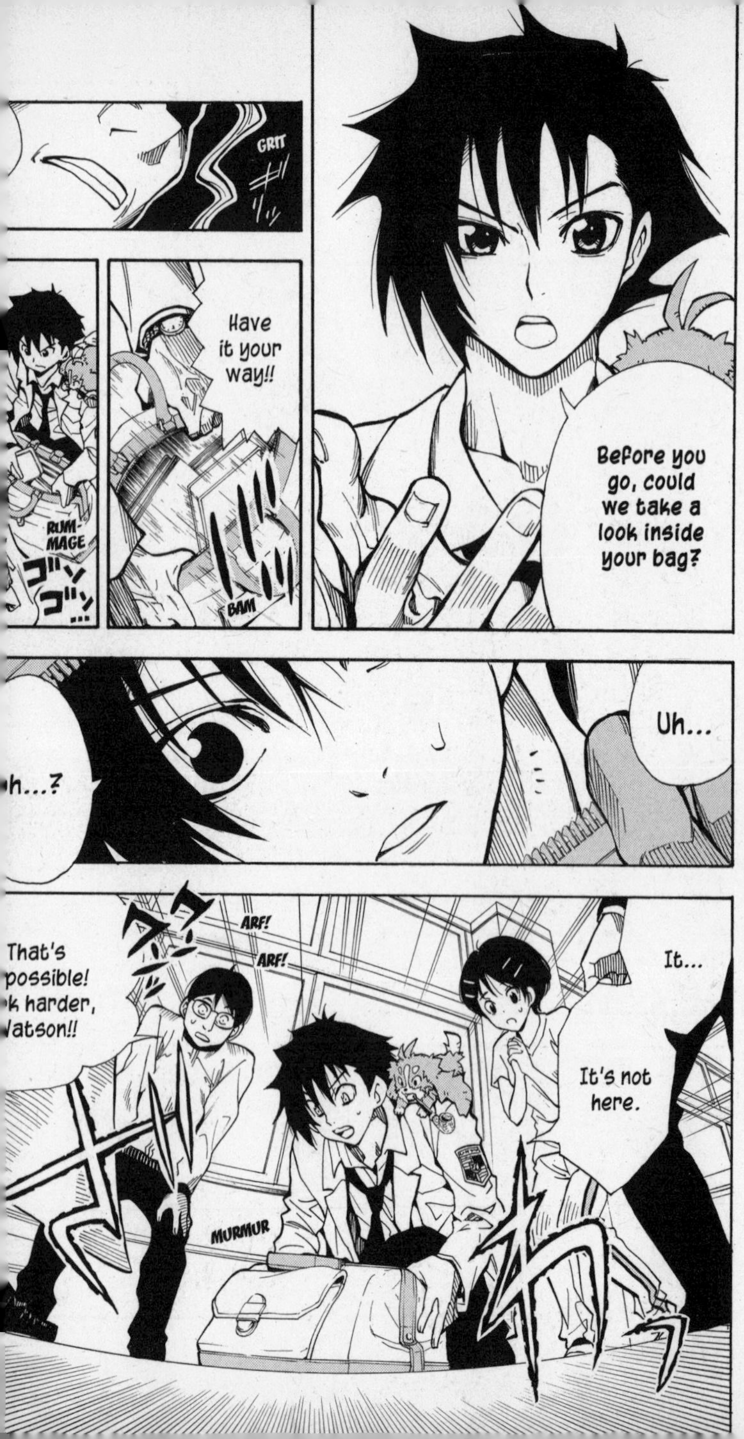
Before you go, could we take a look inside your bag?
GRIT
ギリッ
Have it your way!!
BAM
RUM-MAGE
ゴソゴソ...
Uh...
h...?
It...
It's not here.
ARF!
ARF!
That's possible! k harder, Watson!!
MURMUR

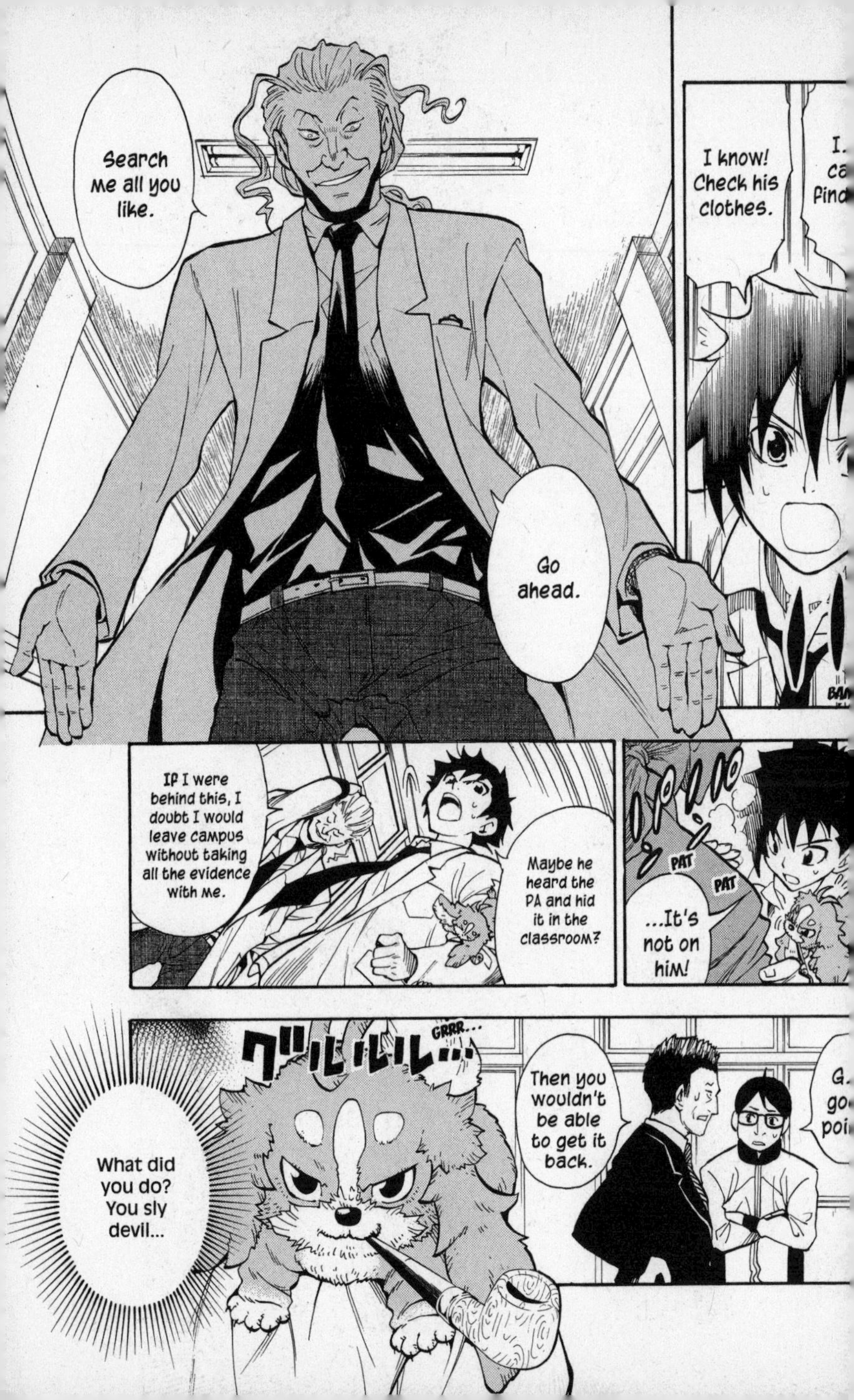
I. ca find
I know! Check his clothes.
Search me all you like.
Go ahead.
PAT
PAT
...It's not on him!
Maybe he heard the PA and hid it in the classroom?
If I were behind this, I doubt I would leave campus without taking all the evidence with me.
G. go poi
Then you wouldn't be able to get it back.
GRRR...
What did you do? You sly devil...

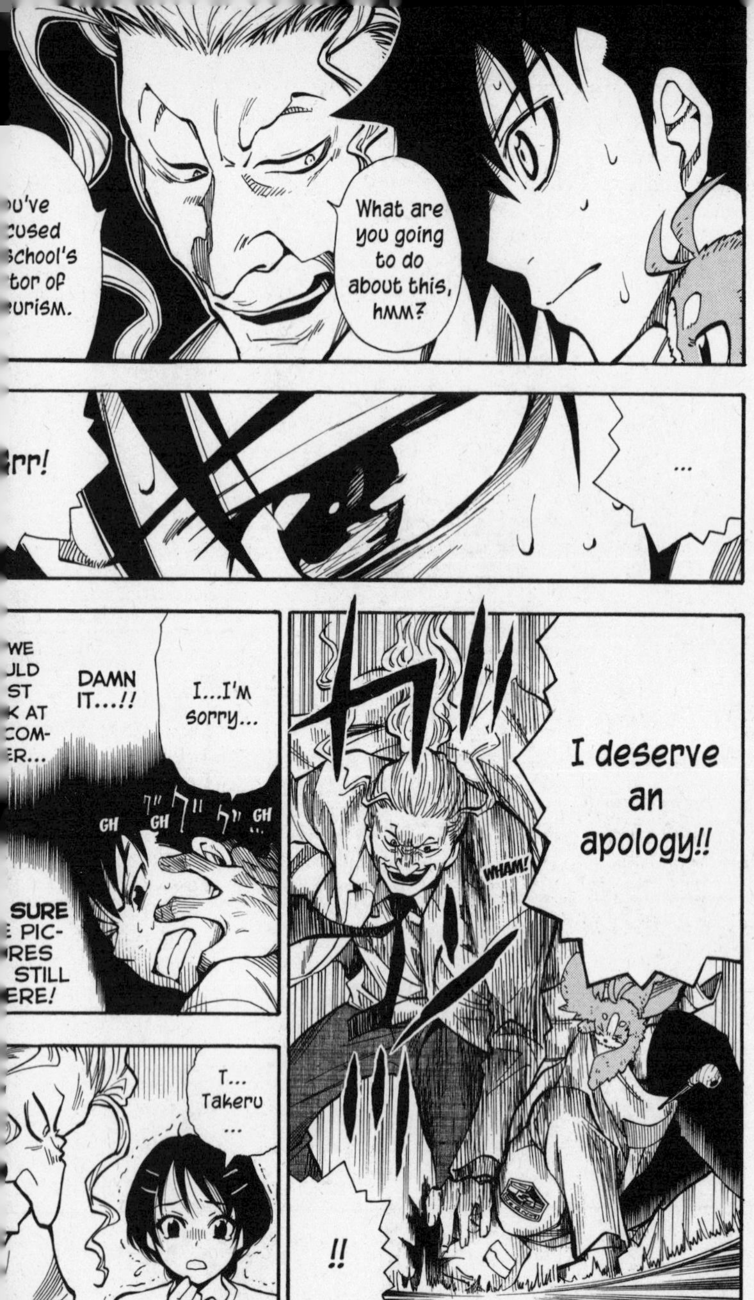
What are you going to do about this, hmm?
ou've
cused
school's
tor of
urism.
...
rr!
I deserve an apology!!
WHAM!
!!
I...I'm sorry...
DAMN IT...!!
WE
ULD
ST
K AT
COM-
ER...
GH GH GH
SURE
E PIC-
RES
STILL
ERE!
T... Takeru ...

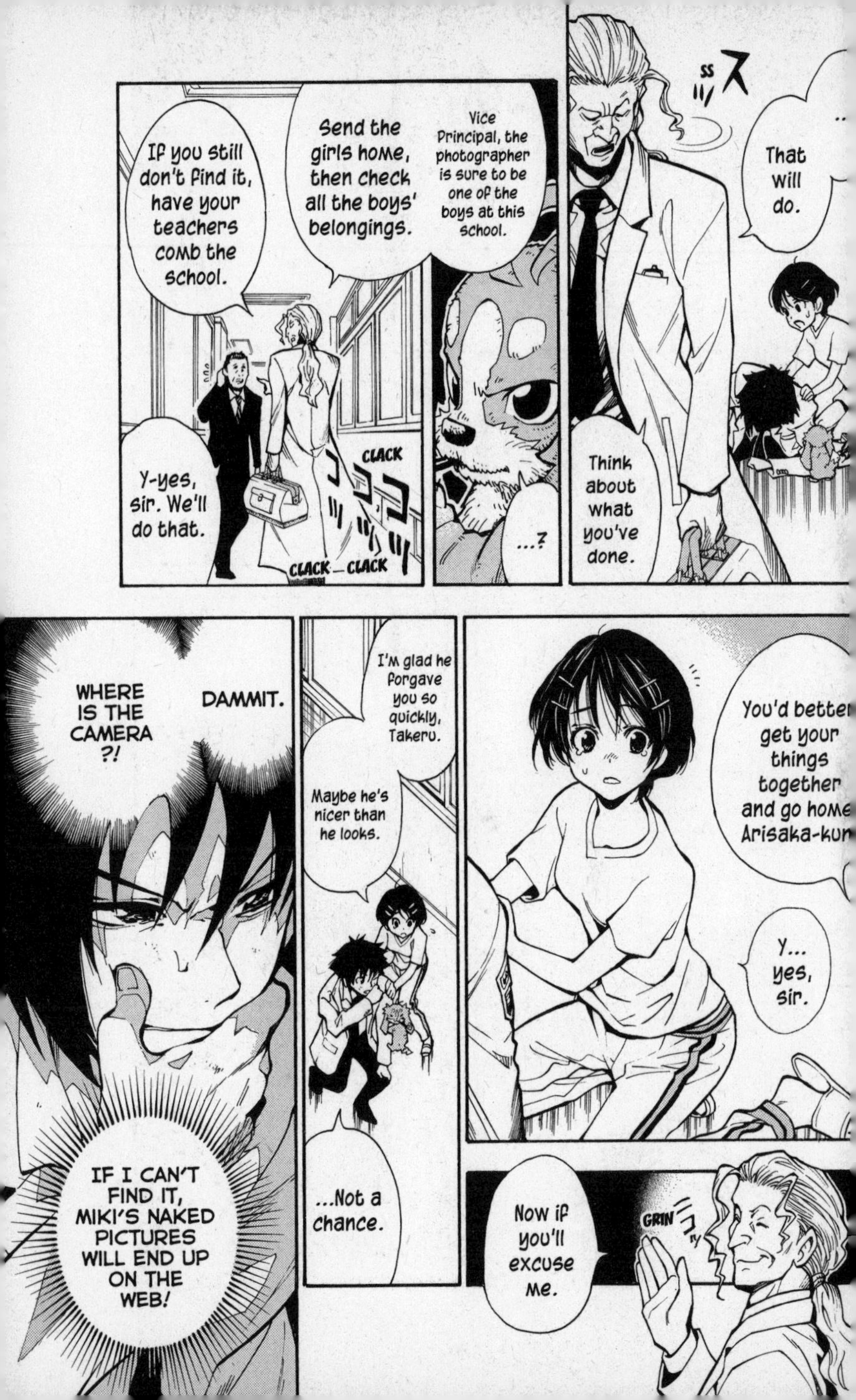
SS
That will do.
Think about what you've done.
Vice Principal, the photographer is sure to be one of the boys at this school.
...?
Send the girls home, then check all the boys' belongings.
If you still don't find it, have your teachers comb the school.
CLACK
CLACK CLACK
Y-yes, sir. We'll do that.
You'd better get your things together and go home Arisaka-kun
Y... yes, sir.
GRIN
Now if you'll excuse me.
I'm glad he forgave you so quickly, Takeru.
Maybe he's nicer than he looks.
...Not a chance.
DAMMIT.
WHERE IS THE CAMERA?!
IF I CAN'T FIND IT, MIKI'S NAKED PICTURES WILL END UP ON THE WEB!

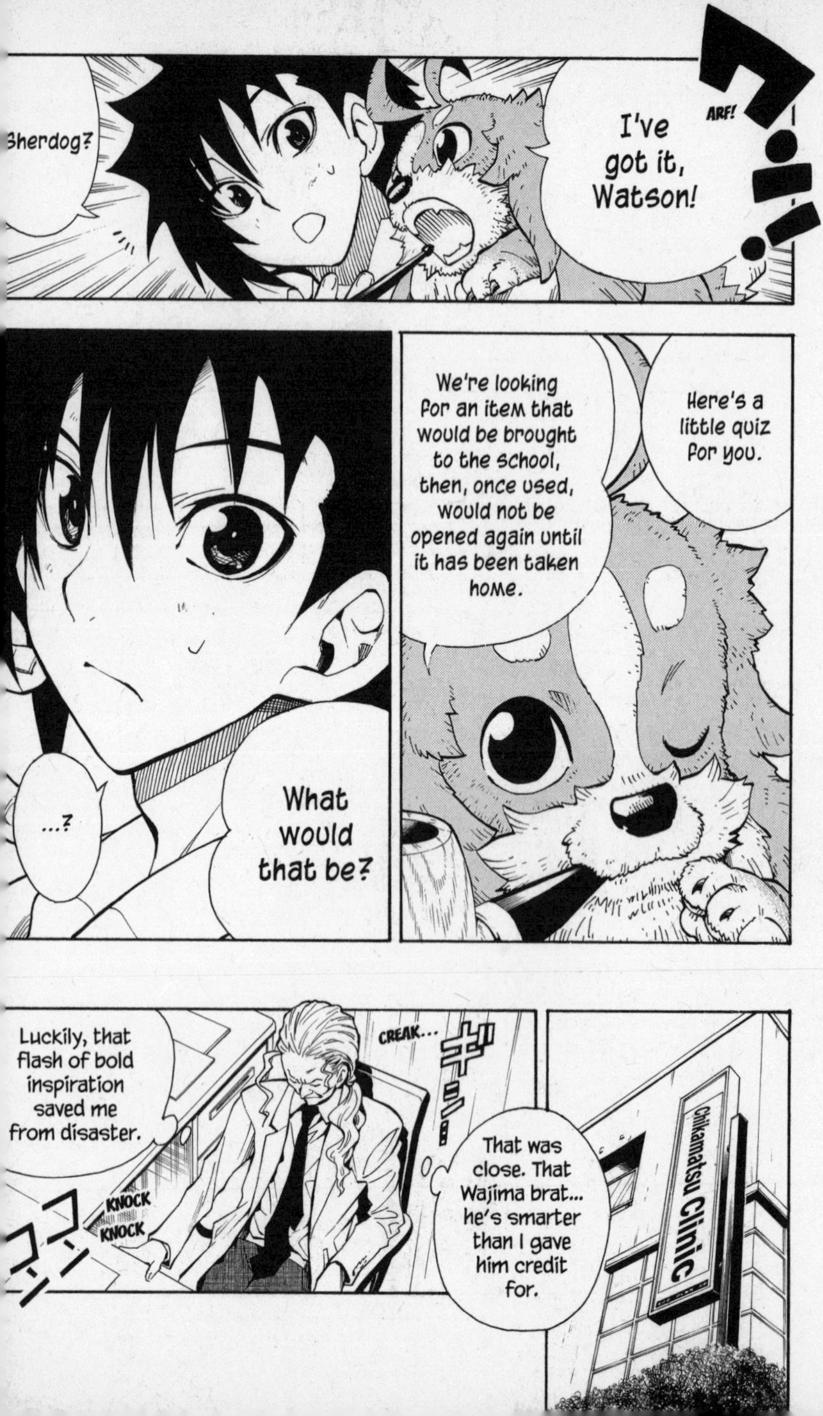
ARF!
I've got it, Watson!
Sherdog?
Here's a little quiz for you.
We're looking for an item that would be brought to the school, then, once used, would not be opened again until it has been taken home.
What would that be?
...?
Chikamatsu Clinic
CREAK...
That was close. That Wajima brat... he's smarter than I gave him credit for.
Luckily, that flash of bold inspiration saved me from disaster.
KNOCK
KNOCK

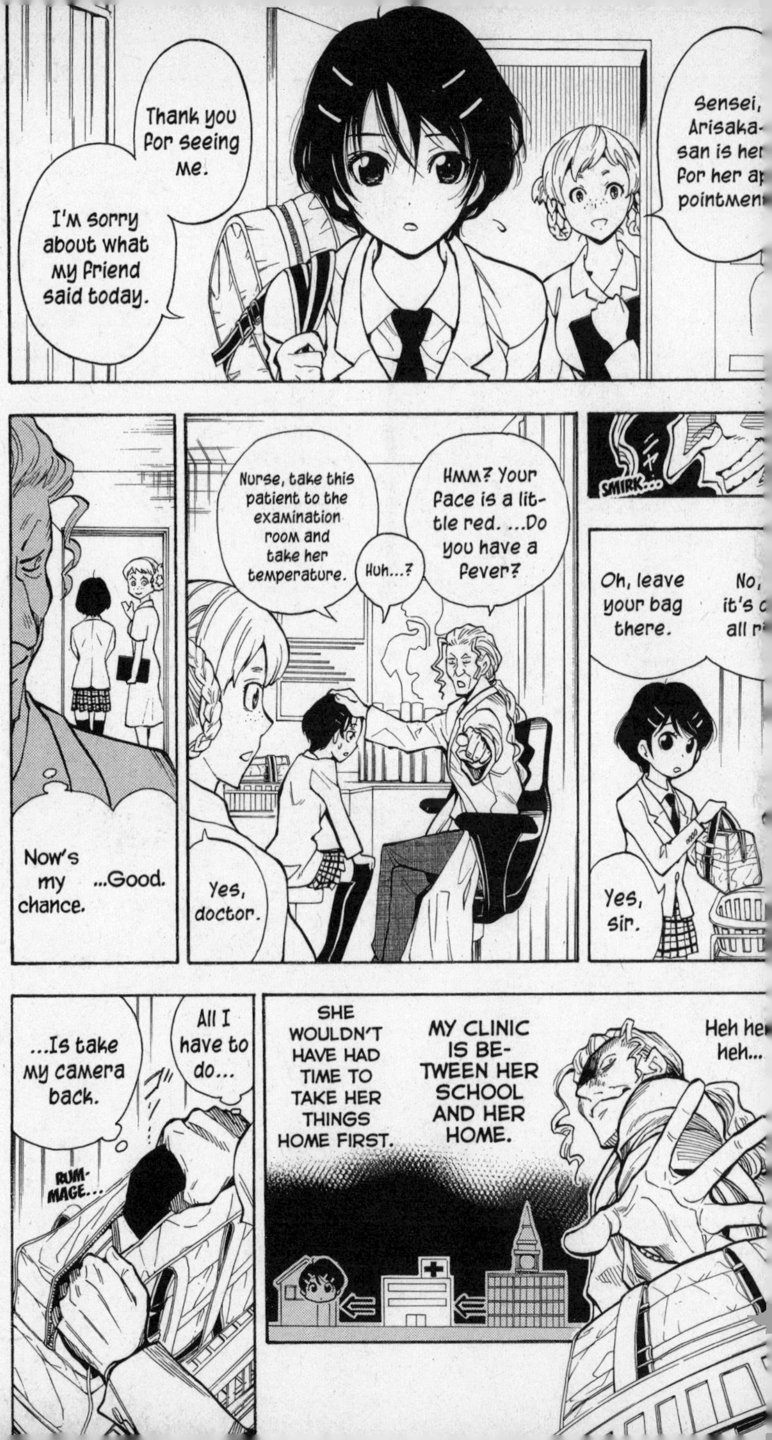
Sensei, Arisaka-san is her for her ap pointmen
Thank you for seeing me.
I'm sorry about what my friend said today.
ニヤ
SMIRK...
No, it's o all r
Oh, leave your bag there.
Yes, sir.
HMM? Your face is a lit-tle red. ...Do you have a fever?
Huh...?
Nurse, take this patient to the examination room and take her temperature.
Yes, doctor.
...Good.
Now's my chance.
Heh heh heh...
MY CLINIC IS BE-TWEEN HER SCHOOL AND HER HOME.
SHE WOULDN'T HAVE HAD TIME TO TAKE HER THINGS HOME FIRST.
All I have to do...
...Is take my camera back.
RUM-MAGE...

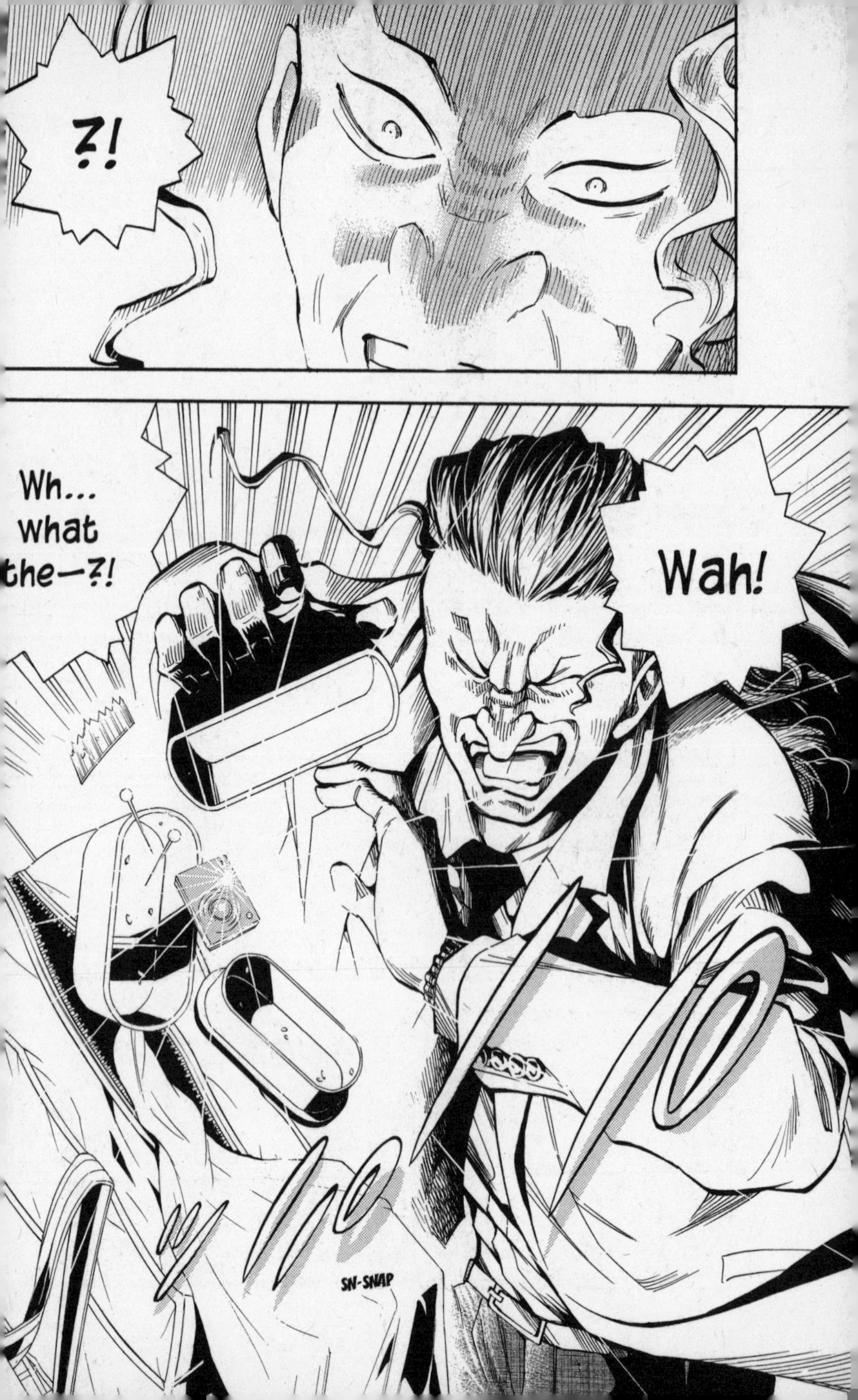
?!
Wah!
Wh... what the—?!
SN-SNAP

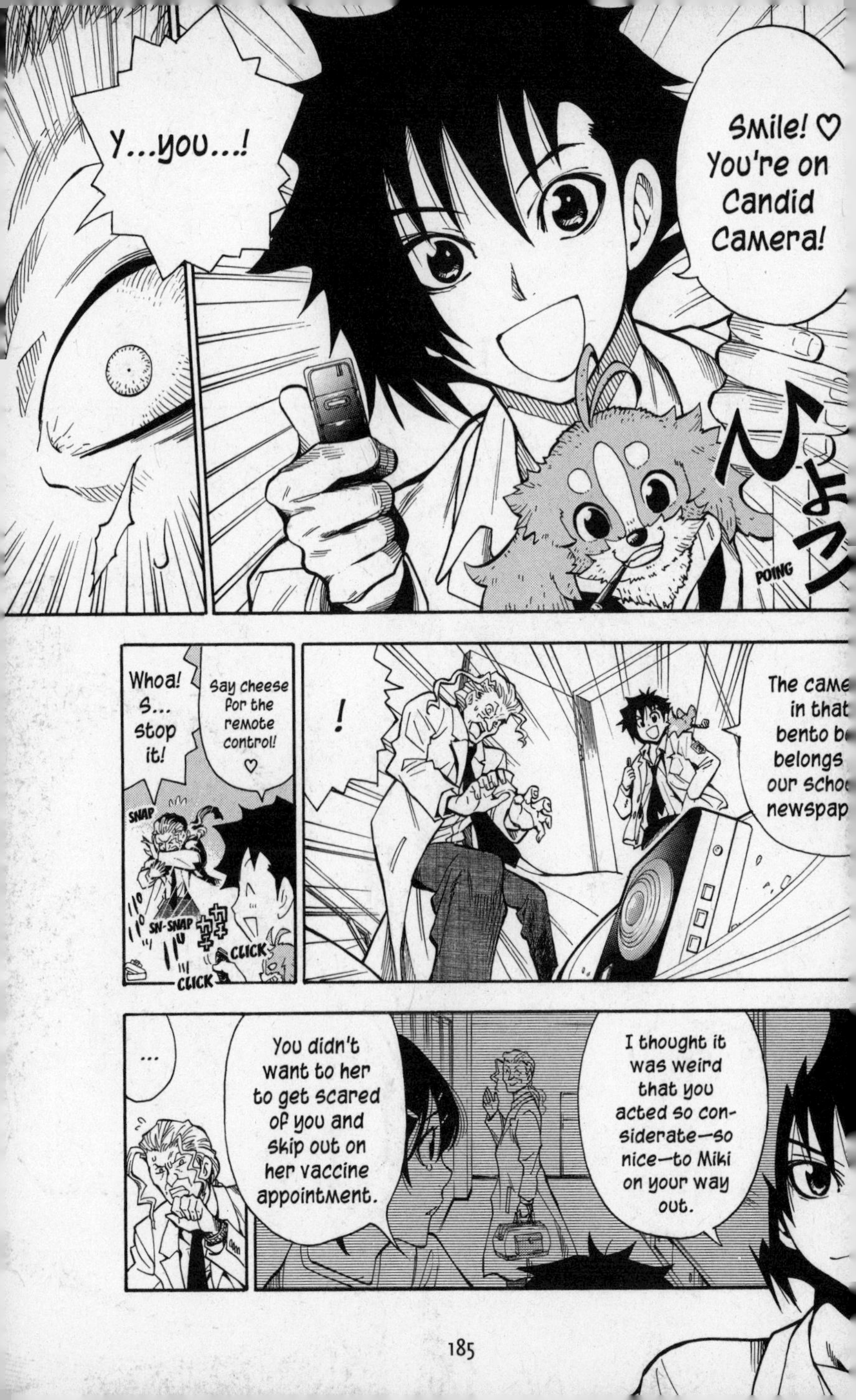
Smile! ♡ You're on Candid Camera!
POING
Y...you...!
The came
in that
bento b
belongs
our scho
newspap
!
Say cheese for the remote control! ♡
Whoa! S... stop it!
SNAP
SN-SNAP
CLICK
CLICK
I thought it was weird that you acted so con-siderate—so nice—to Miki on your way out.
You didn't want to her to get scared of you and skip out on her vaccine appointment.
...

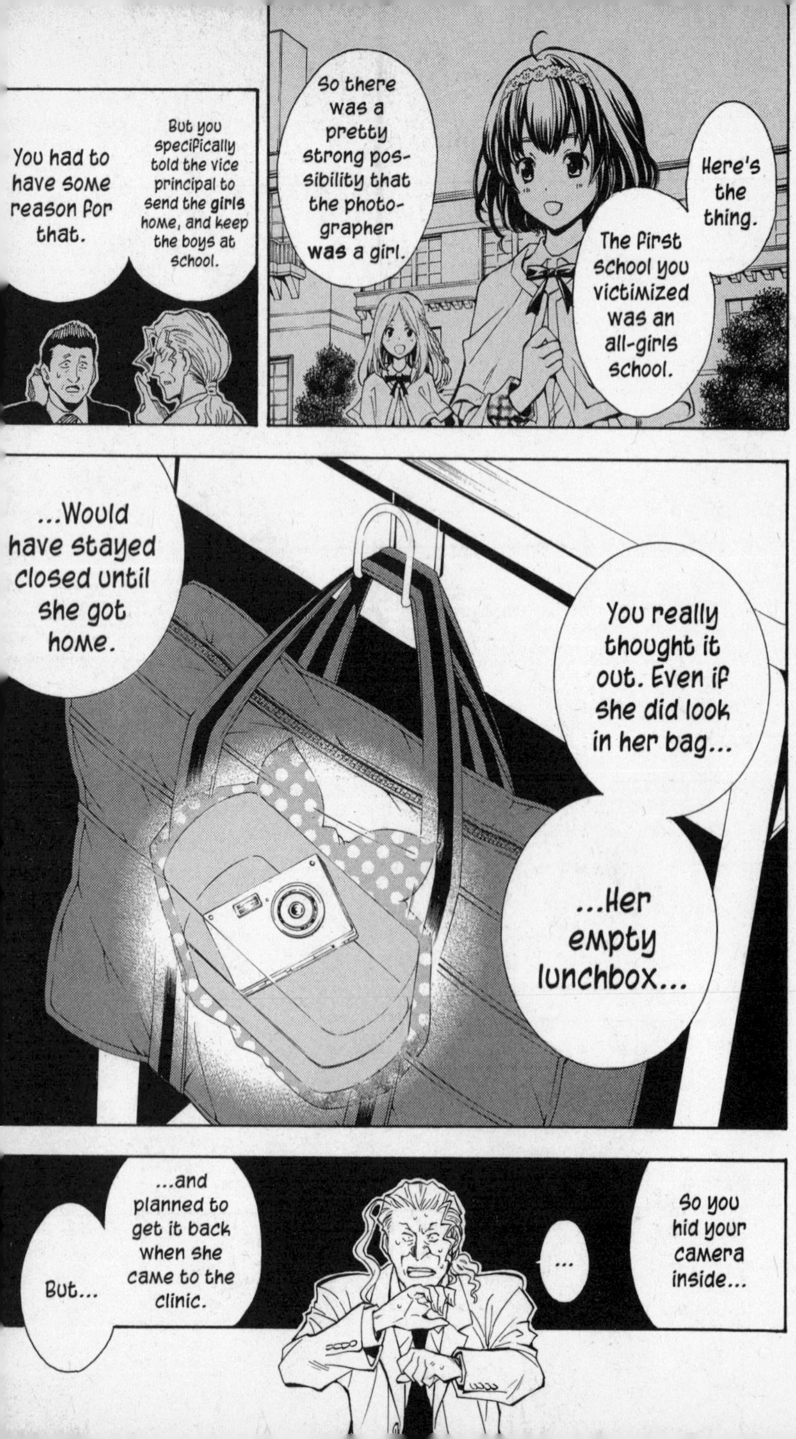
Here's the thing.
The first school you victimized was an all-girls school.
So there was a pretty strong possibility that the photographer was a girl.
But you specifically told the vice principal to send the girls home, and keep the boys at school.
You had to have some reason for that.
You really thought it out. Even if she did look in her bag...
...Her empty lunchbox...
...Would have stayed closed until she got home.
So you hid your camera inside...
...
...and planned to get it back when she came to the clinic.
But...

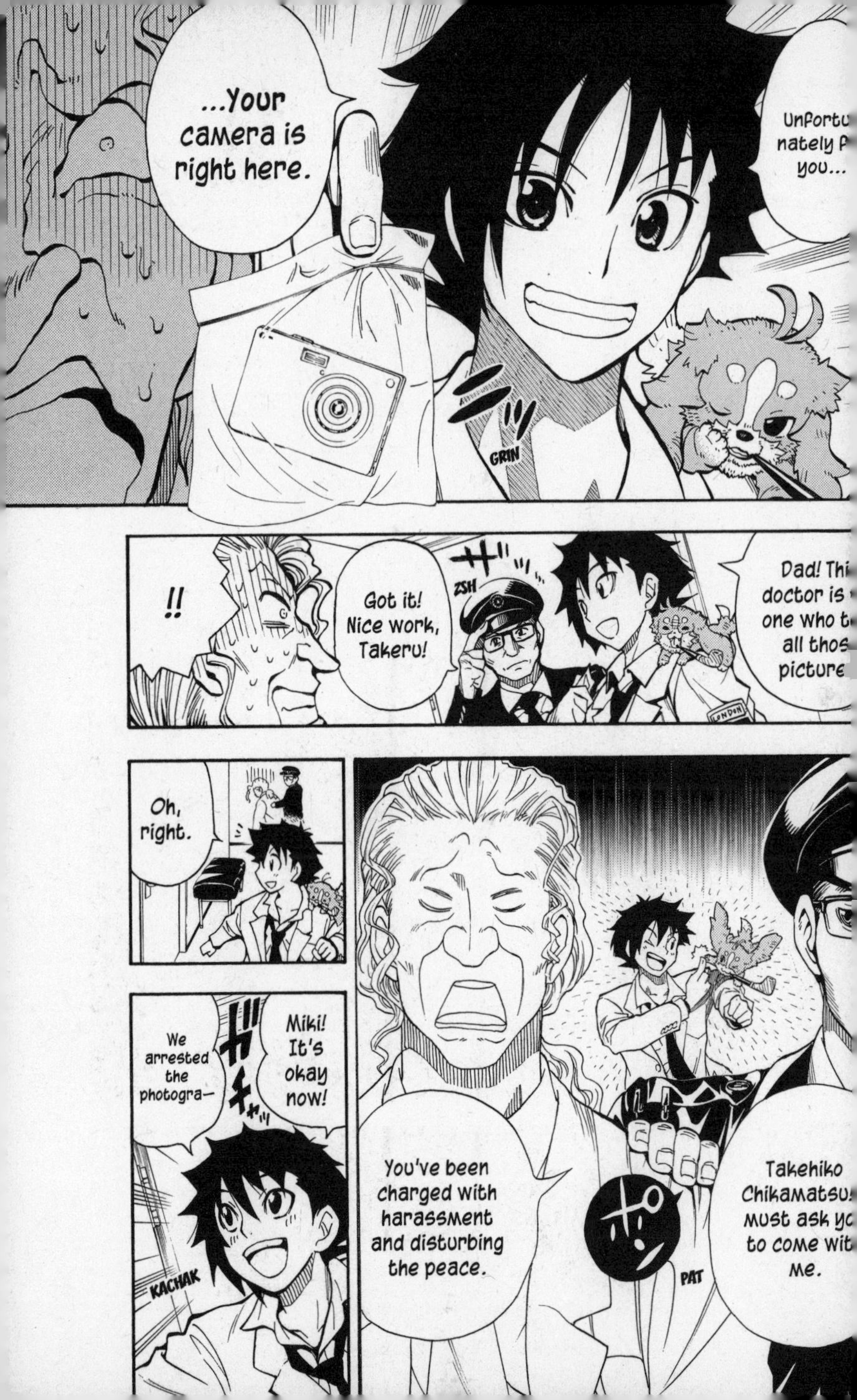
Unfortu nately f you...
...Your camera is right here.
GRIN
Dad! Thi doctor is one who t all thos picture
ZSH
Got it! Nice work, Takeru!
!!
Takehiko Chikamatsu! Must ask yo to come wit me.
PAT
You've been charged with harassment and disturbing the peace.
Oh, right.
Miki! It's okay now!
We arrested the photogra—
KACHAK

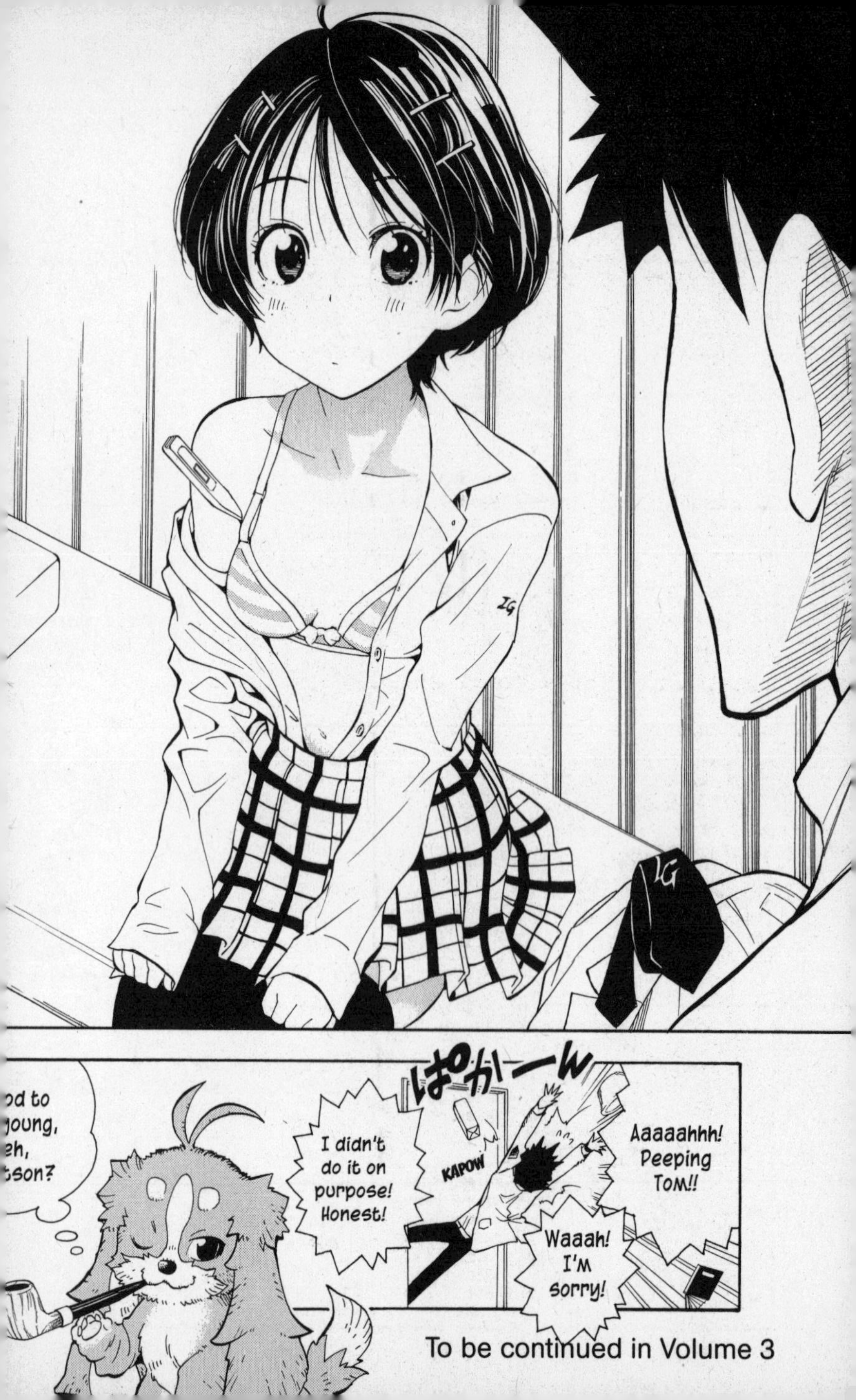
ぱかーん
Aaaaahhh! Peeping Tom!!
KAPOW
Waaah! I'm sorry!
I didn't do it on purpose! Honest!
od to
young,
eh,
tson?

To be continued in Volume 3

Bonus

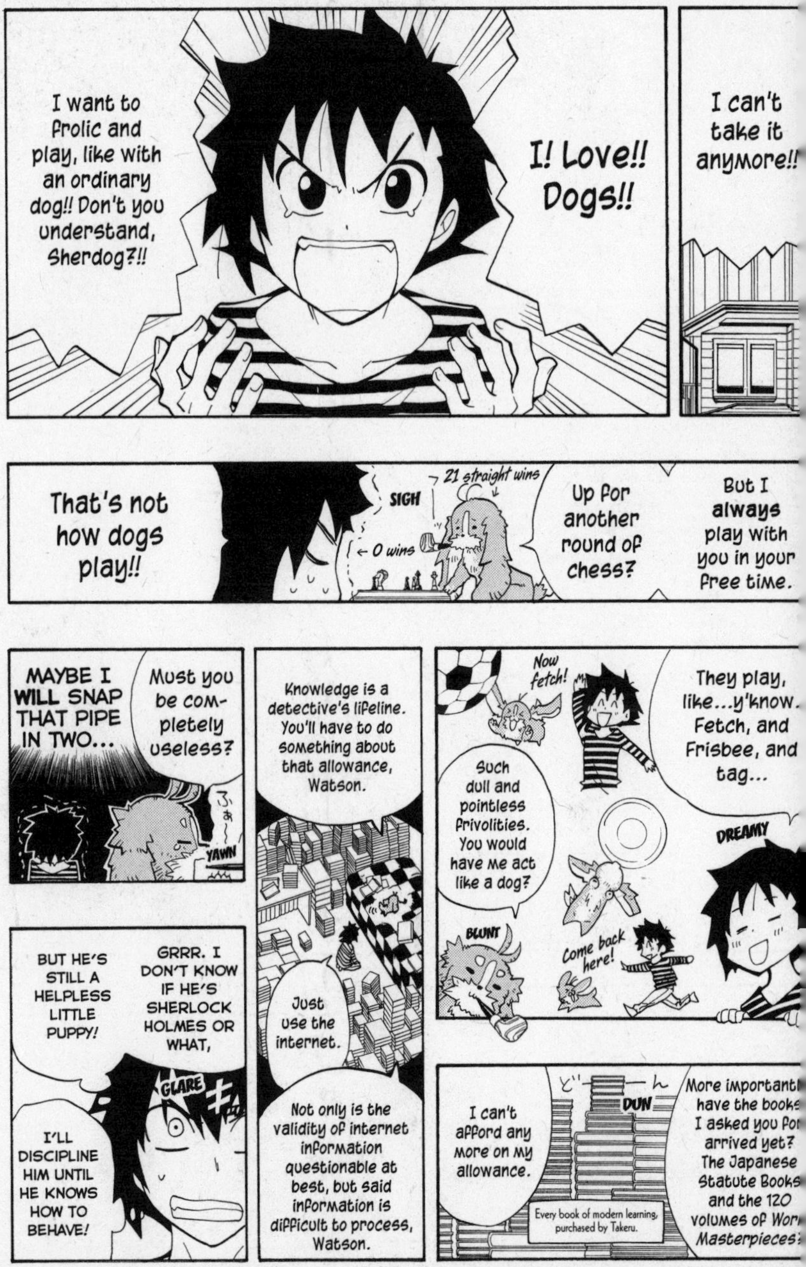

I can't take it anymore!!
I! Love!! Dogs!!
I want to frolic and play, like with an ordinary dog!! Don't you understand, Sherdog?!!
But I always play with you in your free time.
Up for another round of chess?
21 straight wins
SIGH
← 0 wins
That's not how dogs play!!
They play, like...y'know. Fetch, and Frisbee, and tag...
Now fetch!
DREAMY
Such dull and pointless frivolities. You would have me act like a dog?
BLUNT
Come back here!
More important have the books I asked you for arrived yet? The Japanese Statute Books and the 120 volumes of Wor Masterpieces?
DUN
I can't afford any more on my allowance.
Every book of modern learning, purchased by Takeru.
Knowledge is a detective's lifeline. You'll have to do something about that allowance, Watson.
Just use the internet.
Not only is the validity of internet information questionable at best, but said information is difficult to process, Watson.
Must you be completely useless?
MAYBE I WILL SNAP THAT PIPE IN TWO...
ふぁ～
YAWN
GRRR. I DON'T KNOW IF HE'S SHERLOCK HOLMES OR WHAT,
BUT HE'S STILL A HELPLESS LITTLE PUPPY!
GLARE
I'LL DISCIPLINE HIM UNTIL HE KNOWS HOW TO BEHAVE!

Ando-sensei, Editor I-san, my staff, my mentor, my friends, my family, and all my readers—thanks...

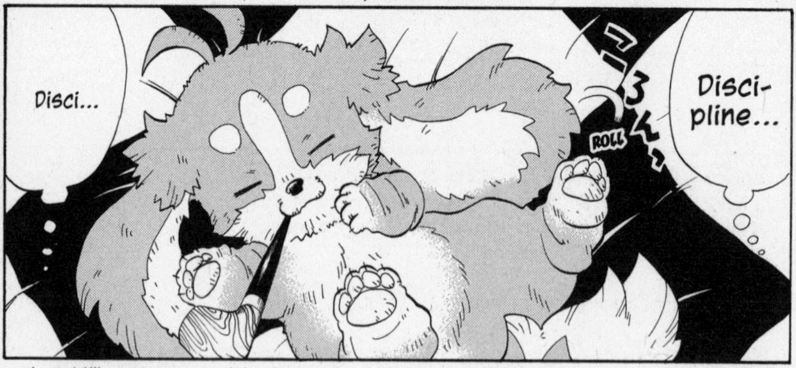
Disci-pline...
ころん
ROLL
Disci...

...always! I'll continue to work hard every day. Yuki

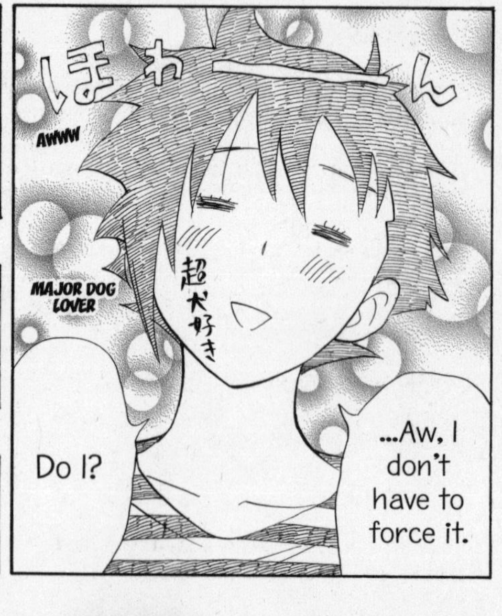
ほわーん
AWWW
MAJOR DOG LOVER
超犬好き
...Aw, I don't have to force it.
Do I?

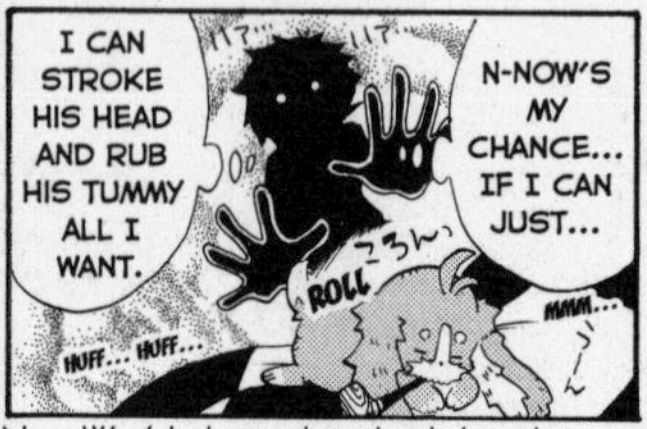
N-NOW'S MY CHANCE... IF I CAN JUST...
I CAN STROKE HIS HEAD AND RUB HIS TUMMY ALL I WANT.
ころん
ROLL
MMM...
HUFF... HUFF...

Note: Won't let him pet him when he's awake.

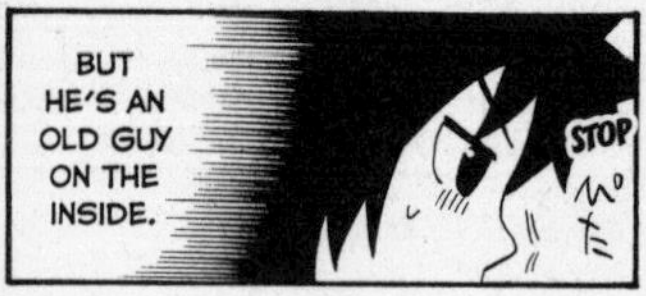
STOP
ぴた
BUT HE'S AN OLD GUY ON THE INSIDE.

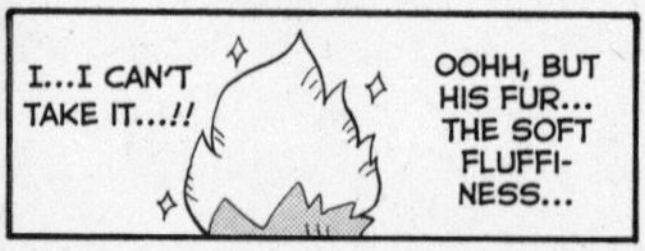
OOHH, BUT HIS FUR... THE SOFT FLUFFINESS...
I...I CAN'T TAKE IT...!!

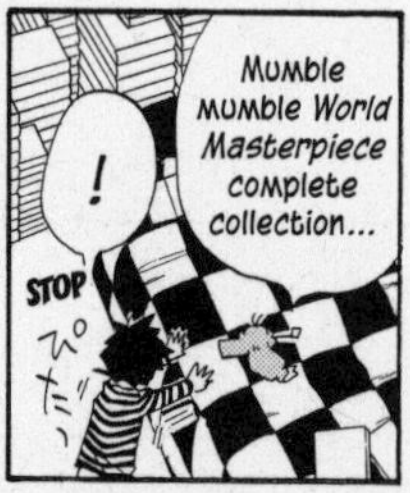
Mumble mumble World Masterpiece complete collection...
!
STOP
ぴた

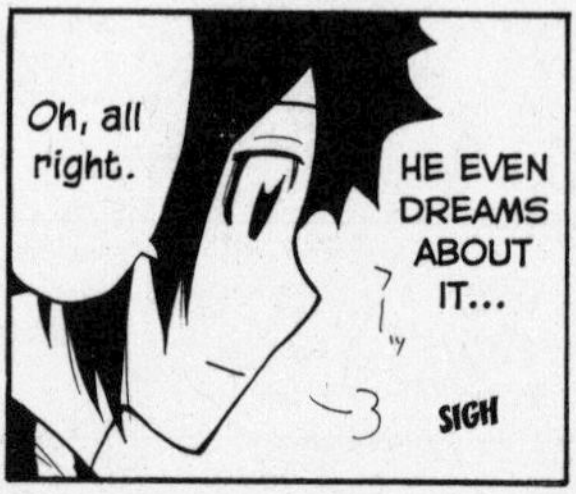
HE EVEN DREAMS ABOUT IT...
Oh, all right.
SIGH

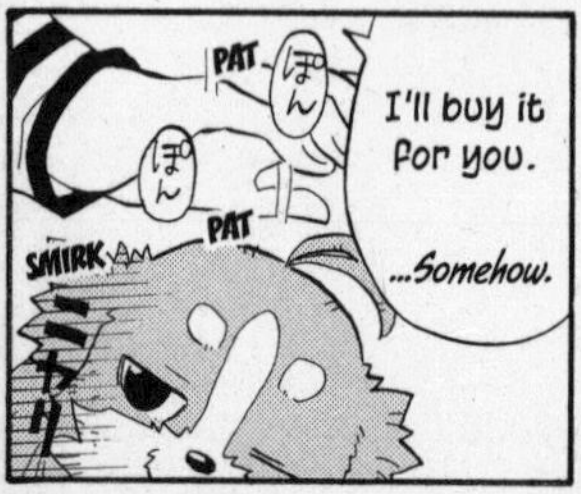
I'll buy it for you.
...Somehow.
PAT
ぽん
ぽん
PAT
SMIRK
ニヤリ

To be continued next volume! (I think.)

A Kodansha Comics Trade Paperback Original.

Sherlock Bones volume 2 copyright © 2012 Yuma Ando & Yuki Sato
English translation copyright © 2013 Yuma Ando & Yuki Sato

Published in the United States by Kodansha Comics,
an imprint of Kodansha USA Publishing, LLC, New York.

Publication rights for this English edition arranged through Kodansha Ltd., Tokyo.

First published in Japan in 2012 by Kodansha Ltd., Tokyo, as *Tanteiken Sherdock* volume 2.

ISBN 978-1-61262-445-7

Printed in the United States of America.

www.kodanshacomics.com

9 8 7 6 5 4 3 2 1

Translator: Alethea Nibley and Athena Nibley
Lettering: Kiyoko Shiromasa

You are going the wrong way!

Manga is a completely different type of reading experience.

To start at the beginning, go to the end!

That's right! Authentic manga is read the traditional Japanese way—from right to left, exactly the opposite of how American books are read. It's easy to follow: Just go to the other end of the book, and read each page—and each panel—from right side to left side, starting at the top right. Now you're experiencing manga as it was meant to be.